STATS™ 1997 BASEBALL SCOREBOARD

John Dewan, Don Zminda, and STATS, Inc.

Ethan D. Cooperson, Kevin Fullam, Jim Henzler, Chuck Miller, Tony Nistler and Mat Olkin, Assistant Editors

Published by STATS Publishing

A division of Sports Team Analysis & Tracking Systems, Inc.

Dr. Richard Cramer, Chairman • John Dewan, President

This book is dedicated to my father Bill, who gave me a love of numbers, my mother Judy, who gave me a love of writing, and my brother Dave, a great older brother and a great friend too.
—Drew Faust

Cover photo by David Seelig

First Edition: March, 1997

ISBN 1-884064-34-5

Table of Contents

Acknowledgments

Here at STATS, Inc., the *Baseball Scoreboard* is one of our most ambitious undertakings. We want to thank all the people who had a hand in its production.

Dozens of insightful essays were penned by publications staff members Ethan D. Cooperson, Kevin Fullam, Jim Henzler, Tony Nistler and Mat Olkin. Drew Faust and loyal reader Steve Schulman also chipped in with some prose. Steve Moyer, Jim Osborne and Pat Quinn contributed ideas for essays, as did Bill James—who even wrote one himself.

Stefan Kretschmann, Jeff Schinski, Kevin Thomas, Steve Moyer, David Pinto and Brent Osland were the programmers responsible for masterfully extracting the data from our considerable database. As always, Chuck Miller wrestled with our publications software and ultimately persuaded it to cooperate. Tony tag-teamed with Chuck and stepped in whenever Chuck got winded.

Ethan did the stat-checking, which was no mean feat. Ethan, Kevin, Tony and Mat did preliminary edits, while Don and I did the final touch-ups. The illustrations which appear throughout the book come courtesy of John Grimwade, who made the *Scoreboard's* charts spring to life for the eighth straight year.

Thanks as always to the other full-time employees at STATS, starting with our managers: Art Ashley, Mike Canter and Sue Dewan (Systems); Doug Abel (Operations); Bob Meyerhoff (Vice President of Finances and Human Resources); Stephanie Seburn (Marketing Support and Administration); and Jim Capuano (Vice President of National Sales). Thanks also to staff members Kristen Beauregard, Grant Blair, Dave Carlson, Jeff Chernow, Marty Couvillon, Marc Elman, Ron Freer, Ken Gilbert, Ginny Hamill, Mike Hammer, Tiffany Heingarten, Mark Hong, Jason Kinsey, Dave Klotz, Betty Moy, Jim Musso, Jim Osborne, Oscar Palacios, Dean Peterson, John Sasman, Heather Schwarze, Matt Senter, Leena Sheth, Lori Smith, Allan Spear, Mike Wenz and Peter Woelflein.

And finally, we'd like to thank Bill James. If he hadn't taught us how to think analytically about the game of baseball, there wouldn't even *be* a *Baseball Scoreboard.*

—John Dewan and Don Zminda

Foreword

by Bill Bavasi

A variety of talented individuals and progressive companies have created technology that allows us to analyze the game of baseball as never before. The efforts of one such company, STATS, Inc., have culminated in perhaps the ultimate analytical baseball book, the *1997 STATS Baseball Scoreboard*. It is a publication utilized by individuals at all levels of the sport, from those in the front office who strive to constuct winning teams year after year, to managers and coaches who make key in-game decisions, to those who truly support the game of baseball—the fans.

Baseball, unlike any other sport, is a game that is played, expressed and analyzed through numbers. These numbers are simply tools, whether they're being used on the business side, or in the actual preparation and playing of a game. They can be used to explain, justify or even rationalize countless decisions. The *Baseball Scoreboard* uses objective criteria to provide insight into baseball's trends, the kind of information a decision-maker uses to make subjective decisions. Over time, as the statistical evidence builds to undeniable conclusions, these trends graduate from theory to *fact*. We in the front office incorporate these facts into our decision-making process, and the results make the game even more interesting.

During the early stages of a player's professional career, no set of numbers can accurately project his potential. His development depends upon the efforts of dedicated scouts and instructors as well as his own physical and emotional efforts. However, once a player begins his major league career, more times than not the player is evaluated by numbers. The "normal" statistics like batting average and RBI are documented daily in box scores and utilized in television and radio broadcasts. Many of us view these numbers as only the first step in formulating decisions on player personnel. But the *Baseball Scoreboard* goes well beyond the elementary statistics, providing unique breakdowns of player performance and delivering insights that are truly captivating.

The debate between "going by the book" and "playing a hunch" has always been part of baseball's intrigue. The data in this book may help a manager or general manager weigh the pros and cons for certain key strategic decisions on and off the field. Playing a hunch will always have its place in baseball, but the *Scoreboard* helps us all to better understand what's at stake.

The outcome of a particular baseball game does not depend only upon the relative strengths of the two teams. Rather, it is the end result of hundreds of decisions by managers, coaches and players during the course of the game. The knowledge contained in this book facilitates informed decision-making in areas such as defensing particular hitters, creating favorable batter-pitcher match-ups, and choosing when to go for the extra base.

I have been around or involved in baseball all my life. Over the years, I have witnessed baseball's evolution from a sport once merely described by performance and outcome, to a more complex entity subjected to sophisticated statistical analysis. It has been a rapid and fascinating enlightenment in which STATS, Inc., and the *Baseball Scoreboard* have played a significant role. This book is not just for industry decision-makers but also for the dedicated and devoted fan who wants to understand and comprehend everything he or she can about this great game.

Bill Bavasi is the Vice President and General Manager of the Anaheim Angels.

Introduction

Hundreds of years ago, the only satellite that orbited the earth was the moon. As a result, cartographers had to go to great lengths to gather information about the earth. Their primary source was often the returning explorer, who provided descriptions of far-away lands. Based on those tales, the cartographers created maps that helped to shape people's view of the world. Of course, the travelers' misperceptions and fabrications helped to distort the results. My father's old English map, for example, depicts California as an *island.* Apparently, an old sailor had convinced the map-maker that the Gulf of California stretched all the way north to Puget Sound, completely separating the future Golden State from the mainland of North America.

Before the computer age, our perception of the game of baseball was subject to similar gaps and distortions. Even basic knowledge like how a hitter performed against left-handed pitchers relied entirely upon anecdotal evidence, and the resulting degree of accuracy was predictably low.

Today, it's all different. Just as satellites enabled the cartographers to map the earth down to the most minute break in the coastline, computers allow us to analyze the game of baseball in breathtaking detail. In the past, a player could acquire a reputation as a clutch hitter with just a single memorable hit in the postseason. Today, we can simply check the records to see who *really* comes through in the clutch.

Thanks to modern technology, we can address issues that used to be limited to the realm of speculation. The result is the *STATS Baseball Scoreboard*, where we ask dozens of insightful questions about baseball and then proceed to *answer them.*

The greatest thing about baseball is that, unlike the surface of the globe, the avenues of analysis are virtually infinite. This is the eighth edition of the *Scoreboard,* and we're not even *close* to running out of new ways to analyze the game. This year, we've tackled new questions, like "Which pitchers throw the most strikes?", "What's the best home-run park in the American League?" and "Is Joe DiMaggio's streak in any danger?"

Of course, we've developed a collection of old favorites over the years. As we do every year, we'll show you the relievers who stranded the most inherited runners last year and the pitchers who received the most run support. And you'll also find the leaders in Bill James-invented categories like pitchers' game scores, secondary average and runs created. Bill even contributed an essay himself this year, applying his "Favorite Toy" system to project pitchers' chances to win 300 games. You'll find the essay on page 200.

Our goal, as always, is to make our essays enjoyable as well as informative. John Grimwade's illustrations liven up the essays, while the appendix in the back of the book supplements the essays with comprehensive data from our STATS database.

Once again, we invite you to write to us with comments and suggestions for future editions of the *Scoreboard.* One reader, Steve Schulmann, sent us an idea for an essay so intriguing that we invited him to write about it for this year's book. You'll find his piece on page 188. With readers like Steve, we know that the *Scoreboard* will continue to evolve and improve.

Today, we no longer need to wonder what lies beyond the horizon, but the game of baseball still holds secrets for us to unlock. Turn the page, and join us on a journey of discovery.

— Mat Olkin

I. TEAM QUESTIONS

Anaheim Angels: Should it Be "An' a Home Run!" Stadium?

When people talk about the difference in the levels of offense between the two leagues, the "cozier" American League ballparks are often cited as a major cause of the disparity. It certainly *seems* like most of the better home run parks—besides Coors Field, of course, which is completely off the charts—belong to Junior Circuit clubs.

If you asked 100 people to name the best home-run park in the American League, many would guess Tiger Stadium. Camden Yards would also be a popular choice, and Skydome would certainly get some votes. So, too, would Jacobs Field. Some would choose the Metrodome or the Kingdome, while others still consider Fenway to be a good home-run park. Hardly anyone would guess Anaheim Stadium.

And therefore, hardly anyone would guess the right answer. Over the last three years, the "Big A" has been the best longball park in the league—better than Tiger Stadium, Camden Yards. . . or even Fenway.

From 1994 through 1996, the Angels and their opponents have combined to hit 18 percent more homers during the Angels' home games than during their road games. That translates into a "Park Index" of 118, the highest figure in the league (Park Index is defined in the Glossary). Here are the six most favorable home run parks in the American League:

Best A.L. Home Run Parks—1994-96

Park	Index
Anaheim Stadium	118
Tiger Stadium	114
Hubert H. Humphrey Metrodome	109
Oriole Park at Camden Yards	109
Skydome	108
Kingdome*	107

(* index since dimensions changed in 1995.)

Why is it that Anaheim Stadium's tendencies have been largely overlooked? Perhaps it's because it used to be such an extreme *pitcher's* park. Back in the 1960s and '70s, the visibility was very poor and a prevailing wind blew in from the outfield. Nolan Ryan threw two no-hitters there, and from 1972 to 1979, an Angels pitcher—either Ryan or Frank Tanana—led the A.L. in strikeouts every single year.

Then, after the '79 season, Anaheim officials changed the park to suit their new football tenant, the since-departed Los Angeles Rams. Triple-decked seats were constructed behind the outfield walls, completely enclosing the stadium and cutting off the wind. Since then, it's been a hitter's park, although 17 years later, its reputation still hasn't caught up with reality.

That isn't all that surprising; once a stadium acquires a reputation as either a hitters' or pitchers' park, that label isn't likely to change—even if the park's characteristics do. Labels tend to stick, and subtle changes in the wind or the lighting can easily escape the public's perception.

As we noted above, many people still think that Fenway is a big home run park. That used to be true; through the 1970s, it was one of the best launching pads around. But in 1982 and '83, they installed luxury boxes on the roof along the left and right field foul lines. The roof used to be only about as high as the Green Monster, and in the summer months, a hitter's breeze often blew out from over the roof, helping many fly balls over the Wall and into the net. But since the construction of the luxury boxes, the ball simply hasn't carried as well. As a result, the park has completely changed: although it's retained its title as one of the best singles and doubles parks around, it's become a completely *neutral* home run park, registering a park index of only 98 over the last three years. (Some trace the change to the construction of a new, higher press box behind home plate in 1989. However, the trend began earlier. During the six-year period *before* the "600 Club" was built, Fenway actually favored the home run *less* than the average park.)

In any event, there are still people who marvel at a slugger like Mark McGwire and ask, "I wonder what he could do in Fenway?" Perhaps it would be better to speculate about what he might do in *Anaheim*.

—Mat Olkin

A more complete listing for this category can be found on page 236.

Baltimore Orioles: Did Brady Have the Biggest Home Run Jump Ever?

As a team, the Baltimore Orioles cranked out a major league record 257 home runs in 1996. Without question, Brady Anderson's incredible total of 50 homers came as the biggest surprise. How big? Perhaps the biggest *ever*.

Let's look at Anderson's career home run production prior to 1996. From 1988 through 1991, he hit no more than four homers in a season. In 1992, he hit 21 longballs—a career-high until mid-June of last year—and followed that with seasons of 13, 12, and a modest 16 in 1995. Let's face it: heading into the 1996 season, Brady was better known for sideburns than swats.

Then what? Anderson rewrote the record books, leading off 12 games with a home run, passing Frank Robinson as the Orioles' all-time single-season home-run leader, and becoming the 14th player in major league history to hit 50. With Anderson accomplishing all of this after hitting just 16 homers in 1995, we decided to look at the largest single-season home-run jumps in major league history by a player who had logged at least 100 games in the majors the previous season:

Largest Single-Season Home-Run Jumps

Player, Team	Year	Age	HR	Prev Yr	Jump
Dave Johnson, Atl	1973	30	43	5	38
Brady Anderson, Bal	1996	32	50	16	34
Harmon Killebrew, Min	1969	33	49	17	32
Lou Gehrig, Yanks	1927	24	47	16	31
Johnny Mize, Giants	1947	34	51	22	29
Andre Dawson, Cubs	1987	32	49	20	29
Jimmie Foxx, A's	1932	24	58	30	28
Ralph Kiner, Pit	1947	24	51	23	28
Carl Yastrzemski, Bos	1967	27	44	16	28
Rico Petrocelli, Bos	1969	26	40	12	28
Kevin Mitchell, SF	1989	27	47	19	28

(Minimum 100 games played in previous season. Age as of July 1 in second season.)

Who's that topping the list? Well, you probably know him better as *Davey* Johnson, the current Orioles' manager! Johnson was never a serious long-ball threat until his 1973 season, and as it turned out, was never much of a threat thereafter. He hit just five home runs in 1972 while playing with the Orioles, then hit 43 for Atlanta in 1973, a best-ever jump of 38 home runs from one season to the next.

Anderson's jump of 34 home runs in 1996 places second, and the remainder of the list is made up of some pretty fair sluggers. Though each of the players enjoyed a tremendous jump in home runs in the seasons listed above, most had a pretty reasonable explanation.

Harmon Killebrew and Johnny Mize made the list after playing short seasons the previous year. In 1968, "Killer" was slowed by a hamstring injury and played just 100 games, and in 1946, Mize returned from a three-year stint in the military and played just 101 games. Lou Gehrig, Jimmie Foxx and Ralph Kiner were simply young. In each case, the big jump season came at the tender age of 24.

Andre Dawson made the move from the Montreal Expos to the Chicago Cubs for the 1987 season. The "Hawk" played virtually his entire Montreal career with Olympic Stadium—hardly a hitters' haven—as his home park, then adjusted quickly to the friendly confines of Wrigley Field. Still, Dawson was a pretty well-known slugger prior to 1987, having averaged more than 22 home runs a season going all the way back to 1977.

Carl Yastrzemski was a little different. He had already won a batting title prior to the 1967 season, but he'd never hit more than 20 homers in a year. In '67, he bulked up and made a conscious effort to swing for the fences—and he wound up leading the Red Sox to a pennant. (Interestingly, he was able to win another batting title, as well as the Triple Crown).

Kevin Mitchell and Rico Petrocelli are the oddball cases. Mitchell had always shown potential prior to 1989, but a difficult personal life held him back. That year he finally blossomed. . . and while he has never approached 47 homers since, he has proven to be a legitimate slugger when healthy and motivated. Petrocelli was more of a fluke, although his 40-homer explosion in '69 did coincide with the lowering of the mound and the shrinking of the strike zone.

We also wondered whether Anderson had experienced the biggest home-run jump by a veteran player from his previous career high. The following illustration lists the largest increase in home runs from a previous career high for players who had played at least 100 major league games in three or more previous seasons.

From this perspective, Anderson's 1996 campaign is perhaps the most surprising home-run season ever. Will he ever have another season like 1996? Not surprisingly, the evidence points to "No." Even though five of the seven players who join Anderson on the above list made their jump between the ages of 26 and 28, none ever surpassed the home-run total achieved in the jump season.

LARGEST HOME RUN JUMPS BY A VETERAN PLAYER

	Age	HR	Previous high	Difference
Brady Anderson, 1996	32	50	21	29
Dave Johnson, 1973	30	43	18	25
Kevin Mitchell, 1989	27	47	22	25
Carl Yastrzemski, 1967	27	44	20	24
George Foster, 1977	28	52	29	23
Walker Cooper, 1947	32	35	13	22
Roger Maris, 1961	26	61	39	22
Rico Petrocelli, 1969	26	40	18	22

Minimum 100 games in at least 3 previous seasons.
Age as of July 1 in the "jump" season.

The two older players, Johnson and Walker Cooper, never even came close. Johnson's career went quickly downhill after 1973: in '74 he hit 15 home runs, and between 1975 and the end of his career in 1978, he hit just 16 more (although he did hit 39 in two seasons with the Yomiuri Giants in the Japanese Central League during that time). Cooper stayed productive for the next five seasons, hitting 16, 20, 14, 18 and 10 home runs over that span, but he never approached the 35 he hit in 1947.

What do we expect from Brady Anderson in 1997? Bill James and STATS project him to hit 32 home runs next year, and that seems about right. He certainly won't sneak up on any pitchers, and he's likely to see more junk than heat. It will be interesting to see whether *manager* Davey Johnson moves Anderson out of the leadoff spot to try and take advantage of his "newly found" power, or if he chalks up 1996 as a one-year fluke—something like his own—and lets him stay put.

—Drew Faust

A more complete listing for this category can be found on page 237.

Boston Red Sox: Did Kennedy Abuse His Pitchers' Arms?

In 1995, Kevin Kennedy's Boston Red Sox surprised everyone by capturing the American League East flag, but last year was quite different. The team got off to a woeful start, and the bullpen was a mess in the early going. Kennedy, under fire from all sides, responded by leaning more and more heavily on his starters. While the team came on strong down the stretch, and Roger Clemens survived well enough to tie his own nine-inning, single-game record with a 20-strikeout performance on September 18, questions linger about the long-term effects of Kennedy's handling of the staff.

A high-pitch outing can be a pitcher's most hazardous professional endeavor. In the late 1980s, for example, Fernando Valenzuela, Orel Hershiser and Al Leiter each suffered major arm injuries within months of topping the 160-pitch mark. Major league managers seem to have taken notice, and *none* allowed their pitchers to throw close to 150 pitches in a game last year—with one exception. Here are the only five occasions where a starter threw more than 144 pitches in '96:

Highest Pitch Counts—1996

Pitcher, Team	Date	#Pitches
Roger Clemens, Bos	7/21	162
Tim Wakefield, Bos	6/10	162
Roger Clemens, Bos	6/13	157
Tom Gordon, Bos	9/24	151
Roger Clemens, Bos	9/18	151

That's right—Kennedy allowed *each* of his top three starters to venture into territory well beyond the point where any other manager dared to let his pitchers tread. And this is just the tip of the iceberg: even beyond the five games listed above, Kennedy had his pitchers working deep into games more frequently than any other manager. His starters topped the 120-pitch count on 49 occasions, the most of any major league team.

Let's take a closer look at how each of the Red Sox starters fared under Kennedy. In particular, let's focus on how their arms responded after their high-pitch outings.

As you can see from the chart above, Kennedy was especially cavalier in his handling of Roger Clemens. Going into the season, Clemens hadn't topped the 140-pitch mark since early 1993, but Kennedy let him throw 143 pitches on June 8th. In Clemens' very next start, Kennedy left him out there for 157 pitches, and Roger wasn't the same for a while afterward. In his next six starts, he went 1-3 with a 4.14 ERA.

Still, Kennedy kept pushing. In the seventh start following his 157-pitch outing, Clemens was allowed to throw 162 pitches against the Orioles. This time, the result was even worse: Clemens lost his next two starts with a 6.92 ERA, and then was forced to miss a start. He returned to enjoy an amazing stretch run, before Kennedy let him top the 150-pitch mark again on September 18 (Clemens' 20-strikeout game). He started two more times after that, and pitched decently but failed to register another win.

During the 1996 season, Clemens averaged 125 pitches per start, the highest figure in the majors (Alex Fernandez was a very distant second, averaging 117). The Rocket had not exceeded 121 pitches per start in any of his previous eight seasons.

Wakefield's story was similar. After his 162-pitch outing on June 10, he posted a 7.54 ERA over his next seven starts. But the most perplexing case was that of Tom Gordon. In his next-to-last start of the season, Gordon—who had never thrown more than 143 pitches in his major league career—wearily hurled 151 pitches in a win over the Orioles. It was the fifth time that he'd reached the 130-pitch mark during the 1996 season; coming into 1996, he'd thrown 130 pitches just five times in 144 career starts.

Although his arm didn't last long enough to join the 150-pitch club, highly-touted youngster Jeff Suppan warrants a brief mention. The 21-year-old righthander threw 120 pitches on August 14, and experienced extreme difficulties soon afterward (120 might not seem excessive, but it's rather high for a pitcher that young. Tom Glavine, for example, wasn't allowed to top 120 pitches until his 41st major league start).

In Suppan's next start, he was knocked out in the first inning, and in the game after that, he was forced to leave after three pitches after feeling something "pop" in his elbow. He was diagnosed with a stretched elbow ligament and missed the rest of the season.

In case you were wondering, the Red Sox pitchers' adverse reactions to their overuse was far from unusual. In the entire decade of the 1990s, Clemens' and Wakefield's totals of 162 pitches have been topped only three times, and all three times, the resulting damage was both obvious and immediate. Ironically, Clemens and Wakefield were the victims in two of those three games. Their reactions back then forewarned that they wouldn't respond well to Kennedy's rough handling in 1996.

A marathon mound performance by Roger Clemens nearly cost Boston the A.L. East title in 1990. Manager Joe Morgan allowed Clemens to throw 165 pitches against the Tigers on August 4 of that season. Clemens pitched well for six starts after that, but came down with shoulder problems in early September. The injury knocked him out for three weeks, and by the time he returned, the Sox' lead over the Blue Jays had dwindled from 6.5 games down to just a single contest. Boston hung on to win, only to be swept by Oakland in the playoffs.

Wakefield fared even worse after logging the highest pitch count of the '90s on April 27, 1993. He threw 172 pitches for the Pirates in that game, and subsequently proved that even a knuckleballer's arm can't handle such abuse. After going 0-5 with a 7.59 ERA over his next eight starts, he was demoted, twice—first to the bullpen, and then to the minors. He wasn't able to make it back to the majors for good until 1995.

The third and final pitcher to exceed 162 pitches was David Cone, who threw a ridiculous total of 166 pitches on July 17, 1992. During that game, Mets manager Jeff Torborg made a highly dubious decision. The Mets led, 1-0, as Cone was due to bat with one out and no one on base in the bottom of the eighth. He was pitching brilliantly, working on a shutout, but he'd already thrown around 150 pitches. Closer Anthony Young had converted three straight save opportunities and hadn't worked in four days. Still, Torborg refused to pinch-hit for Cone, who went on to complete the shutout. The win raised his record to 10-4 and lowered his ERA to 2.41.

Cone's normally-indestructible arm paid the price. In his next nine starts he posted a 5.13 ERA, during which time he was traded to Toronto. He rebounded to reclaim his position as one of the game's top pitchers, and Clemens has shown that he too may be able to withstand the toll and remain effective. The Toronto Blue Jays certainly hope so, and they've gambled several million dollars in hopes that he can.

Wakefield's and Gordon's futures remain uncertain, but Kennedy won't be around to witness the results of his handiwork. He was fired after the season, and former Atlanta coach Jimy Williams was brought in to replace him. Williams may turn out to be an excellent choice—after all, Atlanta's staff has been the most injury-free in all of baseball. It's probably no coincidence that the Braves' starters topped the 130-pitch mark only five times all last season. Expect the Red Sox starters to rebound under Williams' more careful handling.

—Mat Olkin

Chicago White Sox: How Much Will Belle Help the Sox?

Without a doubt, the most important free-agent deal of the winter was Chicago's signing of slugging outfielder Albert Belle. Set on overtaking the powerful Cleveland Indians, White Sox owner Jerry Reinsdorf emptied the vaults to sign the superstar to an incredible $55-million contract. Belle will head into Comiskey Park with a lot of personal baggage, but if he can help the Sox capture the A.L. Central Division next season, he'll be a local hero—and Reinsdorf, who drew a lot of heat for the dollars he shelled out to sign Belle, will be hailed as a genius.

One important aspect of the Belle signing is this: not only did the White Sox gain a great player, but the Indians lost one as well. Will his move push Chicago past Cleveland? To try and answer this question, we're going to refer to an old staple of our books: the Bill James' "runs created" formula. The advantage of runs created is that it consolidates offensive statistics into a single number that can be used to assess a player's value to his organization in terms of wins and losses. Our first step is to find out exactly how many games the loss of Belle will cost Cleveland in 1996.

With 156 runs created in 442 outs last season, Belle generated approximately 60 more runs than the average A.L. left fielder would have, given the same number of chances. But will Cleveland be able to replace Belle with an "average" left fielder? Prospect Brian Giles might snare a large amount of the playing time; Giles has produced excellent numbers over the past couple of years at Triple-A, and the Indians are planning to use him in at least a platoon role until they're confident in his abilities. In our 1997 *Major League Handbook*, we projected Giles to be a .300/20 HR hitter—pretty good numbers from an inexperienced youngster. While we can't guarantee he'll be *that* effective, we think it's a reasonable assessment of what he can accomplish if given a fair opportunity.

We projected Giles to create about 6.4 runs per 27 outs next season. If Giles starts off poorly and is sent down to the minors, he's obviously not going to rack up those numbers, so we'll need to compute the value of a "replacement" player for the team. With the average American League left fielder creating 5.9 runs/27 outs, we can safely project the Indians' fill-in to produce one run below this average, or 4.9 runs/27 outs. According to Bill James' "Pythagorean Theorem," it's possible to calculate a team's winning percentage based on the total number of runs scored and allowed over the season. Assuming the performance of other players remains constant, here's how the situation stands, using Belle's numbers as a basis for comparison. (Note: Cleveland actually went 99-62 in '96 instead of the 97-65 record that the data projected for them. There's usually a small variation between what the formula predicts and what actually occurs.)

Belle '96 vs. Replacements '97—Cleveland Indians

Player	Runs Created	Run Diff.	Tm Win %	W-L
Albert Belle '96	156	—	.596	97-65
Brian Giles '97	105	–51	.572	93-69
Replacement LF '97	80	–76	.559	91-71

(runs created for all players based on Belle's 442 outs used)

Ouch. Even *if* Giles lives up to our expectations, the Tribe will sorely miss Belle's bat in the lineup. But how much will the addition of Belle help the White Sox? Figuring that one is a little trickier. Belle will be taking over for Tony Phillips in left field, and at press time the plan was to shift Phillips to right, a position manned last year by departed free agent Danny Tartabull. To simplify the analysis, we'll compare last year's outfielder totals with our 1997 projections by substituting Belle for Tartabull. Keep in mind that Belle's numbers in Chicago have been adjusted downward since Jacobs Field is a better hitter's park than Comiskey (his 156 RC were lowered by about 10 percent). Here's what we found:

Tartabull '96 vs. Belle '97

Player	Runs Created	Run Diff.	Tm Win %	W-L
Danny Tartabull '96	95	—	.556	90-72
Albert Belle '97	140	+45	.578	94-68

(runs created based on Belle's 442 outs used)

The first thing that strikes us is the number of games the White Sox *should* have won last season according to the RC formula: 90 instead of the 85 they actually wound up with. So even without Belle, Chicago should post more victories next year; they were just hit by bad luck in '96. With Belle, however, they're a clear threat to overtake the Indians. Phillips might slip a bit at age 38, but Tartabull played only 122 games in right field last season (his RC number was pro-rated) and had to be frequently replaced in the field by Dave Martinez. With Belle in left, Phillips and rookie Mike Cameron should be able to handle right field, freeing Martinez to man center.

All other factors remaining constant, it seems that Belle's signing with Chicago should tighten the A.L. Central considerably. Depending on how the positional moves on both sides work out, the White Sox could indeed have closed the gap between themselves and the Indian frontrunners.

—Kevin Fullam

Cleveland Indians: What Happens When a Good Team Loses a Superstar?

In the Chicago White Sox essay, we assessed the potential impact of superstar Albert Belle's free-agent signing. Mixing an assortment of formulas with a few hypothetical scenarios, we predicted the approximate effect that Belle's move to Comiskey Park might have on the 1997 A.L. Central race. While we concluded that the loss of Belle would cost the Indians several games in the standings, the question piqued our interest about the subject of how other teams responded to the loss of a star player. We researched a few similar scenarios from baseball's past to help us forecast what might happen to Cleveland over the next few seasons:

Roberto Clemente—Pittsburgh Pirates

After losing the services of their Hall of Fame outfielder to a fatal plane crash on New Year's Eve of 1972, the Pittsburgh Pirates went into a tailspin. After claiming three straight N.L. East championships from 1970-72, Pittsburgh struggled the following season and finished with a disappointing 80-82 record—their only losing mark of the decade.

In truth, though, the absence of Clemente had little to do with the team's troubles. Though Pittsburgh certainly missed his presence in the clubhouse, the Pirates' bats hardly felt the impact of Clemente's death. In fact, with the emergence of Richie Zisk and the tremendous season turned in by Willie Stargell, Pittsburgh was actually able to maintain its 1972 division-leading offense. What was the real cause of their post-Clemente woes? The Pirates' pitching staff, which saw its ERA rise from a division-leading 2.81 in '72 to a lackluster 3.73 a year later. Much of the decline can be attributed to one man: Steve Blass. After turning in a stellar campaign (19-8, 2.48 ERA) a season earlier, Blass suffered a complete disintegration, losing any and all ability to find the strike zone. Succumbing what is now known as "Steve Blass Disease," the hurler turned in one of the worst pitching seasons in modern baseball, posting an incredible 9.81 ERA with 84 walks in 89 innings. His struggles effectively sabotaged the Pirates' efforts in '73.

But with young southpaw Jerry Reuss taking over Blass' mantle of staff ace, Pittsburgh quickly rebounded to seize the next two division titles. Throughout the remainder of the 1970s, the Bucs finished no worse than second in the N.L. East.

Pirates' Performance With (1972) & Without Clemente (1973-75)

Year	Record	Position	Runs/Game	Team ERA
1972	96-59	1st	4.46	2.81
1973	80-82	3rd	4.35	3.73
1974	88-74	1st	4.64	3.49
1975	92-69	1st	4.42	3.01

While Clemente was certainly one of the greatest players of his generation, Pittsburgh had to have been prepared for the erosion of the Hall of Famer's skills. Clemente was 38 years old at the time of his death and had played only 102 games in his last season, so the ballclub probably had plans for his decline and/or retirement before the tragedy occurred.

Reggie Jackson—New York Yankees

Changing uniforms for the third time in six years, Reggie Jackson left the New York Yankees via free agency following the 1981 season. His departure ended a five-year stint that had seen the club win two world championships, three pennants, and four A.L. East titles. After making a name for himself as one of the game's greatest sluggers, "Mr. October's" lackluster performance in his final season in pinstripes (.237-15-54 in 94 games) led some to believe that the outspoken 35-year-old's days were numbered. With Yankee owner George Steinbrenner making little effort to re-sign him, Jackson returned to the West Coast to sign a multi-year contract with the California Angels.

As soon as Jackson left, the Yankees' fortunes took a turn for the worse. The 1982 season saw Steinbrenner churn through a trio of managers as the club stumbled to a fifth-place finish, and although Billy Martin eventually righted the team upon his return in 1983, New York was unable to make it back to the postseason. During the early 1980s, the A.L. East was tremendously competitive, with the Orioles, Tigers, and Blue Jays *all* fielding strong teams. As a result, the Yanks—while solid—came up short each year. Was Reggie's defection the main cause of New York's fall from baseball's elite?

Yankees' Performance With (1981) & Without Jackson (1982-84)

Year	Record	Position	Runs/Game	Team ERA
1981	59-48	1st	3.93	2.90
1982	79-83	5th	4.38	3.99
1983	91-71	3rd	4.75	3.86
1984	87-75	3rd	4.68	3.78

The answer appears to be no. Though Jackson led the Angels to the A.L. West title in his first season in California ('82), his production dropped off quickly thereafter. Meanwhile, Dave Winfield, who arrived on the scene during Jackson's last season in New York, provided the Yankees with Reggie's annual output of 25-30 homers through the remainder of the decade. As was the case with the post-Clemente Pirates, New York was stung more by a sudden pitching decline. After posting the A.L.'s top ERA in '81 with a sparkling 2.90 mark, the Yankees' staff steadily dropped out of prominence, as hurlers Ron Guidry and Tommy John eventually succumbed to the effects of age and fatigue; the 39-year-old John was dealt to the Angels late in the '82 season. In addition, Dave Righetti, who was extremely effective as a starter upon entering the majors in '81, wasn't able to withstand the strain of starting and had to be relegated to the bullpen a few seasons later. In retrospect, it's doubtful that the Yanks would have continued to dominate even if Jackson *had* stayed in the Big Apple.

Sandy Koufax—Los Angles Dodgers

It would be pretty hard to name a pitching superstar who vanished more abruptly than Sandy Koufax. After leading the Los Angeles Dodgers to two World Championships and racking up five consecutive ERA titles, Koufax stunned the baseball world in 1966 by announcing his retirement at the age of 31—citing an arthritic elbow. Talk about letting the air out of the Dodgers' pennant chances! Take a look at what happened:

Dodgers With (1966) & Without Koufax (1967-69)

Year	Record	Position	Runs/Game	Team ERA
1966	95-67	1st	3.74	2.62
1967	73-89	8th	3.20	3.21
1968	76-86	7th	2.90	2.69
1969	85-77	4th	3.98	3.08

Even without Koufax, the Dodgers continued to post fine team ERAs, but that's a little deceptive: the league ERA was very low in 1967 and 1968. Here's the team ERA relative to the league in Sandy's last two seasons, and then the first two years without him (Relative ERA is simply team ERA divided by league ERA):

Dodgers With (1965-66) & Without Koufax (1967-68)

Year	LA ERA	NL ERA	Relative ERA
1965	2.81	3.54	0.79
1966	2.62	3.61	0.73
1967	3.21	3.38	0.95
1968	2.69	2.99	0.90

Koufax had gone 26-8, 2.04 while working 335.2 innings in 1965 and 27-9, 1.73 in 323 innings in 1966. Without him, the Dodgers lost their dominant stature. While other factors—like weak hitting and a decline in the bullpen's effectiveness—were involved in the club's failure to return to the postseason until 1974, the loss of Koufax was devastating.

A few more examples of winning teams losing superstars in the expansion era:

1. After winning three straight world championships from 1972 to 1974, the Oakland A's lost superstar righthander Catfish Hunter to free agency due to a contract irregularity. Despite the loss of Hunter, the A's won eight more games in 1975 than they did in 1974, and took home another division title. Oakland was then swept in the '75 ALCS by the Red Sox, and it's doubtful that Hunter's presence would have helped them win the series. The A's began to decline after that, but that was due more to the loss of additional players through free agency and trades forced by salary considerations than just the loss of Hunter.

2. After winning the 1979 A.L. West title, the Calfornia Angels lost their top pitcher, Nolan Ryan, to free agency. Without Ryan, the Angels went from 88 wins in '79 to 65 wins and sixth place in '80, though there were other factors involved than just the loss of Ryan. The Angels would eventually recover, returning to the playoffs in 1982.

3. Free agent signee Jack Morris helped the Twins go from last place in 1990 to the World Championship in 1991. After winning 18 games in the regular season and two more—including the clincher—in the World Series, Morris left the Twins to sign with the Blue Jays. The Twins were solid in '92, but Morris' loss was a factor in their drop to second place.

In conclusion, we'd have to say that a club *can* survive the loss of a superstar, but it sure isn't easy. Without Belle, the Tribe could conceivably win the A.L. Central again in 1997, but don't expect the ride to be nearly as smooth as it's been the last two seasons.

—Kevin Fullam and Don Zminda

Detroit Tigers: Is There Hope for Their Pitching Staff?

In case you hadn't noticed, the Detroit Tigers were *bad* last year—especially their pitching staff. Detroit's team ERA of 6.38 was the worst in American League history, and the second-worst for any major league team in this century. Only the 1930 Philadelphia Phillies, who had the handicap of working in a hitters' paradise known as Baker Bowl, were worse with an ERA of 6.71.

Any staff this bad would figure to improve the next year, but by how much? This chart shows the clubs with the 10 highest ERAs since 1901, and how those teams fared over the next three seasons:

Worst ERAs Since 1901

		Year 1		Year 2		Year 3		Year 4	
Year	Team	ERA	W%	ERA	W%	ERA	W%	ERA	W%
1930	Philadelphia Phillies	6.71	.338	4.58	.429	4.47	.506	4.34	.395
1996	Detroit Tigers	6.38	.327	—	—	—	—	—	—
1936	St. Louis Browns	6.24	.375	6.01	.299	5.80	.362	6.01	.279
1929	Philadelphia Phillies	6.13	.464	6.71	.338	4.58	.429	4.47	.506
1936	Philadelphia Athletics	6.07	.346	4.85	.358	5.49	.349	5.79	.362
1939	St. Louis Browns	6.01	.279	5.12	.435	4.72	.455	3.59	.543
1937	St. Louis Browns	6.01	.299	5.80	.362	6.01	.279	5.12	.435
1938	St. Louis Browns	5.80	.362	6.01	.279	5.12	.435	4.72	.455
1939	Philadelphia Athletics	5.79	.362	5.23	.351	4.84	.416	4.44	.357
1995	Minnesota Twins	5.77	.389	5.30	.481	—	—	—	—

Of the nine teams that had a Year 2, seven improved their ERAs, but all of them remained pretty bad. It might be a good omen for the Tigers that the club with the highest ERA, the 1930 Phillies, lowered their team ERA by over two runs in 1931. The Phils' improvement wasn't *quite* as dramatic as it appears. The 1930 season was the best hitters' year in modern National League history, and the overall league ERA that year was 4.97. Legend has it that N.L. magnates, feeling that things had gotten out of control, made sure the ball was a lot deader in 1931. Whether that actually happened or not, the league ERA dropped by over one full run in 1931, to 3.86, and never again approached the levels seen in 1930.

Relative to the league, the Phils' ERA in 1931 improved by almost exactly a run over their '30 mark. That's still quite an improvement—especially for a club playing in what was probably the best hitters' park of all time next to Coors Field (for more on this, see the essay on p. 84). How'd the Phillies do it? A big factor was the improvement of starter Ray Benge, who lowered his ERA from 5.69 in 1930 to 3.17 in '31—a fabulous mark for a pitcher working in Baker Bowl. Another big factor was the addition of Jumbo Jim Elliott in a deal with the Dodgers. A workhorse, Elliott went 19-14 with a decent 4.27 ERA while starting 30 games and relieving in 22 others. Note to Buddy Bell: don't try this with any of *your* pitchers.

The other team to lower its ERA by more than a run in Year 2 was the American League's Philadelphia club, the Athletics. The 1936 American League season was another great one for hitters—the overall league ERA was 5.04, the highest league ERA in this century. Like the 1931 National League, things normalized a little in the 1937 A.L., though not quite as much—the league ERA dropped 42 points to 4.62. Relative to the league, the '37 A's ERA improved by about 0.80 runs over their 1936 mark, which is still quite good. The biggest factor in the A's improvement in 1937 was the sudden development of righthander George Caster. Out of the majors in 1936, Caster returned to The Show in '37 and became a reliable starter, winning 12 games with a decent 4.42 ERA.

While most of the other teams on the list improved their ERA in Year 2, the improvement usually wasn't dramatic, and most of them remained bad teams in subsequent years. The list is top-heavy with the sad-sack Browns and A's of the '30s—teams which were underfinanced, ineptly run and basically hopeless. Sounds a lot like the Tigers of recent vintage, doesn't it?

Detroit, at least, is working hard to improve the situation. Bell seems like a bright young manager, and general manager Randy Smith is youthful, energetic and unafraid to wheel and deal. And Detroit has a couple of possible candidates to break through with a good season in 1997, just like Ray Benge did with the '31 Phillies. Felipe Lira and Justin Thompson look like the best candidates to give the Tigers some hope. But when you consider that the Tigers could have lowered their 1996 ERA by a run and *still* had the worst mark in the league. . . well, let's just say there's work to be done.

— Don Zminda

Kansas City Royals: Relatively Speaking, Can They Slug?

Hey, Kansas City Royals! Didn't anyone tell you that 1996 was "The Year of the Hitter"?

Looking at the numbers, the answer appears to be no. The Royals finished last in the league in runs scored (746), last in slugging average (.398) and second-to-last in home runs (123). Meanwhile, they were *first* in the "one-run strategy" categories of sacrifice hits (66) and stolen bases (195). Their leading "slugger" was Craig Paquette with 22 homers and 67 RBI—figures that might have looked normal leading a team in 1968, but not in 1996. The Royals were so underpowered that they played Jose Offerman—all five home runs and 47 RBI of him—at first base. After considering the alternatives on the Royals roster, Bill James defended this as a good move.

The Royals were so out of kilter with the rest of the '96 American League that we began to wonder whether their team slugging average—.398 in a league that slugged .445—was historically low relative to the league figure. We asked our programmers to create a "relative slugging percentage" by dividing team slugging average by the league mark for that year. Here are the 10 poorest-slugging teams of this century, relative to their league:

Lowest Team Relative Slugging Averages—Since 1901

Team	Yr	Pct of League	SLG	BA	HR	W	L
Houston Colt .45s	1963	82.6	.301	.220	62	66	96
Chicago White Sox	1910	83.4	.261	.211	7	68	85
Boston Braves	1924	83.5	.327	.256	25	53	100
Baltimore Orioles	1955	83.9	.320	.240	54	57	97
Houston Colt .45s	1964	84.1	.315	.229	70	66	96
Boston Braves	1922	84.3	.341	.263	32	53	100
Texas Rangers	1972	84.6	.290	.217	56	54	100
Oakland Athletics	1979	84.8	.346	.239	108	54	108
St. Louis Cardinals	1986	85.9	.327	.236	58	79	82
Pittsburgh Pirates	1954	86.1	.350	.248	76	53	101

As it turned out, the '96 Royals didn't make the bottom 10; in fact, it wasn't even close. KC's relative slugging percentage of 89.5 finished in 85th place, which is nothing to brag about considering that there were more than 1,800 teams in the study. But they weren't last. . . far from it.

The teams that did rank near the bottom were an interesting bunch, however. Worst of all were the 1963 Houston Colt .45s, a second-year expansion club that slugged a pathetic .301 in a league where the norm was .364. Craig Paquette would have been another Mark McGwire if he'd played for this squad—their home run leader was catcher John Bateman with 10. The .45s did have some good hitters on the roster—Rusty Staub and Jimmy Wynn, to name two, and Hall of Famer Joe Morgan for eight games. But this was before they became good players.

A deadball-era team, the 1910 Chicago White Sox, are next. And we do mean "dead." The Sox hit only seven home runs all year, and their .261 slugging average was the worst for any team this century. The Sox were so pathetic on offense that Big Ed Walsh posted a 1.27 ERA. . . and still lost 20 games! That's hard to do.

The rest of the bottom 10 includes an interesting mix of teams from all eras. In general they had two things in common along with their extreme lack of power: they usually played in parks designed for pitchers, and they usually had terrible won-lost records. The most surprising team on the list was probably the 1986 St. Louis Cardinals, a club which was good enough to play in the World Series in both 1985 and 1987. Busch Stadium was a very tough home run park in those days, but not that bad for hitting overall, and the Cardinal roster included such talented hitters as Willie McGee, Jack Clark, Terry Pendleton and Andy Van Slyke. All played poorly in 1986—Van Slyke was the home run leader with 13—but even so, the '86 Redbirds were easily the strongest team on this list.

Which teams had the *highest* relative slugging averages? Here's the top 10 (actually top 11, since there's a tie for 10th):

Highest Team Relative Slugging Averages—Since 1901

Team	Yr	Pct of League	SLG	BA	HR	W	L
New York Yankees	1927	122.3	.488	.307	158	110	44
Cincinnati Reds	1976	117.5	.424	.280	141	102	60
Pittsburgh Pirates	1902	117.4	.374	.286	19	103	36
Cincinnati Reds	1965	117.3	.439	.273	183	89	73
New York Giants	1947	116.3	.454	.271	221	81	73
New York Yankees	1930	115.9	.488	.309	152	86	68
Colorado Rockies	1996	115.8	.472	.287	221	83	79
Colorado Rockies	1995	115.5	.471	.282	200	77	67
New York Yankees	1931	115.5	.457	.297	155	94	59
Boston Red Sox	1950	115.2	.464	.302	161	94	60
Brooklyn Dodgers	1953	115.2	.474	.285	208	105	49

Every underpowered club—including, we're certain, the 1996 Royals—probably gets described somewhere along the way as being "not exactly the '27 Yankees." With good reason, too, because the legendary Yanks of Ruth and Gehrig were the most dominant collection of sluggers in history, relative to their league. There are a *lot* of dominant offensive teams on this list: the Big Red Machine of 1976, with Johnny Bench, Joe Morgan, Pete Rose, Tony Perez and George Foster; the 1947 New York Giants, the first team to hit more than 200 homers in a season; the 1931 Yanks, the highest-scoring club in this century (1,067 runs); the 1950 Red Sox, the last major league team to hit over .300 *and* score more than 1,000 runs; and the mighty 1953 Dodgers of Snider, Campanella, Hodges and Robinson.

Many, though not all, of these teams had the advantage of playing in great parks for hitting. Most were legitimate powerhouses anyway, but we'll state without hesitation that the 1995-96 Rockies make this list only *because* they played in a great hitters' park. Away from Coors, they were about as powerful as the 1996 Royals.

— Don Zminda

A more complete listing for this category can be found on page 238.

Milwaukee Brewers: Were Vaughn and Fielder the Biggest "Hired Guns" of All Time?

Money is power, it's been said. With modern baseball's rent-a-star mentality, the inverse is often true: power is money. On the eve of last year's trading deadline, two of the game's leading home run hitters were dealt from also-rans to contenders, and in each case, money was a major consideration. The Padres landed Greg Vaughn, and the Yankees picked up Cecil Fielder.

Ultimately, both Vaughn and Fielder made it to the postseason with their new teams, but their seasons were notable for another reason: each of them blasted more home runs in 1996 than any other player in history who changed teams in midseason.

Most Home Runs in a Year—Midseason Acquisitions

Player, Teams	Year	HR
Greg Vaughn, Mil/SD	1996	41
Cecil Fielder, Det/Yanks	1996	39
Goose Goslin, Was/Browns	1930	37
Fred McGriff, SD/Atl	1993	37
Ralph Kiner, Pit/Cubs	1953	35
Gus Zernial, WSox/A's	1951	33
Hank Sauer, Cin/Cubs	1949	31
Bobby Bonds, WSox/Tex	1978	31
Rico Carty, Tor/Oak	1978	31
Andy Pafko, Cubs/Bro	1951	30
Ken Harrelson, Bos/Cle	1969	30

The Padres, who were in desperate need of power, snagged Vaughn from the Brewers, who were happy to unload his considerable salary. (Ironically, these were the same Padres who unloaded Fred McGriff for prospects only three years before). San Diego didn't have an opening in the outfield, but it was so eager to add a bona fide run producer that the club took on Vaughn anyway. He played semi-regularly as part of a four-outfielder rotation, and though his batting average was a disappointment, he did swat 10 home runs for the Padres to finish with 41—the most ever by a player who changed teams in mid-season.

Meanwhile, the Yankees added Fielder, who at the time was the highest-paid player in the game. He drove in 37 runs during his two months in New York; only Tino Martinez drove in more for the Yanks over the same span. In the postseason, Fielder more than earned his keep, batting .308 with three homers and 14 RBI in 14 games.

Some see the system as inherently flawed when a team like the Brewers can't afford to keep a Greg Vaughn, while a team like the Yankees can take on a Cecil Fielder whenever the need arises. Still, the money game is hardly a modern phenomenon. From baseball's earliest days, general managers have made deals with one eye on the bottom line. For example, take the case of Ralph Kiner, who was traded in mid-1953 at the height of his stardom.

When Branch Rickey took over the Pittsburgh Pirates in 1951, he inherited a terrible club with one big star—Kiner, one of the game's most highly-paid players. It wasn't long before Rickey uttered his famous line, "We can finish last *without* you," and dealt Kiner to the Cubs in June of 1953.

Although 10 players changed hands in the deal—three went with Kiner to Chicago and six were sent to the Pirates—the main consideration in the transaction was *money*. The Pirates received $150,000 in the deal, and Rickey, characteristically, invested most of it in his farm system.

Although Rickey's quip proved prophetic—Pittsburgh, without Kiner, finished last in 1953, '54 and '55—the farm system soon produced good young players like Bill Mazeroski and Dick Groat. For the sum of $4,000, they also drafted a little-known outfielder out of the Dodgers' farm system. His name was Roberto Clemente. In 1960, they became world champions by defeating the Yankees in one of the most dramatic World Series ever. But Rickey wasn't around to see it—he had stepped down as general manager of the Pirates four years earlier.

—Mat Olkin

A more complete listing for this category can be found on page 239.

Minnesota Twins: Can Molitor Keep Holding Off Father Time?

In a season of remarkable batting feats—and 1996 was definitely a remarkable year—Paul Molitor's accomplishments should not be overlooked. Consider some of his exploits: he became only the second player since 1950 to drive in at least 100 runs in a single season while socking fewer than 10 homers; his 113 RBI set a career high, and his 41 doubles tied his career best; he scored 99 runs, hit .341 and missed only one game all season. But wait, there's more. He *led* the American League with 225 hits, led the *majors* with 167 singles, and his march on the 3,000-hit plateau was so swift and sure that he barely allowed fans a chance to prepare for his milestone.

Perhaps most remarkable of all was the fact that Molitor accomplished these feats at an age when most players have long since hung up their spikes. Though he turned 40 years of age last August 22, Molitor showed no signs of giving in to the demands of Father Time. If anything, he's gotten *better* with age.

"Seasonal age" is based upon the age of a player entering July 1 of any given year, so Molitor's seasonal age for 1996 is listed as 39. His performance last season ranks among the greatest of all-time for players that "old." His .341 batting average in '96 was the best since 1931 for a player age 39 or older, his 113 RBI were the most since 1900 for a player 38 or older and his 225 hits were the most ever, period, for a player 36 or older.

It's not as though Molitor's renaissance is a recent phenomenon, either. He boasts the highest hit total of this decade, with 1,263 since 1990. Though he's always been considered a good offensive player, there's little question Molitor has been a better hitter in his late 30s than he was in his 20s. Take a look at the following chart:

Paul Molitor, by Five-Year Increments

Years	Age	Avg	Hits	HR	RBI
1978-81	21-24	.296	534	26	163
1982-86	25-29	.287	669	53	227
1987-91	30-34	.319	883	69	311
1992-96	35-39	.322	928	72	448

Wow, that's some learning curve. I think we can forget about the typical age-27 peak for Molitor. If he keeps up this trend, he should be reaching his prime right around the turn of the century. Just how amazing has Molitor's late surge been? To answer that, let's examine the players with the most hits between the ages of 35 and 39. We'll also include how many hits each of the players in this group managed to produce after blowing out the 40th candle on their cake.

Most Hits, Age 35-39

Player	Age 35-39	Age 40+
Sam Rice	1,023	551
Pete Rose	1,010	699
Paul Molitor	928	?
Tris Speaker	887	51
Bill Terry	865	0
Ty Cobb	847	289
Doc Cramer	846	102
Eddie Collins	846	87
Jake Daubert	825	114
Lave Cross	824	162

Molitor's performance is truly exceptional. Only two other players in the history of baseball generated *more* hits between the ages of 35 and 39. Those two, Sam Rice and Pete Rose, also rank third and second, respectively, on the list of most hits after the age of *40* (Cap Anson, who played until age 45, has the most, with 822 hits after turning 40). If Molitor can match Rice and Rose, he has a chance to finish his career with around 3,600 total hits, which would place him in the top five all-time.

Of course, most of the players on the above list fared poorer after reaching the big four-oh. Three of them couldn't muster as many as 100 more base knocks. In Molitor's case, however, that scenario seems unlikely entering 1997. For one thing, he seems to be over the injury problems which plagued his early career. After missing 509 team games in his first 13 seasons, he's been a virtual ironman since '91, playing in all but 25 of his teams' games. Molitor has also led the A.L. in hits three times over the last six years, averaging 191 per year—and that includes two seasons shortened by strikes. Though he may have trouble duplicating last year's total of 225 hits, it would be an upset if Molitor doesn't continue to do his best imitation of Methuselah, defying the age on his birth certificate.

—Jim Henzler

A more complete listing for this category can be found on page 240.

New York Yankees: Do Old Pennant-Winners Just Fade, Fade Away?

Bill James suggested the topic for this essay:

> Did you guys ever do anything in the *Scoreboard* about team age? . . . I thought of this watching the Yankees, with Boggs, Strawberry, Fielder, M. Duncan, K. Rogers, Gooden, Key, Cone, O'Neill, Girardi, Raines, Sojo, Charlie Hayes. . . I don't know if it is or not, but it struck me that this must be one of the older teams ever to play in the World Series. We have the data to calculate it in the Encyclopedia, and it would be interesting to know what the oldest teams ever to play in the World Series were, and whether the age of a World Series contender tended to predict future World Series appearances by that team.

It's a good question. The Yankees *did* seem like an exceptionally old team to be playing in the Series. Was that the case. . . and is that a bad sign for their future?

The first thing we needed to do was select a formula for computing team age. You can't just add up the ages of all the players on the roster and then divide by the number of players; to cite one example on the Yankees, Derek Jeter, age 22 last year, played a lot more (582 at-bats) than 36-year-old Tim Raines (201 AB), and it's silly to give them the same weight. So slightly modifying a formula Bill used in his *Baseball Abstracts* a few years ago, we computed team age as follows:

1. Position players count for 65 percent of the weighting, pitchers for 35 percent.
2. Batters' age is computed on the basis of average age per plate appearance.
3. Pitchers' age is computed on the basis of average age per batter faced.

Bill used at-bats and innings pitched rather than PA and BFP when he was compiling average ages for the *Abstract*, but he was figuring them by hand, and our system is a little more precise. At any rate, we found a total of 16 teams with an average age of 30 or older who had played in the World Series. They're listed in the following chart.

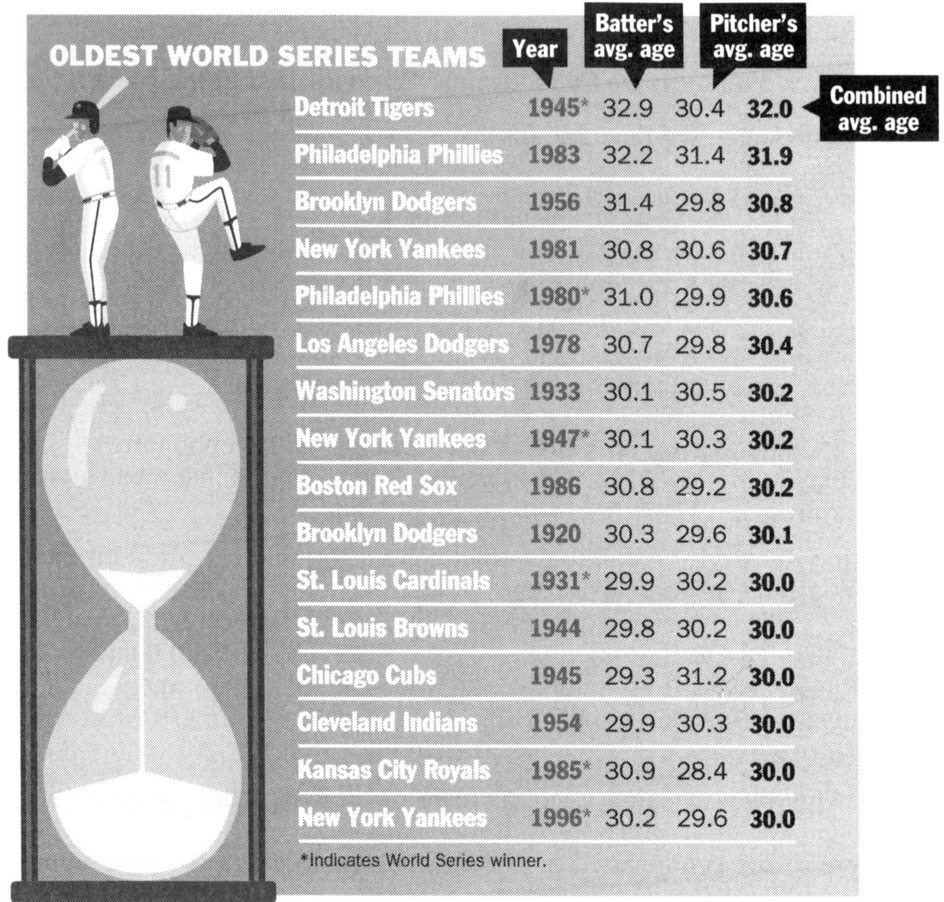

OLDEST WORLD SERIES TEAMS

Team	Year	Batter's avg. age	Pitcher's avg. age	Combined avg. age
Detroit Tigers	1945*	32.9	30.4	**32.0**
Philadelphia Phillies	1983	32.2	31.4	**31.9**
Brooklyn Dodgers	1956	31.4	29.8	**30.8**
New York Yankees	1981	30.8	30.6	**30.7**
Philadelphia Phillies	1980*	31.0	29.9	**30.6**
Los Angeles Dodgers	1978	30.7	29.8	**30.4**
Washington Senators	1933	30.1	30.5	**30.2**
New York Yankees	1947*	30.1	30.3	**30.2**
Boston Red Sox	1986	30.8	29.2	**30.2**
Brooklyn Dodgers	1920	30.3	29.6	**30.1**
St. Louis Cardinals	1931*	29.9	30.2	**30.0**
St. Louis Browns	1944	29.8	30.2	**30.0**
Chicago Cubs	1945	29.3	31.2	**30.0**
Cleveland Indians	1954	29.9	30.3	**30.0**
Kansas City Royals	1985*	30.9	28.4	**30.0**
New York Yankees	1996*	30.2	29.6	**30.0**

*Indicates World Series winner.

As you can see, the 1996 Yankees, with an average age of 30.0, did not rank among the top 10 oldest teams to play in a World Series. They did wind up in a six-way tie for 11th place. The '96 Yanks were the fourth-oldest team to *win* a World Series, along with the 1985 Royals and 1931 Cardinals. Only the wartime 1945 Tigers, the 1980 Phillies and the 1947 Yankees were older.

What about the future performance of these aged pennant-winners? We should probably eliminate the 1945 Tigers, 1945 Cubs and 1944 Browns from consideration, since their rosters by necessity included a lot of aging wartime fill-ins. Among the others, *none* made it back to the World Series the next year, which is not a great harbinger for the '97 Yankees. However, many of the teams on this list returned to the top fairly quickly. For, instance, the 1947 Yankees were back in the Fall Classic two years later—beginning a string of five straight victorious World Series appearances.

Four more teams—the 1956 Dodgers, 1980 Phillies, 1978 Dodgers and 1931 Cardinals—were back in the Series three years later. Another team on the list, the 1986 Red Sox, didn't make it to a Series, but they did win a division title in 1988.

Most of the other teams on the list remained contenders, at least for a couple more years. Only one team on the list got bad the next year and then stayed bad. The 1933 Senators tumbled to seventh place in 1934, and except for one fourth-place finish, remained in the second division until 1943. But Clark Griffith's underfinanced Senators of the '30s don't exactly have much in common with George Steinbrenner's Yankee teams.

How about the *youngest* teams to play in the Series? Here are the 10 youngest:

Youngest Teams to Play in a World Series

Team, Year	Batter's Age	Pitcher's Age	Combined Age
Boston Braves, 1914*	25.3	25.3	25.3
New York Giants, 1911	25.2	26.2	25.5
Boston Red Sox, 1967	25.1	26.2	25.5
Philadelphia Athletics, 1913*	25.5	25.7	25.6
Philadelphia Athletics, 1914	25.8	25.7	25.8
New York Mets, 1969*	25.9	25.8	25.8
Cincinnati Reds, 1970	26.0	25.5	25.8
Boston Red Sox, 1912*	26.1	25.6	25.9
New York Giants, 1912	25.6	26.6	26.0
Philadelphia Phillies, 1950	26.0	26.1	26.0

* Indicates WS winner

In general these teams fared better in the short term than the older teams, which is what you'd expect. The 1911 Giants, 1913 A's and 1912 Giants all made repeat trips to the Series the next year. The 1970 Reds were back in the Fall Classic two years later, and the 1912 Red Sox returned to the Series in 1915. Only one team fell completely on its face the next year, and that was under unique circumstances. Connie Mack unloaded most of the stars of his 1914 A's for economic reasons after that season, and the A's immediately dropped to last place. . . and stayed there for years.

While you'd obviously prefer to have a young pennant-winner than an old one, there's nothing in this data that indicates the Yankees won't remain a contending club if they continue to get good management. But a return trip to the Series in 1997? That's a long shot.

— Don Zminda

A more complete listing for this category can be found on page 241.

Oakland A's: What If McGwire Could Stay Healthy?

Mark McGwire continues to amaze. Last year he hit 52 homers, the most by any player since 1977, despite the fact that he missed 32 games because of injuries. He also broke one of Babe Ruth's more impressive records by averaging a homer every 8.1 at-bats. Ruth's old mark, once considered unbreakable, was one homer every 8.5 AB in 1920.

Looking at McGwire's career, one is struck by two things: what an awesome slugger he's been. . . and how great his numbers *might* have been if he hadn't been hurt so much. The last five years are particularly maddening. Here are McGwire's key stats for 1992-96, with the last line showing the totals for his entire career:

Mark McGwire 1992-96—Actual Totals

Year	G	AB	H	HR	RBI	BB	Avg	OBP	SLG
1992	139	467	125	42	104	90	.268	.385	.585
1993	27	84	28	9	24	21	.333	.467	.726
1994	47	135	34	9	25	37	.252	.413	.474
1995	104	317	87	39	90	88	.274	.441	.685
1996	130	423	132	52	113	116	.312	.467	.730
Career	1224	4082	1053	329	860	789	.258	.380	.544

McGwire missed 23 Oakland games in 1992. In 1993, he was out of action for 135 of Oakland's 162 games. The 1994 and 1995 seasons were shortened by strikes, but McGwire's seasons were shortened even more; he missed 67 of the Athletics' 114 games in 1994, and 40 of their 144 contests in 1995. Add in the 32 missed games from '96, and you come up with 297 missed games—nearly two seasons worth—in the last five years.

What if we gave him those games back, or at least a realistic proportion of them? In the five seasons from 1987 to 1991, McGwire played between 150 and 155 games four times, averaging a little over 625 plate appearances a year in those four seasons; in the other season, 1989, he spent a couple of weeks on the DL and played in 143 games with 587 PA. Figuring 625 PA for a "full McGwire season" and adjusting downward for the strike-shortened years of 1994-1995, let's see what his figures would look like if he'd had 625 plate appearances in 1989, 1992, 1993 and 1996, and give him 450 PA for 1994 and 550 PA for 1995. We'll take his actual figures from those seasons and project them out to the allotted number of PA. Here's his career reconstructed, including his actual numbers for the years in which he wasn't injured.

Mark McGwire Projected Totals

Year	AB	H	HR	RBI	BB	Avg	OBP	SLG
1986*	53	10	3	9	4	.189	.259	.377
1987*	557	161	49	118	71	.289	.370	.618
1988*	550	143	32	99	76	.260	.352	.478
1989	522	120	35	101	88	.230	.338	.466
1990*	523	123	39	108	110	.235	.370	.489
1991*	483	97	22	75	93	.201	.330	.383
1992	511	137	46	114	99	.268	.386	.585
1993	491	164	53	140	123	.334	.468	.729
1994	353	89	24	65	97	.252	.413	.479
1995	413	113	51	117	115	.274	.440	.685
1996	482	151	59	129	132	.313	.468	.730
Total	4938	1308	413	1075	1008	.265	.391	.561

(*Actual numbers; projected numbers for other seasons)

The projections show McGwire just missing Maris' record in 1996 with 59 homers. But if we'd upped the projection a bit to 650 PA—a figure McGwire reached in 1990 and came close to reaching in 1987 (he had 641)—he would have been projected to hit 62 dingers.

Record season or not, the projection shows McGwire with three seasons of 50-plus homers; only Ruth has had more than two. Of just as much interest to us is McGwire's "new" career home run total of 413—84 more dingers than his already-impressive total of 329. McGwire was 32 years old last year, and only seven players in baseball history had more than 413 homers through age 32: Jimmie Foxx (500), Mickey Mantle (454), Eddie Mathews (445), Hank Aaron (442), Frank Robinson (418), Babe Ruth (416) and Mel Ott (415). All those players wound up with more than 500 homers, as did Willie Mays (406 homers through age 32) and Harmon Killebrew (397), the next two players on the list. And of course, a few of those guys hit a *lot* more than 500 homers, led by Aaron (755) and Ruth (714). Could McGwire have challenged Aaron and Ruth's career totals, given good health? That seems perfectly reasonable.

He won't, of course, but even with all his injuries, McGwire could still reach 500 homers. Even better, he's still capable of making a serious challenge to Maris' single-season mark. All he needs to do is stay healthy.

Isn't that where we came in?

— Don Zminda

Seattle Mariners: Where Will Griffey Rank in History?

Can anything stop Ken Griffey Jr.? Last season Junior missed 22 games with a broken hand, yet he still hit 49 homers and drove in 140 runs—averaging exactly one RBI a game. Because of injuries and work stoppages, Griffey has played only 323 games over the last three seasons, meaning that he's missed the equivalent of one entire 162-game season. Yet Griffey, who was only 26 when the 1996 season ended, continues to have one of the most impressive starts to a career of any player in major league history. This chart shows the all-time leaders in home runs through the age of 26, based on the player's age as of July 1:

Most HR at Age 26

Player	HR	Season
Jimmie Foxx	266	1934
Eddie Mathews	253	1958
Mickey Mantle	249	1958
Mel Ott	242	1935
Frank Robinson	241	1962
Ken Griffey Jr.	238	1996
Orlando Cepeda	222	1964
Hank Aaron	219	1960
Juan Gonzalez	214	1996
Johnny Bench	212	1974

Despite all his lost time, Griffey still ranks sixth all-time in home runs through age 26. . . behind five Hall of Famers, all of whom hit more than 500 homers in their careers. Pretty fast company, but Junior seems to fit right in, doesn't he?

Griffey has sometimes been compared with Hank Aaron and Mickey Mantle. We should probably add Frank Robinson to the list:

Griffey, Aaron, Mantle and Robinson—Through Age 26

Player	G	AB	R	H	2B	3B	HR	RBI	BB	Avg	OBP	SLG
Griffey	1057	3985	695	1204	227	21	238	725	504	.302	.381	.549
Aaron	1039	4114	714	1309	225	57	219	743	341	.318	.369	.560
Mantle	1102	3937	890	1238	185	50	249	766	799	.314	.431	.577
Robinson	1050	3895	752	1202	228	36	241	709	468	.309	.390	.571

Of the four, Mantle had the most impressive stats at this point of his career, but Mickey wound up with "only" 536 home runs, far fewer than Robinson (586) or Aaron (755). Injuries and a penchant for fast living helped shorten Mantle's career; Junior—who seems to be a model citizen and whose injuries have tended to be broken bones rather than the chronic type—figures to last a little longer than the Mick. But you never know.

Griffey has hit at least 40 homers in three of the last four years, and he'll need to keep cranking out those 40-homer seasons if he's going to finish among the all-time leaders. To get an idea what fast company he's in, five straight 40-homer seasons would leave him with 438 homers at age 31. This total would bump Junior up to second place on the leaders-by-age chart—but he'd still be a good distance back of the leader, Jimmie Foxx (464 homers at age 31), and not very far ahead of Mathews (422), Mantle (419) and Robinson (403), the only other players with 400-plus homers through age 31. Aaron had 398 homers at that age. . . with a lot of great years still ahead of him.

Barring more serious injuries, our hunch is that Griffey will be able to keep pace with the greats. . . and perhaps even challenge Aaron's career record before he's through.

— Don Zminda

A more complete listing for this category can be found on page 242.

Texas Rangers: Did Juan Gonzalez Deserve the MVP Award?

After the MVP tallies were announced last year, a large contingent of fans and media weren't convinced that Juan Gonzalez was really the most *valuable* player in the A.L. . . but if he wasn't, who was? While he's certainly an outstanding player, we hope to convince you that his performance last season wasn't even one of the year's top 10. How, you ask? Read on. . .

When people evaluate a group of players offensively, they're usually comparing "apples and oranges." That's because they make judgments in a static environment—without regard to the fact that there are vast differences between the replacement-level production of men at different positions. For example, given a first baseman and a shortstop with the same offensive abilities, the shortstop is bound to be far more valuable than his counterpart. Why? If the first baseman breaks down or retires, it's not as critical a loss, since there will be many available players at his position who can hit at a comparable level. However, if a big-hitting *shortstop* needs to be replaced, it's a much more devastating blow, simply because there are far fewer players at that position who are offensive superstars.

Here's a rundown of exactly how potent the average player at each position was last season at the plate. The values given are "runs created per 27 outs"—a Bill James statistic that calculates the number of runs a nine-man lineup consisting of player X would score per 27 outs:

Average Offensive Production By Position—1996 AL

Position	RC/27 Outs
Catcher	4.4
First Base	6.8
Second Base	5.0
Third Base	5.7
Shortstop	4.5
Left Field	5.9
Center Field	5.5
Right Field	6.3
Designated Hitter	6.2

It's not surprising when you think about it. At what positions do teams seem to have the hardest times finding "quality hitters"? Catcher and shortstop. You shouldn't compare right fielders to shortstops anymore than you would compare Coors Field hitters to those playing in the Astrodome.

Instead of directly weighing the players' offensive statistics against one another, we have to first compare them to the replacement-level averages at their positions. After all, that's the level of talent a team will be drawing from if they actually *did* have to find a substitute for a particular player. By rating all the major MVP candidates relative to their respective positions, we'll be able to find who was more valuable to his club in terms of wins and losses. Incidentally, the replacement-level average is generally defined as one run below the average production of a player at a given position.

Gonzalez vs. A.L.'s Top 10 in Runs Created—1996

Player, Team	RC	RC/ Repl.	Diff.
Alex Rodriguez, Sea	157	54	+103
Chuck Knoblauch, Min	147	61	+86
Mark McGwire, Oak	149	66	+83
Jim Thome, Cle	146	64	+82
Brady Anderson, Bal	150	73	+77
Albert Belle, Cle	156	80	+76
Ken Griffey Jr., Sea	142	66	+76
Edgar Martinez, Sea	144	69	+75
Frank Thomas, WSox	150	81	+69
Mo Vaughn, Bos	159	97	+62
Juan Gonzalez, Tex	126	75	+51

Rodriguez' season has to be considered one of the greatest offensive years of the decade—if not *the* greatest. At 103 runs better than the average A.L. replacement-level shortstop, we estimate that his loss would have cost Seattle 10 wins in 1996—an incredible sum. While Gonzalez definitely had an outstanding year at the plate, last season's performance wasn't even on a par with those turned in by McGwire, Griffey Jr. or Edgar Martinez—players, who, like Gonzalez, missed considerable time with injuries in 1996. As for Rodriguez, *his* numbers speak for themselves.

Note that we haven't entered defense into the calculations; it would be difficult to compare players who field eight different positions. However, we can safely assume that Gonzalez isn't going to close the gap on Rodriguez with his glove. The key to Gonzalez winning the MVP wasn't his bat alone, but the fact that the Rangers captured their first-ever division title.

— Kevin Fullam

Toronto Blue Jays: How Long Can "The Rocket" Keep Launching?

More than a few heads rolled last winter when the Toronto Blue Jays lured Roger Clemens away from Boston with truckloads of money and a three-year deal. The signing was definitely the subject of much debate around the entire league, as well as around the office at STATS. Pitchers are *always* risky free-agent signings, and hurlers at Clemens' age with a history of heavy use—well, this appears to have all the markings of a disaster waiting to happen. . . or does it? Is it possible that Toronto is one step ahead of the rest of us, or will the Jays' flight of fancy crash and burn?

Past research shows that the most important indicator of a pitcher's chances for continued success is his strikeout rate. Pitchers who have high strikeout rates will, on average, perform *much* better over a period of time than those who have poor ones. This is not to say that finesse pitchers never succeed (take Bob Tewksbury, for example), but rather that those who *are* effective are definitely in the minority and tend to have much shorter careers than their fireballing counterparts. Pitchers like Mark Fidrych, LaMarr Hoyt and Pete Vuckovich all had relatively low strikeout rates, and they each enjoyed success—but only briefly.

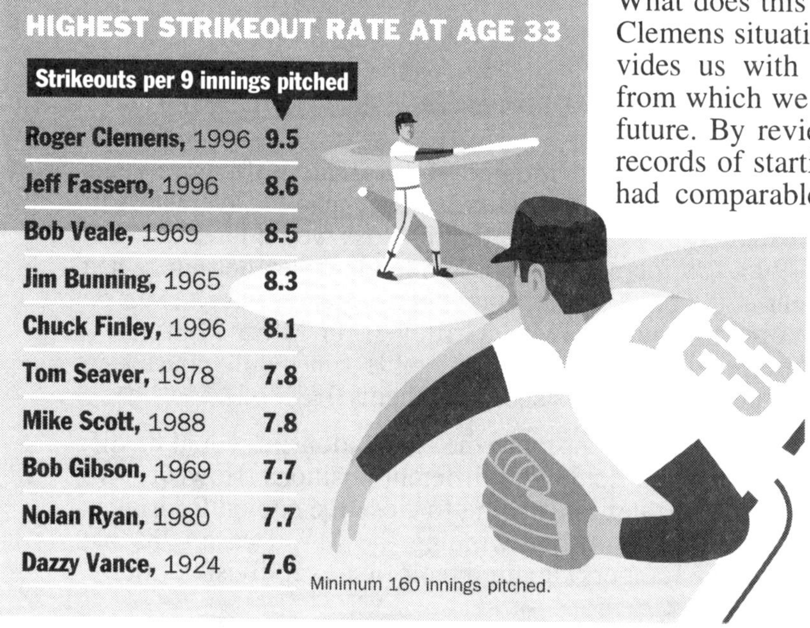

HIGHEST STRIKEOUT RATE AT AGE 33

Strikeouts per 9 innings pitched	
Roger Clemens, 1996	**9.5**
Jeff Fassero, 1996	**8.6**
Bob Veale, 1969	**8.5**
Jim Bunning, 1965	**8.3**
Chuck Finley, 1996	**8.1**
Tom Seaver, 1978	**7.8**
Mike Scott, 1988	**7.8**
Bob Gibson, 1969	**7.7**
Nolan Ryan, 1980	**7.7**
Dazzy Vance, 1924	**7.6**

Minimum 160 innings pitched.

What does this tell us about the Clemens situation? Well, it provides us with a starting point from which we can evaluate his future. By reviewing the career records of starting pitchers who had comparable strikeout rates to Clemens at the same age, we can see if a track record has been established that might predict how long he will remain effective.

With 9.5 strikeouts per nine innings last season, Clemens

posted the highest strikeout rate in baseball history for a 33-year-old pitcher. Without a doubt, 1996 was the year of the veteran power pitcher, as two more of last season's hurlers also placed among the all-time top 10. Since we can't look to Jeff Fassero or Chuck Finley to answer our question, let's examine Bob Veale and Jim Bunning:

Bob Veale—Remainder of Career

Year	Age	W-L	ERA	Lg ERA	IP	H	K/9
1970	34	10-15	3.92	4.05	202.0	189	7.9
1971	35	6-0	7.04	3.47	46.0	59	7.8
1972	36	2-0	3.18	3.07	17.0	12	8.5
1973	37	2-3	3.50	3.82	36.0	37	6.2
1974	38	0-1	5.54	3.63	13.0	15	11.1

Jim Bunning—Remainder of Career

Year	Age	W-L	ERA	Lg ERA	IP	H	K/9
1966	34	19-14	2.41	3.61	314.0	260	7.2
1967	35	17-15	2.29	3.38	302.0	241	7.5
1968	36	4-14	3.88	2.98	160.0	168	5.3
1969	37	13-10	3.69	3.60	212.1	212	6.7
1970	38	10-15	4.11	4.05	219.0	233	6.0
1971	39	5-12	5.48	3.47	110.0	126	4.7

To be lumped with these two hurlers is definitely a compliment: Veale was one of the N.L.'s elite starters in the 1960s, and Bunning is a Hall of Famer. How did their careers wind down? In Veale's case, after he turned 33, a crop of young Pirate starters forced him to the bullpen—where he lost his effectiveness. Bunning had two more great seasons at age 34 and 35, then experienced a sharp dropoff in both his strikeout rate and his ERA. Neither of these pitchers became full-fledged starters until their mid-to-late 20's; by contrast, Clemens already had over 450 major league innings under his belt at the age of just 23. Perhaps a better comparison can be made between Clemens and Tom Seaver, who as a 23 year old was firmly entrenched in the Mets starting rotation.

Tom Seaver—Remainder of Career

Year	Age	W-L	ERA	Lg ERA	IP	H	K/9
1979	34	16-6	3.14	3.74	215.0	187	5.5
1980	35	10-8	3.64	3.61	168.0	140	5.4
1981	36	14-2	2.55	3.49	166.0	120	4.7
1982	37	5-13	5.50	3.61	111.1	136	5.0
1983	38	9-14	3.55	3.64	231.0	201	5.3
1984	39	15-11	3.95	4.00	236.2	216	5.0
1985	40	16-11	3.17	4.15	238.2	223	5.1
1986	41	7-13	4.03	4.19	176.1	180	5.3

After turning 34, Seaver suffered a dramatic loss in his strikeout rates. However, his career stabilized; while he wasn't the dominating pitcher he had once been, he wasn't a *bad* pitcher either—in fact his ERA was close to or better than the league average in six of his final seven seasons. What's surprising about Seaver is that he didn't call it quits after 1982, when it clearly looked as though "Tom Terrific's" career was in mortal danger. Not only did he return at age 38, but he also posted three straight seasons of 200-plus innings—an amazing feat.

Are there any other hurlers on the list that we can examine for possible insight into Clemens' situation? Well, Mike Scott is definitely an historian's anomaly: he rose to prominence at the age of 30 on the strength of the split-fingered fastball and was out of baseball six years later. As for the rest, Bob Gibson and Dazzy Vance both started their careers later than Clemens did, and I don't think we can compare *anybody* to Nolan Ryan.

In an age of frequent rotator cuff tears and ligament sprains, the Sox extracted an average of over 250 innings a year from the Rocket between 1986 and '92. He's completed over a quarter of his career starts (100 of 382), and despite the fact that he entered 1996 coming off arm problems, Boston pushed him for 242.2 more innings last season. That said, there's clearly a precedent for those who believe he'll continue to be effective; after all, Seaver was worked just as hard as Clemens throughout his career, if not harder. From the age of 34 on, Seaver had three seasons of 15-plus wins, not to mention his 14-2, 2.55 campaign in strike-shortened 1981. If Clemens has a few years like those left in him—and Bill James says he is "still a great, great pitcher. . . one of the three or four best starters in baseball *right now*"—the Jays will be more than satisfied.

— Kevin Fullam

A more complete listing for this category can be found on page 243.

Atlanta Braves: The Best Pitching Staff of All Time?

When John Smoltz took home the National League Cy Young Award last fall, it marked the fifth time in six years that a Braves pitcher had won the award: three for Greg Maddux (1993-94-95), one for Tom Glavine (1991) and one for Smoltz. The only time the Braves missed during that period was in 1992. . . and even then, it went to Maddux, who was then a member of the Cubs.

This naturally caused us to wonder whether the Braves have had the best pitching staff in baseball history over a sustained period of time. . . say six years. We asked our programmers to compute the composite ERA for every team in the majors since 1901 in six-year intervals. We then had them compare these composite ERAs with the league ERA figures over the same period. That would enable us to compare teams from big-hitting periods like the 1930s with pitching-dominated eras like the first decade of the century.

The chart lists the top 15 staffs since 1901, and we were as surprised by the results as you are. The top spots are totally dom-

BIGGEST TEAM/LEAGUE ERA DIFFERENTIALS, 6-YEAR PERIOD

Years	Team	ERA	League	Difference	W–L%
1934–39	New York Yankees	3.74	4.67	–0.93	.648
1935–40	New York Yankees	3.76	4.65	–0.89	.641
1936–41	New York Yankees	3.75	4.60	–0.85	.651
1937–42	New York Yankees	3.53	4.37	–0.83	.651
1938–43	New York Yankees	3.41	4.14	–0.73	.647
1933–38	New York Yankees	3.91	4.61	–0.70	.633
1948–53	Cleveland Indians	3.44	4.14	–0.70	.601
1905–10	Chicago Cubs	1.99	2.67	–0.69	.678
1947–52	Cleveland Indians	3.41	4.09	–0.68	.588
1902–07	Chicago Cubs	2.12	2.80	–0.68	.631
1949–54	Cleveland Indians	3.37	4.05	–0.68	.617
1904–09	Chicago Cubs	1.95	2.62	–0.67	.666
1942–47	St. Louis Cardinals	2.93	3.60	–0.67	.646
1926–31	Philadelphia Athletics	3.58	4.24	–0.66	.641
1941–46	St. Louis Cardinals	2.87	3.53	–0.65	.655

Since 1901.

inated by the New York Yankee staffs in the years from 1933 to 1943. Those Yankees didn't always have the sparkling team ERAs of staffs from many other eras, but remember that this was one of the biggest-hitting eras in baseball history. In the context they were performing in, the Yanks *did* have a great staff; they totally blew away the competition. Led by Hall of Famers Red Ruffing and Lefty Gomez and a rotating cast of good pitchers like Johnny Allen, Spud Chandler, Bump Hadley and reliever Johnny Murphy, these guys were good. And obviously very underrated.

Three other staffs make multiple appearances on the leaders list, most notably the Cleveland Indians in the years from 1947 to 1954 and the Chicago Cub staffs from 1902 to 1910. The Indian staff, led by Hall of Famers Bob Lemon, Early Wynn and Bob Feller, is justifiably considered one of the best of all time. That goes double for the Cub staffs of the deadball era, which were led by Hall of Famer Three Finger Brown.

Where are the Braves? As it turned out, the 1991-96 Braves finished all the way down in 31st place, with an ERA differential of -0.60 (3.38 vs. the league figure of 3.98). We'd have to say that this greatly underestimates their value. For one thing, there's only a slight difference between their fantastic -0.60 figure and the differentials recorded by most of the teams in the top 15. We didn't adjust for park factors, but the Braves, playing in Atlanta's Launching Pad, obviously had it tougher than most teams.

Then there's the matter of depth. With Maddux, Glavine and Smoltz, the Braves have three pitchers who have won five Cy Young Awards for Atlanta, and six overall. In addition, former Cy Young winner Steve Bedrosian (Philadelphia, 1987) pitched for Atlanta from 1993 to 1995. No staff in history can match the Braves' collection of hardware. The Cy Young Award didn't exist prior to 1956, but a few years ago SABR polled its membership to create retroactive awards for the missing seasons. The 1933-43 Yankee staff won four of these awards—two went to Gomez (1934 and '37), one to Ruffing (1938), one to Chandler (1943). The 1948-55 Indians also won a total of four, three of them going to Lemon (1948, 1950, 1954), the other to reliever Ray Narleski (1955). The 1902-10 Cubs took just two, to Jack Taylor in 1902 and Three Finger Brown in 1906.

The Braves' trio ranks with any threesome that ever pitched together for an extended period of time, and they've had a number of other excellent pitchers on their staff over the last six years. But the best staff ever over an extended period? We're not sure we could say that just yet.

—Don Zminda

A more complete listing for this category can be found on page 244.

Chicago Cubs: Is 100 Innings Too Much for a Modern Reliever?

The Chicago Cubs are rightfully proud of their young relief pitcher, Terry Adams. He's got one of the best arms in the league, and many expect him to become a fine closer down the road. However, the workload he shouldered last year may be a cause for concern. Adams threw 101 innings of relief, and was one of only three major league relievers to top the 100-inning mark last year. Will his heavy load last year affect his performance in the upcoming season?

To explore that question, let's take a look at the 19 relievers who threw at least 100 innings in a season from 1990 to 1995 (note that three of the relievers broke into triple-digits more than once). Below, we summarize these pitchers' performances during their 100-inning year and in the following season, focusing on the change in their ERA.

100-Inning Seasons By Relievers In The 1990s

Player	Year 1	G	IP	ERA	Year 2	G	IP	ERA	Diff
Greg A. Harris	1993	80	112.1	3.77	1994	38	50.2	7.99	+4.23
Rusty Meacham	1992	64	101.2	2.74	1993	15	21.0	5.57	+2.83
Doug Jones	1992	80	111.2	1.85	1993	71	85.1	4.54	+2.68
Alan Mills	1993	45	100.1	3.23	1994	47	45.1	5.16	+1.93
Dave Veres	1995	72	103.1	2.26	1996	68	77.2	4.17	+1.91
Chuck McElroy	1991	71	101.1	1.95	1992	72	83.2	3.55	+1.60
Mel Rojas	1992	68	100.2	1.43	1993	66	88.1	2.95	+1.52
Todd Frohwirth	1992	65	106.0	2.46	1993	70	96.1	3.83	+1.37
Roger McDowell	1991	71	101.1	2.93	1992	65	83.2	4.09	+1.16
Joe Boever	1992	81	111.1	2.51	1993	61	102.1	3.61	+1.10
	1993	61	102.1	3.61	1994	46	81.1	3.98	+0.37
Tim Burke	1991	72	101.2	3.36	1992	38	43.1	4.15	+0.79
John Doherty	1995	48	113.0	5.10	1996	3	6.1	5.68	+0.59
Xavier Hernandez	1992	77	111.0	2.11	1993	72	96.2	2.61	+0.50
Paul Assenmacher	1990	74	103.0	2.80	1991	75	102.2	3.24	+0.45
	1991	75	102.2	3.24	1992	70	68.0	4.10	+0.86
Dennis Lamp	1990	47	105.2	4.68	1991	51	92.0	4.70	+0.01
Greg W. Harris	1990	73	117.1	2.30	1991	20	133.0	2.23	–0.07
Duane Ward	1990	73	127.2	3.45	1991	81	107.1	2.77	–0.69
	1991	81	107.1	2.77	1992	79	101.1	1.95	–0.81
	1992	79	101.1	1.95	1993	71	71.2	2.13	+0.18
Jeremy Hernandez	1993	70	111.2	3.63	1994	21	23.1	2.70	–0.93
Juan Berenguer	1990	51	100.1	3.41	1991	49	64.1	2.24	–1.17

You'll notice that out of the 23 seasons in which a reliever topped 100 innings, 18 times his ERA went up in the following year. For some, like Greg A. Harris, Alan Mills and Doug Jones, the collapse was both severe and immediate. Others, like Xavier Hernandez, Joe Boever and Chuck McElroy, lost effectiveness in the following season, but fell apart completely the year *after* that (we didn't include the third year in the chart, but if we had, you'd see that many of these guys ultimately declined even further).

Admittedly, when you take a group of relievers who threw 100 innings in a season, you should *expect* many of them to decline in the following year, for reasons *other* than arm fatigue. When you look only at 100-inning seasons, you're necessarily going to be including a lot of "career" years. In order for a pitcher to get the ball enough to pile up all those innings, he must be pitching pretty well (John Doherty and the pitching-starved Tigers notwithstanding). So when you look at a bunch of guys who put together career years, it's quite natural to expect most of them to come back to earth soon afterward.

But the pattern we're seeing here goes far beyond that. As we've noted, almost *all* of the pitchers suffered an immediate decline of some sort in the following season, and several of them dropped off even further after that. But what about the four exceptions, you ask? Let's take a closer look at how they fared.

First we have Greg W. Harris—the Greg Harris who could only pitch with *one* arm. He threw 117.1 innings for the Padres in 1990. In the following season, he was moved into the starting rotation, and missed most of the first half with a sore elbow. He pitched well in the second half, but he's been plagued by injuries and ineffectiveness ever since.

Juan Berenguer gave the Twins 100.1 innings of relief in 1990. In 1991, he became the Braves' closer and performed surprisingly well, until he went down for the season in August with a stress fracture in his arm. He posted a 5.00+ ERA for two teams in '92 and never pitched in the majors again.

Jeremy Hernandez lowered his ERA following his 111.2-inning season, but that's because a neck injury limited him to only 23.1 innings in the latter year. He underwent spinal fusion surgery and hasn't been healthy since, so it's impossible to gauge the impact all those innings had on his arm.

For several years, Duane Ward seemed like the only reliever in baseball who could handle the heavy workload. He threw 127.2 innings in 1990, and the following year, his ERA went *down* by almost three-quarters of a run. Toronto gave him over 100 innings again in '91, and the year after that, his ERA dropped by an even *greater* margin. By then, the Blue Jays felt that they were keeping Ward within reasonable limits, so they gave him a 100-inning workload for the third straight year in 1992. His ERA rose a little bit the year after that, but he continued to excel as he moved from a set-up role into the closer's spot. Then it happened: after the '93 season, Ward tore his rotator cuff. He's pitched just four games in the major leagues since then.

We can summarize the 100-inning men as follows: almost all of them suffered a decline in the season following their heavy workload. Several fared even more poorly in subsequent seasons. The four pitchers who were able to survive the heavy work and improve their ERAs really didn't "survive" at all: three of them suffered a career-threatening or career-ending arm injury soon afterward.

To determine whether or not this was just a recent phenomenon, we went back and looked at how the 100-inning relievers fared in the '50s, '60s, '70s and '80s. Here are their cumulative ERAs in their 100-inning seasons and in the following season:

ERA Change in Season After 100+ Inning Season—By Decade

Decade	# of 100-IP Seasons	Year 1 ERA	Year 2 ERA	%Change
1950s	24	2.94	3.73	+27%
1960s	91	2.72	3.33	+22%
1970s	121	2.79	3.34	+20%
1980s	134	2.95	3.48	+18%
1990s	23	2.95	3.53	+20%

As you can see, the 100-inning pitchers from the 1990s are hardly unique. Over the last 50 years, pitchers have consistently declined in the year following a 100-inning season. While the 1990s pitchers' collective ERA rose 20 percent in the following season, the dropoff was no more severe than it had been for similar pitchers in previous years. That doesn't tell the whole story, however.

As we detailed above, several of the recent 100-inning pitchers suffered arm injuries soon after their heaviest use. Pitchers sidelined with injuries wouldn't affect the numbers on the ERA chart above, but their absence *would* show up if we totaled up *innings* instead of ERA. Let's take a look at the average number of innings groups of pitchers threw before and after:

Average Innings Pitched, Before and After—By Decade

Decade	Year 1 Avg IP	Year 2 Avg IP	%Change
1950s	120.0	91.1	–24%
1960s	119.1	92.1	–23%
1970s	119.2	100.0	–16%
1980s	114.1	91.1	–20%
1990s	106.2	75.0	–30%

Now we get a much a clearer picture. It's obvious that in recent years, relievers haven't been able to throw nearly as many innings in the following season. Even though they threw *fewer* innings during their big seasons than relievers had in the past, their innings totals plunged by 30 percent, almost *twice* the rate of decline for relievers in the '70s, and 50 percent more than that of relievers from the '80s. While some of the decline in innings would be the result of reduced effectiveness—pitchers with higher ERAs would naturally be given less work—a drop as large as 30 percent would almost have to be related to injuries. We consider this compelling evidence that throwing 100 innings in today's game is even more risky than ever.

Still, many are understandably skeptical of the notion that 100 innings represents a dangerous workload. After all, the top short relievers in the '70s regularly threw well over 100 innings per season. Why should 100 innings represent a dangerous amount of use today, when it was a quite unremarkable workload only 20 years ago?

In response, we would submit that throwing 100 innings today requires more effort than it ever has. Why is that? First, the typical pattern of use for short relievers has changed. For a pitcher like Goose Gossage, it wasn't unusual to enter the game in the seventh or eighth inning. As a result, he piled up a good number of two- and three-inning stints. Today's short men are rarely brought in before the ninth inning; they accumulate innings one at a time. To reach the 100-inning mark, today's pitchers must make many more appearances. Perhaps it is harder on the arm to throw one inning three days in a row than it is to throw three innings after two days off.

Another consideration is the fact that it takes more *pitches* to throw the same number of innings today. Batters are taking more pitches and working deeper counts than they used to. We've been keeping complete pitch count information since 1989, and during the '89 season, the average plate appearance took 3.52 pitches. That number has gone up steadily since then, to an average of 3.75 pitches in 1996—a six percent increase in only seven seasons. As to how much that figure has changed since the 1970s, we can only speculate. But we certainly do see the effects of it in starting pitchers' workloads. The 300-inning season—commonplace in the '70s—is virtually extinct today. Steve Carlton posted the last one, in 1980, and we're not likely to see another one for a long time, if ever.

A similar trend has taken hold among relievers. The 100-inning season is dying a slow death, just as the 300-inning season did in the '70s and '80s for starters. So far, there have been only 23 100-inning seasons in the '90s—far less than the 90-plus 100-inning seasons recorded each decade in the '60s, '70s and '80s. Of course, the work stoppage in '94 cut into that total, and the decade obviously isn't over yet, but there's still been a pretty dramatic decline in the heavy use of relievers. Perhaps managers are responding to the increasing challenges of modern pitching, recognizing that many pitchers have been victimized by its demands.

When we last studied the issue, back in the 1993 *Baseball Scoreboard*, we examined relievers who worked 110 innings in a single season between 1987 and 1991, and reached the same conclusion: "The relievers have seldom followed a season of heavy usage with another good year. And except for [Duane] Ward, they've all run into arm problems or had alarming increases in ERA within two years—usually both." Soon after we wrote that, Ward became an illustration of the rule, rather than an exception to it.

While we will concede that there are a lot of reasons to feel optimistic about Terry Adams' chances for stardom, we believe that the charts above should at least give us pause. Will Adams be one of the only pitchers of this decade to show no ill effects at all from his heavy usage? Perhaps he will be, but we wouldn't advise investing your savings in his baseball cards.

The same holds true for the other two relievers who worked over 100 innings last year. Jeff Shaw's case isn't nearly as significant; if he suddenly goes into the tank, no one will demand a reason. But Mariano Rivera is widely expected to excel as the Yankee's closer, and anything less than immediate success will be a huge disappointment to many fans. If his arm suddenly goes dead, or his pitches turn fat, tell the head-scratchers that you saw it coming all along.

—Mat Olkin

Cincinnati Reds: How Remarkable was Eric Davis' Comeback?

For a number of players, 1996 was the "The Year of the Comeback." Chicago Cubs icon Ryne Sandberg returned after nearly two years of retirement to blast 25 home runs; Julio Franco returned to Cleveland and proved he could still hit anywhere on the globe; Dwight Gooden helped the Yankees get a head start on the rest of the A.L. East; and Kevin Elster came out of nowhere to blast 24 home runs—although after playing 36 games in 1995, technically, he'd never been away.

While each of their stories were remarkable in their own way, perhaps the most impressive comeback of all was that of Eric Davis of the Reds. His potential seemed unlimited in 1987, when he batted .293 with 37 homers and 50 stolen bases, but a constant string of injuries stalled his development. After lacerating his kidney in the 1990 World Series, his health and skills deteriorated further, and a herniated disk in his neck precipitated his retirement in 1994, after a season in which played in only 37 games and batted just .183. After taking the 1995 season off, he returned last year to enjoy one of his best all-around seasons, smacking 26 home runs and batting .287, his highest average since his golden summer of 1987. But the most impressive aspect of his comeback may have been the fact that he pulled it off at the ripe old age of 34.

All things considered, it was the most productive comeback season ever for a player his age. Here's a complete list of the players, aged 34 and older, who took an entire season off and returned to hit at least nine homers the following year:

Most Home Runs in Comeback Season—Age 34 and Older

Player	Year	HR
Eric Davis	1996	26
Ryne Sandberg	1996	25
Dave Winfield	1990	21
Julio Franco	1996	14
Jackie Jensen	1961	13
Hank Greenberg	1945	13
Home Run Baker	1921	9
Chick Hafey	1937	9

(min 500 gm played before temp. retirement)

The first thing that stands out is that three of the top four players staged their comebacks last season. It was a great year for home runs, so you might say that Davis, Sandberg and Franco each had impeccable timing. But don't discount their accomplishments; apart from Dave Winfield's strong return from back surgery in 1990, no player has ever returned after a year's layoff and hit more than 13 home runs.

Jackie Jensen's story illustrates just how hard it can be to find the groove after sitting out a year. Jensen won the A.L. MVP Award in 1958 and a Gold Glove in '59, but retired the following year due to a difficult divorce and his fear of flying. When he returned in 1961 and tried to pick up where he'd left off, he found that he couldn't produce anything close to his old power numbers. After his home run total dropped by more than half in 1961, Jensen called it quits for good.

Hank Greenberg took a while to regain his power stroke when he returned from the army in 1945. He clouted 13 home runs in 78 games—a respectable total by normal standards, but a far cry from the 41 round-trippers he collected during his last full season in 1940. When the lifeless wartime baseballs were junked in 1946, Greenberg shook off the rust and pushed his home run total back up to 44.

One player who *appeared* to hit for more power upon his return was—ironically—Frank "Home Run" Baker. He sat out the 1920 season due to the illness and subsequent death of his wife. In 1919, he hit 10 home runs in 141 games, and when he returned in 1921, he came within one homer of matching that total while playing only *94* games. But the game had changed tremendously since he'd been away: the dawn of the lively ball era had sent home run totals skyrocketing, and the homer rate in the A.L. in 1921 was nearly *double* what it had been in 1919. When you take that into account, it's apparent that during the layoff, Baker's power had in fact declined, not improved.

The list illustrates just how unique Davis' comeback really was. Who could have guessed that a man whose career was virtually destroyed by injuries would return a year later, and show no ill effects from age and inactivity? Hats off to Eric Davis, who finally made it all the way back in 1996.

—Mat Olkin

Colorado Rockies: What if McGwire (Thomas, Belle, Sheffield. . .) Called Coors Home?

It's no secret that Coors Field has a profound effect on offensive production—we devote an essay to examining whether it's the best hitters' park in baseball history (see p. 84). It's also no secret that Rockies hitters have been the prime beneficiaries. Check out the 1996 home/road splits for the following Rockies:

Colorado Rockies at Home and on the Road—1996

	Home				Road			
Batter	**HR**	**Avg**	**OBP**	**SLG**	**HR**	**Avg**	**OBP**	**SLG**
Dante Bichette	22	.366	.413	.646	9	.253	.296	.401
Ellis Burks	23	.390	.443	.728	17	.291	.367	.535
Vinny Castilla	27	.345	.389	.659	13	.259	.291	.429
Andres Galarraga	32	.359	.419	.738	15	.245	.290	.458
Eric Young	7	.412	.473	.549	1	.219	.298	.269
Team Totals	149	.343	.408	.579	72	.228	.295	.357

The Rockies hit more than two-thirds of their home runs, batted 115 points higher and slugged an incredible 222 points higher at Coors Field than on the road.

That got us thinking: What if we put some of today's great hitters in Coors? Interesting, but how can we do that? By using park indexes. In a nutshell, a park index tells you whether the park favors a particular stat. For example, let's compute the park index at Coors for home runs in 1996. On the season, there were 271 home runs hit in 5,875 at-bats at Coors, a frequency of .046 HR per AB; in Rockies road games, the frequency was .028 HR per AB (148/5,311). Dividing the Home frequency by the Road frequency gives us a figure of 1.66. We multiply that figure by 100 to get the Park Index for home runs in 1996 at Coors Field: 166. What does an Index of 166 mean? It means that it was 66 percent easier for players to hit home runs in Coors than in an average National League park last season.

We took baseball's top offensive players and reworked their 1996 stats as if they had played last season in Coors Field. Since home-run frequencies can differ significantly at a park depending on what side of the plate a batter is hitting from, we used the 1996 *Major League Handbook* park indexes based on batting righty or lefty. Let's use Mark McGwire as an example. McGwire plays his home games in the Oakland Coliseum, which had a home-run index of 95 for right-handed hitters last year. The home-run index for righties at Coors in 1996 was 169. Since McGwire only played about half of his games at home, what we need to do is reduce the impact of both indexes to account for the fact that the "new McGwire" will also be playing only half of his games at Coors. So, the Coors index of 169 becomes 134.5, and the Coliseum index of 95 becomes 97.5 (again, we had to halve the effect of the pitcher's park as well). Dividing 134.5 by 97.5, we obtain a conversion factor of 1.38, meaning that McGwire could be expected to hit 1.38 times the 52 homers he actually hit last year. Doing the multiplication, we found that McGwire would reach the staggering total of 72 homers. Bye-bye, Roger Maris. And remember that McGwire played in only 130 games last year, and had just 423 at-bats! Albert Belle (68), Juan Gonzalez (67), and Brady Anderson (65) would also have topped Maris' mark, with Todd Hundley (61) close behind. (For switch-hitters like Hundley, we used the overall home-run index at each park.)

But Coors isn't just a park for home runs. It has dramatic effects on almost every offensive statistic—just take another look at the home/road splits the Rockies compiled. The 1996 index for batting average was 132, vaulting Alex Rodriguez to a .414 season. Though nobody else cleared .400, Mike Piazza (.397) and Frank Thomas (.389) would have flirted with the mark throughout the dog days of summer. The index for doubles was 130, and this list is also topped by Alex Rodriguez with 59, just eight shy of Earl Webb's record of 67 set in 1931. The 136 Index for triples means Lance Johnson would have legged out 28 three-base hits, not far from Chief Wilson's longtime record of 36 set in 1912.

All of the dramatic effects on offense at Coors result in a Park Index of 172 for runs scored. Who would lead that list? Once again, it's Alex Rodriguez, who with 197 runs scored would have shattered Babe Ruth's 20th-century record of 177, set in 1921. Roberto Alomar (190) and Steve Finley (183) would also have topped Ruth's mark.

Here are the Top 10 "Could Have Been" seasons, based on players' 1996 stats and ranked by OBS (on-base percentage + slugging average):

Great Seasons that Could Have Been at Coors—1996

Batter, Team	R	HR	Avg	OBP	SLG	OBS
Mark McGwire, Oak	142	72	.350	.499	.886	1.385
Frank Thomas, WSox	163	55	.389	.488	.742	1.230
Gary Sheffield, Fla	172	58	.357	.490	.745	1.235
Alex Rodriguez, Sea	197	48	.414	.462	.737	1.199
Edgar Martinez, Sea	169	35	.378	.498	.696	1.194
Jeff Bagwell, Hou	163	48	.365	.488	.704	1.192
Mike Piazza, LA	132	55	.397	.473	.716	1.189
Albert Belle, Cle	164	68	.343	.430	.740	1.170
Jim Thome, Cle	162	55	.330	.453	.717	1.170
Juan Gonzalez, Tex	113	67	.343	.391	.772	1.163

If you haven't already flipped to the Appendix on page 245 for a more complete listing of the data, we're sure you're about to. There, many of the top sluggers in the game today get the "chance" to play 81 games in the rare air.

These numbers go a long way toward showing what many observers have been saying since Coors opened: put a really *good* hitter there—sorry, but Dante Bichette and Vinny Castilla don't qualify—and the results would be truly awe-inspiring. It's bound to happen soon—and when it does, look out!

—Drew Faust

A more complete listing for this category can be found on page 245.

Florida Marlins: Was Kevin Brown the Best Pitcher in Baseball Last Year?

On Opening Day, 1996, Kevin Brown took the hill for the Florida Marlins against the Pittsburgh Pirates. He allowed just one run over seven innings, but was saddled with a loss when the Marlins offense was shut out. That was a sign of things to come for Brown: in seven of his 11 losses, he allowed three or fewer earned runs while working at least seven innings. Brown finished the season with a major league best 1.89 ERA along with a 17-11 record. There's nothing wrong with 17-11, but consider that National League Cy Young Award winner John Smoltz posted an ERA of 2.94 and he went 24-8. Should Kevin Brown have won more games?

Longtime *Scoreboard* readers know that every year we write about the Bill James batting statistic "runs created" and its derivative, "offensive winning percentage." Runs created combines all of a player's offensive contributions into one number; 100 runs created is a benchmark akin to 100 runs scored or 100 RBI. Offensive winning percentage takes a player's runs created and computes the theoretical winning percentage of a team made up of nine players with that runs created figure. Since pitchers *allow* all the runs that hitters create, we can compute "opponents' runs created" and "opponents' offensive winning percentage" for any pitcher.

Using those formulas (see the Glossary for complete definitions), we predict that if a team had faced Kevin Brown every day in 1996, they would have had a winning percentage of .226 (a 37-125 record over 162 games). By subtracting the opponents' winning percentage from 1, we get Brown's expected winning percentage (EWP) of .774.

Taking this a step further, we can predict Brown's expected won-lost record. Since 1987, starting pitchers have picked up a decision for every eight and one-half innings pitched. Since Brown pitched 233 innings in 1996, we'd expect him to have 27 decisions. This works out to 21 wins (27 times .774) and six losses, and confirms the fact that Brown was indeed a bit unlucky to have compiled his 17-11 record.

Here are the 10 highest expected winning percentages in baseball from 1996:

Best Expected Winning Percentages—1996

		Actual		Expected	
Player, Team	**ERA**	**W-L**	**WPct**	**W-L**	**EWP**
Kevin Brown, Fla	1.89	17-11	.607	21-6	.774
Al Leiter, Fla	2.93	16-12	.571	17-9	.658

Greg Maddux, Atl	2.72	15-11	.577	19-10	.654
Juan Guzman, Tor	2.93	11-8	.579	14-8	.634
John Smoltz, Atl	2.94	24-8	.750	19-11	.629
Curt Schilling, Phi	3.19	9-10	.474	13-8	.616
Tom Glavine, Atl	2.98	15-10	.600	17-11	.603
Pat Hentgen, Tor	3.22	20-10	.667	19-13	.593
Andy Ashby, SD	3.23	9-5	.643	10-7	.589
Steve Trachsel, Cubs	3.03	13-9	.591	14-10	.587

(minimum 20 starts)

Kevin Brown finishes way ahead of the pack. His EWP is more than 100 points better than the next best mark in the majors—that of teammate Al Leiter. Smoltz finishes fifth, but we'd guess that had Smoltz and Brown posted their expected records, Brown would have taken home the Cy Young Award.

In addition to leading the majors by a wide margin in EWP, Brown also led the majors by a wide margin in ERA (two very related events). His ERA of 1.89 was 2.32 runs better than the league mark of 4.21—one of the largest differentials ever. Here are the top 10 in history:

Outpitching the League

Player, Team	Lg	Year	ERA	Lg ERA	Diff
Greg Maddux, Atl	N.L.	1994	1.56	4.21	–2.65
Greg Maddux, Atl	N.L.	1995	1.63	4.18	–2.55
Amos Rusie, Giants	N.L.	1894	2.78	5.32	–2.54
Dazzy Vance, Bro	N.L.	1930	2.61	4.97	–2.36
Al Maul, Was	N.L.	1895	2.45	4.78	–2.33
Lefty Grove, A's	A.L.	1931	2.06	4.38	–2.32
Kevin Brown, Fla	N.L.	1996	1.89	4.21	–2.32
Lefty Gomez, Yanks	A.L.	1937	2.33	4.62	–2.29
Lefty Grove, Bos	A.L.	1936	2.81	5.04	–2.23
Randy Johnson, Sea	A.L.	1995	2.48	4.71	–2.23

(ERA qualifiers since 1876)

While we doubt that Brown's 1996 campaign will be remembered as one of the best *ever*, wins and losses aside, it *was* the best of 1996.

—Drew Faust

A more complete listing for this category can be found on page 246.

Houston Astros: Does Dierker Have a Chance?

The Houston Astros made a surprising choice this winter when they named Larry Dierker their new manager. Dierker, an Astros' broadcaster for almost two decades, has never managed at any level, nor has he been a coach. He *has* been watching the Astros play on a daily basis, perhaps gaining some advantage.

Are there any precedents for this sort of thing? One is obvious—Jerry Coleman, the San Diego Padres' broadcaster, took over the reins of his club in 1980, just as Dierker will do in 1997. We'll get into Coleman's situation in a minute, but we also found two other managers who had backgrounds roughly similar to Dierker's. Similarities among the four:

- All played in the major leagues.
- None had managed previously in the majors.
- Two had managed in the minors, but only briefly, and it had been at least 15 years since they'd last skippered a team at any level. The other two had never managed professionally.
- All had been around the major league team they were picked to manage for several years, either as broadcasters or scouts.

Who were these guys and how did they make out? Here's a brief rundown:

Tom Sheehan

A pitcher for several major league teams in the teens and '20s, Tom Sheehan was working as a "superscout" for the San Francisco Giants when the club fired manager Bill Rigney about a third of the way through the 1960 season. Giants owner Horace Stoneham, an old buddy of Sheehan's, surprised the baseball world by naming the 66-year-old Sheehan the club's manager. Sheehan had managed in the minor leagues for a few years in the early 1940s, but he hadn't worn a uniform in over 15 years. However, he'd been around the club for some time and he knew the Giants' roster, which was loaded with talented players like Willie Mays, Willie McCovey and Orlando Cepeda; Juan Marichal would join the club about a month after Sheehan took over (and pitch a one-hitter in his first start). Under Rigney, the Giants had contended until the final days of the 1959 season, winding up four games out, and they were in second place with a 33-25 record when Sheehan replaced Rigney. He might have known the players, but Sheehan apparently didn't know how to manage. The Giants went 46-50 under Sheehan the rest of the way, dropping from second to fifth. When the season was over, they replaced Sheehan with Alvin Dark, who immediately got the Giants back into contention.

Tom Sheehan				
Year	**Team**	**Record**	**Pct**	**Finish**
1960	Giants	46-50	.479	5th

Bobby Mattick

After joining the American League as an expansion team in 1977, the Toronto Blue Jays went 54-107, 59-102 and 53-109 in their first three years under manager Roy Hartsfield. Deciding that they needed to take a different approach, the Jays replaced Hartsfield with long-time major league scout Bobby Mattick. Mattick's only previous managerial experience had been a 57-game stint in the Pioneer League back in 1948. He was 64 years old, but having been around the Toronto operation from the beginning, he knew the Blue Jay players. Mattick's main asset was that he had an eye for young talent, having signed or developed players such as Frank Robinson, Vada Pinson, Curt Flood, Rusty Staub and Don Baylor in his days as a scout. Under Mattick, the Blue Jays remained a last-place club, but they improved by 14 wins to 67-95 in 1980. In 1981, the year of the strike and split season, they went 37-69, which was a definite regression, and at that point they decided to replace Mattick with a more conventional manager, Bobby Cox. But Mattick, who returned to the Toronto front office, had done his job. Among the players who got their first real chance to play during his two-year stint were Damaso Garcia, Lloyd Moseby, Ernie Whitt, Garth Iorg and Jesse Barfield. All would become mainstays of the fine Toronto teams of the mid-to-late 1980s.

Bobby Mattick				
Year	**Team**	**Record**	**Pct**	**Finish**
1980	Blue Jays	67-95	.414	7th
1981	Blue Jays	37-69	.349	7th

Jerry Coleman

The same year the Jays hired Mattick, the San Diego Padres pulled an even more shocking move, hiring radio announcer Jerry Coleman to replace Roger Craig as the club's manager. Coleman, who was 55 years old, was best known for his malapropisms ("He's throwing up in the bullpen. . ."), and he had neither managed nor coached at the professional level prior to being hired by the Padres. The club went from fifth place under Craig to last under Coleman, but it wasn't as much of a disaster as some people describe it. The Padres actually *improved* by five wins under Coleman, and their .451 winning percentage was much better than either the .422 mark they posted under Craig in 1979 or the .373 mark they would compile in 1981 under Coleman's successor, Frank Howard. The main problem was that Coleman didn't have much starting pitching to work with; the club's leading winners were relievers Rollie Fingers and Bob Shirley with 11 victories apiece. All in all, Coleman probably did as much with the team as anyone could have reasonably expected. . . but the Padres—who just three years earlier had shelled out big bucks for free agents like Fingers and Gene Tenace—thought they should be doing better.

Jerry Coleman

Year	Team	Record	Pct	Finish
1980	Padres	73-89	.451	6th

Though the managerial regimes of Sheehan, Mattick and Coleman were all viewed as failures at the time, only Sheehan fell flat on his face. Mattick did the job he was hired to do—develop some young players—and Coleman did reasonably well with a club whose level of talent was greatly overrated. At 50 years old, Dierker is younger than all three of these guys, he's an intelligent person and the Houston players seem extremely comfortable with his selection as manager. It might be an unconventional choice, but there's no reason why Dierker can't succeed as a manager.

—Don Zminda

Los Angeles Dodgers: Will Piazza Be the Best-Hitting Catcher Ever?

There's a big debate in Los Angeles these days about whether or not catcher Mike Piazza should be shifted to another position. Piazza may not be the greatest defensive catcher around, but one thing's for sure: judged on the basis of his first four full seasons, Piazza is on his way to ranking as one of the best-hitting catchers of all time. . . quite possibly *the* best.

This chart shows the top 10 catchers in career on-base plus slugging percentage (minimum 500 games caught and 1,500 career plate appearances). Piazza not only ranks first, he's first by a whopping 50 points.

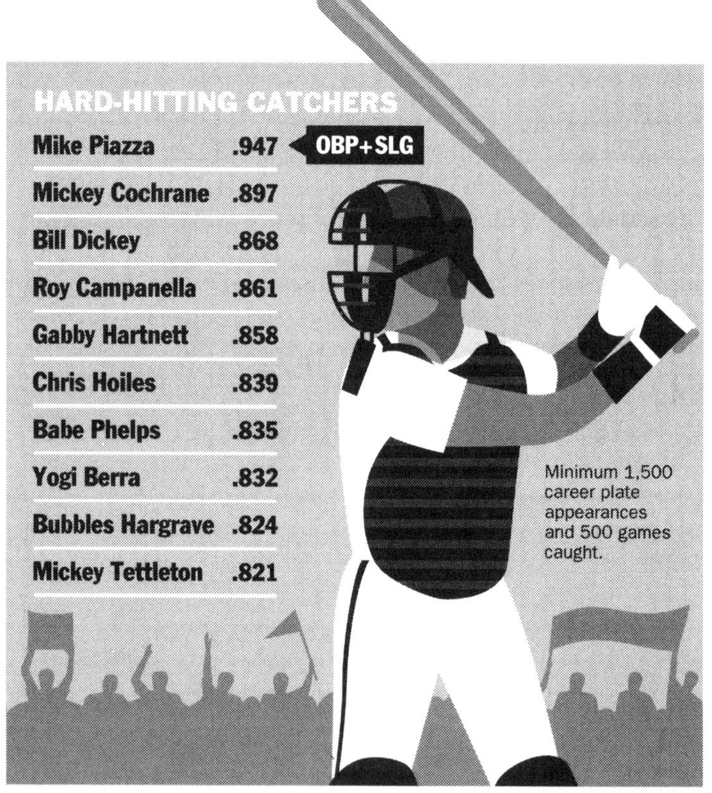

HARD-HITTING CATCHERS
Mike Piazza .947
OBP+SLG
Mickey Cochrane .897
Bill Dickey .868
Roy Campanella .861
Gabby Hartnett .858
Chris Hoiles .839
Babe Phelps .835
Yogi Berra .832
Bubbles Hargrave .824
Mickey Tettleton .821
Minimum 1,500 career plate appearances and 500 games caught.

While Piazza's OBS would figure to decline by the time his career ends, he'd still be a good bet to hold onto first. Neil Munro, who suggested this article, sent us a chart comparing Piazza with the best-hitting catchers of all time through the first four years of their careers. We expanded his chart to include more players; rather than using the first four full years, which gets tricky because of partial seasons, we used the player's stats through the season in which he played his 500th career game. Here's the list:

All-Time Great Catchers: Through First 500+ Games

Player	Age	G	AB	H	HR	RBI	BB	SB	Avg	OBP	SLG
Mike Piazza	27	537	2002	653	128	409	203	5	.326	.388	.559
Johnny Bench	23	635	2349	636	114	387	188	14	.271	.323	.476
Yogi Berra	26	623	2343	701	102	459	160	14	.299	.347	.498
Roy Campanella	30	610	2125	610	117	421	268	16	.287	.370	.510
Gary Carter	24	555	1896	499	75	268	223	22	.263	.341	.432
Mickey Cochrane	25	511	1690	523	36	239	226	28	.309	.393	.456
Bill Dickey	26	617	2206	711	50	391	155	18	.322	.368	.476
Carlton Fisk	28	547	1955	541	88	274	197	33	.277	.349	.480
Gabby Hartnett	26	564	1788	507	66	298	182	18	.284	.355	.482
Ernie Lombardi	27	550	1694	519	40	264	101	3	.306	.350	.453
Lance Parrish	26	613	2214	589	102	328	170	17	.266	.320	.468
Ted Simmons	23	535	2024	600	39	291	165	6	.296	.349	.424
Joe Torre	24	639	2253	668	76	328	191	7	.296	.356	.458

(Records & age through season in which player reached 500 career games)

We couldn't squeeze on-base plus slugging onto this chart, but Piazza ranks first again, and his lead is actually *greater* than on the previous list; the number-two man is Roy Campanella at .880. Piazza also ranks first in batting average, first in slugging and second in on-base average. And though he has fewer at-bats than most of the catchers on the list, he ranks first in home runs, and only Campanella and Yogi Berra have more RBI.

Piazza's number-one ranking is even more impressive when you note that he plays in Dodger Stadium, probably the toughest hitter's park in the majors. Away from Dodger Stadium, he's batted .347, slugged .601 and recorded a .412 on-base average during his career. Awesome.

Catching is rough on a player's body, of course, and that's a good reason why many great-hitting catchers had shorter careers than the superstars at other positions. Johnny Bench is a great example. Given that Piazza is not considered a great receiver, it probably *would* be a good idea for the Dodgers to move him to another position soon. . . even though Piazza seems resistant to the notion. But looking at his amazing numbers, we sort of find ourselves wishing that they'd keep him behind the plate for a few more years—long enough to secure his ranking as the best-hitting catcher ever.

—Don Zminda

A more complete listing for this category can be found on page 248.

Montreal Expos: Were Lansing and Grudzielanek "Identical Twins"?

Last year, Felipe Alou installed Mark Gruzdielanek as the starting shortstop and leadoff man in the Expos' lineup. Grudzielanek's play was a revelation, and he teamed with second baseman Mike Lansing to form one of the most potent double-play combos in the league. Oddly, the two seemed to keep pace with each other, step for step. Batting first and second in the order, they compiled stats that looked amazingly similar:

Grudzielanek vs. Lansing—1996

Player	G	AB	R	H	2B	3B	HR	RBI	SB	BB	SO	Avg	OBP	Slg
Grudzielanek	153	657	99	201	34	4	6	49	33	26	83	.306	.340	.397
Lansing	159	641	99	183	40	2	11	53	23	44	85	.285	.341	.406

Of course, that got us thinking—were these guys the most "identical" middle-infield pair of all time? As it turns out, we've got a perfect way to address that question: a method called the "similarity score." Bill James invented it to measure the degree of similarity between two stat lines. A score of 1,000 is the upper ceiling, but it's pretty much impossible to find two players whose stat lines, without adjusting for age and position, are *that* similar. Like snowflakes, no two are exactly alike.

As it turns out, the Expos' twins were pretty darned identical, although they didn't even come close to being the most similar pair of all time. That honor would go to two different pairs of double-play partners. The first pair of names is instantly recognizable: Billy Herman and Pee Wee Reese. Playing for the 1942 Brooklyn Dodgers, Herman batted .256 with a .333 slugging percentage, while Reese finished just one point behind Herman in each category. It's no wonder that the other carbon-copy combo has been long-since forgotten: the 1917 Pittsburgh Pirates' middle infielders, Jake Pitler and Chuck Ward, batted only .233 and .236, respectively. Neither of them recorded a single four-base hit all season. Their only notable accomplishment was that they recorded a similarity score of 974, which ties Herman and Reese for the highest mark of all time among middle infielders.

Lansing and Grudzielanek placed a little bit farther down the list with a similarity score of 955, which was still the fourth-highest score of the decade. Here are the 10 most identical pairs of the '90s:

Most Similar Double-Play Combos Of The 1990s

Year	Tm	Pos	Player	Avg	HR	RBI	OBP	SLG	Score
1993	Mil	2B	Bill Spiers	.238	2	36	.302	.303	960
		SS	Pat Listach	.244	3	30	.319	.317	
1994	SF	2B	John Patterson	.238	4	50	.315	.325	960
		SS	Royce Clayton	.236	8	48	.295	.327	
1990	Phi	2B	Tom Herr	.264	4	50	.320	.351	958
		SS	Dickie Thon	.255	8	48	.305	.350	
1996	Mon	2B	Mike Lansing	.285	11	53	.341	.406	955
		SS	Mark Grudzielanek	.306	6	49	.340	.397	
1996	SF	2B	Steve Scarsone	.219	5	23	.286	.322	955
		SS	Rich Aurilia	.239	3	26	.295	.296	
1993	SD	2B	Jeff Gardner	.262	1	24	.337	.356	952
		SS	Ricky Gutierrez	.251	5	26	.334	.331	
1990	StL	2B	Jose Oquendo	.252	1	37	.350	.316	951
		SS	Ozzie Smith	.254	1	50	.330	.305	
1991	Atl	2B	Mark Lemke	.234	2	23	.305	.312	951
		SS	Rafael Belliard	.249	0	27	.296	.286	
1990	Atl	2B	Jeff Treadway	.283	11	59	.320	.403	946
		SS	Jeff Blauser	.269	8	39	.338	.409	
1990	Oak	2B	Willie Randolph	.257	1	21	.331	.318	946
		SS	Walt Weiss	.265	2	35	.337	.321	

Although a couple of twosomes put up more similar numbers than the Expos' clones, not a single pair in the entire top 10 were able to duplicate Lansing and Grudzielanek's offensive production. The only duo that even came close was the Braves' 1990 tandem of Jeff Treadway and Jeff Blauser—and a funny thing happened to *them.* The following season, they were replaced by an even *more* similar combo, Mark Lemke and Rafael Belliard. The new guys didn't hit nearly as well as their predecessors, but their glovework more than made up for it, and the Braves captured the first of several pennants. Two years later, however, Blauser reclaimed the bulk of the shortstop's duties from Belliard. . . which serves to illustrate an obvious pattern here. You see, every single duo on the list was ultimately broken up within two years. Still, we can't see Lansing and Grudzielanek parting ways anytime soon—at least until Lansing becomes eligible for free agency.

When we take a glance at the all-time list of similar partners (see Appendix), some interesting combinations pop up. We told you about the two most similar pairs above, but guess who's tied for third? One point behind, with a similarity score of 973, are the second baseman and shortstop for the 1903 Cubs. We'll bet you could guess their names if we gave you a "chance." Give up? Do the names "Johnny Evers" and "Joe Tinker" ring a bell? The 1954 Cubs had quite a pair of rookies in the middle infield. The second baseman hit .275 with 13 homers, while the shortstop hit .275 with 19 homers. Together, they produced a similarity score of 967. The second baseman, Gene Baker, steadily declined and played regularly for only four more seasons, while the shortstop was able to hang around for quite a bit longer. His name was Ernie Banks.

How about the most *productive* pair of twins? Try this on for size: in 1950, Boston second baseman Bobby Doerr batted .294 with 27 homers, while his double play partner, Vern Stephens, batted .295 with 30 homers for a similarity score of 963. How's *that* for a one-two punch? But wait, there's more. Stephens drove in an incredible total of 144 runs, but that didn't even give him sole possession of the league lead in that category. It seems that *another* Red Sox infielder, first baseman Walt Dropo, *also* chalked up exactly 144 RBI. Nice infield.

The *least* similar combo in history was the 1928 Boston Braves' comical keystone mismatch. At second base they had future Hall-of-Famer Rogers Hornsby, who won the batting title with a .387 average and led the league in slugging percentage as well. At shortstop was Doc Farrell, who evidently was a very competent dentist. With a bat in his hand, it was a completely different story, however; Farrell batted .215 with three home runs in 1928, and never played regularly again.

The most dissimilar duo of the '90s shared many resemblances—except at the plate. The 1991 Orioles got an MVP season out of their shortstop, Cal Ripken, who batted .323 with 34 home runs and 114 RBI. Their second baseman was an equally slick fielder with the same last name, but he batted only .216 with no home runs and 14 RBI. Yes, it was quite clear that brother Billy hadn't been fortunate enough to inherit the "hitting" gene.

Numbers aside, there may never be another pair as similar as the 1953 Pittsburgh Pirates' DP combo, Johnny and Eddie O'Brien. That year, Johnny (.247 in 89 games) and Eddie (.238 in 89 games) produced a similarity score of 943, but the resemblance didn't end there. The O'Briens, you see, were the real deal—identical twins.

—Mat Olkin

A more complete listing for this category can be found on page 249.

New York Mets: Who Are the Fastest Players in Baseball?

When asked who the fastest players in baseball are, most fans would probably do no more than check among the stolen base leaders to identify the top candidates. After all, Rickey Henderson, Lou Brock and Maury Wills all were very fast, and they stole tons of bases.

Well, stolen bases are fine, and they *are* a useful tool. But they shouldn't be the only factors considered when measuring a player's *baseball* speed. Some players may not have the inclination or the opportunity to use their speed to steal bases. Others may be fast, but just don't appear to have the talent to read pitchers and get the good jumps necessary to steal bases.

Bill James recognized the limitations of the stolen base when he devised a method to calculate a player's "speed score" in his *Baseball Abstracts*. To generate a number that would attempt to gauge a player's true baseball speed, James developed a formula which utilized six different factors—triples rate, runs scored rate, grounding into double play rate and range factor, in addition to stolen base percentage and stolen base frequency.

A player is awarded points, between zero and 10, in each of those six categories. The lowest score is dropped, and the other five scores are averaged to produce his speed score. Here are the results for 1996. The players at the top of this list may not possess the greatest straight-line speed, but they do appear to apply their speed most effectively to the game of baseball. We think you'll agree the list makes intuitive sense.

Speed Score Leaders—1996

Player, Team	Pos	Speed Score
Lance Johnson, Mets	CF	8.50
Kenny Lofton, Cle	CF	8.42
Tom Goodwin, KC	CF	8.28
Brian L. Hunter, Hou	CF	7.89
Chuck Knoblauch, Min	2B	7.77
Otis Nixon, Tor	CF	7.68
Dave Martinez, WSox	CF	7.67
Ray Lankford, StL	CF	7.65
Eric Young, Col	2B	7.51
Delino DeShields, LA	2B	7.47

(Minimum 450 plate appearances)

It turns out that most of the players on the list are, in fact, good basestealers, with Lance Johnson of the Mets leading the way. Johnson, for instance, ranked second in the National League with 50 thefts. But Johnson has always excelled in hitting triples, and he bagged a remarkable 21 in 1996. He also posted strong grounding into double play and runs scored rates.

Lofton didn't hit many triples (four), but he nevertheless generated strong rates across the board, and he did lead the majors with 75 stolen bases. Goodwin also ran quite often when on base, although with less success than his speed might indicate. The KC center fielder was caught stealing 22 times, the most in baseball.

With the Top 10 list dominated by center fielders, it might be nice to take a peek at the speed score leaders at the other positions in 1996. We'll also throw in the *trailers* by position.

Best/Worst Speed Scores by Position—1996

Pos	Player, Team	Speed Score	Player, Team	Speed Score
C	Joe Girardi, Yanks	5.27	Scott Servais, Cubs	1.27
1B	Jose Offerman, KC	6.40	Mark McGwire, Oak	1.33
2B	Chuck Knoblauch, Min	7.77	Carlos Baerga, Cle/Mets	3.17
3B	Chipper Jones, Atl	5.53	Todd Zeile, Phi/Bal	2.64
SS	Jose Valentin, Mil	7.44	Cal Ripken, Bal	3.13
LF	Ellis Burks, Col	7.36	Jeff Conine, Fla	3.65
CF	Lance Johnson, Mets	8.50	Ernie Young, Oak	5.62
RF	Brian Jordan, StL	6.98	Paul O'Neill, Yanks	2.95
DH	Paul Molitor, Min	5.33	Harold Baines, WSox	2.47

Not surprisingly, catchers dominate the bottom of the list for speed scores, and Servais generated the lowest score in the majors last year. Though McGwire ranked right behind Servais, we don't think the Athletics are complaining.

Who would win a real game between the fastest and slowest players in baseball? Hard to tell, but one thing should be clear. The groundskeepers for the fast guys would have little reason to soak down the basepaths or allow the grass to grow tall.

—Jim Henzler

A more complete listing for this category can be found on page 250.

Philadelphia Phillies: How Bad Was Their Injury Problem?

As everyone knows, injuries are an inevitable fact of life in professional sports. They also make great excuses for owners, managers and players when explaining why Team X or Pitcher Y didn't have a successful season. "We just didn't count on having all those injuries," has to be one of most popular refrains in sports today. Well, which teams can honestly make the claim that they were hit especially hard by the "injury bug"?

We decided to focus on Philadelphia's recent health record because it's been impossible to overlook the impact of their rash of calamities. All-Stars like Darren Daulton, Lenny Dykstra and Curt Schilling have missed huge chunks of time over the past three seasons, and, not coincidentally, the Phillies have sunk like a rock to the bottom of the N.L. East. Of course, their injury problems transcend their stars; in 1996, the Phils lost most of their starting rotation at one point or another, and rookie phenom 3B Scott Rolen barely lasted a month after making his major league debut in August before going down for the season with a broken forearm. While it can be argued that they didn't have an abundance of talent to begin with, the heavy casualties that Philly sustained definitely were felt in the team's final won-lost record. So who occupied the most seats in baseball's "infirmary" last year? Well, let's take a look:

Most DL Days Lost—1996

Team	Days
Phillies	1,700
Red Sox	1,173
Angels	1,083
Mariners	930
Yankees	919

Wow. As we expected, Philadelphia took home the injury crown, but what's amazing about the results of the study is the size of the margin between their number of days lost to the DL and Boston's second-place total. The Phils didn't just lead the rush to sick bay, they lost a whopping 45 percent more days than the second-place finisher! Our injury data goes back to 1983 (coinciding with the beginning of Cal Ripken's streak) and not only does Philly hold the highest single-season mark since then with their 1996 total, but they also had the *second-highest* single-season total, losing 1,400 player-days to the disabled list in 1992. Over the last five years, here are the top five *M*A*S*H* camps in the majors:

Average DL Days Lost—1992-1996

Team	Avg DL Days Lost
Phillies	975
Rangers	816
Marlins	810
Brewers	802
Angels	784

Not surprisingly, Philly's "walking wounded" again finished at the top of the list. Interestingly enough, the one year they didn't finish in the top seven was 1993, the year they won the N.L. pennant. In '93, they actually lost the *fewest* number of DL days in the majors—just 96. That was the last healthy season (some might say the only one) for many of the players on that team. In addition to the aforementioned Dykstra, Daulton, and Schilling, Dave Hollins and Tommy Greene also haven't been the same since. Of course, the fact that they were exceptionally healthy that year makes their five-year DL average all the more daunting. In the other four years of the study, they lost an average of nearly *1,200* DL days a season! That's equivalent to losing 6.5 players per year for an entire campaign—or about 13 players for half a season each. Even if some of them aren't regulars, it's still pretty hard to compete at those levels.

Who's responsible for the Phillies' recent medical catastrophes? Ex-manager Jim Fregosi should probably shoulder some of the blame. Forcing Daulton to catch 145-plus games in the 1992 and '93 seasons probably contributed to his serious knee injuries, and loading Schilling with high pitch counts in the beginning of his career likely contributed to his bone spurs and rotator cuff problems. Incredibly, Fregosi worked Schilling hard in '96 as well—even in meaningless late-season games—despite the fact that his ace was just one year removed from a major shoulder operation. That may have been one of the reasons GM Lee Thomas axed Fregosi when the season ended.

—Kevin Fullam

A more complete listing for this category can be found on page 251.

Pittsburgh Pirates: What Kind of Manager is Jim Leyland?

He's one of the best, no doubt. Perhaps the better question is: what is he going to do with the Marlins, now that he has so much talent at his disposal? One could make a strong case that despite managing the Pirates to three straight N.L. East crowns in the early 1990s, Leyland has never had a team with this much talent.

The Marlins will require a different touch than Leyland's Pirates did. Florida has a solid starter at every position, three of the best starting pitchers in baseball, an established closer and several promising middle relief candidates. The Pirates of the early '90s, on the other hand, were a patchwork team built around several blue-chip players. Leyland's ongoing task was to fill the gaps with platoons and role players. It will be interesting to see how he adjusts to this new, radically different situation.

During his career in Pittsburgh, Leyland displayed several traits that aren't likely to change. Let's analyze his characteristics and try to predict how he will adjust to his new team:

1. As Mike LaValliere aptly put it, Leyland "puts players in situations where they have the greatest chance of succeeding."

Some managers look at roles that need to be filled—for example, leadoff man, cleanup hitter, closer—and try to match up their players with those roles. Leyland, however, does it backwards: he focuses on the player's needs first and the team's second. You may recall that Barry Bonds, a natural number-three hitter if there ever was one, didn't like the pressure that went with batting third. Rather than force Bonds into a spot where he wasn't comfortable, Leyland batted him fifth and looked around for someone else to bat third. From the number-five spot, Bonds put together his first MVP season. One might reason that the Pirates would have been better off if he'd produced that season from the number-three spot, but that assumes too much. In the final analysis, Leyland's handling allowed Bonds to relax and produce MVP-caliber numbers.

Leyland believes that one of the biggest obstacles to achieving success is pressure or self-doubt, and he goes to great lengths to put players into situations where they feel comfortable. To give another example: when Denny Neagle came over to the Pirates in the John Smiley deal, Leyland made sure that Neagle wouldn't expect himself to be Smiley's "replacement." He put the kid in middle relief for two years, until he felt Neagle had enough confidence to move into the rotation. When Neagle finally did become a starter, it didn't take long for him to become one of the game's top southpaws.

This year, we can expect that Leyland will continue to handle his youngsters with care. After Edgar Renteria's tremendous debut last year, the 21-year-old shortstop may be in danger of falling short of expectations. If he gets off to a slow start, Leyland may try to take the pressure off by dropping him down to the lower part of the order. The same goes for his double-play partner, Luis Castillo. If the young second baseman falls into a slump, a brief return to Triple-A may not be out of the question.

Much fanfare will accompany the debut of young pitcher Livan Hernandez, and Leyland may prefer to use him in middle relief until he gets his feet on the ground. Like Neagle, Hernandez will be dealing with steep expectations.

2. Leyland gets as much mileage out of his bench as any major league manager.

Leyland has always kept his bench well-stocked with pinch hitters, especially left-handed hitters or switch-hitters like Dave Clark, John Cangelosi, Gary Varsho and R.J. Reynolds. He makes it clear that his bench players are an integral part of the team, and he keeps them sharp through frequent use and occasional spot starts.

This year, he'll have a tremendous bench—even by his own standards. Outfielders Jim Eisenreich and Joe Orsulak (both left-handed hitters) and John Cangelosi (a switch-hitter) give him enviable flexibility, and Kurt Abbott and Alex Arias give him good depth on the infield. With such a strong starting lineup, the only question is who Leyland will pinch hit for. The obvious candidates are young catcher Charles Johnson and second baseman Luis Castillo (and the pitcher, of course).

3. A deep pitching staff, and in particular, a deep and balanced bullpen are important to Leyland.

Whenever possible, Leyland likes to keep at least two and sometimes as many as three lefties in the bullpen (in Pittsburgh, this even led to the improbable resurrection of the career of Jeff Ballard). Rather than confining himself by assigning "closer" and "set-up" duties to specific pitchers, he prefers to spread out the work. The only *sure* thing is that when the game's on the line, he'll use those southpaws to left-right his opponent to death, creating favorable match-ups at the most critical moments.

This is good news for Marlins reliever Felix Heredia. Although he's only 20 years old, he held lefties to a .143 average during a 21-game stint with the Marlins last season. Despite his youth, he figures to stick in Leyland's bullpen this year. Robb Nen gives Leyland a top-flight closer, so the bullpen-by-committee may finally be put to rest.

4. Leyland relies heavily on his top starters, and fills out the rotation with lesser pitchers.

In Pittsburgh, Leyland usually kept Doug Drabek and John Smiley working on four days' rest, skipping the fifth spot in the rotation to keep them on schedule. When a fifth starter became necessary, he'd often slot in a guy like Bob Walk—someone who could give him six decent innings when a starter was needed and work out of the pen between starts.

Now, Leyland's rotation has the best front three he's ever had: Kevin Brown, Al Leiter and Alex Fernandez. Each have been among the league's most durable pitchers over the last two years, and they figure to handle the bulk of the load this year. Leyland's got plenty of candidates for the other two spots in the rotation, including Rick Helling, Mark Hutton, Pat Rapp and Livan Hernandez. He may settle on a particular pitcher for one or both spots, but it will be an upset if any starter besides the Big Three wins more than 10 games.

5. Leyland is not a high-pressure manager, but he's good at motivating his troops and getting the most out of players with strong personalities.

Leyland will forever be remembered for his spring training confrontation with Barry Bonds in 1991. Leyland goes out of his way to credit his players for the team's success, and the respect he pays them is almost always returned. But when Bonds openly challenged him, Leyland made it abundantly clear that no player—not even the team's biggest star—would undermine his authority.

The following spring, the Pirates dealt 20-game-winner John Smiley to the Twins three weeks before the season opener. The players could have read it as an obvious message that the front office was throwing in the towel on the season, but Leyland pulled the team together and won his third straight division title.

He'll likely need to employ his full powers of persuasion to balance all the strong personalities on the Marlins. At some point, outfielder Gary Sheffield may need to be given a Bonds-like talking-to. His complaints have been an ongoing annoyance for the front office, and Leyland may have to re-focus Sheffield's attention on more team-oriented goals.

Leyland will also have to contend with Bobby Bonilla, who openly rebelled when Orioles' manager Davey Johnson used him as a DH last year.

Bonilla never had problems under Leyland in Pittsburgh, but that was before he became one of the game's highest-paid players. Kevin Brown has been outspoken in the past, although his presence didn't seem to be a disruption last year.

Perhaps Leyland's greatest challenge will be to win with a team that's *expected* to win. The ownership has spent many millions of dollars to build a winner, and immediate results are expected. In addition, Leyland's reputation as a "great manager" will be on the line. The recent poor showings in Pittsburgh have been excused for lack of talent, but now there will be no excuse for losing. Still, our hunch is that come October, no excuses will be necessary.

—Mat Olkin

St. Louis Cardinals: Is La Russa the Master of the "One-Batter Match-Up?"

Over the last 10 years, the left-handed, one-out specialist has become a staple of the modern bullpen. Tony La Russa has been one of the biggest proponents of the strategy, enjoying great success with it in Oakland and, more recently, St. Louis. He loves to bring in a southpaw to face a big left-handed hitter when the game is on the line, and he doesn't mind making the switch even if it means he has to make another pitching change one batter later. This requires a deep bullpen, so over the last seven years, La Russa has made it a habit to keep not one, but *two* left-handed, one-out specialists in the pen.

Last year, he moved over to the National League, where more pitching changes occur between innings when the pitcher is removed for a pinch-hitter. Despite this impediment, La Russa stuck to his game plan, using lefties Rick Honeycutt and Tony Fossas for one batter at a time. He called in a reliever to pitch to only one hitter on 47 occasions, 12 more times than any other N.L. manager. The White Sox' Terry Bevington was the only manager in the majors who called for more one-batter appearances (48).

Since La Russa was always maneuvering to produce favorable batter-pitcher match-ups, it's natural to assume that his pitchers probably got the job done when he called on them to pitch to one specific hitter. But did they perform more effectively in that role than any other team's relievers? Here are the five managers whose pitchers produced the best results in that situation:

Best Results In One-Batter Appearances—1996

Manager, Team	Times	AB	H	RBI	Avg	Slg
Jim Fregosi, Phi	26	23	0	3	.000	.000
Jim Riggleman, Cubs	34	30	1	1	.033	.033
Bobby Cox, Atl	24	24	1	0	.042	.042
Cito Gaston, Tor	17	15	1	3	.067	.067
Don Baylor, Col	31	30	2	2	.067	.167
MLB Average	31	28	5	4	.167	.265

(minimum: 15 one-batter match-ups)

The surprise here is that La Russa's pitchers—while effective—didn't even rate in the top five. They allowed seven hits in 44 at-bats for a .159 average, which was still eighth-best in the majors. Even more amazing is the 0-for-23 performance that Jim Fregosi coaxed out of his otherwise unremarkable middle-relief corps. Dave Leiper was a perfect eight-for-eight in one-batter appearances, but he pitched so poorly the rest of the time that he earned his release by the middle of June. And look at Bobby Cox—his specialists didn't allow a single RBI, despite Pedro Borbon's absence late in the year.

Here are the five managers who fared the *worst* with their one-out specialists. Keep in mind, the league batting average in one-batter appearances was .167 last year. Anything over .300 is distinctly subpar:

Worst Results In One-Batter Appearances—1996

Manager, Team	Times	AB	H	RBI	Avg	Slg
Art Howe, Oak	35	29	11	9	.379	.690
Tom Kelly, Min	33	30	10	7	.333	.667
Marcel Lachemann, Cal	23	22	7	6	.318	.500
Buddy Bell, Det	34	30	9	8	.300	.533
Ray Knight, Cin	24	21	6	5	.286	.333

They sure must miss La Russa in Oakland. Art Howe had no luck at all in trying to find the right match-ups with the Athletics' relievers. In fact, three of the 11 hits they allowed were home runs. Buddy Groom was the worst offender of the bunch. He was used for only one batter on eight occasions, and he allowed five hits—including a homer—and two walks. He recorded exactly one out.

—Mat Olkin

A more complete listing for this category can be found on page 252.

San Diego Padres: Are Things Heating Up at the Hot Corner?

It all came down to the final weekend of the 1996 regular season. Clinging to a two-game lead in the National League West, the Dodgers and Mike Piazza welcomed the second-place Padres and Ken Caminiti to Dodger Stadium for a three-game set—a mano-a-mano battle between two teams fighting for a title and two players fighting for an N.L. MVP Award.

In the end, it was no contest.

The Pads swept the series to claim their first West flag since '84, and Caminiti left Piazza holding his batting donut, outhitting the Dodger catcher .545 to .167 in the three games and *outslugging* him .909 to .167. The rest, as they say, is MVP history. Undoubtedly swayed by the convincing exclamation point, MVP voters made Caminiti just the second third baseman in the past 10 years from *either* league to win the award.

Caminiti's stellar .326-40-130 campaign actually led a procession of outstanding offensive seasons by third sackers around the league—guys like Chipper Jones, Dean Palmer, Vinny Castilla, Robin Ventura, Jim Thome, Ed Sprague and Jeff Cirillo all registered the best numbers of their careers. That, of course, got us to wondering. . .

Using on-base plus slugging percentage (OBS), a way to measure a hitter's all-around effectiveness, we looked at the top offensive seasons by third basemen in the 1990s. We took their numbers when they were actually playing third base, as opposed to those stats they accumulated as pinch hitters, designated hitters or when they played at another position. Using a 400 at-bat minimum, it's not hard to see that '96 was a pretty good year.

Highest On-Base + Slugging Pct As 3B—1990-96

Player, Team	Year	OBS
Jim Thome, Cle	1996	1.061
Ken Caminiti, SD	1996	1.032
Jim Thome, Cle	1995	1.002
Gary Sheffield, SD	1992	.965
Chipper Jones, Atl	1996	.946
Matt Williams, SF	1994	.930
Scott Brosius, Oak	1996	.924
Vinny Castilla, Col	1995	.904
Jeff Cirillo, Mil	1996	.898
Ken Caminiti, SD	1995	.894

(minimum 400 AB while playing third base)

Five of the top 10 single-season performances of this decade by third sackers came last season, and all but two came during the past two years. In fact, when we looked a little further down our list, we found that *eight* of the top 16 names were from 1996, and that number rose to 12 when we included 1995. If not for Gary Sheffield's Triple Crown bid in '92 and Matt Williams' 43 dingers in '94, the first five seasons of this decade at the hot corner would be left out in the cold. Yes, all of baseball is upping the offensive ante, but third basemen are more than keeping up with the crowd.

Kudos go to Jim Thome, who beat out our MVP for top billing in 1996 after an outstanding showing in 1995. Unfortunately for this essay's premise, Thome appears to be headed for first base following the Tribe's acquisition of Matt Williams. Still, Williams, Jones, Cirillo, Brosius, Castilla, Palmer, Ventura and Sprague, along with Travis Fryman and power-prospect Shane Andrews, all enter '97 under the age of 32, and Caminiti is just 34. With such a solid foundation, look for the following trend to continue:

Average Team Offensive Output As 3B—MLB

Year	Avg	HR	RBI	OBP	SLG
1990	.260	14	70	.325	.385
1991	.262	16	73	.326	.397
1992	.264	14	75	.328	.391
1993	.269	17	83	.335	.416
1994*	.268	21	88	.335	.436
1995*	.271	20	86	.346	.433
1996	.272	23	92	.342	.446

(*Projected for strike-shortened seasons)

We did a study two years ago that showed average production of each position by decade since the turn of the century. Through 1994, the '90s were not projecting to be a banner stretch at the hot corner in terms of offense. Over the past two years, that prognosis has changed. Ask the Padres, who went from the three-headed monster of Craig Shipley, Scott Livingstone and Archi Cianfrocco at third in '94 to Caminiti in '95. Now the question will be consistency; if this present group avoids the '90s black hole that sucked up the likes of Kelly Gruber, Chris Sabo, Howard Johnson, Scott Cooper, Dave Hollins, etc., Caminiti may be the first in a long line of third sackers giving MVP voters plenty to think about over the next few years.

—Tony Nistler

A more complete listing for this category can be found on page 253.

San Francisco Giants: What Will the Rest of Bonds' Career Look Like?

Along with being the son of former Giant great Bobby Bonds, Barry Bonds is the godson of Willie Mays. Bonds will be 32 when the 1997 season starts, and his career is progressing in a way that bears more than a slight resemblance to "The Godfather." Just check out the chart on this page, which compares Bonds' current career totals with Mays' at the same point of his career (through age 31). We'd have to give Willie a slight edge overall, but not by much. Bonds more than holds his own in the comparison, and in categories like walks and stolen bases, Barry is well ahead.

BARRY BONDS AND WILLIE MAYS (THROUGH AGE 31)

	G	AB	R	H	2B	3B	HR	RBI	BB	SB	Avg.	OBP	SLG
MAYS	1534	5862	1143	1846	301	99	368	1076	724	240	.315	.392	.588
BONDS	1583	5537	1121	1595	333	51	334	993	1082	380	.288	.404	.548

We all know that Mays went on to compile some awesome career totals, but is there a way to project how Bonds will perform the rest of the way? There is, thanks to Bill James. More than a decade ago, Bill invented what he called the "Brock2 System." As Bill put it in the 1985 *Bill James Baseball Abstract*, "What the Brock2 system does is to take the records that a player has produced up to this point in his career, and project out the rest of his career." The formulas Bill uses are very complicated, and it's probably safe to say that he's the one who best knows how to make the adjustments for performance and aging needed to make the system work.

The system is now known as Brock6, and in past editions of this book Bill has run projections for the careers of Cal Ripken and Frank Thomas. Does it work? Well, following the 1991 season, the system predicted that Ripken would remain healthy and go on to break Lou Gehrig's consecutive-game record in 1995; it also predicted that in '95, Ripken would bat .269 with 22 homers and 85 RBI. Ripken did break the record, of course, and his 1995 triple crown numbers were .262-17-88. Want more? Two years ago, Bill's system projected that Frank Thomas would hit 82 homers and drive in 240 runs in 1995-96; his actual totals were 80 and 245. It's not perfect, of course, and sometimes the system will turn out to be dead wrong. But overall the results have been quite good.

We asked Bill to use Brock6 to project the rest of Bonds' career. This is what he came up with:

Brock6 Projections—Rest of Barry Bonds' Career

Year	AB	R	H	HR	RBI	BB	SB	Avg
1997	526	113	149	38	109	131	34	.283
1998	520	110	144	36	108	138	33	.277
1999	506	108	138	34	105	138	32	.273
2000	492	102	132	32	98	132	30	.268
2001	476	95	126	30	93	130	28	.265
2002	459	90	120	28	88	127	27	.261
2003	443	84	114	26	81	123	23	.257
2004	426	79	107	24	76	120	22	.251
2005	410	74	101	22	71	117	20	.246
2006	392	68	95	20	66	113	18	.242
2007	327	55	78	14	52	95	14	.239
2008	226	37	53	9	35	66	9	.235
Career Total	10740	2136	2952	647	1975	2512	670	.275

A few comments:

1. The system predicts that Bonds will retire with 2,952 hits. That's just the computer spilling out numbers, and the computer doesn't understand milestones like 3,000 hits. As Bill pointed out, it's a virtual certainty that if Bonds got this close to 3,000, he'd keep on playing.

2. Bill says that it's clear to him now that Bonds, not Frank Thomas, will be the one to break Babe Ruth's career record for walks. According to the projection, Bonds won't just break the record, he'll destroy it. Ruth drew 2,056 walks; the system predicts Bonds to get 2,512.

3. Bobby *and* Barry Bonds, Mays and Andre Dawson are the only players in history with both 300 homers and 300 stolen bases. The system predicts that Bonds will be in a world of his own with more than *600* of each.

4. Did we say that Bonds was a little like Mays? Willie retired with 660 homers and 1,903 RBI; the system predicts Barry Bonds to get 647 homers and 1,975 ribbies.

Will all of this come true, or will Bonds get hurt, fade out early or take his millions and pack it in after a few more years? Who knows, but we'll all have fun watching.

— Don Zminda

II. GENERAL BASEBALL QUESTIONS

Who Has the Fastest Team?

In the New York Mets essay on page 61, we determine who the fastest players in baseball are, based on a formula Bill James devised in his old *Baseball Abstracts*. Here, we'll look at the fastest *teams*.

In football, the straight-line speed of every player is well known, even for those whose positions are not necessarily dependent upon it. That's *not* the case in baseball, though speed is still a very important component of a player's ability. But while a ballplayer's 40-yard time may not be common knowledge, his triples rate and stolen base frequency can be. It's that kind of accessible information which Bill James' procedure puts to use.

The formula James created attempts to reflect a player's true baseball speed, using events and situations which are unique to the game. The formula has six components—stolen base rate, stolen base frequency, triples rate, runs scored rate, grounding into double play rate, and range factor. Those six factors each receive a "score" between zero and 10, based on the player's performance. The lowest score is then dropped and the remaining five factors averaged to produce his "speed score."

We're going to make a couple of adjustments to the formula when generating the team speed scores. We're going to eliminate range factor from the calculation, and cease dropping the lowest score from the remaining five. Why? Well, we actually figured the team range factors using James' formula. The formula employs different calculations to determine range factors, depending on the position considered. We averaged the eight positional scores by team to compute their range factor. It turns out that the Milwaukee Brewers posted the highest range factor score last year; the Atlanta Braves the lowest. Not coincidentally, the Brewers pitching staff had the fewest strikeouts; the Braves the most. The inverse correlation between strikeouts and range factor makes intuitive sense. Since teams shouldn't be rewarded nor penalized based on the strikeout ability of their pitching staffs, we're dropping range factor from the calculation.

When we crunch the numbers, we get the following results:

Team Speed Scores—1996

Team	Speed Score
Rockies	5.98
Royals	5.79
Reds	5.62
Dodgers	5.48
Pirates	5.45
Astros	5.45
Blue Jays	5.42
Mets	5.36
Brewers	5.32
Cardinals	5.30
Phillies	5.23
Expos	5.21
Twins	5.19
Rangers	5.14
White Sox	4.97
Indians	4.97
Giants	4.89
Mariners	4.85
Cubs	4.79
Orioles	4.78
Red Sox	4.73
Yankees	4.70
Marlins	4.58
Braves	4.51
Padres	4.44
Tigers	4.38
Athletics	4.17
Angels	3.80

And the winner is. . . the Colorado Rockies? Yes, they may be better known for their supposed slugging ability, but the Rockies actually led the majors last year with 201 stolen bases. Their runs scored rate also ranked as baseball's best according to the formula. Individually, Ellis Burks boasted the highest speed score among left fielders, while Andres Galarraga and Eric Young ranked second at first and second base, respectively.

The Royals rank right behind the Rockies on the team chart, due in large measure to their stolen base frequency (they led the majors with 280 attempts) and grounding into double play rate (their 99 GDP's were the majors' fewest). Kansas City, you might notice, is the only American League team ranked in the top six, so it appears the National League continues to be the "speed" league.

The *slowest* team in baseball last year? Unquestionably, the California Angels. The Angels attempted the fewest steals in the majors, and they evidently knew what they were doing—their 57.6 percent success rate was also the worst in baseball. Among players with at least 450 plate appearances last season, the Angels had four who ranked in the lower six in speed rating at their positions. And that doesn't even include Chili Davis, who ranked second to last as a designated hitter.

How important is speed to a team's success? That's debatable, at least if speed scores are any indication. Take a look at where last year's World Series participants ended up on the list. The Braves and Yankees both ranked in the bottom seven, and only the Padres ranked lower than Atlanta among National League teams. Although four teams in the bottom nine made it to October, the Dodgers were the only team in the *top* nine to play in the postseason. While speed can definitely be an integral component of a team's success, it appears other factors, such as power, pitching and defense, are more critical.

—Jim Henzler

Is This Another Golden Age?

Though people disagreed violently about what caused it—and disagreed even more violently about whether they liked it or not—everyone can agree that the hitters went a little crazy in 1996. There was so *much* offense in 1996 that we thought it would be instructive to put the numbers into historical perspective. It's undeniably true that the hitters completely dominated the pitchers last season. . . but it's also undeniable that this sort of thing has happened before.

MOST RUNS PER GAME 1901–96
1930 11.10
1936 10.38
1929 10.37
1925 10.25
1996 10.07
1901 9.98
1994 9.85
1932 9.82
1934 9.81
1935 9.79

Let's begin by looking at the chart, which shows the highest-scoring seasons of the 20th century. The 1996 season does not rank first, but it's one of only five seasons in which the average game produced a score in double figures. To put this in context, here are a few brief highlights of the other double-digit years:

1930. In 1930, the entire National League—pitchers, third-string catchers, everybody—combined to bat .303. The Giants had a team batting average of .319, the Phillies hit .315, the Cardinals .314. Bill Terry batted .401 and had 254 hits. Hack Wilson hit 56 homers and drove in a record 190 runs. Chuck Klein batted .386 with 250 hits, including 59 doubles. Klein also drove in 170 runs and scored 158. Babe Herman batted .393. In the American League, Lou Gehrig had 174 RBI. Babe Ruth, at the age of 35, hit .359 with 49 homers, 153 RBI and a .493 on-base average. Pitching? Well, Lefty Grove went 28-5 with a 2.54 ERA, but then, he was Lefty Grove. More typical was the National League, which had exactly *one* ERA qualifier with a figure under 3.87. The overall National League ERA in 1930 was 4.97, virtually identical to the 1996 American League figure of 4.99. The 1930 Phillies had a team ERA of 6.71, which topped anything that pitching-starved 1996 could produce.

1936. Among other things, this was the rookie season for Joe DiMaggio (.323-29-125, 132 runs scored), Johnny Mize (.329-19-93) and 17-year-old Bob Feller (5-3, 3.34, 76 strikeouts in 62 innings). As in 1996, most of the offense was in the American League. Lou Gehrig, still going strong, hit .354 with 49 homers, 152 RBI and 167 runs scored. Luke Appling hit .388, a record for a shortstop, and Indian first baseman Hal Trosky—all but forgotten now—had 42 homers and 162 RBI. Charlie Gehringer (60) and National Leaguer Ducky Medwick (64) each reached the 60-double mark. Pitching? There wasn't much of it in the A.L., where Grove (2.81) was the only pitcher with an ERA under 3.00. In the N.L., Carl Hubbell went 26-6, 2.31 and Dizzy Dean was 24-13, 3.15. They were the exceptions, however. In the A.L., the league ERA was 5.04, the highest of the century. How 'bout those 1936 Browns (6.24 ERA) and A's (6.08) staffs?

1929. Another fun year. . . except if you were a pitcher. Lefty O'Doul, another all-but-forgotten player, hit .398 with 254 hits. Hack Wilson (159), Al Simmons (157), Babe Ruth (154) and Mel Ott (151) all topped 150 RBI. Three National League teams batted better than .300, and the overall N.L. batting average was .294. Pitching? This time only one ERA qualifier in the major leagues had an ERA under 3.00 (Grove, of course, at 2.81). The Phillies had a team ERA of 6.13.

1925. More of the same. The American League, as a group, batted .292; so did the National League. Rogers Hornsby batted .403, Harry Heilmann .393, Tris Speaker .389, Al Simmons .387. Ty Cobb, at age 38, hit .378. Simmons had 253 hits. There was a *little* more pitching this time—two guys in each league had ERAs under 3.00. Grove wasn't one of them, however; he was only a 25-year-old rookie at the time.

All these years were part of what later became known as baseball's "golden age," the 1920s and 1930s. The 1996 season fits right in with them, numbers-wise. Perhaps the only difference is that not many people look back at 1930 and say, "Yeah, Terry hit .401, but the ball was juiced and the pitching was lousy and the parks were small and. . ." They just say it was great. Catch our drift?

We'll show you a couple of lists that put the '96 season into further context. First, the home-run thing. It was, to be sure, the best home run season ever, but not that much better than 1987 or 1994 or 1995 or even 1961. Here's the top 10:

Top 10 Seasons, HR per Game—1901-96

Year	HR/G
1996	2.19
1987	2.12
1994	2.07
1995	2.02
1961	1.91
1956	1.85
1962	1.85
1959	1.82
1958	1.81
1986	1.81

Interesting—lots of seasons from the 1950s and '60s, along with the more recent years. And aren't the '50s and '60s considered another "golden age"? Still, the 1996 figures are a good 20 percent higher than those of 1958-59, and nearly 15 percent higher than Maris' year, 1961. Perhaps things are out of kilter a little, but didn't they say the same thing after Maris hit 61?

The final numbers show the top 10 seasons in slugging percentage.

Top 10 Seasons, Slugging Pct—1901-96

Year	SLG
1930	.434
1996	.427
1994	.424
1995	.417
1929	.417
1987	.415
1925	.411
1936	.404
1993	.403
1921	.403

That amazing 1930 season claims the top spot again, followed by the three most recent campaigns. All 10 seasons are either in the period from 1921 to 1930, or in the years from 1987 to 1996. So if you're going to say that "the game has been wrenched out of its context," as Bob Costas grumpily announced in his All-Star game broadcast, don't you have to say the same thing about the '20s? And what context is that, anyway? The context of 1930, maybe? Or 1968 (a year in which the *pitchers* were in total control)? Or 1908 (another pitching-dominated year)? Does every season have to strike some bland, undefined "balance" between hitting and pitching to be considered legitimate? Aren't the extremes part of the history, too? And aren't the extremes more than a little *fun*?

To return to the central issue: what's happening right now is *not* unprecedented. . . well maybe the home-run surge is, to some degree, but not the fact that the hitters are dominating the pitchers. The phrase "these things go in cycles" may seem trite, but in this case it's absolutely true. There's a lot of offense in the game these days, for a number of reasons, but one *big* reason for that is that there are simply a lot of great offensive players. Frank Thomas and Barry Bonds and Alex Rodriguez and their ilk are truly special players. Our guess is that, 20 or 30 years from now, we'll look back on this era the way people look back on the '20s and '30s: as a Golden Age for the game.

— Don Zminda

A more complete listing for this category can be found on page 254.

Is Coors Field the Best Hitters' Park of All Time?

Several articles in this book are dedicated to the subject of Coors Field and its amazing effect on offense. We won't cover the same ground again in this article; instead, we'd like to try to put the "Coors phenomenon" in historical perspective by asking this question: is Coors the best hitter's park of all time?

The best way to answer this question, we believe, is to rank the "park indexes" for each major league team since 1901. Park indexes, a Bill James creation, are familiar to readers of Bill's old *Baseball Abstracts*, and to those of you who read our (and Bill's) *STATS Major League Handbook.* You can create park indexes for batting average, errors or any stat. An index of 100 indicates a neutral park for the stat in question; the higher the index goes, the more favorable the home park is for that particular statistic. The formula is in the glossary.

Now let's look at the Coors Field numbers for 1996. Last year the Rockies and their opponents scored the staggering total of 1,217 runs in 81 games at Coors, an average of 15.02 runs per game. In 81 Colorado road games, the Rockies and their opponents combined to score just 708 runs, an average of only 8.74 runs per game. The park index computes to 172, meaning that scoring was a whopping 72 percent higher at Coors than at a neutral park.

That makes Coors the best hitter's park currently in use, and by a pretty good margin; The Ballpark in Arlington, which had the *second-highest* park index for scoring in 1996, was far back with an index of 114. So how does the Coors index compare with all other parks since 1901? Here are the teams with the 20 highest scoring indexes over that period:

Highest Home Park Scoring Indexes—1901-96

			–Home–		–Away–	
Year	**Home Team**	**Index**	**Run**	**Gm**	**Run**	**Gm**
1996	Colorado Rockies	171.9	1217	81	708	81
1995	Colorado Rockies	164.4	975	72	593	72
1955	Boston Red Sox	155.5	865	78	542	76
1933	Philadelphia Phillies	153.3	792	72	574	80
1993	Colorado Rockies	151.8	1040	81	685	81
1925	Philadelphia Phillies	144.5	1035	77	707	76
1923	Philadelphia Phillies	144.3	1015	75	741	79
1970	Chicago Cubs	143.0	865	80	620	82

Year	Home Team	Index	-Home- Run	Gm	-Away- Run	Gm
1922	Philadelphia Phillies	142.7	966	76	686	77
1985	Chicago Cubs	140.4	822	80	593	81
1933	St. Louis Browns	138.5	869	76	619	75
1906	New York Yankees	138.5	692	76	493	75
1916	Chicago Cubs	138.4	626	78	435	75
1906	Cincinnati Reds	138.3	649	76	463	75
1935	Philadelphia Phillies	136.8	915	78	643	75
1977	Boston Red Sox	136.5	902	80	669	81
1977	Atlanta Braves	135.1	904	81	669	81
1950	Boston Red Sox	135.0	1052	77	779	77
1973	Atlanta Braves	134.4	897	80	676	81
1910	Boston Braves	133.9	688	77	507	76

Wow. Coors Field not only ranks first for its 1996 numbers, but the number-two spot goes to Coors for the only other year it's been in existence, 1995. Coors really does look like the best hitter's park *ever*. . . or at least in this century, since we didn't look at figures for 19th-century parks.

Fans of old-time ballparks will identify many of the teams on this list with their legendary hitter-friendly parks. The Coors Field of the 1920s and '30s was Baker Bowl in Philadelphia, the place where Chuck Klein went crazy. Baker Bowl makes an amazing *five* appearances in the top 20, all of them in the years between 1922 and 1935. Fenway Park shows up three times, as does Wrigley Field. Atlanta's "Launching Pad," Fulton County Stadium, makes two appearances. And Colorado's former park, Mile High Stadium, shows up in the number-five spot for the 1993 season.

The older parks we mentioned have been greatly loved by baseball fans, so maybe we criticize Coors too much. It's important to recognize that however much the place distorts offensive statistics, a game at Coors is *fun*—a good reason why the stands are always packed.

It's also important to realize the extent of the distortion, and to recognize that Vinny Castilla is not a future Hall of Famer (or at least we hope not). But for now, let's salute Coors Field, the best hitter's park of the 20th century. . . and a fun place to watch a game.

—Don Zminda

A more complete listing for this category can be found on page 255.

How Unlikely Was Nomo's No-No?

On September 17, 1996, Hideo Nomo tossed the first no-hitter ever in Coors Field. He did it in the best hitters' park in baseball against a Colorado Rockies club which hit an incredible .343 at home last season. It goes without saying that the odds are stacked pretty heavily against any no-hitter, but how steep were the odds Nomo overcame?

To figure the odds against Nomo's no-hitter, we looked at the batting averages of the 11 hitters he faced, the park he threw it in, and the effect he had during the 1996 season on the batting averages of opposing hitters. Our formula computed the odds of his no-hitter as 1 in 21,294.

How does that compare to the odds against a "typical" no-hitter? Since 1989 there have been about three no-hitters per season. With 26 to 28 teams playing a 162-game schedule, there are between 2,100 and 2,300 games per season. For each game played, there are two chances to pitch a no-hitter, one for each starting pitcher. To get a rough idea of the odds against a no-hitter, figure that there are three per season in about 4,500 chances (2 x 2,250), which works out to odds of about 1 in 1,500.

At 1 in 21,294, Hideo Nomo's no-hitter bucked some pretty steep odds. Were they the steepest? Employing the same formula we used to compute the odds against Nomo's gem, we found the odds against each nine-inning no-hitter thrown by a single pitcher since 1989. "Opp Avg" in the chart is the overall batting average against the pitcher for the year in which he threw his no-no. Here are the 10 toughest:

Most Unlikely No-Hitters Since 1989

Pitcher, Team	Date	Opp	Park	Opp Avg	Odds
Dwight Gooden, Yanks	5/14/96	Sea	Yankee Stadium	.259	1 in 62,568
Scott Erickson, Min	4/27/94	Mil	Metrodome	.299	1 in 35,513
Hideo Nomo, LA	9/17/96	Col	Coors Field	.218	1 in 21,294
Fernando Valenzuela, LA	6/29/90	StL	Dodger Stadium	.276	1 in 19,286
Jim Abbott, Yanks	9/04/93	Cle	Yankee Stadium	.271	1 in 7,242
Wilson Alvarez, WSox	8/11/91	Bal	Memorial Stadium	.230	1 in 4,544
Terry Mulholland, Phi	8/15/90	SF	Veterans Stadium	.252	1 in 4,384
Kevin Gross, LA	8/17/92	SF	Dodger Stadium	.241	1 in 4,225
Kenny Rogers, Tex	7/28/94	Cal	Ballpark in Arlington	.260	1 in 3,226
Dave Stewart, Oak	6/29/90	Tor	SkyDome	.231	1 in 2,757

We'll be honest. When Hideo Nomo threw his no-hitter at Coors, we wondered if it was the most unlikely no-hitter *ever.* As it turns out, it wasn't even the most unlikely no-hitter of last season. That honor belongs to Dwight Gooden. What made Gooden's masterpiece so tough? Well, he was facing some fantastic hitters—Alex Rodriguez, Edgar Martinez, and Ken Griffey Jr. among them—and Doc was barely above average in terms of opposition batting average last year. His mark of .259 was only six percent better than the A.L. average of .277. In contrast, Nomo's opposition batting average of .218 was the third-best mark in the National League last year, lowering batting averages by about 17 percent. How significant is opposition batting average when computing the odds of a no-hitter? For comparison, take a look at the five easiest no-hitters since 1989, and the opposition batting averages of these pitchers:

"Easiest" No-Hitters Since 1989

Pitcher, Team	Date	Opp	Park	Opp Avg	Odds
Nolan Ryan, Tex	5/01/91	Tor	Arlington Stadium	.172	1 in 239
Nolan Ryan, Tex	6/11/90	Oak	Oakland Coliseum	.188	1 in 255
Al Leiter, Fla	5/11/96	Col	Joe Robbie Stadium	.202	1 in 648
Chris Bosio, Sea	4/22/93	Bos	Kingdome	.229	1 in 702
Ramon Martinez, LA	7/14/95	Fla	Dodger Stadium	.231	1 in 724

We weren't at all surprised when Nolan Ryan landed on the top of this list. In 1990 and 1991 (and throughout his career, for that matter), batters had a heck of a time getting hits off him *any* time he took the hill. Ryan's total of seven no-hitters underscores the fact that a great pitcher—one with a very low opposition batting average—has a *much* better chance of throwing a no-hitter than an average pitcher.

If we remove the individual pitcher's effect on the odds from the equation and assume an average pitcher is on the hill, the odds against throwing a no-hitter can change dramatically. In Nomo's case, the odds of an average pitcher throwing a no-hitter on September 17, 1996 in Coors Field were an astronomical 1 in 314,806, by far the steepest odds for an average pitcher since 1989. In comparison, the odds of the second most-difficult no-hitter, Dwight Gooden's, work out to 1 in 161,505 for an average pitcher.

Regardless of how we compute the odds, Nomo's no-no was truly remarkable, and it could be many years before we see another thrown in that park.

—Drew Faust

Who Went to the Moon in '96?

The longest home run of 1996? Many would guess this to be a Mark McGwire moon-shot. Or, if it didn't come off McGwire's bat, then 1996's longest blast would have to be a Coors Field special, right?

Wrong. The longest home run of the season, and the only fair ball to travel 500 feet, came off the bat of Chicago Cubs' slugger Sammy Sosa, on an April afternoon at Wrigley. Here's the short list of last season's longest homers:

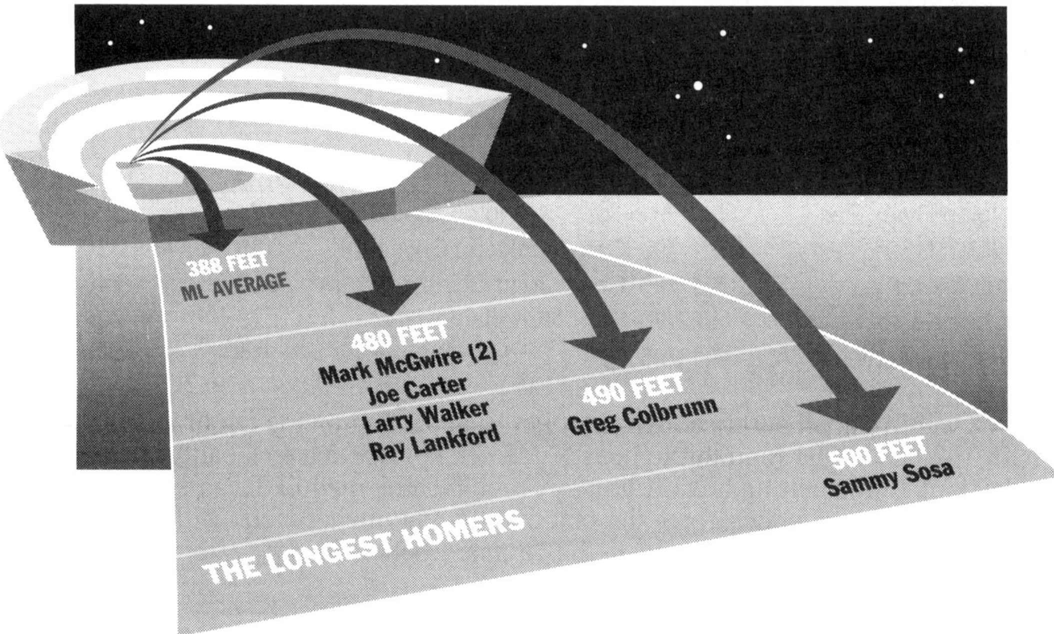

McGwire is well represented among the long home runs, but Sosa topped him with his center-field smash off San Francisco's Allen Watson. And lo and behold, 1996's second-longest homer, off the bat of Florida's Greg Colbrunn, was surrendered by. . . Allen Watson. Is there a reason why Watson is susceptible to long homers? Well, if nothing else, he does tend to give up homers—lots of them. Watson tied for fifth in the National League in home runs allowed last year, with 28. Take Watson out of Candlestick Park, however, and he becomes far *more* susceptible to the longball. Pitching on the road—where Watson allowed the mammoth shots by Sosa and Colbrunn—the lefthander gave up an amazing 25 home runs in just 109.1 innings.

OK, so Mark McGwire finishes a disappointing *third* on our chart. But did McGwire really fall short of expectations when it came to long blasts? Not by a long shot! Consider that McGwire hit two of the seven longest home runs of 1996. Looking a little further down the list of long home runs, we found that McGwire led all MLB sluggers with five blasts that traveled at least 450 feet last year. Even more impressively, he did it against some pretty decent pitchers: Cleveland's Orel Hershiser and Chicago's James Baldwin and Alex Fernandez were all victimized by long McGwire blasts in 1996.

What about Coors Field? What did the park that last year yielded 34 more longballs than any other major league stadium contribute to the list of long home runs? Two of 1996's longest homers were hit in Denver—no more than in Toronto. But again, we checked out the longer list, and the numbers are striking: of the 57 450-foot homers, *16* of them were hit in Coors; the most in any other park was just four! And don't believe that balls flew farther out of the yard on Blake Street just because of the players who were swinging the bats. No fewer than 10 different players—six Rockies and four visitors—connected for 450-foot bombs in Coors Field.

As an aside, we're happy to note that perhaps the most potent moon-shot scenario imaginable is set up for the 1997 season. The wise MLB schedule-maker (who we swear had never seen this data) has slated the A's for a two-game series in Colorado this year. That's right—on August 30 and 31, 1997, Mark McGwire will take aim for the Coors Field fences. Keep in mind: the longest major league home run in the last decade was a 550-footer by Cecil Fielder in 1990. Surely that's within McGwire's reach.

One final interesting note about our data: of the 10 longest home runs that were hit outdoors, six of them came in day games. Roughly two-thirds of all major league games are played at night, but it seems that games played under the sun result in the highest percentage of moon-shots. Does the ball carry better in the daylight? Our numbers certainly suggest it does. All the more exciting for Mark McGwire fans—the A's second game in Colorado will be played in the afternoon.

—Ethan D. Cooperson

A more complete listing for this category can be found on page 256.

Who Had the Best Months of the Year?

In a sport like baseball, with its 162-game marathon schedule, much emphasis is placed on consistency, and a great deal of attention is given to the players who perform well over the grueling six months. Rightfully so. But while we're sure to recognize the players who lead the league's statistical categories for the entire season, it's always fun to examine who the top *sprinters* are—i.e. the guys who perform best over shorter stretches of the season. We looked at each month of the 1996 campaign, and came up with the following list of the top batting averages in each month:

Best Averages by Month—1996

Player, Team	Month	AVG	OBP	SLG	AB	R	H	HR	RBI
Wally Joyner, SD	April	.407	.528	.605	86	17	35	1	14
Roberto Alomar, Bal	May	.421	.491	.621	95	22	40	5	25
Mark McLemore, Tex	June	.472	.563	.597	72	24	34	1	11
Juan Gonzalez, Tex	July	.407	.472	.917	108	22	44	15	38
Jim Eisenreich, Phi	Aug	.446	.460	.639	83	13	37	1	14
Lance Johnson, Mets	Sept	.405	.426	.595	111	20	45	1	10

(Minimum 75 plate appearances)

What a novelty, to see a hitter with a .400 average next to his name—even if it's not for a full season! More importantly, doesn't our chart tell us that hitters are more likely to get hot when the weather does likewise? Two *different* Texas players had the hottest months of June and July, including Mark McLemore's .472 in June, the best batting average by any player for a single month last year. McLemore's average the rest of the year was a more human .261. And while most of baseball played through frigid weather in April, Wally Joyner—who enjoyed 14 games in temperate San Diego—had the majors' best month. Hot weather seems to equal hot bats.

We might expect pitchers to show the opposite trend, and do their best work in the colder months. But the data shows otherwise:

Best ERAs By Month—1996

Pitcher, Team	Month	ERA	W	L	IP	H	BB	K
Juan Guzman, Tor	April	1.88	3	1	43.0	29	8	39
Chuck Finley, Cal	May	0.79	4	0	45.2	31	16	45
Danny Darwin, Pit	June	1.06	4	1	34.0	27	4	8
Jeff Fassero, Mon	July	1.00	3	2	45.0	31	15	44
Greg Maddux, Atl	Aug	1.60	3	1	45.0	37	7	30
Pedro Martinez, Mon	Sept	1.67	2	1	32.1	28	12	39

(Minimum 25 innings)

Chuck Finley had the best ERA in any month last year, and was the only pitcher on the chart who did not lose a game during his dominant month. Note that Greg Maddux had the best August—despite making three starts in the sweltering heat of Atlanta. Conversely, Juan Guzman had the best month of April, but his 1.88 ERA was only the *21st* best by any pitcher for a single month in '96. Perhaps some pitchers didn't work as hard as they should have last offseason, and didn't round into form until later in the year.

Going beyond batting average and ERA, we wanted to look at some other statistics, to see which other players had dominant months last year, and to choose our annual award for *best* month of the year. Here's a look at the best month in each important category:

On-Base Percentage. Mark McLemore, June, .563; Gary Sheffield, Sept., .556; Jim Thome, Aug., .538; Wally Joyner, April, .528; Barry Bonds, Sept., .528. Bonds and Sheffield each had more than 30 walks in September. In his run at 40 stolen bases, Bonds drew a whopping 35 walks in September. McLemore's June was the best month in both batting average *and* on-base percentage; no other player made the top seven on both lists. We'd have to make McLemore a semi-finalist.

Slugging Average. Juan Gonzalez, July, .917; Mark McGwire, June, .915; Ken Griffey Jr., July, .861; Mark McGwire, July, .859; Ken Caminiti, Aug., .844. Juan Gonzalez' 15-homer July was the best single month for slugging last year, and the A.L. MVP voting may have been a sign that a single spectacular stretch was given more weight than a better overall season. Meanwhile, Mark McGwire, who led the majors in slugging with a .730 mark for the season, had two of the top five slugging months last year, and his June was a narrow second to Gonzalez' July. Gonzalez and McGwire are definitely contenders for best month honors.

Hits. Alex Rodriguez, Aug., 54; Dante Bichette, June, 48; Eric Young, June, 47; Paul Molitor, Aug., 47; Alex Rodriguez, July, 46. Speaking of the American League MVP voting, Alex Rodriguez—who many think should have won the award—had a total of 100 hits in July and August, two of the top five totals for the season. Dante Bichette and Eric Young each hit over .370 in June, when the Rockies played 17 games in hitter-friendly Coors Field. Of course, their hit totals were aided by the fact the Rockies hit .315 as a team, assuring that Bichette and Young would keep coming up to the dish. Rodriguez' 54-hit August deserves consideration for our prize.

Home Runs. Juan Gonzalez, July, 15; Mark McGwire, June, 14; Ken Caminiti, Aug., 14; Tim Salmon, June, 13; Mark McGwire, July, 13. We've discussed the heroics of Gonzalez in July, as well as McGwire's tremendous season, so here we pay tribute to Ken Caminiti. Caminiti's 14 homers and .844 slugging in August were the best months in either category by a National Leaguer. We all know about Caminiti's performance in Mexico, where he homered while on the verge of dehydration, but let the record show that he did not play a single August game in Colorado. No one can question that the N.L. MVP earned his stripes during his best month. Yet another finalist.

RBI. Dante Bichette, June, 39; Juan Gonzalez, July, 38; Ken Caminiti, Aug., 38; Greg Vaughn, June, 35; four players with 33. Bichette also topped this list for the 1995 season, when he knocked in 35 runs in July.

Stolen Bases. Kenny Lofton, April, 17-for-21; Otis Nixon, Aug., 16-for-18; five players with 15. Lofton stole 32 bases in April and May, then averaged less than 11 per month after that. Did he lose interest in stealing bases once the Indians raced to a huge lead in the A.L. Central?

Wins. Charles Nagy, May, 6-0; John Smoltz, May, 6-0; Andy Benes, Aug., 6-1; five pitchers tied at 5-0. Smoltz put a strangle-hold on the N.L. Cy Young Award during May, when he went 6-0 with a 1.73 ERA.

Strikeouts. Curt Schilling, Aug., 56; Roger Clemens, Sept., 54; Roger Clemens, May, 53; John Smoltz, April, 51; Darryl Kile, June, 49. Salary drives for Schilling and Clemens? Perhaps. What's certain is that only one of these pitchers, Smoltz, had an ERA under 3.00 in his big strikeout month.

After careful consideration, we've chosen four finalists for best hitting month of the year:

Best-Hitting Months of 1996

Hitter	Month	AVG	OBP	SLG	AB	R	H	2B	3B	HR	RBI	BB
Mark McGwire	June	.329	.513	.915	82	26	27	6	0	14	25	31
Juan Gonzalez	July	.407	.472	.917	108	22	44	10	0	15	38	14
Ken Caminiti	Aug	.344	.427	.844	96	24	33	4	1	14	38	17
Alex Rodriguez	Aug	.435	.474	.758	124	30	54	11	1	9	28	11

As impressive as McGwire and Caminiti were, we'd have to lean towards the other two, who did much more than hit home runs. And as amazing as 15 homers in a month is, 54 hits in a 31-day span is great. We'll take Rodriguez.

Our top pitching months:

Best-Pitching Months of 1996

Pitcher	Month	ERA	W	L	G	GS	CG	ShO	IP	H	HR	BB	SO
Chuck Finley	May	0.79	4	0	6	6	1	0	45.2	31	2	16	45
Danny Darwin	June	1.06	4	1	5	5	0	0	34.0	27	0	4	8
John Smoltz	May	1.73	6	0	6	6	1	1	41.2	26	3	11	46

Darwin's one loss and low strikeout total would eliminate him, leaving us to choose between Finley and Smoltz. And although each pitched a quality start in every outing, Smoltz did give up six unearned runs against the Phillies, and was bailed out only because the Braves scored 11. Plus, Finley pitched more innings, and gave up fewer homers. The nod goes to Finley.

Finally, who had the worst months of '96?

Worst Months—1996

Month	Hitter, Team	AVG	HR	RBI	Pitcher, Team	W	L	ERA
April	Vince Coleman, Cin	.153	1	4	Todd Van Poppel, Oak	0	2	8.64
May	Chad Fonville, LA	.123	0	1	Alan Benes, StL	1	2	7.67
June	Rey Ordonez, Mets	.155	0	1	Steve Avery, Atl	0	3	9.47
July	Darren Lewis, WSox	.143	0	6	Mark Leiter, SF	0	4	8.28
Aug	Joe Carter, Tor	.138	2	9	Kevin Jarvis, Cin	3	4	8.84
Sept	Alex Gonzalez, Tor	.147	3	6	Tom Gordon, Bos	2	3	7.57

Well, if you're young and promising, like Rey Ordonez or Alan Benes, you can get away with a bad month; it also might help if your brother is the team's ace pitcher! Otherwise, you might sort of disappear: Chad Fonville got less than 100 big league at-bats after May, while Todd Van Poppel, Steve Avery and Mark Leiter got changes of scenery either during or after the 1996 campaign. And Coleman fared the worst—it looks like he'll be subbing in the Detroit Tigers' outfield.

—Ethan D. Cooperson

A more complete listing for this category can be found on page 257.

Is DiMaggio's Streak in Any Danger?

On May 30 it almost ended, but a ninth-inning single off Earl Johnson saved the day. On June 17 it almost ended, but a bad hop off the shoulder of Luke Appling in the seventh inning was ruled a hit. On June 24 it almost ended, but an eighth-inning single—this time off Bob Muncrief—kept it alive. Two days later it almost ended again, but a two-out, eighth-inning double off Eldon Auker allowed the march to continue. Finally, on July 17, it *did* end, but not before Joe DiMaggio had tempted fastballs and curveballs and change-ups and fate for 56 straight games.

As Michael Seidel prefaced his 1988 book *Streak* (Penguin):

> No sustained performance in the history of baseball builds with the drama and explodes with the energy of DiMaggio's 56-game consecutive hitting streak. . . Surely, none is more memorable.

And surely, none is more unattainable.

Or is that really the case? Since DiMaggio set baseball's immortal standard in 1941, only Pete Rose (44 straight games) in 1978, Paul Molitor (39) in 1987 and Tommy Holmes (37) in 1945 have posted hitting streaks of longer than 35 games. Even DiMaggio would probably admit that a couple of late-inning singles here and a fortuitous bounce there could have pushed those streaks even closer to, if not over, his "unreachable" plateau. To see just how close some major leaguers *really* have come to duplicating Joltin' Joe's journey, we took a look at those players who have hit safely in the most games over any 56-game stretch during the past decade.

Most Games With A Hit, 56-Game Stretch—Since 1987

Player, Team	Year	Games With Hit
Paul Molitor, Mil	1987	51
Benito Santiago, SD	1987	51
Wade Boggs, Bos	1988	51
Don Mattingly, Yanks	1988	51
Mike Greenwell, Bos	1989	51
John Olerud, Tor	1993	51
Kenny Lofton, Cle	1994	51

Over the past 10 seasons, seven players have amassed 51 games with at least one base knock over a 56-game stretch, though only two of those efforts have come in the 1990s. We looked only at single-season stretches; otherwise Benito Santiago's best 56-game total would have shown up as

53 if we included the end of his 1987 campaign and the beginning of '88.

For the above seven players, it must be a source of either great pride or great frustration to know that a mere five hitless games separates them from immortality. Certainly Molitor, Boggs and Mattingly can take solace in the fact that they were, and still are, some of the premier hitters of their generation. Boggs, in fact, had produced a hit in *50* of 56 games just a year prior to his stellar 1988 stretch. Santiago's and Olerud's efforts, on the other hand, appear to be little more than blips on their career radars. Kenny Lofton led the American League with 160 hits in '94 and posted a career-high 210 base knocks last year; he's got the speed-plus-average combination that *could* make him a threat to DiMaggio for a few years to come.

It's interesting to note, and perhaps comforting to DiMaggio fans, that only Molitor, Santiago and Olerud had hitting streaks of 25 or more games on the way to their totals of 51. But two of those streaks came nearly a decade ago, and runs of 30-plus have been unheard of in this decade.

Longest Hitting Streaks—1990s

Player, Team	Year	Games
Hal Morris, Cin	1996	29
Marquis Grissom, Atl	1996	28
John Flaherty, SD	1996	27
John Olerud, Tor	1993	26
Brian Harper, Min	1990	25
Lance Johnson, WSox	1992	25

Not one hitter in the '90s has been able to break the 30 mark, though three National Leaguers came very close in 1996. You may be wondering, then, if the odds of catching DiMaggio are diminishing. Well, not exactly. Only two players have hit safely in as many as 51 of 56 games in the '90s, but *seven* other hitters have strung together hits in *50* contests over a 56-game run. . . including an amazing total of four in 1996. The Reds' Hal Morris, the Red Sox' Mo Vaughn, the Brewers' Kevin Seitzer and the Mariners' Alex Rodriguez needed just a few scratch singles or a couple of bad hops in a mere six games to tie DiMaggio's mark. Sounds so simple. . .

Of course, it's the elusiveness of those "scratch" singles and those "bad" hops that continues to make DiMaggio's achievement one of the game's everlasting milestones. . . and continues to make "56" one of the most daunting numbers in all of sports.

—Tony Nistler

Do Heavily-Used Catchers Wind Up Paying at The Plate?

As the employers of the best-hitting catcher in baseball, the Los Angeles Dodgers have come under heavy fire over the workload they've given their superstar, Mike Piazza. Since breaking into the majors full-time in 1993, Piazza has compiled eye-popping numbers with the bat—but he's also racked up a *lot* of time behind the plate. Over the last four seasons, "Iron Mike" has caught 87 percent of his team's games (509 out of 582), the highest figure in the majors. Most of his missed games were the result of a thumb ligament injury he suffered in '95—over the other three seasons, he actually caught *91 percent* of the Dodgers' contests.

Not surprisingly, Los Angeles has drawn criticism from those who feel that subjecting Piazza to heavy abuse will have major repercussions later in his career. Is the superstar catcher *really* being used too frequently, or are the worrisome fans and sportswriters getting riled up for no reason? Also, even if he is racking up a lot of time behind the plate, does that necessarily mean that he'll fade at an early age? The Dodgers barely squeaked into the postseason last year; they can't afford to let backup catcher Tom Prince, a career .195 hitter, get *too* many of Piazza's at-bats.

We compiled a list of the highest percentages of games caught by a player over three consecutive seasons. Why percentages instead of total games? To even the playing field for those backstops who worked before 1961—when the baseball season was 154 games long instead of 162. However, we didn't treat the strike years ('81, '94-95) in the same manner since we believe that carrying a heavy load over a much shorter period of time just doesn't have the same impact as being overworked for an entire season. Because of the strike-shortened seasons and his aforementioned thumb injury, Piazza himself doesn't make the list, even though it can be argued that he *might* have if not for the unusual circumstances.

Highest Three-Year Percentages of Games Caught

Player	Gms Caught	Years	Pct
Randy Hundley	463	1967-1969	94.9
George Gibson	433	1908-1910	93.5
Yogi Berra	427	1953-1955	92.8
Jim Sundberg	449	1978-1980	92.2
Ted Simmons	448	1973-1975	92.2
Cy Perkins	428	1920-1922	91.8
Jim Hegan	427	1947-1949	91.4
Tony Pena	441	1983-1985	90.9
Gary Carter	439	1978-1980	90.7
Ray Schalk	419	1920-1922	90.5

(Only Highest Figure for Each Catcher Was Used)

Gary Carter deserves special recognition; not counting the strike year in 1981 (during which he caught 100 of a possible 108 games), Carter caught an average of 146 games per season from 1977 through 1985. No other catcher in baseball history has had a comparable stretch of work over such an extended period.

Did these heavy workloads have any effect on catchers' hitting performances? This proved to be a difficult problem to solve. Initially, we tried to evaluate the production decline of the players on the preceding list by calculating their changes in slugging and on-base percentages as they aged. However, since we evaluated the players in their early 30s, it would be natural to expect offensive declines *regardless* of the number of games that they caught. To isolate the drop in performance due to workload, we used the following approach:

1.) We selected a Bill James tool to help us hammer out our solution—the Approximate Value (AV) Method. It's a broad-based formula that takes into account a player's yearly accomplishments and assigns a "value" to his season between 0 and 20, with 15 signifying an "MVP" caliber year.

2.) We used the method to rate the "overworked" catchers (the 10 players on the preceding list) and a control sample during each season of their careers. The control sample consisted of 143 players who had caught at least 750 games. Then, we obtained the total AVs of the groups on a year-by-year basis, where AVs at a given age were summed. Finally, we found the "peak value" of both groups, with peak value defined as the highest collective AV total of any age (which, incidentally, occured at age 27).

3.) We obtained the AVs that both groups produced from ages 30-36. Dividing those totals by their respective peak values, we were able to calculate the percentage of peak value that they had retained at a given age.

What did we find? Take a look:

Percentage of Peak Value Retained

Age	"Overworked" Catchers	Control Group
30	71%	93%
31	65%	82%
32	54%	71%
33	57%	56%
34	41%	48%
35	35%	39%
36	21%	23%

Interesting results. There's no doubt that the overworked catchers started to fade much faster than the control group, but the differences narrowed as they got older. Notice that at age 33, the overworked catchers actually experienced a slight *increase* in performance; this irregularity can be attributed to the unusual increase in playing time of both George Gibson and Jim Hegan. Gibson, a pioneer in the use of catching equipment, returned from a broken ankle to catch 101 games (up from 48 the year before) for the 1914 Pirates. At the same age, Hegan also saw a marked increase in action when it was apparent that his '54 Indians were actually going to have a shot at interrupting the Yankees' perennial reign atop the American League (and they did). After weighing the entire study, however, we conclude that the overall effects of catching a large amount of games in a short stretch of time are detrimental to a player's offensive performance.

How did the most overworked catcher in major league history, Randy Hundley, fare? After several seasons of toiling under the sun in Wrigley Field, Hundley was reduced to a burned-out husk of a player. At age 27, Hundley generated a peak value of 12 AV points; after turning 32, however, he would total only *one* point throughout the remainder of his career. He wasn't the last receiver to wither with the Cubs, either. Although he barely missed placing on the "highest percentage" list, backstop Jody Davis spent most of the mid-'80s racking up dangerously high totals of games behind the plate. After Davis was traded from Chicago to Atlanta during the 1988 season at age 31, he batted just .161 in limited action before calling it quits two years later.

Which catchers were able to best withstand the effects of aging and overuse? Without a doubt, Yogi Berra and Ted Simmons. However, while both Berra and Simmons were used extensively at catcher early in their careers, their teams eventually tried to conserve their hitting prowess by rotating them through other positions for about 30-40 games a year. As a result, they were able to prolong their careers (Berra especially) by reducing the amount of time they spent behind the plate. Because Berra was a much better defensive backstop than Simmons was, they were shifted defensively at different stages in their careers.

How does this affect the Mike Piazza situation? Well, the Dodgers recently signed Piazza to a $15 million two-year contract to avoid going to arbitration. When he becomes a free agent after the 1998 season at age 30, Piazza will probably be commanding huge sums of money and a long-term contract.

As we see it, LA has two options, and the manner in which they use Piazza over the next couple of seasons will play a big factor in whether they will make a huge fiscal investment in their slugger as he enters his 30s. If the Dodgers decide that they can't afford to give him more rest—or if he proves incapable of handling another fielding position, they probably will choose not to re-sign Piazza in the future. From their standpoint, it'd be a terribly risky investment to empty the vaults on an overworked 30-year-old catcher.

On the other hand, the organization may come to the conclusion that preserving Piazza's incredible offensive ability must be achieved at all costs, and that his long-term future is worth more than the team's short-term potential. Obviously, LA would then attempt to relieve Piazza of some of the catching workload in the future so that re-signing him in '98 will be a more sound move. Though he is not in the "danger zone" as of yet, he probably *will* be—unless manager Bill Russell starts reducing his time behind the plate.

—Kevin Fullam

A more complete listing for this category can be found on page 258.

Who Were the Best Players Never to Play in the World Series?

No baseball fan will forget the image of Yankee captain Don Mattingly striding to the plate in Game 1 of the 1995 Division Series to take his first postseason cuts. "It was everything I had supposed it would be. It was wild. It was a great place to be tonight," Mattingly would say after the game. No baseball fan also will forget the feelings of empathy for Donnie Baseball when the M's ousted the Pinstripes in that incredible Game 5, denying him a chance at the World Series.

And certainly no baseball fan missed the irony of last season, when Mattingly hung up his cleats just in time to watch his Yankees make their first World Series appearance since 1981.

Andre Dawson announced his retirement in 1996. Though he reached the postseason with both the Expos and Cubs, "The Hawk" never played in a World Series in his 2,627-game career. No one in the history of the game has appeared in more contests without playing for baseball's ultimate prize.

Before Mattingly and Dawson, there was two-time MVP Dale Murphy. Murphy spent the better part of 15 very productive but World Series-less seasons with the Braves before they traded him to the Phillies in 1990. Atlanta would wind up in four of the next five Fall Classics, but Murphy would never play for a title. Before Murphy, there was Hall of Famer Billy Williams, who spent 16 World Series-less seasons with the Cubs before joining the A's in 1975—ironically, the season *after* they won their third straight world championship. Oakland would not return to the World Series in '75. . . and Williams would never play for a title.

The annals of baseball history are littered with the stories of great players who never got the chance to play in the greatest of games. We thought it might be appropriate, then, on the heels of Mattingly's "official" retirement, to take a look at some of the legends who fell short. We only looked at those players whose careers started in 1903 or later—the year the first World Series was held.

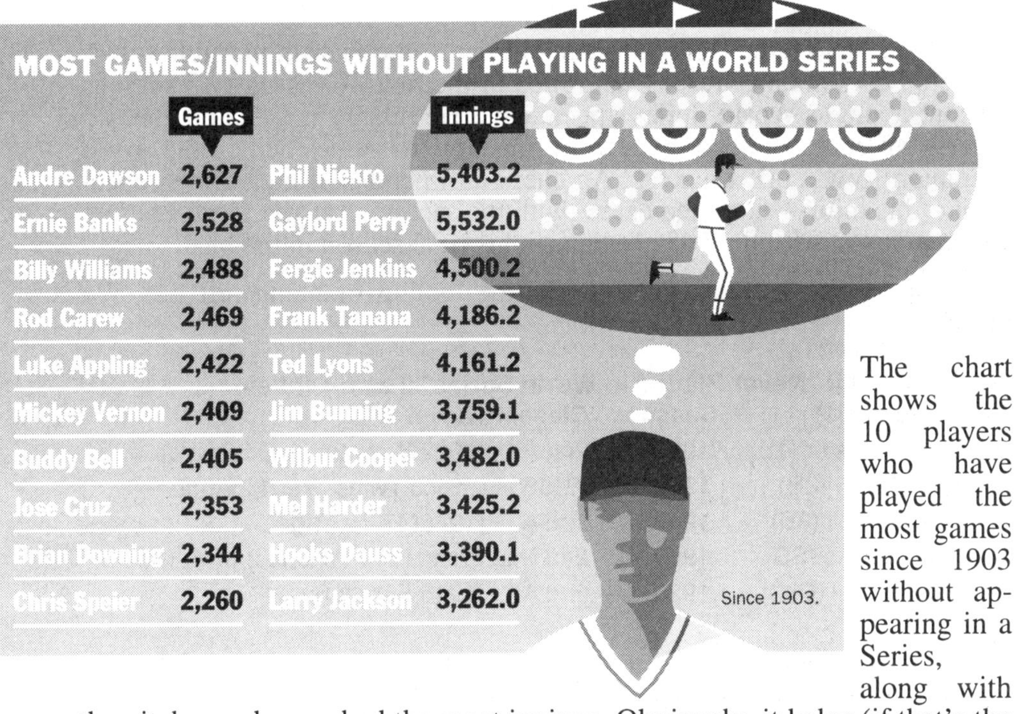

MOST GAMES/INNINGS WITHOUT PLAYING IN A WORLD SERIES

Player	Games	Pitcher	Innings
Andre Dawson	2,627	Phil Niekro	5,403.2
Ernie Banks	2,528	Gaylord Perry	5,532.0
Billy Williams	2,488	Fergie Jenkins	4,500.2
Rod Carew	2,469	Frank Tanana	4,186.2
Luke Appling	2,422	Ted Lyons	4,161.2
Mickey Vernon	2,409	Jim Bunning	3,759.1
Buddy Bell	2,405	Wilbur Cooper	3,482.0
Jose Cruz	2,353	Mel Harder	3,425.2
Brian Downing	2,344	Hooks Dauss	3,390.1
Chris Speier	2,260	Larry Jackson	3,262.0

Since 1903.

The chart shows the 10 players who have played the most games since 1903 without appearing in a Series, along with the pitchers who worked the most innings. Obviously, it helps (if that's the word) to have played for the Cubs—the top three in games played are Dawson, Ernie Banks and Williams, while Fergie Jenkins ranks third on the pitchers' list. The number-10 pitcher, Larry Jackson, also spent several years on the North Side, and the number-10 position player, Chris Speier, wore Cub blue for two years, as did Wilbur Cooper. Ron Santo, another Cub great from the 1960s and '70s, just missed the top 10, ranking 11th with 2,243 games played. No one, however, knew frustration quite the way Banks did. Not only did Mr. Cub never play in a Series—he never even got into a postseason game in his 2,528-game career.

How about a "Never Played in the World Series" All-Star team? We'll start in the outfield:

All "Never Played In World Series" Team—Outfield

Player	Seasons	Closest They Got
Andre Dawson	1976-96	NLCS (1981 Expos, 1989 Cubs)
Harry Heilmann	1914-32	2nd A.L. (1923 Tigers)
Ralph Kiner	1946-55	2nd A.L. (1955 Indians)
Dale Murphy	1976-93	NLCS (1982 Braves)
Billy Williams	1959-76	ALCS (1975 A's)

Hall of Famers Harry Heilmann and Williams, along with possible future HOFers Dawson and Murphy, all toiled in the field for at least 17 seasons without a single World Series appearance. Heilmann hit .403 for the '23 Tigers, but couldn't keep them from finishing 16 games behind the world champion New York Yankees. Another Hall member, Ralph Kiner, spent most of his injury-shortened career with the second-division Pirates before coming closest with the 1955 Indians in his final season in the bigs.

Some legendary infielders also knew the feeling of being left out. We picked our "best" from each position:

All "Never Played In World Series" Team—Infield

Player (Pos)	Seasons	Closest They Got
George Sisler (1B)	1915-30	2nd A.L. (1922 Browns)
Rod Carew (2B)	1967-85	ALCS (1969-70 Twins, '79, '82 Angels)
George Kell (3B)	1943-57	2nd A.L. (1946-47, '50 Tigers)
Ernie Banks (SS)	1953-71	2nd N.L. East (1969-70 Cubs)
Rick Ferrell (C)	1929-47	2nd A.L. (1945 Senators)

Five Hall members here, with Banks leading the way. Fifteen players in the history of major league baseball have slugged 500 or more home runs; "Mr. Cub" is the only one never to get the *opportunity* to hit one out in the World Series. In both '69 and '70, the North Siders either led the N.L. East or were in a virtual tie for the top spot at the beginning of September, but faltered down the stretch. Second sacker Rod Carew certainly tempted fate on more than a few occasions, playing in four different ALCS with two different teams. If it wasn't for the Baltimore Orioles, he may just have eaten his cake, too, but the O's eliminated Carew's Twins in '69 and '70, then disposed of his Angels in '79. He joins Nap Lajoie as the only other player with 3,000 hits and no World Series appearances. Sisler, who hit an amazing .420 for that 1922 St. Louis team, and Kell also enjoyed lengthy stays in the majors, but never played into October. As a cruel twist of fate would have it, Kell joined a strong Tiger team in '46—the season *after* they won a world championship, and Ferrell left the Browns after the '43 campaign, a year *before* they went to the World Series.

Finally, here are the moundsmen:

All "Never Played In World Series" Team—Pitchers

Pitcher	Seasons	Closest They Got
Fergie Jenkins	1965-83	2nd N.L. East (3), A.L. West (2), A.L. East (1)
Ted Lyons	1923-46	3rd A.L. (1936-37, '41 White Sox)
Phil Niekro	1964-87	NLCS (1969, '82 Braves)
Gaylord Perry	1962-83	NLCS (1971 Giants)
Lee Smith	1980-96	NLCS (1984 Cubs), ALCS (1988 Red Sox)

Phil Niekro now sits alongside Jenkins, Lyons and Perry in the Hall, with Lee Smith most likely joining them in a few years. Between them, they have amassed 1,247 wins and 543 saves. Niekro's Braves were swept out of the NLCS on both occasions, while Perry and his '71 Giants scratched out just a single win. Jenkins played bridesmaid in the division races on six different occasions with three different clubs, but never even broke through to the playoffs, much less the World Series. Lyons toiled an amazing 21 seasons for the South Siders, but never had better than a third-place finish to show for it. The closest call of all was turned in by Smith, who nearly tasted the champagne in 1984 when his Cubs won the first two games of the NLCS before dropping three in a row to the Padres.

This is by no means an exhaustive compendium, and you may even feel a few glaring omissions have been made (all you Luke Appling or Jim Bunning fans out there, unite!). But you'll have a hard time convincing us that the above players weren't as deserving as any in the history of the game for a crack at baseball's ultimate prize. And even if you're not a Yankee fan, you'd have a hard time convincing us that a little piece of the *baseball* fan in you wouldn't have loved to have seen Don Mattingly join Wade Boggs on the back of a horse. . . riding around a frenzied Yankee Stadium.

—Tony Nistler

A more complete listing for this category can be found on page 259.

Was the Ball Really Livelier Last Year?

Last year, it seemed that everywhere you looked, home run records were being threatened or even obliterated. Mark McGwire cranked out longballs at a pace that would have approached Roger Maris' single-season record if he'd stayed healthy. His club, the Athletics, was one of *three* teams that shattered the 1961 Yankees' team record for homers. In Baltimore, Brady Anderson—a *leadoff* man, for heaven's sake—broke out with a 50-homer season after hitting only 41 the previous three years combined. Over in the National League, Todd Hundley hit 41 homers, eclipsing Roy Campanella's single-season record for catchers. All of which leads us to ask: what's going on? Why the sudden power surge?

One of the first theories to find favor was that the major leagues had secretly introduced a "rabbit ball." Although this tired story seems to be revived every time the offense jumps, there actually was some evidence to support it last year. As you can see from the chart below, the average distances of both fly balls to the outfield and home runs have been climbing steadily since 1992, with each number reaching or maintaining an eight-year high last year. You'll also notice that these trends correlate with the increase in home runs and runs per game over the same period:

Average Distances of Fly Balls and Home Runs—1989-1996

Year	Avg OF Fly	Avg HR	HR/G	R/G
1989	314	381	1.46	8.26
1990	311	382	1.58	8.51
1991	313	382	1.61	8.62
1992	314	380	1.44	8.23
1993	317	385	1.78	9.20
1994	319	386	2.07	9.85
1995	320	387	2.02	9.69
1996	320	388	2.19	10.07

Be careful to note that longer fly balls and home runs don't necessarily indicate a change in the nature of the baseballs. The manufacturers maintain, as always, that today's balls are no more resilient than in years past.

Other theories have been offered to explain the trend. The prevalence of modern weight-training programs has been fingered; it's no coincidence that McGwire makes an excellent poster boy for this theory. While we would agree that in general, today's hitters are bigger and stronger than those from the 1960s and '70s, the increase in muscle still fails to explain the obvious change in the game over the last four years. If memory serves, the hitters in 1992 were hardly a bunch of underdeveloped weaklings.

Some people attribute the phenomenon to the "woeful" state of modern pitching. This line of thinking holds that the expansion in 1993 elevated a bunch of Triple-A-quality pitchers to the majors, resulting in an increase in offense. This doesn't explain much; *hitters* were promoted, too. In the past, expansion has led to a rise in offense, but in every instance, the offense receded shortly thereafter. This time, however, the trend has picked up momentum during subsequent seasons.

We do have one answer that no one will dispute: Colorado. The ball travels better there, and the Rockies' entrance into the league in '93 was met with a corresponding increase in fly ball and home run distances. But the overall increase wasn't due to the addition of Colorado:

Average Distances of Fly Balls and Home Runs—1992-1996

	Colorado		All Other Parks	
Year	Avg OF Fly	Avg HR	Avg OF Fly	Avg HR
1992	—	—	314	380
1993	336	392	316	385
1994	336	393	319	386
1995	340	406	319	386
1996	338	407	320	387

Even when you remove Colorado from the equation, you're still left with the same trend. The ball's been carrying better and better—at *all* elevations.

The theory we find most convincing is the "incredible shrinking strike zone." When the strike zone contracts, the hitter knows he's less likely to see a strike, and he has less incentive to swing. As a result, he will take more pitches and work deeper counts. Over the last four years, we have seen strong evidence that this is exactly what's happening. Hitters saw 3.62 pitches per plate appearance in 1992; this figure has risen steadily to last year's high of 3.75 pitches per plate appearance.

Of course, with a smaller strike zone, hitters can work the count in their favor more often. This results in not only more hits and home runs, but more *hard-hit* balls in general. For this reason, we think the smaller strike zone is the root cause of the longer flight paths of today's home runs.

But regardless of the cause, the longball barrage shows no signs of slowing down. Unless the rabbit dies, weight training is banned, the Rockies move to Sarasota, or the umpires start calling strikes above the belt, the slugfest figures to continue.

—Mat Olkin

Will Kirby Make it to Cooperstown?

In 20 spring training games last season, Kirby Puckett tore it up. He was hitting .344 with two home runs and 14 RBI when he woke up on March 28 with a blind spot in his right eye. On July 12, he announced his retirement from baseball due to glaucoma, prematurely ending a brilliant career.

Was it a Hall-of-Fame career? Bill James' book *The Politics of Glory* examines the history of the Hall and presents several methods for predicting a player's chances for induction. We'll start by comparing Puckett to players with similar career totals by using Similarity Scores (SS). If two players had identical career totals and played the same position, their similarity score would be 1,000. For each difference between them, we subtract something (see the glossary for a complete definition). Among those players whose careers are over, here are the three most similar to Kirby Puckett:

Retired Players Most Similar to Kirby Puckett

Player	G	AB	R	H	2B	3B	HR	RBI	BB	Avg	OBP	SLG	SS
Kirby Puckett	1783	7244	1071	2304	414	57	207	1085	450	.318	.360	.477	—
Don Mattingly	1785	7003	1007	2153	442	20	222	1099	588	.307	.358	.471	883
Cecil Cooper	1896	7349	1012	2192	415	47	241	1125	448	.298	.337	.466	880
Tony Oliva	1676	6301	870	1917	329	48	220	947	448	.304	.353	.476	871

Interestingly enough, a process based entirely on numbers chose Don Mattingly as the most-similar player in baseball history to Puckett. Puckett and Mattingly have similarities that go beyond numbers. They played at the same time (they were born roughly a month apart in 1961) and in the same league, and are two of the best-liked and most respected ballplayers of our generation. They were both true franchise players, spending their entire careers with just one team. And unfortunately, they were both prematurely forced into retirement by injury.

Though their final *totals* are strikingly similar, Puckett and Mattingly had different types of careers. Mattingly burst onto the scene in his first full season (1984), winning the batting title while leading the league in hits and doubles. The following season, he won the American League MVP Award while leading the league in RBI (145), doubles and total bases. He continued to play at the top of his game in 1986 and 1987, finishing second and seventh in the MVP voting. For a three or four-year stretch, any discussion of the best player in baseball had to include Don Mattingly. After 1987, his production dropped off, and he suffered through some mediocre seasons with the bad back that eventually forced his early retirement.

Puckett was probably not as good as Mattingly was in his prime—he never won an MVP—but he strung together many more quality seasons than the Yankee first sacker. As evidence, here are his top 10 finishes in the MVP vote: sixth (1986), third (1987), third (1988), seventh (1989), seventh (1991), second (1992), and seventh (1994). That's an amazing run in a nine-year span. Though Mattingly did win the award, he finished in the top 10 only four times (1984-87).

Looking further down the list we find Cecil Cooper and Tony Oliva, neither of whom is in the Hall of Fame. Cooper played first base for Boston and Milwaukee from 1971 through 1987. Though similar to Puckett, he has a significantly lower batting average, and lower on-base and slugging percentages as well.

Tony Oliva is the most similar outfielder to Puckett, and the commonalities here also go beyond the numbers. Oliva patrolled right field for the same club as Puckett, the Minnesota Twins. It should be noted that Bill James lists him as the best eligible right-field candidate *not* enshrined at Cooperstown. Like Puckett and Mattingly, Oliva's career was cut short by injury. A bad right knee required surgery seven times and ultimately ended his career in 1976. Though their careers are similar, Puckett does appear to have a slight edge. He played longer and compiled higher marks for average, on-base and slugging percentage. Yes, Oliva played in more of a pitchers' era, but he finished in the top 10 of the MVP vote five times—two fewer than Puckett.

The second item we'll look at in evaluating Kirby Puckett's chances for making it to Cooperstown is Bill James' Hall of Fame Career Monitor. The Monitor awards points for accomplishments during a player's career. If the player scores more than 100 points, the system predicts he will make it into the Hall of Fame; a score of 130 makes him almost a lock for Cooperstown. Let's walk through this for Kirby, as we did with Mattingly in last year's *Scoreboard.*

1. For batting average, award 2-1/2 points for each season of hitting .300 (in a hundred or more games), 5 points for hitting .350, 15 points for hitting .400. Seasons are never double-counted: a .350 season is not also counted as a .300 season. Puckett hit .350 once and .300 in seven other seasons. He scores 22.5 points.

2. Award the player 5 points for each season of 200 hits, 3 points for each season of 100 runs, and 3 points for each season of 100 RBI. Puckett had 200 hits five times, three seasons with 100 runs scored, and three seasons with 100 RBI. He scores 43 points, 65.5 so far.

3. Award the player 10 points for hitting 50 home runs in a season, 4 points for hitting 40 HRs, and 2 points for hitting 30 HRs. Puckett topped 30 HRs once for two points. He has 67.5 so far.

4. Award the player 2 points for hitting 45 doubles in a season, one point for hitting 35. Puckett hit 45 doubles once and 35 in six other seasons, scoring eight points. He now has 76.5 points.

5. Award the player 8 points for each MVP award, 3 points for playing in an All-Star game, 2 points for winning a Gold Glove as a catcher, shortstop or second baseman, one point for a Gold Glove at another position, and one point for either of the recognized Rookie of the Year Awards. Puckett played in 10 All-Star games and won six Gold Glove Awards for 36 points, bringing his total to 112.5 points.

6. If the player was a regular on a world championship team, award him 6 points if he was the shortstop or catcher, 5 points if he was the second baseman or center fielder, 3 points if he was the third baseman, 2 points if he player left field or right, and one point if he was the first baseman. Puckett earns five points each for his play during the Twins 1987 and 1991 world championship seasons. He now has 122.5 points.

7, 8. These award points for playing on league or division championship teams. Both times that the Twins made the postseason during Kirby's career, they won the World Series, and those points are covered in (6).

9. Award additional points for leading the league in batting average (6 points), home runs (4), RBI (4), runs scored (4), hits or stolen bases (2), doubles or triples (1). Puckett led the league in average once, in RBI once, and in hits four times. That adds 18 points to bring his total to 140.5 points.

10. For career totals, give the player 50 points for 3,500 career hits, 40 points for 3,000, 15 points for 2,500 and 4 points for 2,000. Puckett scores four points, and now has 144.5.

11. Award the player 30 points for 600 career HRs, 20 points for 500 career HRs, 10 points for 400 HRs, 3 points for 300 HRs. Puckett does not score.

12. Give the player 24 points for a lifetime average of .330, 16 points for .315, and eight points for .300. Puckett's .318 average earns 16 points. He now totals 160.5.

The rest of the system awards points for playing tougher defensive positions, and Puckett does not earn any further points.

The Monitor touches on a point that we haven't yet discussed: postseason play. Kirby Puckett was the best player on two world championship editions of the Minnesota Twins: 1987 and 1991. The defining moment of Puckett's career was Game 6 of the 1991 World Series. When he came to the plate in the bottom of the 11th of a 3-3 game to face the Braves' Charlie Leibrandt, Puckett had already driven in two of the Twins runs and made a run-saving catch against the plexiglass in left-center at the Metrodome. He hit a game-winning home run, and the Twins captured the Series the following night.

To answer the original question posed, Kirby Puckett *will* make it to Cooperstown. He scores extremely well on the Hall of Fame Career Monitor, and compares favorably to those players who were most similar to him. Unlike Mattingly, Puckett was still going strong when his injury forced him into retirement. Voters will remember a player like Kirby who played on an elite level throughout his career.

—Drew Faust

Are Smaller Parks Causing the Home Run Explosion?

It's no secret that hitters cranked out home runs at a record pace in 1996. But why? Is the ball juiced? Is it a lingering effect of expansion? Are hitters stronger these days? Are new ballparks more home-run friendly?

Let's examine that last theory. We identified the 12 ballparks that have had the same dimensions and same surface between 1989 and 1996. These parks make up our control, or "unchanged," group. They are: Atlanta-Fulton County Stadium, Fenway Park, Anaheim Stadium, Wrigley Field, Riverfront Stadium/Cinergy Field, Tiger Stadium, Dodger Stadium, County Stadium, Shea Stadium, Yankee Stadium, Veterans Stadium and Three Rivers Stadium.

Since 1989, eight new parks have been christened. By year, these are: 1989 SkyDome, 1991 New Comiskey Park, 1992 Oriole Park at Camden Yards, 1993 Mile High Stadium and Joe Robbie Stadium (renamed Pro Players Stadium), 1994 The Ballpark in Arlington and Jacobs Field and 1995 Coors Field.

First, we'll look at the home run per game (HR/G) ratio from '89 to '96 for three groups of parks: all major league stadiums, the 12 parks in our unchanged group and the eight new parks.

Let's look at a few items "in theory." If the home run explosion was caused *solely* by new, smaller parks, the 12 parks in our unchanged group would have a constant HR/G ratio over the course of the study. Any increase in HR/G in all of baseball over that span would be due to new parks and changes made to existing parks.

If the new parks were completely neutral in terms of home runs hit, meaning they had *nothing* to do with the home run explosion, the HR/G ratio of these parks would match the HR/G ratio for all of baseball each year. Of course, it's also possible that we're dead wrong in assuming the new parks are hitters' parks. If the new parks are in fact *less* friendly to home runs, they'll have HR/G ratios below the majors as a whole.

OK, enough theory. Let's look at the results. The following graph has three lines representing HR/G from 1989 to 1996: one for all of baseball (ALL), one for the 12 parks in our control group (UNCHANGED) and one for the new ballparks (NEW).

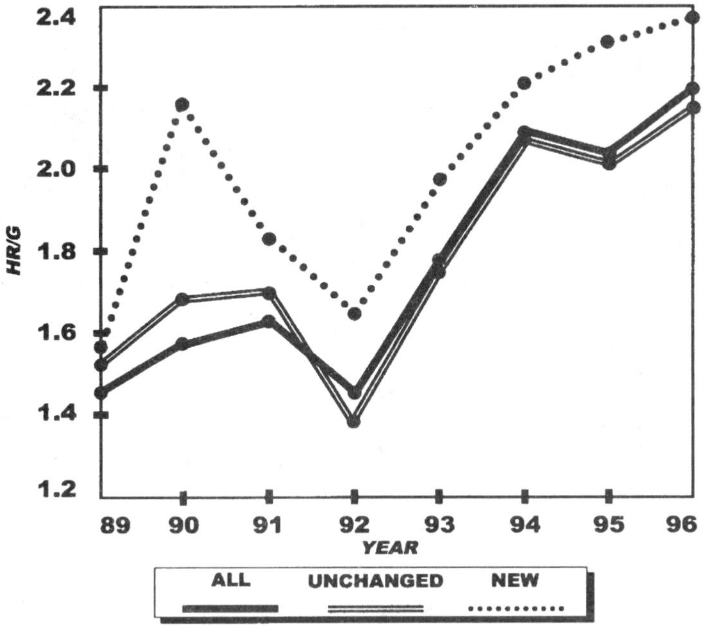

It's obvious from the graph that new parks *are* contributing to the home run explosion. In every season of the study, the new parks have had higher HR/G ratios than the majors as a whole. You can also see that the unchanged group started the study as hitters' parks. From 1989 to 1991, the unchanged group had a HR/G ratio higher than the MLB average. However, in 1992, the HR/G ratio of the unchanged group dipped below the ratio for all of baseball. Ever since, these parks have been acting as pitchers' parks.

What about the parks not in the study? Not included are old stadiums that were replaced by the new ballparks, and parks that underwent dimension or surface changes. To include these in our study, we compared the unchanged group to *all* of the other parks in play each year. We do not show the HR/G ratio for all of baseball, but we will point out that it always falls between the HR/G ratio of the two groups.

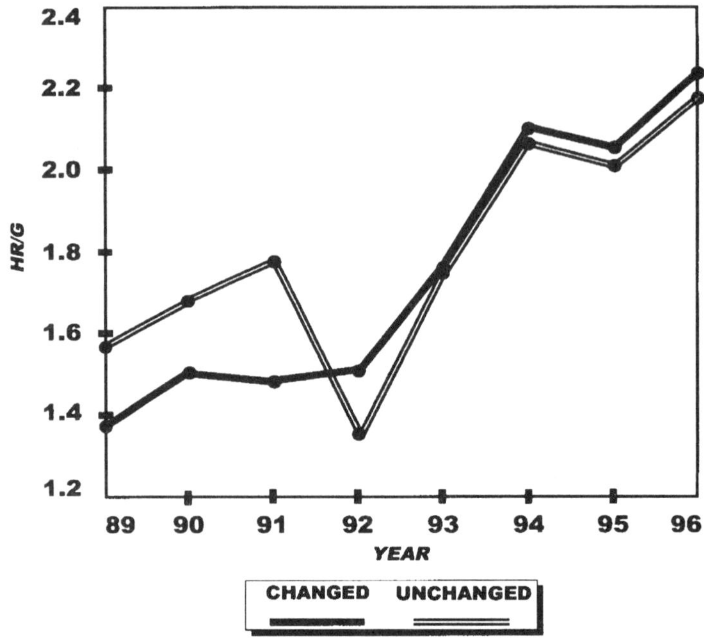

This graph also illustrates that at the start of the study, the 12 unchanged parks were home-run friendly, but over the last five years they were not. In 1989, their HR/G ratio was 1.57, about eight percent higher than the 1.46 HR/G hit in all of baseball. All of the other parks combined exhibited a HR/G ratio of 1.38. The 12 control parks remained home run parks through 1991, but in '92, they dipped dramatically to 1.36 HR/G, about six percent *below* the major league average of 1.44 HR/G. What happened? Not much—Oriole Park at Camden Yards was the only new park in baseball. Perhaps it was a one-year fluke for the rate to drop so dramatically, but ever since, the 12 parks in the unchanged group have been *pitchers'* parks, allowing fewer than average HR/G when compared to the major league average. Most recently, in 1996, the unchanged parks allowed 2.15 HR/G, about two percent below the average in baseball.

What do we conclude? New parks aren't the only factors in the home run explosion, but they are definitely playing a role.

—Drew Faust

A more complete listing for this category can be found on page 260.

III. QUESTIONS ON OFFENSE

Who Gets the "Slidin' Billy Trophy"?

One of the keys to any successful offense is a quality leadoff man: a player who can get on base, disrupt pitchers with his baserunning ability and set the table for the hitters who follow him. In what's become an annual tradition in the *Baseball Scoreboard*, we'd like to recognize this season's most outstanding leadoff man with the "Slidin' Billy Trophy." The award is named for the legendary Slidin' Billy Hamilton, a 19th-century superstar who, with a lifetime on-base percentage of .455, was the game's first great leadoff hitter.

Since a leadoff man's role is to score runs, it's only natural that his most important job is to get on base. The following chart identifies the players with the best OBPs last year while batting at the top of the order.

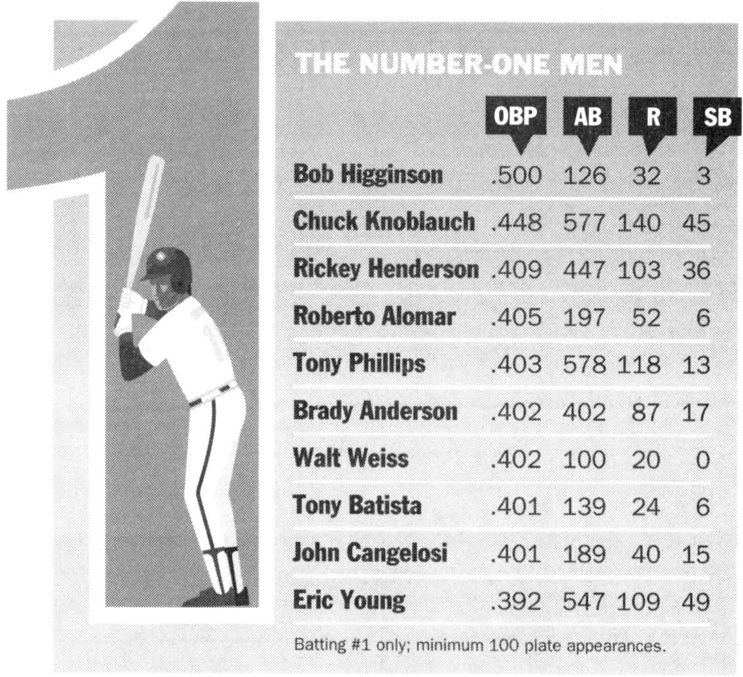

THE NUMBER-ONE MEN

	OBP	AB	R	SB
Bob Higginson	.500	126	32	3
Chuck Knoblauch	.448	577	140	45
Rickey Henderson	.409	447	103	36
Roberto Alomar	.405	197	52	6
Tony Phillips	.403	578	118	13
Brady Anderson	.402	402	87	17
Walt Weiss	.402	100	20	0
Tony Batista	.401	139	24	6
John Cangelosi	.401	189	40	15
Eric Young	.392	547	109	49

Batting #1 only; minimum 100 plate appearances.

You might recognize the name at the top of the list—Detroit's Bob Higginson, who also finished as this year's biggest "gainer" (see essay on p. 120) from last season. Higginson rebounded from a mediocre rookie campaign to have an outstanding year, and really turned it up a notch when heading the Tigers' lineup. Even though he occupied the leadoff slot for only a fraction of the year, Higginson's OBP of .500 was impressive indeed.

We can't give the Slidin' Billy Trophy to Higginson *that* easily, though; since he only had about 150 plate appearances at the top of the lineup, it wouldn't exactly be fair to have him compete with the full-timers. We feel that the following five players are the best regular leadoff men in the game:

Brady Anderson. Is he for real? At age 32, Anderson became one of the game's most unlikely sluggers by cranking out a career-high 50 homers, 35 of which came from the leadoff slot. Despite his great leadoff OBP (.402), the Orioles may be forced to move him down in the lineup to take advantage of his power explosion if it continues.

Rickey Henderson. Despite suffering a huge decline in batting average (.300 in '95 to .241 last year), Henderson actually *improved* his leadoff OBP (.409) by drawing 118 walks. At age 38, he's still a basestealing threat, having swiped 37 sacks in 52 attempts last season.

Chuck Knoblauch. Improving on what was an outstanding 1995 season, Knoblauch set career highs in almost all of the major offensive categories. Among leadoff men with at least 300 plate appearances, he ranked first in OBP (.448), batting average (.341) and runs scored (140), while placing second in slugging average (.518). (These numbers are leadoff stats only).

Kenny Lofton. Baseball's premier basestealer churned out another stellar year, scoring 131 runs from the leadoff slot to rank second behind Knoblauch. Despite his considerable accomplishments, Lofton generated an awful lot of outs for the runs he produced and didn't draw enough walks to be considered a *truly* great leadoff man (only 61 BB's in 736 PA's last season).

Tony Phillips. Whoever said leading off was a young man's job? At age 37, Phillips also posted some phenomenal numbers from the top slot, placing first in walks (123) and third in runs scored (118). His .403 OBP certainly provided Frank Thomas with plenty of RBI opportunities last season. Can you believe he was ready to retire last year?

Unlike past years where we awarded the Slidin' Billy Trophy subjectively, we decided to do things a little differently this time around. With the aid of Bill James and a couple of his computer simulation programs, we were able to find out *in a more scientific way* who was the best leadoff hitter in the majors last year. Bill's programs ran five separate lineups through the equivalent of 100 seasons worth of baseball games; the lineups were filled with identical "phantom" players in batting spots two through nine, with a different candidate occupying the leadoff position in each one. By finding out whose lineup scored the most runs, we were able to identify which player had the greatest influence on his team's offense. What did we find? Take a look:

Simulated Leadoff Runs Scored

Player	Avg Runs/Season	Avg Team Runs/Season	Team W/L Pct
Knoblauch	147	875	.528
Anderson	152	873	.523
Lofton	131	835	.503
Henderson	119	821	.489
Phillips	115	825	.487

(Players' overall offensive statistics used)

As you can see, the race for the Slidin' Billy Trophy was tight, indeed. Anderson actually scored (and drove in) the most runs of anyone in the group, but it was Knoblauch who had the greater impact on his team's performance. The comparison of these two players in particular was fascinating: here we had the prototypical leadoff man (Knoblauch) opposing a supposedly out-of-place slugger (Anderson). Here are some of the more interesting topics Bill James examined in his simulation:

1.) Who scored more runs in the innings in which they led off?

Knoblauch leads this category; his team crossed the plate .702 times per inning led off versus Anderson's mark of .690. However, as Bill wrote, "The leadoff hitter affects the runs scored not only in the innings in which he leads off, but equally as much in the innings in which the eighth or ninth hitter leads off (since he always bats in those innings) and also quite significantly in the innings in which the fifth, sixth or seventh hitter leads off." Here's where Anderson made up ground: late in the inning, his power was far more important than Knoblauch's ability to get on base. With two outs, there's a big difference between the run potential of a single or walk compared to that of a home run.

2.) If Anderson scored more runs per season than Knoblauch did, how come his team didn't finish with a better record?

Because Knoblauch's superior balance of skills increased the offensive efficiency of the team. Anderson may have compiled higher individual numbers, but they came at the expense of the 2-3-4 hitters in the lineup. On the other hand, Knoblauch—who has a better combination of power and on-base percentage—added runs to the performance of the 8-9 hitters *as well as* RBI to the totals of the 2-3-4 hitters.

3.) What effect did the players have on the consistency of their teams' offensive output?

Anderson's power increased the number of one- and two-run innings by five percent as compared to the average leadoff man—the largest difference of any of the players analyzed. But Knoblauch had the greatest impact when it came to helping his club generate rallies of three or more runs; over the 100-year study, his teams posted big innings *10* percent more often than those of the average leadoff hitter. As Bill put it, "a home run hitter in the leadoff spot does not tend to generate BIG innings, as much as he tends to prevent shutout innings."

Based on simulated team performance and overall offensive leadoff skills, we've decided to give this year's Slidin' Billy Trophy to. . . Chuck Knoblauch—his second consecutive award. Congratulations, Chuck, on a job well done!

—Kevin Fullam

A more complete listing for this category can be found on page 261.

Are Switching Switch-Hitters at a Disadvantage?

The biggest reason switch-hitters are prized by managers is that they can exploit the platoon advantage. Let's say it's the ninth inning and the opposing right-handed starter has just been replaced by a left-handed closer. A switch-hitter would theoretically destroy any platoon edge that any pitching change may have gained, since he simply digs in from the other side of the plate. But one of our readers, Issac W. Stephenson, wasn't so sure. Issac asked if "having to switch-hit during the course of a game [is] hard, easy or neither?" To find out, we did some digging of our own. We examined every instance since 1992 in which a switch-hitter (excluding pitchers) made at least his first two plate appearances in a game on one side of the plate, then got turned around. The study covers five years, so it contains a fairly large sample size—and it yields some interesting results.

The chart below shows the totals. We included the first two or more plate appearances from one side of the plate in the "before" row, and all plate appearances following the initial switch in the "after" row.

Switch-Hitters Who Get Turned Around—1992-96

Start as Right-Handed Batter

	AB	H	2B	3B	HR	RBI	BB	K	AVG	OBP	SLG
Before	15298	4417	825	82	375	1843	1510	2199	.289	.354	.427
After	8432	2190	382	54	191	1199	1080	1600	.260	.345	.386

Start as Left-Handed Batter

	AB	H	2B	3B	HR	RBI	BB	K	AVG	OBP	SLG
Before	20354	6276	1157	206	568	3014	2482	2951	.308	.384	.469
After	10475	2844	495	76	246	1537	1346	1800	.272	.355	.404

Overall

	AB	H	2B	3B	HR	RBI	BB	K	AVG	OBP	SLG
Before	35652	10693	1982	288	943	4857	3992	5150	.300	.371	.451
After	18907	5034	877	130	437	2736	2426	3400	.266	.350	.396

As you can see, it doesn't matter whether the switch-hitter opened the game from the left or right side—in either case, he became a poorer batsman after making a midgame switch. If he started from the right side, he lost 29 points from his batting average after making the initial change; if he started from the left side, he lost 36 points. Overall, the batting average dipped 34 points. Furthermore, the midgame switch resulted in a measurable loss in power. Slugging percentages dropped 41 points after opening right-handed, 65 points after starting left-handed.

When digesting these numbers, you may want to keep in mind that mid-game batting side switches typically take place after a pitching change has been made. Could the "after" results therefore be affected by those match-ups against relievers? Well, yes, but consider that over the past five years the overall batting average against relievers has been only nine points lower than against starters (.259 versus .268), while the overall slugging percentage dropped only 19 points after a starter left the game (.415 versus .396). The switch-hitters' drop in production cannot be explained only by the entry of relievers into the equation.

Perhaps the decrease occurs because many switch-hitters are, in fact, better from one side of the plate than the other. They would therefore be more likely to open games facing pitchers against whom they can take advantage. When a pitching change is made, these switch-hitters could be forced to move to their weaker side. Another possible reason for the dropoff is that switch-hitters may prepare for a game by anticipating the starting pitcher. They may take batting practice from only one side of the plate, and when a pitching change is made during the game, they're not prepared for the adjustment.

It's also interesting to note that switch-hitters appeared to be much more consistent batting from the right side than the left. Their batting average was .289 opening games right-handed, and .272 following switches after starting games left-handed (though not all of those plate appearances after making the switch remained right-handed, since subsequent pitching changes may return the batter to the left side). Meanwhile, switch-hitters who opened games batting left-handed hit .308, as opposed to the .260 mark posted by hitters who switched to the left side during a game.

That discrepancy isn't easy to explain. Intuitively, you might have guessed just the reverse. Since there are more right-handed pitchers, there are then more left-handed appearances by switch-hitters, and thus, less chance to get out of practice. Perhaps, as with other unexplained left-handed phenomena, it's simply due to which side of the brain they think with.

In any case, there's no disputing the drop in production when switch-hitters change sides during games. Managers would be wise to consider this, at least somewhat, when making tactical decisions. And the next time an announcer talks about how an upcoming pitching change doesn't affect the team because there's a switch-hitter on-deck, you'll know better.

—Jim Henzler

Who Rose From the Ashes—and Who Crashed to Earth—in 1996?

Without a doubt, one of the most amazing stories of the 1996 season was the resurgence of soon-to-be Hall of Famer Paul Molitor. After a subpar '95 campaign with the Toronto Blue Jays, during which he posted his lowest batting average (.270) in 11 seasons, the 39-year-old superstar was thought by many to be at the end of the line. However, Molitor shocked the baseball world when he exploded out of the gates with Minnesota last spring and jumped out to a .386 average in April. The savvy veteran recorded career highs in hits, RBI and even *games played*, while posting a stellar .341 batting average that was up 71 points from his 1995 figure. It was a remarkable jump for a player his age.

Each year we shine our spotlight on those hitters who experienced the biggest improvements and declines at the plate over the previous season. Molitor didn't account for the biggest increase last year. . . but he was close. Here's the top 10:

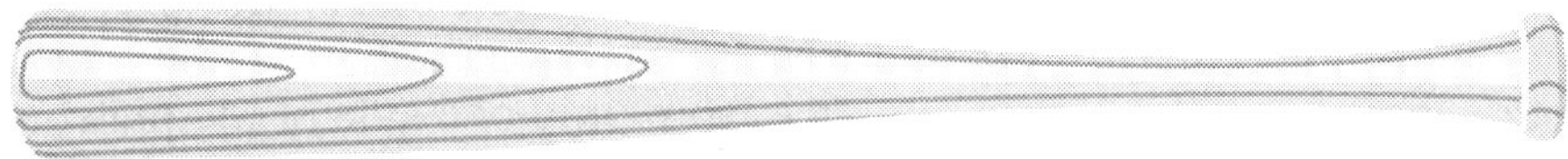

BIGGEST BATTING AVERAGE CHANGES 1995–96

	1995	1996	CHANGE
UP			
Bob Higginson	.224	.320	+96
Ellis Burks	.266	.344	+78
Paul Molitor	.270	.341	+71
Mark Johnson	.208	.274	+66
Rusty Greer	.271	.332	+61
Mark Grudzielanek	.245	.306	+61
DOWN			
Brad Ausmus	.293	.221	–72
Derek Bell	.334	.263	–71
Mike Devereaux	.299	.229	–70
Luis Sojo	.289	.220	–69
Rey Sanchez	.278	.211	–67

Minimum 250 plate appearances each year.

After struggling a bit in his rookie year, Detroit's Bob Higginson turned in the biggest single-season improvement in the majors, raising his batting average from .224 in '95 to a sparkling .320 last year. While Higginson has been considered a bona fide prospect for the past several years, few expected the Tiger outfielder to post such high marks in his second season—especially on the heels of his marginal showing as a rookie. In addition to his outstanding average, Higginson slammed 26 homers and proved to be especially effective when hitting out of Detroit's leadoff slot (which we discuss in a separate essay on p. 114).

Should Higginson be expected to remain at last year's performance level? Probably not; though he's still relatively young at 26, it's likely that his numbers will gravitate towards the average of his first two big league seasons. His stats in the minors projected him as a .260-.275 hitter, and in our 1997 *STATS Major League Handbook*, we project Higginson to drop down to about .280 next year.

Interestingly enough, last season's biggest offensive decline was turned in by one of Higginson's teammates. Catcher Brad Ausmus, traded from San Diego to Detroit in midseason, saw his batting average plummet by a whopping 72 points. While the Tigers certainly weathered their fair share of misery last season, they decided that Ausmus wasn't the solution to their catching problems and traded him to Houston at the conclusion of the season.

The irony of finding Molitor and Ausmus among our leaders is that, at 39, one would expect *Molitor* to be the one experiencing a large drop in offensive production. On the other hand, the 27-year-old Ausmus should have enjoyed the prime season of his career in 1996. The reality is both players turned in 1995 totals that differed greatly from their career averages, and it was only natural that they would respond with counterbalancing years.

—Kevin Fullam

A more complete listing for this category can be found on page 262.

Will Belle and Thomas Be the Greatest Single-Season Power Duo Ever?

Abbott & Costello, Lenny & Squiggy, Starsky & Hutch, Butch Cassidy & The Sundance Kid, Masters & Johnson, Luke & Laura, M & M. . . their names are indelibly linked. So, too, are those of some of baseball's greatest sluggers, joined forever by common teams and powerful swings. Together, Ruth & Gehrig, Mantle & Maris, Mays & McCovey, Aaron & Mathews, Banks & Williams, Hodges & Snider pummelled opposing pitchers, kept opposing mangers awake at night and rewrote the record books with every monster cut. They top the list of the greatest power-hitting pairs in the annals of baseball—as inseparable as Burns & Allen.

And Albert Belle and Frank Thomas are looking to join them.

When the White Sox' Jerry Reinsdorf pulled the shocker of the offseason and inked Belle for five years, fans began to picture a lineup card featuring two of the biggest bats of this decade—if not of all time. Naturally, we felt the waves first-hand at our offices in suburban Chicago, and watched supporters of the South Siders gleefully count potential home runs on their fingers and toes and arms and legs and. . . well, you get the picture. They simply ran out of body parts! "Will this be the greatest power duo ever?" they wondered aloud. Well, let's give the new teammates at least a few seasons together before we get carried away with trying to answer that weighty question. Memorable duos stand the test of time, and Belle and Thomas have yet to stand in the same *dugout.*

But we *can* start looking at the greatest single-season duos, with an eye toward 1997. We'll begin with the top single-season home run duos:

Top Home Run Duos—Single Season

Players, Tm	Year	Combined HR
Maris/Mantle, Yanks	1961	115
Ruth/Gehrig, Yanks	1927	107
Wilson/Hartnett, Cubs	1930	93
Foxx/Simmons, A's	1932	93
Griffey Jr./Buhner, Sea	1996	93
Ruth/Gehrig, Yanks	1931	92
Greenberg/York, Det	1938	91
Mays/McCovey, SF	1965	91
Ruth/Gehrig, Yanks	1930	90
Anderson/Palmeiro, Bal	1996	89

You probably already knew who occupied the top spots. The immortal Yankee combinations of Mantle & Maris and Ruth & Gehrig set standards that may be beyond approach even in this second "gilded age" of hitting. But once you get past *their* otherworldly numbers, the other figures seem very attainable. Belle and Thomas swatted a combined 88 homers last season, which would have placed them just off the bottom of this list. But *two* years ago, they totaled 90 longballs in a strike-shortened campaign, and if you add Belle's best year (50 homers) with Thomas' (41), you have a duo with a great chance to leapfrog a number of legendary partners.

Don't go rewriting the record books just yet, however. Albert and Big Frank face at least two major obstacles: free passes and Comiskey Park. The knock on Thomas as a power hitter has always been his penchant for drawing walks, and Belle's base on balls total fell one short of the century mark in 1996. Of course, walks didn't exactly hurt the likes of Ruth, Gehrig or Mantle. Then there's the ballpark. We've been keeping track of "park indexes" for a number of years, and for a good explanation of how the figures are derived, please see the Colorado Rockies essay (p. 48). For our purposes here, our data has shown that over the past three seasons, Comiskey has been the toughest place in the American League to hit homers, decreasing a player's longball total by 17 percent in games played in the "unfriendly" confines.

So let's take the sole focus off home runs, and include walks, by examining the duos with the best combined OBS (on-base plus slugging percentage) in a single season.

Top OBS Duos—Single Season

Players, Tm	Year	Combined OBS
Ruth/Gehrig, Yanks	1927	1.249
Ruth/Gehrig, Yanks	1930	1.209
Ruth/Gehrig, Yanks	1931	1.148
Ruth/Gehrig, Yanks	1928	1.142
Ruth/Meusel, Yanks	1920	1.137
Ruth/Meusel, Yanks	1921	1.132
Gehrig/Dickey, Yanks	1936	1.121
Wilson/Hartnett, Cubs	1930	1.112
O'Neill/Caruthers, Browns	1887	1.109
Hornsby/Bottomley, StL	1925	1.107

(minimum 400 PA for each hitter)

This category not only measures the ability to smack homers, but also the ability to get on base and generate extra-base hits. Without question, this is the list that Ruth and Gehrig built. The Yankee cornerstones have a say in seven of the top 10 spots, and 12 of the top 19. Also notice that the list is completely void of any duos from the post-WWII era. In fact, the first teammates who show up in this category from a season *after* 1941 are Thomas and Julio Franco, whose combined OBS of 1.063 in 1994 gives them the *32nd*-best mark of all time.

That all may be about to change. . .

With walks now working for them, Belle and the Big Hurt may be about to break into that sacred Ruth-&-Gehrig territory. Combining their numbers from last season, the newest dynamic duo posted a 1.058 OBS—not even as good as the mark set by Thomas and Franco in '94. But two years ago, Belle's and Thomas' combined figure was 1.079, and in 1994, it was an amazing 1.185, which would have been better than all but the two best showings by Ruth & Gehrig. With Belle turning 30 last August, and Thomas not yet 29, there's certainly no reason to believe they can't reach those levels again.

Soon they may be as inseparable as Tom & Jerry, or Siegfried & Roy, or Sonny & Cher. . . well OK, maybe not Sonny & Cher.

—Tony Nistler

A more complete listing for this category can be found on page 263.

You Gotta' Have "Heart," But Can You Live Without One?

As if you needed any more proof of 1996's offensive explosion, we're here to offer Exhibit 125: the outpouring of emotion (not to mention raw numbers) from deep inside baseball's "heart." We're talking about the "heart of the order"—the three, four and five hitters who certainly lived up to their billing for a number of clubs last year. We've been tracking the production of the game's healthiest "hearts" for the past seven seasons now, and our computers are *still* cooling down after churning out these lofty figures:

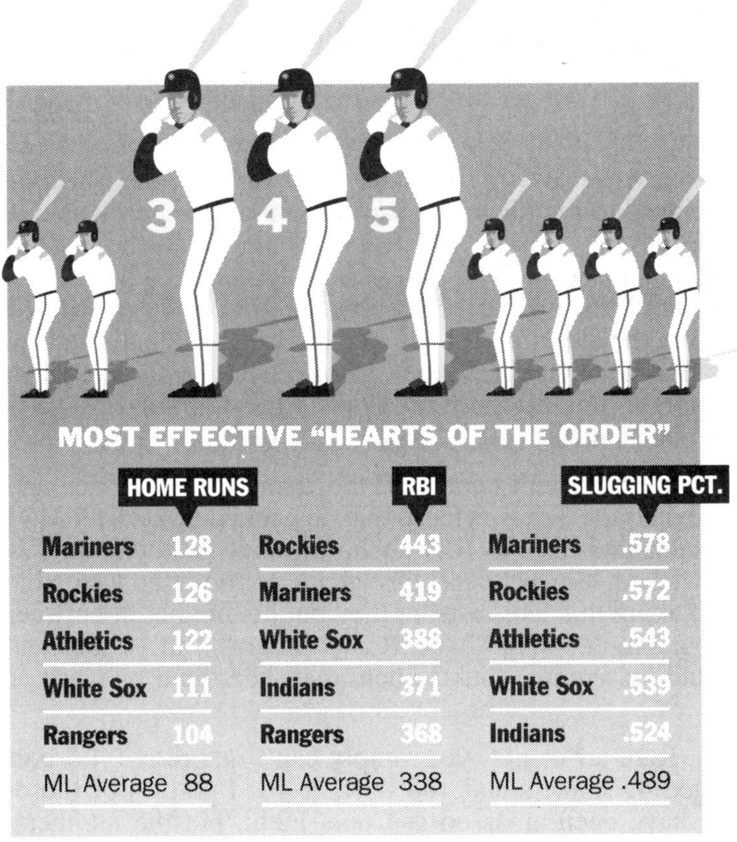

MOST EFFECTIVE "HEARTS OF THE ORDER"

HOME RUNS		RBI		SLUGGING PCT.	
Mariners	128	Rockies	443	Mariners	.578
Rockies	126	Mariners	419	Rockies	.572
Athletics	122	White Sox	388	Athletics	.543
White Sox	111	Indians	371	White Sox	.539
Rangers	104	Rangers	368	Indians	.524
ML Average	88	ML Average	338	ML Average	.489

Since we first introduced our findings on 3-4-5 production in the second edition of the *Baseball Scoreboard* following the 1990 campaign, no "hearts" had ever pumped out as many as 400 RBI in a single season. Also, a *grand total* of four teams from 1990-1995 boasted a 3-4-5 combination which accounted for 100 or more homers. Well, break those old measuring sticks over your knee. Snap! Not one, but two trios crossed the 400-RBI barrier, and no fewer than seven clubs hit at least 100 heart-of-the-order homers. We've made it a tradition to pick the teams with the top five tickers in the league, and here are the results of our 1996 health report:

1. Mariners. For the second straight year, Seattle's heart beat the loudest. In 1995, the M's gained top honors *without* the presence of Ken Griffey Jr. in the lineup for a good chunk of the season. With Junior keeping out of harm's way long enough to log 536 at-bats (along with 48 homers and 139 RBI) in the number-three spot last season, it's hardly surprising that the team found itself in the best shape again in 1996. The other key components for Seattle—Jay Buhner (32 years old) and Edgar Martinez (34)—aren't getting any younger, but they don't appear to be slowing down yet, either.

2. White Sox. After showing the most heart in 1994, the Chisox middle of the order slipped to middle of the pack in 1995. The constants in those two seasons were Frank Thomas and Robin Ventura, but the puzzle lacked a third and final piece in '95. Enter Harold Baines, who returned to the Windy City in 1996 and exceeded everyone's expectations with 18 homers and 66 RBI in the cleanup spot and another three longballs and 21 RBI hitting in the five-hole. Of course the Chisox have to be the early front-runner for top honors in this category in '97 with the addition of Albert Belle to an already potent attack.

3. Rangers. Juan Gonzalez came off the respirator last season and pumped *so much* life into the Texas offense that he walked away with MVP honors. With Gonzalez and his 144 RBI anchoring the cleanup spot, Texas could have sandwiched him between just about *anybody* and still have had a chance at making this list. Instead, they put his big bat in between the formidable foursome of Will Clark, Rusty Greer, Dean Palmer and Mickey Tettleton and erased any doubts about their heart and its place among the elite.

4. Rockies. Rare air or not, you simply can't ignore a 3-4-5 combination that averaged 42 homers and 148 RBI. A good portion of those amazing totals may have been amassed at Coors Field, but the numbers at home should not be entirely discounted: Colorado's 55 home wins were right behind Atlanta's 56 for tops in the majors.

5. Athletics. Oakland was certainly the dark horse on this list, and though the team didn't exactly return to the days of the Bash Brothers, Mark McGwire has found a powerful friend in the form of Geronimo Berroa. The Athletics were one of three teams in 1996 to fell the team home run record set by the 1961 Yankees, and over half their longballs came from the heart.

A strong heart may guarantee production, but it doesn't necessarily ensure a trip to the postseason. Four of our top five teams—with Oakland being the lone exception—finished the 1996 season with a winning record, but only the Rangers took the field in the postseason. The Cardinals, Padres, Braves and Yankees all had hearts which finished out of the top 10 in most of our three categories. They were far from being the worst, however. That distinction goes to the 3-4-5 hitters of the Kansas City Royals, who accounted for only 58 homers, 269 RBI and a .402 slugging percentage to go along with a .249 batting average. Oh, if Bob Hamelin could only find his stroke again. . .

—Tony Nistler

A more complete listing for this category can be found on page 264.

Who Puts Their Team Ahead?

In his autobiography, *Nice Guys Finish Last,* Leo Durocher offered a peculiar estimation of Ron Santo's clutch-hitting abilities. Durocher said that when he took over as manager of the Cubs in '66, other baseball men told him he'd never win a pennant with Santo at third. "Sooner or later," they said, "Santo is going to come up with the game on the [line] and nine times out of 10 he's going to [fail]." Later, Durocher agreed, "They were right."

Ron Santo—a bad clutch hitter? He must have piled up a ton of RBI in blowouts, because he drove in more than 90 runs in each of Durocher's first five seasons with Chicago. It's impossible to say how many of Santo's RBI put the Cubs ahead, but thankfully, we *do* have this information for today's players.

We credit a player with a "go-ahead RBI" whenever he drives in a run which gives his club the lead. By looking at who drove in the greatest number of truly meaningful runs, we can see who really delivered in the clutch. Here are the leaders for 1996:

1996 Leaders—Go-Ahead RBI

Player, Team	RBI
Albert Belle, Cle	55
Rafael Palmeiro, Bal	51
Dante Bichette, Col	49
Gary Sheffield, Fla	49
Barry Bonds, SF	48
Juan Gonzalez, Tex	47
Jay Buhner, Sea	44
Bernard Gilkey, Mets	44
Jeff King, Pit	44
Mark McGwire, Oak	43

It's clear that Albert Belle wasn't just driving in a lot of runs for the Indians—he was driving in a lot of *big* runs. His total of 55 go-ahead RBI led the majors, while teammates Manny Ramirez (36) and Jim Thome (34) didn't even come close.

Some players get more chances to drive in meaningful runs. We keep track of "go-ahead opportunities," which are any at-bats with runners in scoring position who are go-ahead runs. The go-ahead RBI in the following chart are the ones that result only in these particular at-bats. We can now determine which hitters cash in on the highest percentage of their "golden" opportunities. Here are last year's leaders in go-ahead RBI percentage:

1996 Leaders—Go-Ahead RBI Percentage

Player, Team	Opp	RBI	Pct
Albert Belle, Cle	105	33	31.4
Barry Bonds, SF	96	30	31.3
Mark McGwire, Oak	77	24	31.2
Gary Sheffield, Fla	100	31	31.0
Bernard Gilkey, Mets	113	34	30.1
Ron Gant, StL	78	23	29.5
Paul O'Neill, Yanks	95	28	29.5
Juan Gonzalez, Tex	104	30	28.8
Rafael Palmeiro, Bal	119	34	28.6
Mike Piazza, LA	96	27	28.1

(Minimum 50 total RBI)

By this measure, Barry Bonds very nearly knocks Belle out of the top spot. Bonds didn't have as many opportunities to put the woeful Giants in the lead, but he rose to the occasion when the situation presented itself. Bonds was even better in '95, when he led this list by a wide margin with a go-ahead RBI percentage of 36.2.

Here are the players with the *lowest* go-ahead RBI percentages last year:

1996 Trailers—Go-Ahead RBI Percentage

Player, Team	Opp	RBI	Pct
F.P. Santangelo, Mon	58	5	8.6
Jeff Kent, Mets/Cle	69	6	8.7
J.T. Snow, Cal	87	8	9.2
Scott Stahoviak, Min	73	7	9.6
Jason Giambi, Oak	97	10	10.3

We can excuse F.P. Santangelo—after all, he isn't *expected* to drive in runs—but not Jeff Kent. Kent failed to step up his production in clutch situations during the Mets' early-season struggles. Perhaps, years from now, Dallas Green's autobiography will read, "They *told* me I'd never win a pennant with Jeff Kent at third base!"

—Mat Olkin

A more complete listing for this category can be found on page 265.

Runs Created: Did Bonds Get Robbed of Another MVP Award?

If you want to assess a player's *value*, one of the best places to start is with his total of runs created. Invented by Bill James back in his *Baseball Abstract* days, runs created uses a complex formula to estimate how many runs a player contributed to his club's offense. The formula is in the Glossary, and it covers just about everything a player does on offense, both positively and negatively.

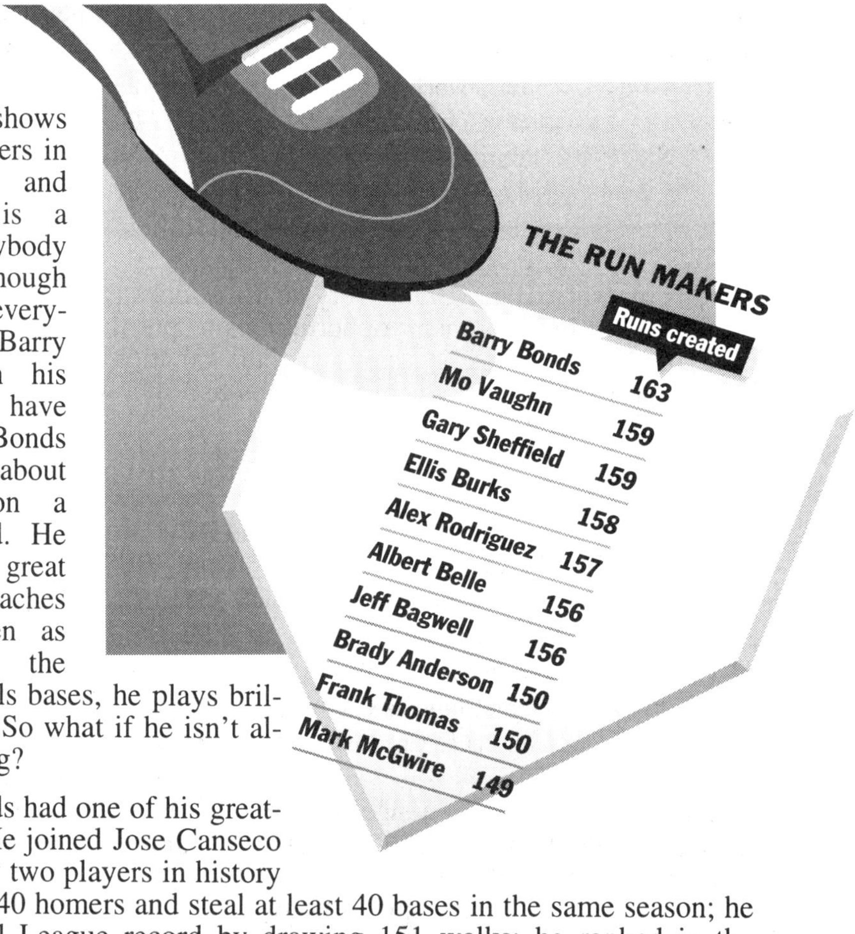

The chart shows the 1996 leaders in runs created, and the leader is a player everybody admires, though not one who everybody loves: Barry Bonds. Even his critics would have to agree that Bonds can do just about everything on a baseball field. He hits with great power, he reaches base as often as anyone in the game, he steals bases, he plays brilliant defense. So what if he isn't always charming?

THE RUN MAKERS

	Runs created
Barry Bonds	163
Mo Vaughn	159
Gary Sheffield	159
Ellis Burks	158
Alex Rodriguez	157
Albert Belle	156
Jeff Bagwell	156
Brady Anderson	150
Frank Thomas	150
Mark McGwire	149

In 1996, Bonds had one of his greatest seasons. He joined Jose Canseco as one of only two players in history to hit at least 40 homers and steal at least 40 bases in the same season; he set a National League record by drawing 151 walks; he ranked in the N.L.'s top five in homers, runs scored, RBI, walks, stolen bases, on-base percentage and slugging. And oh yeah, he won a Gold Glove for the sixth time in the last seven seasons.

Yet when the National League Most Valuable Player voting was announced, Bonds—playing for an also-ran team—was well down the list; the award went unanimously to Ken Caminiti of the Padres. No knock on Caminiti, a brilliant and inspirational performer, but when it comes to offensive production, he couldn't compare with Bonds. Though Caminiti had a great year with 139 runs created, he ranked fifth in the National League after Bonds, Gary Sheffield (159), Ellis Burks (158) and Jeff Bagwell (156).

We won't argue too much with the choice of Caminiti, who did some amazing things while leading his team to a division title. Bonds has three MVP awards of his own, so you can't say he's been ignored. But one could make the argument that Bonds deserved to win *six* MVP awards in the seven seasons of the 1990s. Look at his record in terms of runs created:

Barry Bonds in the 1990s

Year	Bonds RC (NL Rk)	NL MVP (NL RC Rk)
1990	128 (1st)	Bonds (1st)
1991	118 (1st)	Pendleton (5th)
1992	148 (1st)	Bonds (1st)
1993	172 (1st)	Bonds (1st)
1994	115 (2nd)	Bagwell (1st)
1995	134 (1st)	Larkin (7th)
1996	163 (1st)	Caminiti (5th)

What a remarkable run.

We also had problems with the American League MVP choice, Juan Gonzalez, who didn't even make the American League top 10 in runs created. That issue is discussed at length in the Texas Rangers essay (see p. 34), so we won't get into it here. Our choice would have been Alex Rodriguez, who ranked second in the A.L. in runs created.

A twin brother of runs created is "offensive winning percentage," a James creation which uses a player's runs created to estimate the won-lost percentage he would have compiled against a team of league average opposition. Here are the 1996 leaders in OW%:

1996 Leaders—Offensive Winning Percentage

Player, Team	OW%
Barry Bonds, SF	.858
Mark McGwire, Oak	.856
Gary Sheffield, Fla	.848
Jeff Bagwell, Hou	.822
Ellis Burks, Col	.817
Edgar Martinez, Sea	.803
Ken Caminiti, SD	.802
Jim Thome, Cle	.801
Frank Thomas, WSox	.799
Alex Rodriguez, Sea	.779

(Minimum 3.1 PA per scheduled game)

That man Bonds again, just edging his Bay Area rival, Mark McGwire of the Athletics. Two pretty valuable players, we'd say.

—Don Zminda

A more complete listing for this category can be found on page 266.

Who's the Best Bunter?

Welcome to our annual review of the fine—some would say lost—art of bunting. We look at both kinds of bunts: sacrifice attempts and bunts for a hit. Let's start with the sacrifice. Here's a list of the top sacrifice artists of 1996, based on success rate when attempting a sac hit (minimum 10 attempts). For this year, we've taken Greg Crouse's suggestion and charged a bunter with a failed attempt when he fails to record a sacrifice after two foul bunts. . . whether he makes another attempt or not. Makes a lot of sense, doesn't it? Here's the top 10:

Top Sacrifice Bunt %—1996

Bunter, Team	SH	Att	Pct
John Smoltz, Atl	14	14	1.000
Kimera Bartee, Det	12	12	1.000
Rheal Cormier, Mon	11	11	1.000
Mike Morgan, StL/Cin	11	11	1.000
Kevin Elster, Tex	16	17	.941
David Howard, KC	15	16	.938
Shane Reynolds, Hou	14	15	.933
Walt Weiss, Col	14	15	.933
Ozzie Guillen, WSox	12	13	.923
Joey Hamilton, SD	11	12	.917
Quinton McCracken, Col	11	12	.917
MLB Average			.806

(minimum 10 sacrifice attempts)

The new rule makes a difference, as there were only four players with perfect records, down from seven in 1995 under the old format. But National League pitchers John Smoltz, Rheal Cormier and Mike Morgan all succeeded every time out, as did rookie outfielder Kimera Bartee of the Tigers. Also worth noting is the performance of Houston Astro pitcher Shane Reynolds, the only player—pitcher or otherwise—to make the top 10 in both 1995 and 1996.

Who were the *worst* sacrifice bunters of 1996? Pitcher Pat Rapp of the Marlins probably was the single worst bunter; he attempted to lay down four sacrifices last year, and failed on all four. Another pitcher, Steve Avery of the Braves, was no prize, either: six attempts, one success. (Avery's probably happy he won't have to bunt now that he's in the DH league.) Among position players, both Quilvio Veras (Marlins) and Rex Hudler (Angels) were 1-for-4. Shame on you guys.

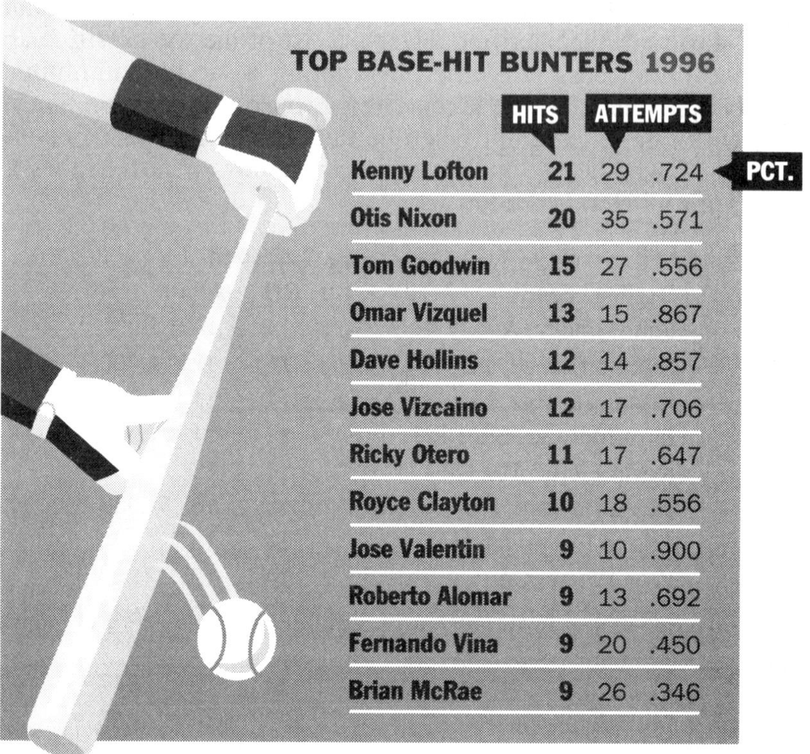

TOP BASE-HIT BUNTERS 1996

	HITS	ATTEMPTS	PCT.
Kenny Lofton	21	29	.724
Otis Nixon	20	35	.571
Tom Goodwin	15	27	.556
Omar Vizquel	13	15	.867
Dave Hollins	12	14	.857
Jose Vizcaino	12	17	.706
Ricky Otero	11	17	.647
Royce Clayton	10	18	.556
Jose Valentin	9	10	.900
Roberto Alomar	9	13	.692
Fernando Vina	9	20	.450
Brian McRae	9	26	.346

The chart shows the 1996 leaders in bunt hits, and there are plenty of repeaters on *this* list: Kenny Lofton, Otis Nixon, Tom Goodwin and Roberto Alomar all made the top 10 in 1995 as well. Lofton, who had something of an off year despite making the top 10 in '95, bounced back to lead the majors in bunt hits for the second time in three years.

Maybe the most surprising name on the list is Dave Hollins, the slugging infielder who's now with the Angels. Hollins has stolen only 20 bases in 37 attempts in his seven-year career, so you wouldn't call him a "speed guy." But he obviously knows how to bunt for a hit.

Conspicuous by his absence from the leaders list was one of the great bunters of all time, Brett Butler, who spent most of 1996 waging an heroic fight against cancer. Also missing was a promising bunter named Deion

Sanders, who didn't even play baseball in 1996. He'll hope to rejoin the leaders list as he returns to the Reds this year.

We annually award the "STATS FlatBat" to the best bunter of the year, and that means displaying prowess in *both* bunting categories. The leading candidates for 1996:

David Howard. He can't hit much, but he sure can field. . . *and* bunt. Howard was 15-for-16 in sacrifice attempts in 1996, and 6-for-7 bunting for a hit. Somehow we don't think that'll be enough to keep Jay Bell from taking his job.

Jose Vizcaino. I'm tellin' ya, these good bunters, they don't get no respect. Vizcaino was 9-for-10 bunting for a sacrifice, and 12-for-17 bunting for a hit. His reward for this was to get traded twice, including the deal that sent him from the Indians to the Giants after the season.

Kenny Lofton. Along with leading the league in bunt hits, Lofton was 7-for-8 when he attempted a sacrifice. Of course, being such a great hitter, he wasn't asked to sacrifice very often.

Otis Nixon. The 1995 FlatBat winner had another great year. He finished second to Lofton in bunt hits, and he was also 7-for-8 sacrificing. Otis could do this in his sleep.

Tom Goodwin. Along with finishing among the leaders with 15 bunt hits, Goodwin led the majors with 21 sacrifice hits. His only negative was that he failed four times in sacrifice situations.

Worthy candidates all, but we think one man sticks out. The 1996 STATS FlatBat goes to Kenny Lofton, who also took home the award in 1994.

—Don Zminda

A more complete listing for this category can be found on page 268.

Who's First in the Secondary?

Batting average is the game's most-quoted offensive statistic, but it only measures one thing—the hitter's ability to get base hits. So Bill James invented "Secondary Average," which measures just about everything *else* a batter can do. Here's the formula:

Secondary Average = (Total Bases - Hits + BB + SB - CS) / AB

If a player can hit for power, draw walks and steal bases efficiently, his Secondary Average will reflect those abilities, even if the player's batting average doesn't make him out to be anything special. Last year, Mark McGwire hit home runs and drew walks at a Ruthian rate. As a result, he led the major leagues in Secondary Average, despite the fact that he didn't steal a single base:

1996 Leaders—Secondary Average

Player, Team	Avg
Mark McGwire, Oak	.693
Barry Bonds, SF	.663
Gary Sheffield, Fla	.597
Jim Thome, Cle	.545
Jeff Bagwell, Hou	.518
Edgar Martinez, Sea	.515
Barry Larkin, Cin	.505
Albert Belle, Cle	.495
Ken Griffey, Jr., Sea	.495
Brady Anderson, Bal	.494
MLB Average	.272

(minimum 502 appearances)

Here we've got two main types of players: on one hand, we've got the guys with across-the-board ability, like Barry Bonds, Barry Larkin and Brady Anderson. On the other hand, we've got pure power-and-walks guys like McGwire, Jim Thome and Albert Belle. Brady Anderson had always been the kind of hitter who made contributions in many areas, but it was his power explosion that enabled him to finally break into the top 10 last year.

The list of players with the *worst* Secondary Averages is equally revealing:

1996 Trailers—Secondary Average

Player, Team	Avg
Rey Ordonez, Mets	.086
Ozzie Guillen, WSox	.126
Gary DiSarcina, Cal	.132
Jose Vizcaino, Mets/Cle	.146
Garret Anderson, Cal	.161
Pat Meares, Min	.166
Jody Reed, SD	.166
Carlos Baerga, Cle/Mets	.168
Brian L. Hunter, Hou	.169
Mark Grudzielanek, Mon	.170

There sure are some interesting names on *this* list. Bringing up the rear is the Mets' rookie shortstop, Rey Ordonez. This should provide a harsh dose of reality for those who insisted that his hitting was acceptable last year. Ordonez registered only 17 extra-base hits and 22 walks—12 of which were intentional—and he was thrown out on three of four stolen base attempts. In fact, if you subtract his intentional walks, his Secondary Average drops below that of the Mets' *pitchers*. It takes a lot of stellar glove work to make up for that.

Another shocker is Garret Anderson, who nearly won the A.L. Rookie of the Year Award in 1995. There were few complaints when he batted .285 last year, and the Angels haven't seemed interested in trading him to relieve their glut of outfielders. Still, he hit only 12 homers last year, drew only 27 walks, and got caught stealing nine times in 16 attempts. He'll have to do more than hit an empty .285 if he wants to help the Angels.

—Mat Olkin

A more complete listing for this category can be found on page 269.

Who Are the Human Air Conditioners?

What happens to a player who comes out of the chute with 21 home runs in his first 202 at-bats of the season? Well, if that player is Henry Rodriguez, a man who had hit only 21 homers in parts of four big league seasons prior to his explosion, he may very well start swinging for the fences. And what happens when a hitter consciously tries to jerk the ball? Well, let's just say it's called the *whhhiiifff*.

Ah, temptation. Henry Rodriguez might argue that he did *not* start trying to hit homers last year, but one thing is certain: Rodriguez topped all major leaguers by swinging at and missing 396 pitches in '96:

Perhaps it's understandable that Rodriguez led the majors in swinging and missing—and in strikeouts—last year; after all, he had never had more than 306 at-bats in any season prior to '96. But his homer and strikeout totals, broken down by month, do support the notion that "Oh Henry" tried to hit too many pitches over the fence after his early-season power surge. In April and May, Rodriguez homered 20 times while striking out in 25.5 percent of his at-bats. By June, National League pitchers woke up and realized they better start pitching him more carefully. The result: just 13 homers in June, July and August combined, and a strikeout in *34.8* percent of his at-bats during those summer months. To Rodriguez' credit, he bounced back in September, bringing his strikeout percentage down to 23.3 while batting .333. He hit only three homers in September, perhaps proving that over the long haul, a home run swing is not the way for Rodriguez to go.

The other four names on our whiff chart are more established home run hitters, who tend to be excused for swinging and missing frequently. Galarraga, Buhner, Sosa and Fielder all homered at least 39 times last year, and let's face it—fans will live with the swinging and missing, because they want to see the longball. Sosa, it should be noted, places fourth on the chart despite missing about a quarter of the season with a broken hand. Project his numbers for a full season, and Sosa would have swung and missed a whopping 499 times last year. That would have made Rodriguez look like a contact hitter. As for Cecil Fielder—well, he's been so well-represented in this chart over the years that the STATS, Inc. editors are thinking of creating a "Cecil Fielder Award," to be given annually to the player who leads the majors in swinging and missing.

One thing's clear about the chart: you have to be pretty productive just to get that many cuts. Perhaps a more revealing list is that of the leaders in swing-and-miss percentage—i.e. the percentage of a batter's swings which found nothing but air:

Highest Percentage of Swings that Missed—1996

Batter, Team	Swings	Missed	Pct
Tony Clark, Det	780	281	36.0
Reggie Sanders, Cin	586	202	34.5
Jayhawk Owens, Col	408	139	34.1
Sammy Sosa, Cubs	1137	382	33.6
Pete Incaviglia, Phi/Bal	624	209	33.5
Henry Rodriguez, Mon	1188	396	33.3
Jay Buhner, Sea	1160	383	33.0
Melvin Nieves, Det	888	293	33.0
Archi Cianfrocco, SD	425	137	32.2
Danny Tartabull, WSox	937	302	32.2
MLB Average			20.2

(Minimum 350 swings)

We can understand Tony Clark leading this list, because rookies are allowed to be overanxious. But Reggie Sanders' second-place ranking is a big disappointment. With more than twice as many strikeouts as walks in his career, Sanders needs to learn a little better discipline, lest his speed go to waste. As for Rodriguez, Buhner and Sosa, who show up among the leaders in both total swings-and-misses and in percentage, there's simply no denying their ranking among the whiff kings. But again, that's OK—for them.

Finally, here are the players who missed on the lowest percentage of their swings last year:

Lowest Percentage of Swings that Missed—1996

Batter, Team	Swings	Missed	Pct
Wade Boggs, Yanks	791	37	4.7
Ozzie Smith, StL	401	23	5.7
Joey Cora, Sea	852	57	6.7
Tony Gwynn, SD	730	49	6.7
Ricky Otero, Phi	680	47	6.9
Luis Sojo, Sea/Yanks	502	35	7.0
Jessie Levis, Mil	372	26	7.0
Fernando Vina, Mil	882	65	7.4
Omar Vizquel, Cle	945	71	7.5
Gregg Jefferies, Phi	677	57	8.4

We've got some future Hall of Famers on this list—Wade Boggs, Ozzie Smith and Tony Gwynn. Boggs and Gywnn, two of the best contact hitters of this generation, proved that their ability to make contact hasn't left them, even as they approach 40 years of age. Boggs was the runner-up on this list in 1995, and finished first in 1996. His total numbers for the past two years: just 79 swing-and-misses in 1,589 cuts. Apparently a chicken-only diet does wonders for the eyesight.

—Ethan D. Cooperson

A more complete listing for this category can be found on page 270.

Which Hitters Will Finish With "Immortal" Numbers?

"If a man paddles his canoe at a speed of four miles per hour against a current going along at a rate of one foot per second, how long will it take him to reach his camp three miles upstream?" Ah, the dreaded word problem. We wrestled with them in some long-ago math class, but today we leave them for our children, content to indulge in one of the privileges of adulthood. However, a simple word problem can take on new life when the subject is baseball. What if we rephrased the above question to read: "If Albert Belle hits 45 home runs per year against an aging process that diminishes his abilities as he gets older, how long will it take him to break Hank Aaron's home run record?"

Have we gotten your full attention now? Don't rush off to sharpen your pencils just yet, though; let us take care of the math. We'd like to address the latter question above, using a method that Bill James invented: the "Favorite Toy." The method gives an insight into Belle's future, but instead of asking "How long will it take him to break Aaron's record?" it asks, "What are the chances that he'll break the record, given his age and recent performance?"

Before we turn our attention to Belle's pursuit of Aaron, let's take a look at the current major leaguers who have established at least a 15 percent chance of reaching the 3,000-hit plateau (age is as of July 1, 1996):

Players Projected to Reach 3,000 Hits

Player	Age	Curr. Hits	Proj. Hits	%Chance
Cal Ripken	35	2549	3166	87
Tony Gwynn	36	2560	3139	81
Wade Boggs	38	2697	3025	58
Roberto Alomar	28	1522	2803	37
Rafael Palmeiro	31	1636	2672	26
Chuck Knoblauch	27	1019	2509	25
Alex Rodriguez	20	259	2151	19
Frank Thomas	28	1077	2355	16
Marquis Grissom	29	1096	2328	15

Both Ripken and Gwynn probably have three good years left in them, so they're strong favorites to make it. Boggs, however, needs to have two more strong seasons at ages 39 and 40, which is considerably less likely (and the Toy doesn't even know that Charlie Hayes is cooling his heels on the Yankees' bench, just waiting to grab some of Boggs' at-bats).

Roberto Alomar is the strongest candidate from the younger generation, but the Toy still recognizes that there's something special about Alex Rodriguez. Some might be surprised to see that Frank Thomas ranks so low on the list—just ahead of Marquis Grissom, who isn't widely regarded as a candidate for Cooperstown. Why does Thomas fare so poorly? As Rob Neyer explained last year, the answer is *walks*. Despite his lusty batting averages, Thomas draws so many free passes that he simply doesn't pile up a ton of base hits. In fact, over the last three seasons, the free-swinging Grissom has accumulated nine more hits than Thomas has.

Poor Frank; he may have to settle for a seat in the 500-homer club. The Favorite Toy estimates that he's got a 61 percent chance to gain entry into that exclusive circle. The chart to the right shows the nine active hitters with at least a 40 percent chance of reaching the 500 home run mark.

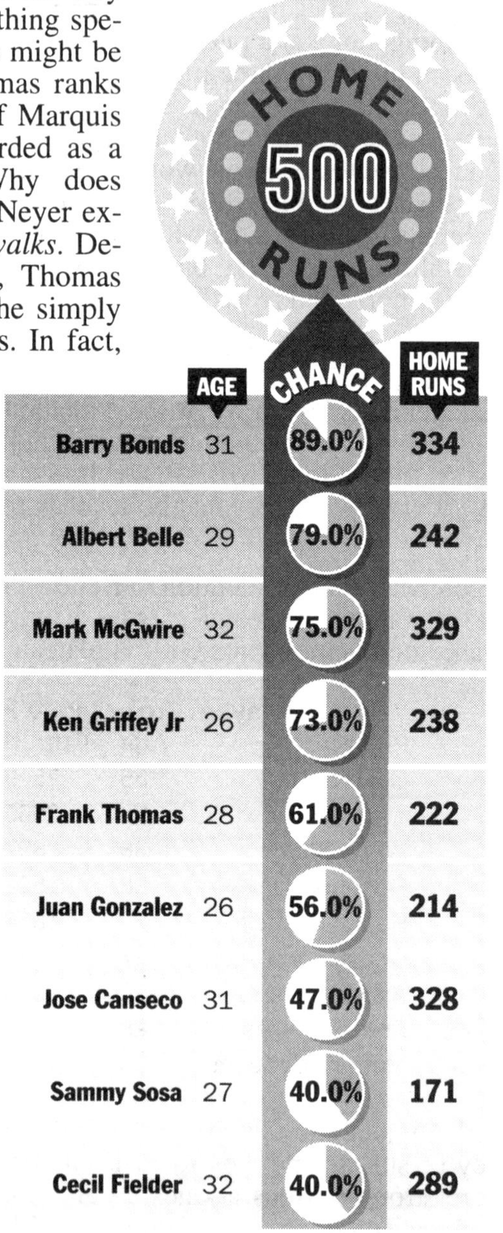

HOME 500 RUNS

	AGE	CHANCE	HOME RUNS
Barry Bonds	31	89.0%	334
Albert Belle	29	79.0%	242
Mark McGwire	32	75.0%	329
Ken Griffey Jr	26	73.0%	238
Frank Thomas	28	61.0%	222
Juan Gonzalez	26	56.0%	214
Jose Canseco	31	47.0%	328
Sammy Sosa	27	40.0%	171
Cecil Fielder	32	40.0%	289

After last year's home run explosion, several players have significantly increased their chances. Mark McGwire's outburst transformed him from a long shot at 16 percent into a strong favorite at 75 percent. Last year, Bonds and Belle registered at 54 and 55 percent, respectively, but they now top the charts.

Since Bonds has the best chance to crack the 500 mark,

you might assume that he would have the best chance to break Aaron's record as well. That's not necessarily the case, however; through age 31, Bonds has 334 home runs, 64 less than Aaron had at the same age. That may not sound like an enormous deficit, but the pace Aaron set in his 30s will be very difficult for Bonds to duplicate. After age 31, Aaron posted *six* more seasons with at least 38 home runs. Bonds, on the other hand, has topped 38 homers only twice in his career (or three times, if you give him the benefit of the doubt on the '94 strike year).

One thing is clear: the hitter who makes a real run at Aaron will need to crank out 40-homer seasons year after year. There are only two hitters in the game who have even a 10 percent chance of maintaining that pace long enough to break Aaron's record: Albert Belle, at 15 percent, and Ken Griffey Jr., at 12 percent. Belle's career total is 100 homers behind Aaron's at the same age, but the formula recognizes that Belle may be the *one* hitter in today's game with the ability to produce enough 50-homer seasons to actually *make up ground* on Aaron. Junior's in a very strong position, 19 homers *ahead* of Aaron at the same age. All he needs to do is prove that he can stay healthy enough to be a perennial 40-homer threat. With the way balls are flying out of the park, it's certainly possible that one of these two sluggers will become baseball's new home run king sometime in the next decade. . . or two.

—Mat Olkin

A more complete listing for this category can be found on page 272.

Who Are the Real RBI Kings?

Who was the better RBI man last year—Andres Galarraga or Barry Bonds? At first, the question seems absurd; Galarraga drove in 150 runs, the highest RBI total in over three decades, while Bonds finished fourth in the National League with 129 RBI. On the surface, there's no comparison.

When you approach the question from a different angle, however, the answer becomes less clear-cut. With Eric Young, Ellis Burks and Dante Bichette batting in front of him, Galarraga had no shortage of runners to drive in. Bonds, on the other hand, batted third in the Giants' injury-ravaged lineup, and didn't see nearly as many ducks on the pond. Instead of simply looking at their RBI totals, perhaps we should look to see which one drove in a higher *percentage* of baserunners.

To that end, we developed the concept of "RBI available." It's simply the number of RBI a hitter would accumulate if he hit a home run every time he stepped to the plate. An at-bat with the bags juiced counts as four RBI available; a bases-empty at-bat counts as one. We make one exception: if a batter stands in with men on and reaches base via a walk, a hit batsman, or catcher's interference, we don't charge him with any RBI available for that time at bat. He may not have gotten the baserunners home, but he got on base for the next man without using up an out.

With respect to Galarraga and Bonds, it's clear that Galarraga had far more opportunities to drive in runs. The Big Cat had 1,008 RBI available while Bonds only tallied 855. Galarraga drove in 150 runs, making good on 14.9 percent of his opportunities. Bonds, however, drove in 129 runs, cashing in on 15.1 percent of his chances. From this perspective, he was the more productive of the two. Here are the 1996 leaders in RBI per opportunity:

Most RBI per Opportunity—1996

Player, Team	RBI Available	RBI	Pct
Mark McGwire, Oak	703	113	16.1
Ken Griffey Jr., Sea	926	140	15.1
Barry Bonds, SF	855	129	15.1
Juan Gonzalez, Tex	961	144	15.0
Andres Galarraga, Col	1008	150	14.9
Frank Thomas, WSox	940	134	14.3
Albert Belle, Cle	1043	148	14.2
Gary Sheffield, Fla	868	120	13.8
Ken Caminiti, SD	945	130	13.8
Rafael Palmeiro, Bal	1066	142	13.3
MLB Average			8.9

(Minimum 350 Opp)

As you can see, Galarraga comes out looking pretty good, despite the unfavorable comparison to Bonds. His conversion rate was the fifth-best in the majors, just ahead of more celebrated sluggers like Frank Thomas and Albert Belle. Mark McGwire led the pack by a comfortable margin for the second straight season. Small wonder—with 91 homers over the last two years, he's always a threat to drive *himself* in, at the very least.

Which players came up empty? We picked 10 players who were expected to produce, but didn't. Each had at least 800 RBI available, and usually hit near the middle of the order. Here are the RBI "Underachievers":

RBI "Underachievers"—1996

Player, Team	RBI Available	RBI	Pct
J.T. Snow, Cal	948	67	7.1
Carlos Baerga, Cle/Mets	886	66	7.4
Ruben Sierra, Yanks/Det	926	72	7.8
Terry Pendleton, Fla/Atl	945	75	7.9
Greg Colbrunn, Fla	860	69	8.0
Eddie Murray, Cle/Bal	971	79	8.1
Kevin Seitzer, Mil/Cle	918	78	8.5
Raul Mondesi, LA	1029	88	8.6
Charlie Hayes, Pit/Yanks	867	75	8.7
Mark Grace, Cubs	864	75	8.7

Eddie Murray has always been known as a run producer, but in 1996 he drove in only 79 runs for two of baseball's most high-powered offenses. Raul Mondesi seemed to have a good year for the Dodgers, but he was unable to get many runners home. The Cubs had similar problems with Mark Grace. They've always regarded him as an ideal number-three hitter, but his lack of home-run power handicaps him in that spot. Despite his .331 batting average and 39 doubles, Grace's RBI percentage of 8.7 was below the major league average of 8.9.

—Mat Olkin

A more complete listing for this category can be found on page 273.

Who Gets the Green Light on 3-and-0?

The 3-and-0 count presents an interesting dilemma for a hitter: do you lay off the next pitch, or do you come out hacking? It can't hurt to let the pitch pass; at best, you'll work a walk, and at worst, you'll still be in the driver's seat with a 3-and-1 count. On the other hand, if you opt for restraint, the pitcher—perhaps desperate to avoid a walk at all costs—may offer up one of the fattest pitches you'll see all day.

It's a tough choice, but many managers take the decision out of the hitter's hands by putting on the take sign. With most hitters, the move makes sense. Giving the red light creates the strong possibility of the base on balls, while turning the hitter loose produces a relatively smaller chance of a more favorable outcome (such as an extra-base hit). However, there are a fair number of hitters who are so dangerous that it often makes more sense to let them take their rips at cripple pitches. Indeed, to get the green light on a 3-and-0 count is one of the greatest signs of respect a manager can show one of his hitters. Here are the 10 hitters who were allowed to swing at the highest percentage of 3-and-0 pitches over the last five years:

Highest Percentage Of Swings, 3-and-0 Counts—1992-1996

Player	Times Swung	3-and-0 Counts	Pct Swung	AB	H	HR	RBI	Avg
Andres Galarraga	41	73	56.2	18	9	2	6	.500
Albert Belle	84	153	54.9	29	8	2	7	.276
Fred McGriff	74	150	49.3	40	18	6	19	.450
Vinny Castilla	28	62	45.2	13	4	1	4	.308
Juan Gonzalez	49	115	42.6	26	12	5	14	.462
Kevin Mitchell	25	64	39.1	16	7	1	4	.438
Ken Griffey Jr.	62	171	36.3	24	10	3	9	.417
Frank Thomas	98	273	35.9	54	21	7	17	.389
Eddie Murray	44	137	32.1	25	8	0	4	.320
Matt Williams	29	91	31.9	9	6	3	6	.667

(minimum 25 3-and-0 swings)

Not surprisingly, we're looking at many of the game's best hitters here. And as expected, they lit up the scoreboard when they went hacking. Juan Gonzalez batted .462 with five home runs in 26 at-bats, Fred McGriff batted .450 with 19 RBI in 40 at-bats, and Matt Williams went 6-for-9 with three home runs. These hitters are all quite aggressive on 3-and-0, mind you. Over the last five years, major league hitters have swung at only 10 percent of 3-and-0 offerings; everyone on the list above at least triples that rate.

The list contained one very big surprise, however: Albert Belle. Despite going after 3-and-0 pitches more often than anyone in baseball except Andres Galarraga, Belle hasn't enjoyed even average success when he's put the ball in play. Over the last five years, major league hitters have batted .381 on 3-and-0 pitches, while Belle's only hit .276 with a pair of homers in 29 at-bats. Of all the hitters on the list, Belle is the one who could benefit the most from sitting back and taking a strike more often. Oddly, when he's able to do that, he enjoys much *greater* success: over the same five-year period, he's batted .465 with 10 home runs in 86 at-bats on 3-and-1 counts.

—Mat Olkin

A more complete listing for this category can be found on page 275.

Is the Big Cat Really Just a Nice, Average Kitty?

Andres Galarraga. The Big Cat. Hall of Fame slugger to Colorado Rockies fans. . . and to me, one of the most overrated hitters in baseball. Granted, I don't necessarily think he's a *bad* player, but he's definitely not *quite* the superstar he's cracked up to be. Why not? You know the reason—Coors Field. As one of the most extreme hitters' parks in baseball history, it sure makes things difficult for us analytical types. Pretty soon, we'll need two tables for everything we do—one for Coors, and the other for everywhere else. Just how outrageous *is* this stadium? Well, we charted the number of runs created by N.L. and A.L. teams (and their opponents) both at home and away last year. Here are the five most favorable hitters' parks:

Largest Offensive Differentials by Park—1996

Park	Team	Home RC/27 outs	Road RC/27 outs	Pct Diff
Coors Field	Col	7.83	4.28	+83.1
Fenway Park	Bos	6.31	5.33	+18.5
Ballpark in Arlington	Tex	6.06	5.26	+15.2
Olympic Stadium	Mon	4.61	4.17	+10.7
Metrodome	Min	5.80	5.32	+9.0

The major league's top pitching park, Dodger Stadium, also had a strong effect on run production last season. While it *reduced* the number of runs scored within its confines by approximately 29 percent, even that figure paled in comparison to the magnitude of the *increase* that Coors Field had on offense. With Coors boosting the offensive totals of its players by an amazing 83 percent, it's no wonder that mediocre sluggers like Dante Bichette and Vinny Castilla are treated like royalty in Colorado.

To evaluate Galarraga's true hitting prowess, we first have to account for the fact that runs he created were inflated by about 41.5 percent—half of Coors' offensive differential—since he played half his games at home. Considering that Galarraga generated 8.02 runs per 27 outs overall last season, we can estimate that in a "neutral park" he would have created about 5.67 runs/27 outs.

How does that figure compare with the average National League first baseman? Well, the typical N.L. first sacker created 5.73 runs/27 outs, so it would appear that Galarraga was actually a *below-average* hitter for his position. Not so fast, however, since:

1.) The N.L. average is artificially inflated because it includes Galarraga's 8.02 mark; and,

2.) The road stats for the other first basemen include a few games at Coors Field, whereas Galarraga's don't.

Can we adjust for these problems? To a certain degree, yes. Roughly estimating that Galarraga's production constitutes 1/14 of the totals posted by N.L. first basemen, we can conclude that the group's average *sans Galarraga* would fall from 5.73 to 5.55 runs/27 outs. Since the average opposing first baseman also played 6.2 games a year—or 3.8 percent of his season—at Coors Field, we should bump their figures down and Galarraga's up by about 3.2 percent (3.8 percent of the park factor's 83 percent). This works out to:

Galarraga vs. Typical N.L. First Baseman—1996

Galarraga	RC/27 Outs	Avg N.L. 1B	RC/27 Outs
In Coors Field	8.02	Original	5.73
In Neutral Park	5.67	W/O "Big Cat"	5.55
After Road Adjustments	5.85	After Road Adjustments	5.38

After all of the numbers have been sifted through, we can safely conclude that Galarraga is a better offensive performer than the average player at his position—albeit marginally. Before those Colorado fans get too excited, however, we should point out that the term "average player" includes *all* of those who played the position, both regulars and backups. N.L. first basemen who started at least 100 games last season posted a road-adjusted average of 6.01 runs/27 outs. . . which again throws a wrench into the debates.

Though we can dance around the numbers back and forth until we're blue in the face, it's safe to argue that Galarraga—150 RBI last year or not—was no better or worse than the typical N.L. first baseman—and definitely no superstar.

— Kevin Fullam

A more complete listing for this category can be found on page 276.

IV. QUESTIONS ON PITCHING

Which Pitchers are the Real "Stoppers"?

When the baseball writers submitted their votes for the American League Cy Young award this past offseason, they faced a tough decision. On the surface, it appeared Toronto righthander Pat Hentgen boasted a decided statistical edge, holding or sharing the league lead in innings pitched, complete games and shutouts. He had also finished second in the A.L. in ERA and wins. His detractors, however, pointed out that Hentgen pitched for a team that finished 14 games under .500 and a distant fourth in its division behind the eventual world champion Yankees. Andy Pettitte had been the top starter on that Yankee pitching staff, and his supporters noted that he had, in fact, led the league with 21 victories.

Pettitte's supporters had another stat at their disposal—one which presumably indicated how valuable he had been to the Yankees' cause. Pettitte was 13-3 last season in games following New York losses, a sterling record which implied he was the closest thing to a "stopper" the Yankees possessed. If Pettitte toed the rubber with New York riding a losing streak, the chances were good that the skid would end.

There's no question that every team could use such a stopper, and that Pettitte's performance last year qualified him for that title with the Yankees. But was he really the best in baseball in that role? Here's the list of the pitchers with the top individual records during 1996 following a team loss:

Pitcher Records after a Team Loss—1996

Player, Team	W-L	Pct
Charles Nagy, Cle	8-0	1.000
Darren Oliver, Tex	6-0	1.000
Ramon Martinez, LA	9-1	.900
Andy Pettitte, Yanks	13-3	.813
Joey Hamilton, SD	11-3	.786
Ismael Valdes, LA	7-2	.778
Rocky Coppinger, Bal	6-2	.750
Jimmy Key, Yanks	6-2	.750
Pat Hentgen, Tor	13-5	.722
Denny Neagle, Pit/Atl	10-4	.714

(minimum 10 starts following losses)

As good as Pettitte's record was, three pitchers actually posted better winning percentages following a team loss. Charles Nagy was undefeated in eight decisions after Cleveland defeats, and the Indians as a team were 11-1 (.917) when Nagy climbed the mound trying to stop a Cleveland losing streak. Darren Oliver and Ramon Martinez were also very good at *starting* winning streaks. Oliver's 6-0 record after a Ranger loss requires a footnote. It includes one victory the night after Texas and Baltimore had played to a 1-1 tie in a game stopped in the sixth inning due to rain. Since tie games don't count in the standings (though player stats from the game do count), and since the Rangers had lost their previous game, we give Oliver credit for ending a Texas losing streak.

Though Pettitte ranked fourth in terms of percentage, his 13 wins after a team loss did tie for the major league lead. The guy with whom Pettitte shared the top spot? Why Pat Hentgen, who ended up edging Pettitte for the A.L. Cy Young award. Hentgen's performance following a Blue Jay defeat virtually negated any edge Pettitte may have held in the category. And Hentgen is the only pitcher in the top 10 who *didn't* work for a club that appeared in last year's playoffs.

One guy who doesn't appear on the list on the previous page is Bill Swift, who started only three games all year and was 0-1 in games following a Colorado loss. Nevertheless, over the last five seasons, no starter has been better at halting his teams' losing skids.

Pitcher Records after a Team Loss—1992-96

Player	W-L	Pct
Bill Swift	26-9	.743
Joey Hamilton	22-9	.710
Dennis Martinez	24-11	.686
Randy Johnson	39-18	.684
Jimmy Key	26-12	.684
Mike Mussina	41-19	.683
Steve Avery	23-11	.676
Greg Maddux	34-17	.667
David Cone	36-19	.655
Roger Clemens	34-18	.654

(minimum 40 starts following losses)

The top two guys may be minor surprises, but the rest of the list is composed of many of the best starters in baseball. It's interesting to note who ranks first among the Braves recent starters in this category. While Greg Maddux, Tom Glavine and John Smoltz have the Cy Young awards, it's actually Steve Avery who posted the best record after team losses over the past five seasons (though Maddux' ledger includes a 12-7 mark while with the Cubs in '92; he's 22-10 (.688) with Atlanta). That might be important for Avery's new team—the Red Sox—since Boston's stopper in recent years, Roger Clemens, has moved on to join Hentgen in Toronto.

Randy Johnson's standing on the five-year list conveys just how much the Mariners missed him last season. Had he been healthy, Seattle would have had a much better chance at reaching the postseason. And Mike Mussina deserves commendation for his consistency. Since 1992, he's posted records of 6-3, 6-2, 9-2, 9-6 and 11-6 following Oriole defeats. His total of 41 wins following a loss by his team ranks as the most for any pitcher over the last five years. If you're looking for someone to label as baseball's top stopper, you could do a lot worse than to choose Mussina.

—Jim Henzler

A more complete listing for this category can be found on page 277.

Which Pitchers Find Hitting "Elementary"?

The above question now takes on added significance for American League fans. With the creation of inter-league play, A.L. pitchers will bat for themselves during the regular season for the first time in 24 years. Perhaps the Junior Circuit's clubs have been preparing for this scenario: after the Angels' trade for Allen Watson and the Red Sox' signing of Chris Hammond, the A.L. now boasts three of the top five best-hitting pitchers in the majors. Here are the top five, ranked by on-base plus slugging percentage, or OBS:

PITCHERS WHO CAN HIT
AVG.
OBS
Allen Watson .255 .632
Chris Hammond .205 .585
Jim Bullinger .180 .581
Omar Olivares .229 .569
Bill Swift .215 .521
Minimum 150 career plate appearances;
OBS=On-base plus slugging pct.

As you can see, Allen Watson stands head-and-shoulders above the rest of the crowd. This shouldn't surprise anyone; Watson was an All-American DH in college, and finished fifth in the nation in hitting among college players in 1991. After batting .321 during his time in the minors, Watson now carries a .271 average in pro ball. He went 1-for-3 as a pinch hitter last year, and may give the Angels some extra punch when they face their N.L. foes this year.

But after leading N.L. pitchers with a .417 average in '95, Watson was eclipsed by a couple of Cub pitchers last year. Here are the best-hitting pitchers of 1996:

Best-Hitting Pitchers—1996

Pitcher, Team	AB	Avg	OBP	Slg	OBS
Kevin Foster, Cubs	27	.296	.406	.519	.923
Jim Bullinger, Cubs	32	.250	.368	.531	.899
Steve Avery, Atl	46	.239	.245	.500	.745
Jason Isringhausen, Mets	51	.255	.291	.412	.703
Tom Glavine, Atl	76	.289	.333	.342	.675

(minimum 30 plate appearances)

Kevin Foster and Jim Bullinger, each former minor league infielders, were by far the best-hitting pitchers in baseball last year. Foster would place second on the career leader list, but he comes up 14 plate appearances short of qualifying. Tom Glavine, who won his third Silver Slugger Award last year, places fifth, but Foster made a strong bid to steal the award from Glavine last year—the Cub righthander had a higher average than Glavine, but did not log enough at-bats to qualify for the award. Foster and Glavine hooked up in a couple of games in late August, and Foster prevailed each time by the score of 3-2. At the plate, he went 2-for-5 and drove in half of his team's six runs, and while on the mound, he held Glavine hitless in five at-bats over the two games.

—Mat Olkin

A more complete listing for this category can be found on page 278.

Who Gets the "Red Barrett Trophy"?

Nobody likes a slow-poke, and pitchers who work fast, throw strikes and keep their fielders attentive are treasured by baseball people. So a few years ago we invented the "Red Barrett Trophy," which goes to the hurler who threw the fewest pitches in a nine-inning complete game. It's named after Boston Braves pitcher Red Barrett, who supposedly threw only 58 pitches in a complete-game performance back in 1944.

Here are the top 10 low-pitch games of 1996:

Fewest Pitches in a Nine-Inning Complete Game—1996

Pitcher, Team	Date	Opp	Fin	W/L	IP	H	ER	BB	K	#Pit
Bob Wolcott, Sea	7/15	@Oak	5-1	W	9.0	5	1	0	6	79
Tim Belcher, KC	9/2	@Tor	2-0	W	9.0	4	0	0	5	90
Jeff Fassero, Mon	4/7	Col	9-1	W	9.0	3	1	0	6	91
Jim Bullinger, Cubs	5/12	@Mets	3-0	W	9.0	2	0	0	4	93
Terry Mulholland, Phi	4/17	@Mon	9-3	W	9.0	10	3	1	1	95
John Smoltz, Atl	6/19	SD	5-1	W	9.0	2	1	0	8	95
Greg Maddux, Atl	9/18	Hou	6-2	W	9.0	6	2	0	3	95
Kevin Foster, Cubs	9/9	Mon	3-1	W	9.0	6	1	0	2	96
Chris Haney, KC	7/1	@Cle	4-2	W	9.0	7	2	0	1	97
Roger Salkeld, Cin	6/16	Mon	7-0	W	9.0	4	0	1	5	98
Donne Wall, Hou	8/30	@Pit	10-0	W	9.0	7	0	0	4	98

The trophy goes to righthander Bob Wolcott of the Mariners, and it wasn't even close. Wolcott threw only 79 pitches in his five-hit, no-walk gem against the A's last July 15—11 fewer pitches than anyone who worked a nine-inning complete game last year. Tim Belcher of the Royals threw the second-fewest number of pitches in a game, but he gets a consolation prize: his 2-0 duel with Toronto's Erik Hanson on September 2 was the fastest nine-inning game of the year, lasting only an hour and 53 minutes. (Wolcott's game lasted 2:13.) Hanson, who also tossed a complete game, threw 115 pitches for Toronto in that contest, meaning that the two hurlers combined to throw only 205 pitches. Heck, sometimes the pitchers on *one* team will throw that many pitches in a game.

Who's the fastest worker in the game in terms of time? No surprise, the 1996 champion was Greg Maddux of the Braves—for the third year in a row. Maddux' 30 starts last year averaged a speedy 2:24, making him the only regular starter in baseball to average less than two and a half hours per start. Maddux was followed (minimum 20 starts) by Joey Hamilton of the Padres (2:35), Kevin Brown of the Marlins (2:37), Mark Clark of the

Mets (2:37) and Curt Schilling of the Phillies (2:38). The fastest American League starter was Cy Young Award winner Pat Hentgen of the Blue Jays, who averaged 2:38, which is very fast for the poky American League. Speaking of poky, the *slowest-working* regular starter last year was—surprise!—Mike Mussina of the Orioles, whose games averaged a shade under 3:06. We're sure all those Oriole home-run trots slowed down his games, but still, the kid should work a little faster, don't you think?

We've been keeping pitch counts since the late 1980s, and we wondered if anyone had been able to beat Wolcott's 79-pitch complete game. The answer is yes. Here are the starters who have thrown the fewest pitches in a nine-inning CG since 1988:

Fewest Pitches in a Nine-Inning Complete Game—1988-96

Pitcher, Team	Date	Opp	Fin	W/L	IP	H	ER	BB	K	#Pit
Bob Tewksbury, StL	8/29/90	@Cin	9-1	W	9.0	6	1	0	0	76
Kevin Brown, Tex	6/20/90	Min	8-0	W	9.0	4	0	0	4	79
Tom Glavine, Atl	6/15/93	Mets	2-1	W	9.0	6	1	0	0	79
Bob Wolcott, Sea	7/15/96	@Oak	5-1	W	9.0	5	1	0	6	79
Ed Whitson, SD	5/6/90	@Cubs	8-3	W	9.0	8	3	0	1	80
Bob Tewksbury, StL	8/17/90	Hou	5-0	W	9.0	1	0	0	3	80
Doug Drabek, Pit	9/30/90	@StL	2-0	W	9.0	3	0	0	2	80
John Smiley, Min	10/2/92	@KC	5-1	W	9.0	4	1	0	4	80
Bobby Munoz, Phi	7/27/94	@Fla	3-1	W	9.0	2	1	0	3	80
Chris Bosio, Mil	9/17/91	@Yanks	2-0	W	9.0	2	0	1	1	82
Teddy Higuera, Mil	6/4/88	Cal	1-0	W	9.0	3	0	2	3	83
Jack McDowell, WSox	7/14/91	@Mil	15-1	W	9.0	1	1	1	4	83

Somehow we're not surprised that the winner was Bob Tewksbury, who throws strikes as consistently as any pitcher in modern history. Tewksbury's 76-pitch game against the Reds in 1990 was a 9-1 laugher for his team, the Cardinals—but despite all the runs the Redbirds scored, the game was over in an even two hours. Amazing.

The Boston Red Sox essay (see p. 9) does a pretty good job of reviewing the *high-pitch* outings of 1996, which were completely dominated by Red Sox pitchers. But we wondered who had thrown the most pitches in a game since 1988. Here's the list:

Most Pitches in a Game—1988-96

Pitcher, Team	Date	Opp	Fin	W/L	IP	H	ER	BB	K	#Pit
Tim Wakefield, Pit	4/27/93	@Atl	6-2	W	10.0	6	2	10	1	172
Al Leiter, Yanks	4/14/89	Min	8-5	W	8.0	5	3	9	10	171
Nolan Ryan, Tex	9/12/89	@KC	5-6	ND	8.0	8	3	3	13	169
Tim Belcher, LA	5/15/88	Phi	9-2	W	9.0	6	2	4	8	167
Greg Maddux, Cubs	5/17/88	StL	0-3	L	10.2	7	3	4	7	167
Don Carman, Phi	5/15/89	SF	3-2	ND	9.0	4	0	7	4	167
Orel Hershiser, LA	10/1/89	@Atl	3-1	W	11.0	10	1	3	8	167
David Cone, Mets	7/17/92	SF	1-0	W	9.0	6	0	4	13	166
Roger Clemens, Bos	8/4/90	Det	3-1	W	8.2	9	1	2	8	165
John Farrell, Cle	9/10/89	Tor	4-5	ND	9.0	9	2	4	6	164

Knuckleballer Tim Wakefield has the recent record for most pitches in a game with 172, but don't blame Kevin Kennedy; Wakefield did it while working for Jim Leyland and the Pirates in 1993. Knuckleballer or no, Wakefield didn't seem to respond well at all to this heavy workload. He didn't pitch again for a week; then, after a couple of reasonably good outings, he fell apart completely and wound up back in the minor leagues, where he languished for most of the next two years. Coincidence? Likely, but whatever your main pitch is, 172 is a lot of pitches to be throwing in a game, and perhaps needlessly risky.

Next to Wakefield, the pitcher who threw the most pitches in a game was Al Leiter, who made 171 pitches for Dallas Green and the Yankees in an April, 1989 game. A couple weeks later, the Yankees traded Leiter to Toronto, and the Blue Jays immediately discovered they'd obtained a pitcher with a very sore arm. Leiter went on the DL after one start with the Jays and wound up missing the rest of the 1989 season. His arm didn't recover for several years. Again, you can hardly blame all that on one start. . . but we're sure the strain of throwing 171 pitches didn't help Leiter's tender arm any.

There are a few more horror stories on this high-pitch outing list:

- Don Carman's career never seemed to be the same after a 167-pitch outing in May of 1989. Carman, who had been one of the Phillies' more dependable starters in 1987 and 1988, went 5-15 with a 5.24 ERA in '89, went back to the bullpen in 1990, and quickly faded out after that.

- Another up-and-coming pitcher, John Farrell of the Indians, threw 164 pitches in a game late in the '89 campaign. Farrell, who'd worked 200+

innings in both 1988 and 1989, broke down the next year and never recovered.

- At the end of the (you guessed it) 1989 season, Tommy Lasorda kept his ace, Orel Hershiser, on the mound for 11 innings and 167 pitches in a totally meaningless game against the Braves. Hershiser, who had led the National League in innings pitched for three straight years from 1987 to 1989, came down with shoulder trouble the next spring and needed major reconstructive surgery. He pitched in only four games in '90, and didn't resume his career as a full-time starter until 1992.

Again, we won't say that these high-pitch outings *caused* the pitchers to break down. But they undoubtedly added to the strain their arms were already under. Most managers now seem to agree that it's risky to have their starters throw 150 pitches in a game, and usually you'll see them being lifted well before that point. A pitcher's arm is a valuable commodity—no sense risking it for the sake of one game.

— Don Zminda

A more complete listing of this category can be found on page 279.

Which Pitchers Have "Bionic Arms"?

With pitching at a premium these days, every manager treasures a pitcher who can take the ball every fifth day, work deep into the game, give a quality effort—and not break down. The last one's the rub. . . a lot of guys can handle a heavy workload for a year or three, but then wind up on the disabled list, nursing a sore arm.

STATS has been counting pitches since the late 1980s, and Jim Osborne of our staff was wondering which starting pitchers had "bionic arms"—that is, which guys had thrown the most total pitches over the last five seasons. Kevin Thomas produced the list, and the results are shown in the chart to the right.

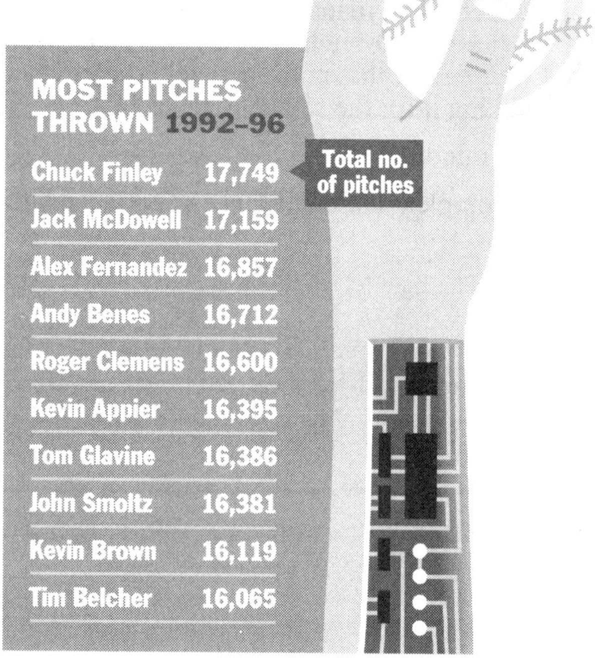

MOST PITCHES THROWN 1992-96	Total no. of pitches
Chuck Finley	17,749
Jack McDowell	17,159
Alex Fernandez	16,857
Andy Benes	16,712
Roger Clemens	16,600
Kevin Appier	16,395
Tom Glavine	16,386
John Smoltz	16,381
Kevin Brown	16,119
Tim Belcher	16,065

Chuck Finley's name seldom comes up when people talk about the top starting pitchers in baseball, but then, when you pitch for the California—make that Anaheim—Angels, you don't get a lot of chances to strut your stuff in the World Series. (Maybe in "Angels in the Outfield, Part II"?) But consider some of Finley's accomplishments:

1. Pitching for generally mediocre clubs, he's won 15 or more games six times in the last eight seasons.

2. He's won in double figures all but one season since 1989.

3. Pitching in a hitter's league in a big-hitting era, he's never had a bad year. His highest ERA since becoming a regular starter in 1988 has been 4.32.

4. He's worked over 190 innings in all but one season since 1988, the year he became a regular starter. The only season he missed, the strike year of 1994, Finley led the American League with 183.1 innings pitched.

5. He's never had a sore arm. Finley has had only two short stints on the disabled list in his career (once in 1989, once in 1992), both times with foot problems.

If this sounds like "dependable" rather than "great," well, dependable means something. Just ask his managers. And anyway, Finley's lack of fame is more a function of the team he's pitching for than anything else.

There *is* plenty of fame on the leaders list, what with Cy Young winners Jack McDowell, Roger Clemens, Tom Glavine and John Smoltz. And plenty of wealth, too, given the big contracts signed by McDowell, Alex Fernandez, Andy Benes, Clemens and Smoltz over the last couple of years. One might say that if you have a rubber arm, you'll never have to sign a rubber check.

One question you've probably asked when looking at this list is, "Where's Maddux?" Greg Maddux has led the National League in innings pitched in five out of the last six seasons, and the year he missed, 1996, he finished second to John Smoltz. Yet Maddux is all the way down in 15th place in pitches thrown over the last five years with 15,598. The reason? Efficiency. With his pinpoint control, Maddux is as efficient as any starter in modern history, and he usually disposes of the hitter in his first few tosses. That's a good reason why many people think Maddux is the one active pitcher who can stay healthy long enough to win 300 games (for more on this, see the essay by Bill James on page 200).

— Don Zminda

A more complete listing of this category can be found on page 280.

Which Pitchers "Scored" the Best?

One of the more popular additions to this book last year was our article on pitchers' "game scores," a tool devised by Bill James back in his *Baseball Abstract* days. Game scores are an attempt to quantify how a starting pitcher performed in a single game. The formula is pretty simple:

1. Start with 50.

2. Add one point for each hitter the pitcher retires, i.e., one point for each third of an inning pitched.

3. Add two points for each inning the pitcher completes after the fourth.

4. Add one point for each strikeout.

5. Subtract one point for each walk.

6. Subtract two points for each hit.

7. Subtract four points for each earned run.

8. Subtract two points for each unearned run.

As we pointed out last year, the great thing about game scores is that they're easy to understand. A score of 50 is about average, one around 70 is pretty good and anything over 90 is outstanding. A score over 100 is so rare that it's been achieved only three times in the last 10 seasons: an 11-inning one-hit performance (with no walks) by Jose DeLeon in 1989 (game score 103), Nolan Ryan's 16-strikeout no-hitter against the Blue Jays in 1991 (101), and Ryan's 10-inning, three-hit, 15-strikeout/no-walk outing against the White Sox in 1990 (101). Obviously you don't see performances like that very often.

Here's a list of all the game scores over 90 in 1996:

Top Game Scores of 1996

Pitcher, Team	Date	Opp	W/L	IP	H	R	ER	BB	K	Score
Roger Clemens, Bos	9/18	@Det	W	9	5	0	0	0	20	97
Curt Schilling, Phi	8/21	@LA	W	9	2	0	0	0	12	95
Jeff Fassero, Mon	6/29	@Phi	W	9	2	0	0	0	11	94
John Smiley, Cin	9/22	StL	W	9	1	0	0	0	8	93
John Smoltz, Atl	4/14	@SD	W	8	1	0	0	1	13	92
Ken Hill, Tex	5/3	@Det	W	9	1	0	0	0	7	92
Hideo Nomo, LA	4/13	Fla	W	9	3	1	1	3	17	91
Al Leiter, Fla	5/11	Col	W	9	0	0	0	2	6	91
Hideo Nomo, LA	9/17	@Col	W	9	0	0	0	4	8	91

Pitcher, Team	Date	Opp	W/L	IP	H	R	ER	BB	K	Score
Rheal Cormier, Mon	4/22	StL	W	9	3	0	0	0	9	90
Mark Gardner, SF	4/25	Atl	W	9	4	0	0	0	11	90
Todd Stottlemyre, StL	5/15	@Fla	W	9	4	0	0	2	13	90
John Smoltz, Atl	5/29	@Cubs	W	9	4	0	0	2	13	90
John Smoltz, Atl	7/13	Fla	W	9	2	0	0	3	10	90
Salomon Torres, Sea	9/15	@Min	W	9	2	0	0	2	9	90

Not surprisingly, the top game score of the year was the 97 awarded to Roger Clemens for his 20-strikeout/no-walk demolition of the Tigers on September 18. You might think the season's three no-hitters would be next, but several performances ranked ahead of them—in fact, one no-hitter, Dwight Gooden's, ranked below the leaders with a score of 86. Why didn't the no-hitters score higher? Because game scores put a big premium on a superior strikeout-to-walk ratio. In Gooden's May 14 no-hitter against the Mariners, he walked six and struck out only five. Similarly, a 17-strikeout three-hitter by Hideo Nomo against the Marlins received the same score (91) as Nomo's unbelievable no-hitter against the Rockies at Coors Field. While the site of the no-hitter puts Nomo's feat in a class by itself, a topic that we tackle in another essay (see p. 86), game scores don't account for the ballpark. That said, it's reasonable to think that when a pitcher strikes out 17 batters and allows only three hits, his stuff is just as good as a pitcher who throws a no-hitter.

These were the *worst* game scores of 1996:

Worst Game Scores of 1996

Pitcher, Team	Date	Opp	W/L	IP	H	R	ER	BB	K	Score
Bryan Rekar, Col	4/28	Mon	L	2.1	10	11	11	4	0	−11
Kevin Jarvis, Cin	8/2	@Mon	L	3.1	13	10	10	1	2	−5
Michael Mimbs, Phi	5/11	Atl	L	3	12	9	9	3	1	−3
Jason Jacome, KC	4/15	WSox	ND	1.1	8	9	9	3	0	−1
Chris Hammond, Fla	4/28	@SF	L	1	9	9	9	0	0	−1

Speaking of Coors Field, we guess that Don Baylor gives his starters a little more leeway in an outing at Coors. He sure did with Bryan Rekar on April 28, letting Rekar absorb an 11-run, 10-hit pounding in two-and-a-third innings before finally giving him the hook.

Game scores can also help us identify the best pitchers' duels of the year. These were the only two games in which both starting pitchers recorded game scores of 80 or better last season:

Top Pitchers Duels of 1996

Pitcher, Team	Date	W/L	IP	H	R	ER	BB	K	Score	Total
Dwight Gooden, Yanks	8/2	ND	9.0	4	0	0	2	3	80	
Kevin Appier, KC		ND	9.0	5	0	0	0	9	86	166
Denny Neagle, Pit	7/31	ND	9.0	6	1	1	0	12	83	
Paul Wilson, Mets		ND	8.0	1	1	1	3	7	80	163

The four pitchers listed here must have wound up feeling frustrated as well as pleased. Denny Neagle of the Pirates and Paul Wilson of the Mets battled to a 1-1 draw on July 31, with Wilson leaving after eight innings and Neagle departing after nine. The Pirates scored a run off Jerry DiPoto in the 10th to take the lead, but the Mets came back with two off Dan Plesac in the bottom of the inning to pull it out, 3-2. Dwight Gooden and Kevin Appier staged an even better duel two days later on August 2, with each pitcher leaving after working nine shutout innings. As in the Met-Pirate game, both offenses came to life after the starters left the game. The Yankees scored three runs off Jeff Montgomery in the top of the 10th, but the Royals scored four off Mariano Rivera in the home half to win it, 4-3.

One last note on game scores. Kevin Brown of the Marlins had an average game score of 63.7 last year, tops in the majors. John Smoltz of the Braves was second with an average of 63.0. The American League leader was A.L. ERA champ Juan Guzman of the Blue Jays, who had an average game score of 59.7.

— Don Zminda

Which Starters Combine Quality With Quantity?

Some starting pitchers are known to grab the headlines with an occasional outstanding outing. These guys might throw a shutout once or twice a season, or hit double digits in strikeouts on occasion, but the question is: how often do they pitch at least a decent game? To gauge which starting pitchers are effective most often, we look at their "quality start percentage," or the percentage of starts in which they work at least six innings while allowing no more than three earned runs.

Looking at the leaders in quality start percentage for 1996, we found a huge disparity between the National and American Leagues. Quite simply, National League starters dominated, as the 12 pitchers who turned in quality starts most often all toiled in the N.L.! For this reason, we felt it necessary to show the two leagues separately. Here is the N.L.'s top 10:

Highest % Of Quality Starts, National League—1996

Pitcher, Team	GS	QS	Pct
Ismael Valdes, LA	33	26	78.8
Kevin Brown, Fla	32	25	78.1
Donovan Osborne, StL	30	23	76.7
Steve Trachsel, Cubs	31	23	74.2
Al Leiter, Fla	33	24	72.7
Hideo Nomo, LA	33	24	72.7
John Smoltz, Atl	35	25	71.4
Curt Schilling, Phi	26	18	69.2
Pedro Astacio, LA	32	22	68.8
Greg Maddux, Atl	35	24	68.6
N.L. Average			49.5

(Minimum 20 games started)

Without question, the list above does include some of baseball's most dominant starting pitchers. John Smoltz won the N.L. Cy Young last year, and Kevin Brown was also worthy of the award. Al Leiter and Hideo Nomo each threw no-hitters. Still, our top 10 does include several lesser-known pitchers, whose quiet efficiency is quite impressive. Although overshadowed by teammate Nomo and the media circus surrounding him, Ismael Valdes led the majors in quality starts—and quality start percentage—last year. The 23 year old never misses his turn, and when he took the ball in '96, he was as likely to be effective as any starter in baseball.

What about Donovan Osborne's high ranking? Think that's a fluke? Guess again. . . over the last five years, Osborne ranks ninth in the majors among pitchers who have logged at least 100 starts with a quality start percentage of 63.5. He missed the entire '94 campaign after shoulder surgery, and he's never won more than 13 games in a single season, but Osborne has been consistent for the Cardinals, posting an ERA of 3.81 or better in each of his four seasons. Who knew?

Meanwhile, a pitcher we all know a lot about, Greg Maddux, dropped to 10th on last year's list. Maddux topped the charts the previous two seasons, and has by far the best quality start percentage in baseball over the past five seasons. Some might consider his 10th-place finish a disappointment, but consider this: only Maddux and Valdes managed to finish in the top 10 in both 1995 and 1996. Apparently, it's awfully tough to be a quality starter year after year.

A final word on our National League list: For the second straight year, the Dodgers placed three pitchers in the top 10—but only one turned in a repeat performance. Ramon Martinez and Tom Candiotti joined Valdes in '95, while Nomo and Pedro Astacio were on last year's leader board. What would happen, we might wonder, if all five Dodgers made the list in the *same season*?

Okay, on to the American League. Who topped the A.L. in quality start percentage?

Highest % of Quality Starts, American League—1996

Pitcher, Team	GS	QS	Pct
Juan Guzman, Tor	27	18	66.7
Ken Hill, Tex	35	23	65.7
Orel Hershiser, Cle	33	21	63.6
Pat Hentgen, Tor	35	22	62.9
Charles Nagy, Cle	32	20	62.5
Wilson Alvarez, WSox	35	20	57.1
Tim Belcher, KC	35	20	57.1
Ben McDonald, Mil	35	20	57.1
Brad Radke, Min	35	20	57.1
Ariel Prieto, Oak	21	12	57.1
A.L. Average			42.1

The league leader, Juan Guzman, finished 13th in the majors in quality start percentage, and by the time you get down to Ariel Prieto, you're talking about the *33rd*–best QS percentage in baseball—yet the 10th-best in the Junior Circuit. National League pitchers simply dominated this category, throwing quality starts in 49.5 percent of their games, as compared to the A.L.'s 42.1 percent. Granted, the DH helps make the A.L. the "hitter's league," but isn't it also true that the standard of starting pitching is simply higher in the N.L.? Maybe we should ask Ken Hill, who was shelled when he pitched for the Cardinals in '95, but rebounded to finish as the A.L. runner-up in quality start percentage last year. Or ask Orel Hershiser, who finished one notch below Hill. Hershiser left the Dodgers after the '94 season, and has pitched well for Cleveland—but he probably wouldn't even make L.A.'s rotation today.

—Ethan D. Cooperson

A more complete listing for this category can be found on page 281.

Could Smiley Have Used Some of Pettitte's Support?

Perhaps the most frustrating thing about being a pitcher is knowing that personal success is only partly based upon one's own performance. A hurler can go out and toss a whale of a ballgame, and still have to answer questions about how his team lost a 2-1 contest.

That's exactly what happened to the Reds' John Smiley in his final outing of 1996.

Facing the St. Louis Cardinals on September 27, Smiley twirled a beauty: nine innings of five-hit, one-run, seven-strikeout, one-walk, 109-pitch baseball. On just about any given day with any given team, those numbers would have been more than enough to earn a victory. Instead, Smiley was pulled after the ninth with the score knotted at 1-1. Two innings later, the Cards completed the 2-1 win. Unfortunately for the veteran lefty, the game pretty much summed up his entire season—a season which saw him go 13-14. All the while, another lefty over in the American League by the name of Andy Pettitte was darn near winning a Cy Young Award for the New York Yankees with remarkably similar statistics as a starter.

As Starters—1996

Pitcher	GS	IP	H	SO	BR/IP	ERA
Pettitte	34	218.0	226	160	1.38	3.92
Smiley	34	217.0	205	171	1.21	3.61

With the same number of starts, the same number of innings, and virtually the same ERA (considering the difference between leagues), Pettitte pocketed 20 wins as a starter against only eight losses. Smiley's final mark paled in comparison, and not once was his name so much as whispered when it came time to talk awards. So why the big difference in final record? Your first big clue is run support. While the Pinstripers were scoring an average of 6.28 runs every nine innings in Pettitte's starts, the Reds were plating a mere 4.27 runs in Smiley's outings. In fact, in 20 of Smiley's 34 starts, Cincinnati scored two or *fewer* runs while he was on the mound. For Pettitte, that happened in only eight of his starts.

Smiley certainly wasn't the only one feeling a bit let down by his team's bats last season. As the following illustration reveals, other pairs of pitchers compiled matching numbers *as starters* in just about every category besides run support and overall record.

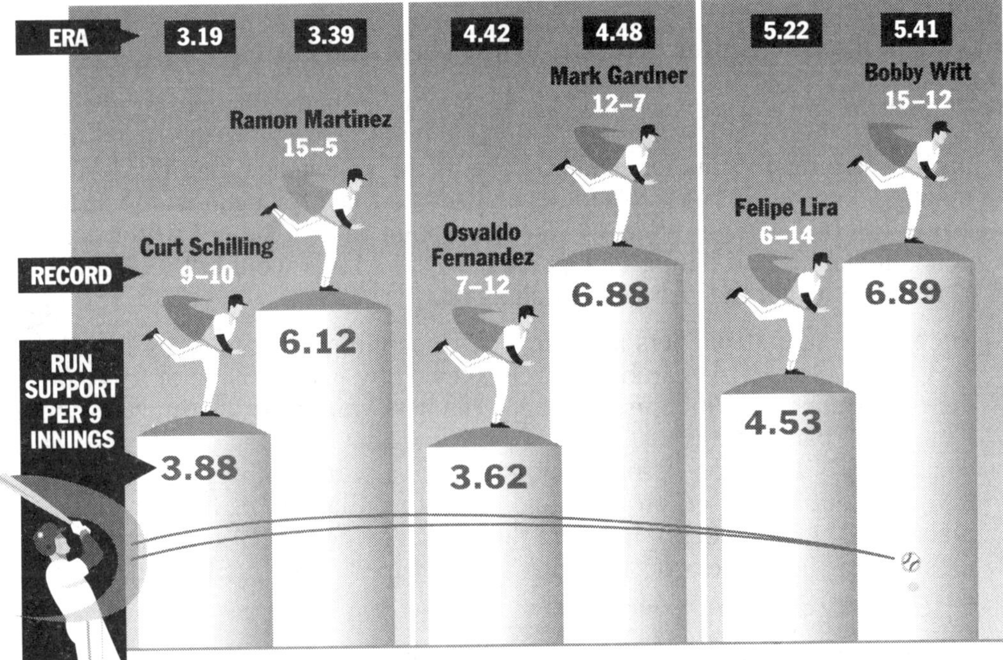

Take the case of Bobby Witt and Felipe Lira, both of whom posted ERAs over 5.00. They came away with remarkably different final records despite the fact that they both started *exactly* 32 games and pitched *exactly* 194.2 innings in a starting role. Boy, were the Rangers generous when Witt was on the mound! When we compare Curt Schilling with Ramon Martinez, it's obvious that Schilling deserved a better fate. The anemic Philadelphia offense could muster only 3.88 runs per nine innings for their ace. Then there's our favorite example from last season of the difference run support, or lack thereof, can make. In 1996, two Giants finished with nearly identical ERAs, identical start totals (28), identical earned run totals (88), identical walk totals (57). . . and exactly *opposite* records!

Osvaldo Fernandez *may*, however, take solace in the fact that what comes around goes around. Just look at Chuck Finley's roller coaster ride: in 1994, he finished third from the bottom in run support (4.22) among A.L. pitchers who qualified for the ERA title; in 1995, he finished fourth from the *top* (6.65); in 1996, he fell all the way back down to second from the bottom (4.24). Of course, that will happen when your team almost goes to Disneyland one season. . . then crashes back to earth the next.

—Tony Nistler

A more complete listing for this category can be found on page 282.

Which Pitchers Suffer the Most From Their Bad Outings?

Several years ago, a group of Little League teammates was poring over a printout of their team's statistics. The topic quickly turned to the first—and only—pitching appearance made by one of the youngsters: one-third of an inning, four earned runs. When several of the players began to mock the boy's 108.00 ERA, he tried in vain to explain that if Steve Carlton happened to have a bad outing on Opening Day, his ERA wouldn't look much better until he got the chance to pitch again.

Such is the fate of pitchers at all levels. Depending on how many innings they work, their ERAs can be severely skewed by just a couple of forgettable performances. Which major league pitchers were most victimized by a handful of bad outings last year? To answer this question, we looked at each hurler's ERA for 1996, excluding his five worst outings. We defined his worst outings based on the game score formula (see p. 162 for an explanation of game scores). Here are the pitchers whose ERAs improved the most when their five worst outings were "wiped away" (ERA qualifiers only):

Best ERA Differential For Pitchers Without Five Worst Games—1996

Pitcher, Team	Actual ERA	Adjusted ERA	Difference
Frank Castillo, Cubs	5.28	3.84	−1.44
Scott Erickson, Bal	5.02	3.58	−1.44
Felipe Lira, Det	5.22	3.81	−1.42
Osvaldo Fernandez, SF	4.42	3.12	−1.30
Shawn Boskie, Cal	5.43	4.20	−1.23
Doug Drabek, Hou	4.57	3.36	−1.21
David Wells, Bal	5.14	3.98	−1.16
Bobby Witt, Tex	5.41	4.25	−1.16
Scott Aldred, Det/Min	6.57	5.44	−1.13
Danny Darwin, Pit/Hou	3.82	2.72	−1.10

(minimum 162 innings pitched)

One thing's for sure about the chart—the pitchers who make the top 10 didn't exactly have good years that suddenly look even stronger when you take away their five clunkers. Seven of the pitchers on the list finished with actual ERAs over 5.00, and only one, Danny Darwin, checked in under 4.00. Let's face it—guys like John Smoltz (-0.73) and Kevin Brown (-0.32) were way too consistent for their five worst outings to have much of an overall effect on their ERA.

For Frank Castillo, whose ERA improved by a whopping 1.44 runs when his worst starts were removed, the lesson is one of consistency. We can trace many of Castillo's problems to a two-start stretch in mid-May, when he allowed an astonishing total of 14 earned runs in just four innings! The two shellings started the Cub righthander on a string of seven straight games without a quality start, virtually guaranteeing that his season's numbers would be pretty unimpressive. Castillo is certainly a serviceable major league starter—he's twice won 10 games, and last year he enjoyed seven outings where he worked at least six innings and held the opposition to one or no runs. But like the fabled Little Girl With the Curl, when he was bad, he was *very* bad. . .

Inexperienced pitchers like Detroit's Felipe Lira and San Francisco's Osvaldo Fernandez should be encouraged by their ranking on our list. As a GM, most of us would be happier knowing that an inexperienced pitcher has shown flashes of brilliance, even while demonstrating that he is susceptible to a few bumps and bruises once in a while. Lira took some beatings last year—allowing 20 earned runs in 7.2 innings in one three-start stretch—but late in the year he showed promising consistency. The Tiger righty allowed no more than four earned runs in each of his last seven starts, posting a 3.04 ERA over that span. It certainly will be interesting to see what Lira and Fernandez do next year. Will they continue to have the occasional nightmare outing, or will experience bring consistency?

One pitcher who *doesn't* show up on our list is Yankee lefty Andy Pettitte, who nearly won the Cy Young Award despite his relatively high 3.92 ERA. Supporters of Pettitte's case may have argued that he was actually a *better pitcher* than that 3.92 mark indicated, but we found 27 pitchers whose ERAs showed more improvement minus their five worst outings. Pettitte's adjusted ERA of 3.03 *was* better than Cy Young Award winner Pat Hentgen's adjusted mark of 3.04. If we use that argument, however, we'd have to label Donovan Osborne a Cy Young candidate, along with Osvaldo Fernandez, Ken Hill, Roger Clemens. . . and a host of others. We wouldn't have any more luck with that argument than the Little Leaguer with the 108.00 ERA.

—Ethan D. Cooperson

A more complete listing for this category can be found on page 283.

Whose Heater is Hottest?

Pitchers who "throw heat" will always be in demand simply because they can dominate hitters with their fastballs. You can record a lot of strikeouts *without* superior heat, of course, so as usual we'll point out that the title of this article can be a little misleading. But most of the pitchers featured here do throw hard. . . and what's more, most are also very successful.

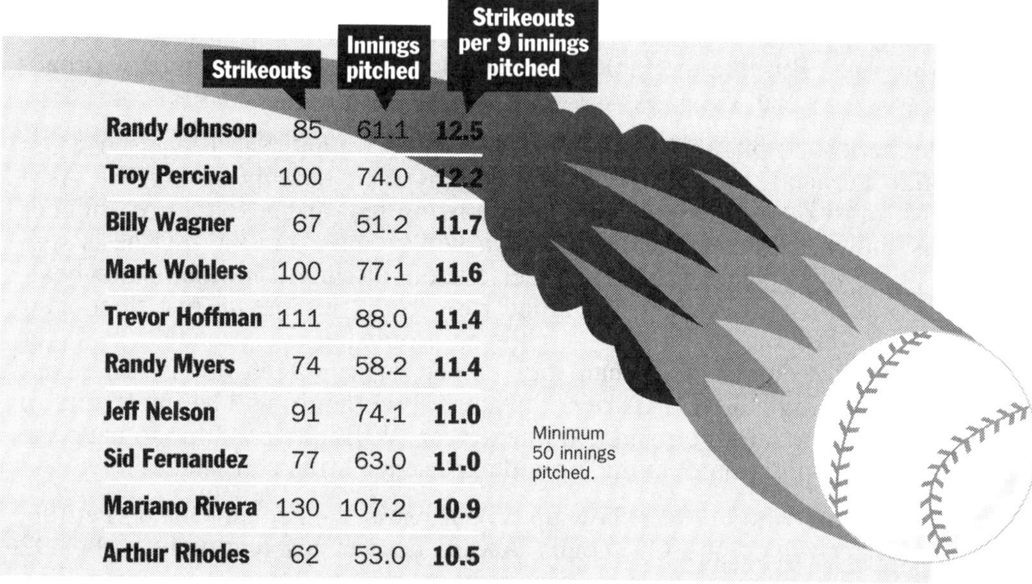

	Strikeouts	Innings pitched	Strikeouts per 9 innings pitched
Randy Johnson	85	61.1	**12.5**
Troy Percival	100	74.0	**12.2**
Billy Wagner	67	51.2	**11.7**
Mark Wohlers	100	77.1	**11.6**
Trevor Hoffman	111	88.0	**11.4**
Randy Myers	74	58.2	**11.4**
Jeff Nelson	91	74.1	**11.0**
Sid Fernandez	77	63.0	**11.0**
Mariano Rivera	130	107.2	**10.9**
Arthur Rhodes	62	53.0	**10.5**

Minimum 50 innings pitched.

The chart lists the pitchers with the highest strikeout rates in 1996. Not surprisingly, relievers tend to dominate; since they usually work an inning or less, relief pitchers don't have to worry about pacing themselves the way starters do. Some of the top firemen in the game are represented here: guys like Troy Percival, Mark Wohlers, Trevor Hoffman and Mariano Rivera. Some *serious* heat there.

Only two starting pitchers crack the leaders list, and neither one of them saw much action last year. The number-one man, the great Randy Johnson, appeared in only 14 games—just eight as a starter—because of back problems which eventually required surgery. When he *was* able to take the mound, however, Johnson was obviously throwing as hard as ever. Sid Fernandez, the other starter on the list, is one of those rare strikeout artists who *doesn't* throw much heat; El Sid gets his Ks with an unorthodox motion that makes it difficult for hitters to pick up the ball. He was as baffling as ever last year, and also as prone to injury; for the fourth year in a row, Fernandez failed to record 20 starts.

Among starters who qualified for the ERA crown, the top strikeout rates belonged to John Smoltz (9.8), Roger Clemens (9.5), Hideo Nomo (9.2), Pedro Martinez (9.2) and Darryl Kile (9.0). It used to be rare for a starter to average a strikeout an inning; now it's commonplace.

These pitchers averaged the *fewest* strikeouts per nine innings in 1996:

Fewest Strikeouts per Nine Innings—1996

Pitcher, Team	IP	K	K/9 IP	ERA
Steve Sparks, Mil	88.2	21	2.1	6.60
Brian Keyser, WSox	59.2	19	2.9	4.98
Roger McDowell, Bal	59.1	20	3.0	4.25
Matt Ruebel, Pit	58.2	22	3.4	4.60
Steve Wojciechowski, Oak	79.2	30	3.4	5.65
Joe Magrane, WSox	53.2	21	3.5	6.88
Jose Bautista, SF	69.2	28	3.6	3.36
Brian Anderson, Cle	51.1	21	3.7	4.91
Jim Abbott, Cal	142.0	58	3.7	7.48
Jeff Russell, Tex	56.0	23	3.7	3.38

A few guys on this list performed reasonably well last year, but we can offer no assurances that their success will continue in '97. On the contrary, we've noticed over the years that appearing on this list is often an ominous sign for a pitcher's future. Among the bottom 10 on the '95 list were Mark Gubicza, who went 4-12, 5.13 in '96; Bob Scanlan, Brian Maxcy and John Doherty, who wound up back in the minors; Ricky Bones, whose '96 mark was 7-14, 6.22; Tim Pugh, who had a 7.27 ERA for two clubs; and Roger Bailey, who had a 6.24 ERA in 24 games for the Rockies. If your heater ain't hot, one might say, neither is your future.

— Don Zminda

A more complete listing for this category can be found on page 284.

Who Gets the Easy Saves?

Let's say you're a player agent, and one of your top clients is a closer. How ecstatic are you to see your guy get called in to start the ninth inning with a three-run lead? A save in that situation should be a sure thing, and let's face it—more saves equals more bargaining power come contract time.

With so many managers going out of their way to ensure that their closers get these types of save opportunities, the save statistic can become quite misleading (see Mitch Williams' 43 saves in 1993). To gain some more insight into closers' performances, we've devised three categories of saves based on how precarious the situation is when a reliever enters the game:

Easy Save: First batter faced is not the tying run *and* the reliever pitches one inning or less. Example: Jose Mesa comes in to start the bottom of the ninth, with the Tribe ahead by a 7-4 score. This is an (agent-friendly) Easy Save opportunity.

Tough Save: The reliever comes in with the tying run anywhere on base. Example: With the Mariners clinging to a 9-7 lead, Norm Charlton enters with runners on first and second and no outs in the ninth. This is considered a Tough Save opportunity.

Regular Save: All save opportunities that fall into neither of the categories above are classified as Regular Save opportunities.

How tough *is* a Tough Save opportunity? Across baseball, they're much tougher to convert than the Easy Save opportunities:

League-Wide Save Conversions—1996

	Easy			Regular			Tough		
League	**Sv**	**Op**	**%**	**Sv**	**Op**	**%**	**Sv**	**Op**	**%**
A.L.	241	266	91	229	353	65	66	190	35
N.L.	258	280	92	261	396	66	61	191	32
MLB Totals	499	546	91	490	749	65	127	381	33

Tough Saves were converted in about one-third of all opportunities, Regular Saves in about two-thirds and Easy Saves—well, let's just say they are converted with such frequency that a blown Easy Save sticks out like a sore rotator cuff. This is very bad news for Lee Smith, who converted just one of four such opportunities in 1996. A future Hall of Famer, Smith has probably seen his last days as a closer.

What about baseball's regular stoppers? How did they fare in Easy, Regular and Tough Save situations? Here is the breakdown for each reliever who saw at least 25 save opportunities in 1996:

Save Conversions—Major League Closers, 1996

	Easy			Regular			Tough			Total		
Pitcher, Team	**Sv**	**Op**	**%**	**Sv**	**Op**	**%**	**Sv**	**Op**	**%**	**Sv**	**Op**	**%**
Troy Percival, Cal	12	12	100	17	18	94	7	9	78	36	39	92
John Wetteland, Yanks	27	29	93	12	13	92	4	5	80	43	47	91
Mel Rojas, Mon	9	9	100	21	23	91	6	8	75	36	40	90
Jeff Brantley, Cin	25	25	100	19	22	86	0	2	0	44	49	90
Ricky Bottalico, Phi	19	22	86	11	12	92	4	4	100	34	38	89
Jose Mesa, Cle	25	26	96	14	18	78	0	0	0	39	44	89
Mark Wohlers, Atl	18	18	100	12	14	86	9	12	75	39	44	89
Dennis Eckersley, StL	13	13	100	15	18	83	2	3	67	30	34	88
Trevor Hoffman, SD	19	19	100	19	23	83	4	7	57	42	49	86
Mike Fetters, Mil	15	17	88	13	17	76	4	4	100	32	38	84
Mike Henneman, Tex	14	16	87	15	18	83	2	3	67	31	37	84
Rod Beck, SF	20	21	95	9	12	75	6	9	67	35	42	83
Robb Nen, Fla	19	20	95	15	18	83	1	4	25	35	42	83
Todd Worrell, LA	23	24	96	19	26	73	2	3	67	44	53	83
Bruce Ruffin, Col	16	17	94	6	7	86	2	5	40	24	29	83
Roberto Hernandez, WSox	19	20	95	18	22	82	1	4	25	38	46	83
Randy Myers, Bal	17	18	94	13	19	68	1	1	100	31	38	82
Mike Timlin, Tor	22	23	96	7	13	54	2	2	100	31	38	82
Heathcliff Slocumb, Bos	20	20	100	10	16	62	1	3	33	31	39	79
John Franco, Mets	13	13	100	14	18	78	1	5	20	28	36	78
Norm Charlton, Sea	6	7	86	11	15	73	3	5	60	20	27	74
Jeff Montgomery, KC	14	16	87	8	15	53	2	3	67	24	34	71

(Minimum 25 save opportunities)

The first thing we noticed about the chart is that justice was served. Troy Percival, who topped the majors in save percentage last year, *earned* his number-one ranking. About 45 percent of all major league saves in 1996 were Easy Saves, but only a third of Percival's 36 saves fell into this category. In addition, Percival finished second in Tough Saves, and tied for second in Tough Save opportunities; only Mark Wohlers had more. Clearly, Percival earned his stripes, making his league–leading overall save percentage all the more impressive.

Similar kudos should be given to Mel Rojas, who placed third on our list with numbers very similar to Percival's. No pitcher in the top 20 had as few Easy Saves as Rojas' nine, and the Montreal stopper earned his money in the heat of a pennant race.

Other than Percival and Rojas, four of the top six pitchers on our list feasted on Easy Save opportunities in 1996. Jeff Brantley went 25-for-25 in save situations when given room for error, while John Wetteland led the majors in Easy Saves and Easy Save opportunities. But let's not criticize Wetteland: after all, he did go 4-for-5 in Tough Save situations, and picked up a (very) Tough Save in Game 5 of the World Series.

We couldn't help but be impressed by the work turned in by Philadelphia's Ricky Bottalico. In just his second full season—and first as a closer—Bottalico was a perfect 4-for-4 in Tough Save chances. Only two other relievers matched Bottalico's perfect mark in as many tough situations—Milwaukee's Mike Fetters and the Cubs' Turk Wendell (who doesn't show up on the chart because he didn't garner enough save opportunities to qualify). Of course the question needs to be asked of Bottalico: if (or when) he ever pitches for a contender, will he be as effective when the pressure is on?

Finally, a word on Cleveland's Jose Mesa. Mesa has 85 saves and a 2.51 ERA over the last two seasons—but only once has he been asked to come in for a Tough Save opportunity. We're not here to negotiate contracts, but Mesa's agent has to like this trend.

—Ethan D. Cooperson

A more complete listing for this category can be found on page 286.

If You Can Hold the Fort, Will You Soon Be Closing the Gate?

It may not be the sexiest stat in baseball, but we've spent the past seven years arguing the validity of the "hold" as an accurate measuring stick for the performance of middle relievers. Though "hold" may not yet roll off the tongue like "save" and "ERA" do, we are now as accustomed to seeing an H in our box scores as we are to finding an S or a W.

Here's a short refresher course: a reliever is credited with a hold when he enters a game in a save situation and records at least one out before passing the save situation over to another reliever. Perfect? Of course not. Just as a closer can look very shaky in a given outing and still register a save, a middle man can give up a run or two or even three and still notch a hold.

In plenty of cases, however, a middle reliever gets that hold the old-fashioned way: he eeeaaarns it. Look no further than the sixth-and-deciding game of last year's World Series for not one, but *three* good examples. After Yankee relievers David Weathers and Graeme Lloyd stranded Chipper Jones at third in the sixth inning of a 3-1 contest to register holds, Mariano Rivera earned one of his own with two frames of hitless relief

HOLDING THE FORT

	HOLDS
Mariano Rivera	27
Steve Reed	22
Jeff Shaw	22
Mike Stanton	22
Doug Bochtler	20
Jeff Russell	20
Rick Honeycutt	19
Jesse Orosco	19
Eddie Guardado	18
Mike James	18
Greg McMichael	18

against the likes of Grissom, Lemke, Jones, McGriff and Lopez. His heroics gave John Wetteland the chance to win the Series—and an MVP Award—in the ninth.

Rivera, in fact, spent the *entire season* helping Wetteland look so good.

An established pattern has developed in the years we've been doing this study: behind the top closers you're likely to find a middle reliever who is among the best at holding the fort. Last year it was Rivera backing Wetteland and Jeff Shaw backing Jeff Brantley—the N.L. co-leader with 44 saves.

But another pattern also seems to be in the works: the top "guards" often turn their success into closing jobs the following year. In 1995, Troy Percival and Ricky Bottalico finished one and three in holds—both became stoppers in 1996. In 1994, Mel Rojas and Heathcliffe Slocumb posted the two highest hold totals—both were finishing games in 1995. In 1992, the top hold duo was Duane Ward and Todd Worrell—you guessed it: both were closing in 1993 (though arm injuries limited Worrell's duties that year). With Wetteland moving on to Texas, all indications point to Rivera continuing this pattern in 1997.

Before we go, let's take a look at how each team fared in this category last year:

1996 Team Leaders—Holds

American League		National League	
Team	**Holds**	**Team**	**Holds**
Rangers	65	Cardinals	68
Yankees	62	Rockies	67
Brewers	58	Reds	56
Indians	58	Padres	50
Red Sox	58	Pirates	50
Orioles	53	Braves	49
Mariners	51	Expos	49
White Sox	50	Dodgers	43
Athletics	43	Phillies	43
Tigers	40	Cubs	43
Angels	39	Marlins	42
Blue Jays	39	Giants	38
Twins	39	Astros	28
Royals	38	Mets	26

For the fourth time in the last six seasons, a Tony La Russa-managed club led its respective league in holds. Judging by its 3.45 ERA, the Cards pen was quite effective, but La Russa was also up to his old tricks. A bullpen can build up a lot of holds when relievers come in to face just a single batter, and no National League skipper could top the 47 one-batter appearances La Russa called for (see the St. Louis Cardinals essay on p. 69 for more on this subject). Over in the Junior Circuit, the Rangers' Johnny Oates nearly kept pace, asking his relievers to face a single batter 44 times—and Texas relievers came through with an A.L.–best 65 holds. The Mets, by the way, have occupied the N.L. cellar in this category four of the last six seasons. Little wonder why their fort has been in disarray for much of this decade.

—Tony Nistler

A more complete listing for this category can be found on page 287.

Which Relievers Can Be Counted On to Convert?

In any introductory statistics course in high school or college, the professor will establish two things from the get-go: 1) statistics can be wonderful tools to support an argument, and 2) statistics can be misleading when they aren't put in proper context. We work very hard in this book to seek out cases of "statistical injustice" and then try to right those wrongs by adding further context. Fairness is always our goal.

A few years ago, we championed the cause of middle relievers, who were being unfairly judged when measured primarily by their save percentages. After all, middle relievers get plenty of chances to *blow* saves, but they seldom have the chance to *earn* one.

Take the case of Doug Bochtler. In 1996, the middle reliever saved three games for San Diego but blew four other opportunities. His .429 save percentage could hardly be construed as a successful campaign. Yet in actuality, Bochtler was a very effective reliever. He fashioned a 3.02 ERA and posted 20 *holds*—the fifth-highest total in the majors. So how does one compare relievers without penalizing the middle-men for not being closers? We offer the "relief conversion percentage," which is simply a catchier way of saying "hold-plus-save percentage." Here are the 1996 leaders:

1996 Leaders—Relief Conversion Percentage

Pitcher, Team	Holds	Saves	Opp	Pct
Ed Vosberg, Tex	11	8	20	95.0
Troy Percival, Cal	2	36	41	92.7
Mike Myers, Det	17	6	25	92.0
Bob Patterson, Cubs	15	8	25	92.0
John Wetteland, Yanks	0	43	47	91.5
Mariano Rivera, Yanks	27	5	35	91.4
Mike Jackson, Sea	15	6	23	91.3
Billy Taylor, Oak	4	17	23	91.3
Terry Mathews, Fla/Bal	15	4	21	90.5
Dave Veres, Mon	15	4	21	90.5
MLB Average				81.5

(minimum 20 opportunities)

As is our intention, middle relievers always rub elbows with the game's best closers at the top of this list. Stoppers Troy Percival and John Wetteland dominated A.L. hitters, but you may not have known about the effectiveness of Ed Vosberg, Mike Myers and Bob Patterson. Each did yeoman's work when it came to holding the fort, and each was up to the task of closing the door when called upon. Mariano Rivera's stellar season has him in line for the role of Yankee closer in 1997. By the way, you may be asking where Bochtler's name is on this list. He didn't crack the top 10, but his 85.2 relief conversion percentage sure looks a heckuva lot better than his save percentage.

What about the bottom of this list for 1996?

1996 Trailers—Relief Conversion Percentage

Pitcher, Team	Holds	Saves	Opp	Pct
Matt Karchner, WSox	13	1	22	63.6
Jeff Montgomery, KC	0	24	34	70.6
Francisco Cordova, Pit	3	12	21	71.4
Bill Simas, WSox	15	2	23	73.9
Todd Jones, Hou	1	17	24	75.0
T.J. Mathews, StL	9	6	20	75.0
Greg McMichael, Atl	18	2	26	76.9
Mike Mohler, Oak	13	7	26	76.9
Tony Fossas, StL	15	2	22	77.3
Doug Henry, Mets	8	9	22	77.3
Graeme Lloyd, Mil/Yanks	17	0	22	77.3

Closers Jeff Montgomery and Todd Jones had as much trouble with their shoulders as they did with opposing hitters last year, and both have big questions marks surrounding their futures. Teammates Matt Karchner and Bill Simas also stand out—though in this category, they probably wish they didn't. The sporadic Chicago bullpen gave the South Siders fits all season.

For the second year in a row, the Cleveland Indians took home the team crown, converting 88.9 percent of their hold-plus-save opportunities (58 holds, 46 saves, 117 opp). Amazingly, they compiled that total without placing a single pitcher in our top 10. The Phillies, of all teams, led all N.L. bullpens, converting 85.9 (43-42-99) percent of their opportunities. The title of shakiest bullpen went to the Astros, who converted only 63 of their 85 opportunities. Perhaps the 'Stros should shelve that push for a new stadium and concentrate more on their relief corps.

—Tony Nistler

A more complete listing for this category can be found on page 288.

Which Pitchers Get a Helping Hand From Their Teammates?

Just as it was for many of his Philadelphia teammates, 1996 was far from the best of years for reliever Toby Borland—to put it mildly. Not only did Borland have to toil all season in the Phillies bullpen (watching loss. . . after loss. . . after mind-numbing loss), but he also had to suffer while his teammates repeatedly invited the runners he left on base to score. It was pretty much like having his credit cards stolen; no matter what kind of expenses someone *else* rang up on them, Borland was the one who got stuck with the bill.

		'Bequeathed runners'	Later scored	PCT.
THEIR BULLPENS DESERTED THEM	Toby Borland	25	17	68.0%
	Vaughn Eshelman	29	19	65.5%
	Dennis Springer	24	14	58.3%
	Jack McDowell	31	18	58.1%
	Tim Wakefield	25	14	56.0%
THEIR BULLPENS RESCUED THEM	Mike Mohler	25	1	4.0%
	Carlos Reyes	23	1	4.3%
	Mark Brandenburg	22	1	4.5%
	Bob Patterson	46	4	8.7%
	Jason Jacome	28	3	10.7%
	ML Totals	7,334	2,581	35.2%

Minimum 20 'bequeathed runners'.

In the last two seasons, Borland is the only relief pitcher to make our "most victimized" list: this is usually a starter's category. If Borland were backed by just an average pitching staff, how much better would he have fared? A great deal better. A typical relief corps in 1996 would have allowed only nine of Borland's 25 bequeathed runners to score—instead of the 17 who actually did cross the plate last season. Assuming that seven of the eight runs saved were destined to be earned (the average MLB ratio is about 9:1), his ERA would have dropped from 4.07 to 3.38—a considerable difference.

At the other end of the scale, we have the Athletics' Mike Mohler, who was possibly the *luckiest* pitcher in baseball last year. On the surface, Mohler appears to have compiled decent stats—a 3.67 ERA, 13 holds, seven saves, 20-for-26 hold/save conversion rate—good numbers for a part-time closer. Delving deeper into his performance last season, however, we found that his bullpen buddies bailed him out of quite a few jams, stranding 24 of the 25 runners he left on base. After doing a little math, we estimated that an average pitching staff would have allowed eight more of those runners to score (seven of them being earned), pushing his ERA from 3.67 to 4.44. With a figure *that* high, it's possible that he wouldn't have lasted the season in Oakland.

In last year's *Scoreboard*, we mentioned that the Astros' Darryl Kile suffered a few unusually heavy blows to his ERA in '95 when his teammates allowed a whopping 78.3 percent (18 of 23) of his bequeathed runners to score. Despite the offensive explosion last season, Kile's ERA dropped from 4.96 to 4.19. While the 'Stros pen may have struggled overall last year, it certainly came to the rescue of Mr. Kile on numerous occasions. Houston relievers allowed just six of his 27 runners to come home in '96.

Not all bequeathed runners are created equal. A man on third, inherited with no outs, is much more likely to score than a man on first, handed over with two outs. However, the statistics certainly paint a clearer picture with regard to the considerable impact—both positive and negative—that a club's bullpen can have on its hurlers.

—Kevin Fullam

A more complete listing for this category can be found on page 289.

Who Knows How to Handle Their Inheritance ?

For a relief pitcher, ERA and win-loss records don't exactly paint the best picture of performance. Since a reliever can enter a game with the bases loaded and allow all three runners to score without suffering a dent to his earned run average, ERA obviously has some flaws. As for wins, the system actually *rewards* pitchers who surrender late-inning leads and then have their teammates bail them out with a couple of well-timed runs.

So what *can* we use to better illustrate the effectiveness of a reliever? One way is to look at the relief conversion percentage, which is the topic of another essay (p. 180). We can also calculate the percentage of inherited baserunners that each relief pitcher allows to score. The relievers who enter a game with the tying runs on base and stifle an enemy rally—*those* are the guys I'd want to have in my bullpen. Which pitchers allowed the lowest percentage of inherited runners to score in 1996? Let's take a look:

Lowest Percentage of Inherited Runners Scored—1996

Reliever, Team	IR	IRS	Pct
Billy Taylor, Oak	34	5	14.7
T.J. Mathews, StL	36	6	16.7
Mark Wohlers, Atl	36	6	16.7
Trevor Hoffman, SD	35	6	17.1
Larry Casian, Cubs	38	7	18.4
Dennis Cook, Tex	81	16	19.8
Norm Charlton, Sea	39	8	20.5
Larry Thomas, WSox	52	11	21.2
Jesse Orosco, Bal	46	10	21.7
Eric Plunk, Cle	49	11	22.5

(minimum 30 inherited runners)

While Billy Taylor and Mark Wohlers both spell certain doom for late-inning enemy rallies, one has to be amazed by the Rangers' Dennis Cook. Cook appeared in 60 games last season and inherited an incredible 81 runners—or 1.4 per appearance. Is there a reason why he racked up such high totals? Well, as a left-handed specialist, Cook entered quite a few games last season with men on base where he was only required to get an out or two. Righthanders are used less frequently in this manner for the simple reason that more hitters bat righty than lefty; as a result, they tend to pitch longer during dangerous situations.

Which bullpens did the best job of shutting down offensive threats collectively? Here's a list of last season's team inherited-runners percentages:

Team Inherited-Runners Percentages—1996

AL Team	IR	IRS	Pct	NL Team	IR	IRS	Pct
Rangers	307	90	29.3	Cardinals	226	65	28.8
Royals	241	74	30.7	Expos	276	80	29.0
Indians	247	78	31.6	Cubs	263	77	29.3
Mariners	342	111	32.5	Padres	257	76	29.6
Blue Jays	155	51	32.9	Braves	196	61	31.1
White Sox	271	90	33.2	Reds	216	73	33.8
Athletics	315	105	33.3	Pirates	224	80	35.7
Orioles	279	103	36.9	Marlins	255	93	36.5
Brewers	324	121	37.4	Astros	228	86	37.7
Angels	339	127	37.5	Mets	189	73	38.6
Tigers	396	154	38.9	Giants	303	118	38.9
Red Sox	305	120	39.3	Dodgers	189	74	39.2
Twins	288	115	39.9	Rockies	215	87	40.5
Yankees	280	114	40.7	Phillies	208	85	40.9
A.L. Totals	4089	1453	35.5	**N.L. Totals**	3245	1128	34.8

With bullpen master Tony La Russa at the helm, it's not hard to see why St. Louis led the majors in allowing the lowest percentage of inherited runners to score. Rotating T.J. Mathews, Cory Bailey, Tony Fossas, Rick Honeycutt and a rejuvenated Dennis Eckersley into the fray, La Russa repeatedly thwarted opponents' scoring threats.

How did the World Champion Yankees wind up with the AL's *worst* inherited-runners percentage? The fact is that the Yankees' best relievers, John Wetteland and Mariano Rivera, rarely came into the game with men on base. In 123 combined appearances, the duo inherited only 36 runners. Of those 36, Wetteland allowed six of 14 to score (42.9 percent), while Rivera permitted six of 22 (27.3 percent) to cross the plate. Manager Joe Torre didn't bring his bullpen aces in the game in mid-inning, preferring to let them come in with clean slates. With the likes of Bob Wickman (52.5 percent of IR scored) and Jim Mecir (51.7 percent) getting the call in dangerous situations, it's no surprise that Yankee relievers didn't grade well overall with regards to allowing inherited runners to score.

— Kevin Fullam

A more complete listing for this category can be found on page 291.

Which Pitchers Really "Lost Out" in 1996?

We've all seen the picture. It's one of the great "agony of defeat" shots in all of baseball: a starting pitcher sitting in the dugout, a towel wrapped around his neck and his white knuckles wrapped around his face. His agonized look speaks volumes as he watches the bullpen blow his lead. . .

Few starters are ever happy about leaving a game, *especially* when they have the lead. Most go kicking and screaming (sometimes literally), and for good reason; once they turn the ball over, their livelihood is in someone else's hands. History will remember a certain pitcher won only nine games one season, but it will quickly forget that that very same hurler exited eight *other* contests with the lead. Unfortunately, there's no category for "should-have-been wins," though Dodger righty Pedro Astacio probably would be the first in line to endorse it. *He* won just nine games in 1996, but failed to come away with a "W" on eight other occasions when he was pulled with the lead after logging at least five innings.

1996 Leaders—No Win After Leaving With Lead

Pitcher, Team	No Win	Pulled With Lead	Pct
Pedro Astacio, LA	8	17	47.1
Brad Radke, Min	8	17	47.1
Wilson Alvarez, WSox	8	23	34.8
Scott Karl, Mil	7	17	41.2
Roger Clemens, Bos	6	11	54.5
Mark Leiter, SF/Mon	6	12	50.0
Armando Reynoso, Col	6	14	42.9
John Burkett, Fla/Tex	6	15	40.0
Kevin Tapani, WSox	6	18	33.3
Andy Benes, StL	6	21	28.6
Tom Glavine, Atl	6	21	28.6

Astacio, Brad Radke and Wilson Alvarez were the biggest "losers" in this category last season, each assuming that agony-of-defeat pose on eight different occasions. Perhaps Roger Clemens can claim even greater mental anguish, however, after watching the Red Sox bullpen lose his leads nearly 55 percent of the time. In a perfect world, then, Astacio would be boasting about a 17-win season and Alvarez about *his* wonderful 23-win campaign. In a perfect world, Tom Glavine would have been a 22-game winner and Clemens may have commanded an even *higher* price tag.

But alas, no world is perfect, no pen is perfect. . . and neither is any starting pitcher. What this chart *doesn't* show is whether Astacio left with the bases loaded eight times, or whether Clemens left with runners in scoring position and no outs on six occasions. What we're trying to point out here, however, is how many *possible* wins a starter lost, and a win is always possible when you leave with a lead after working at least five frames.

So who've been the biggest "losers" over the last four seasons?

1992-96 Leaders—No Win After Leaving With Lead

Pitcher	No Win	Pulled With Lead	Pct
Steve Avery	20	62	32.3
Scott Erickson	18	56	32.1
Andy Benes	18	71	25.4
Chris Bosio	17	53	32.1
Pete Harnisch	17	53	32.1
Ricky Bones	17	58	29.3
Bob Tewksbury	17	66	25.8
Roger Clemens	16	59	27.1
Erik Hanson	16	60	26.7
Jaime Navarro	16	62	25.8

Maybe Steve Avery and his agent have a point when they say he's a better pitcher than his numbers would indicate. Not only does Avery sport the most cases of "no wins" after leaving with the lead, he also had the highest *percentage* of leads blown over the past four years among our top 10. No lead is safe in Fenway, but that's probably no comfort to the Rocket when he starts thinking about the possibility of sitting 16 wins closer to 300.

Then there's the other side of the coin. A total of six starters—John Smoltz (19), Orel Hershiser (15), Darren Oliver (13), Fernando Valenzuela (13), Bobby Witt (13) and Steve Trachsel (10)—left at least 10 games last season with leads and came away with wins *every single time*. Hershiser has been the beneficiary of what may be the most eye-popping stat in this entire book. Over the past two seasons with Cleveland, the Bulldog has left 30 different games with the lead, and he has come away with *30* wins. Not a single blown lead. . . not a single feeling of helplessness. . . not a single set of white knuckles. Now *that's* a perfect world!

—Tony Nistler

A more complete listing of this category can be found on page 292.

Which Reliever is *Really* the Best at Preventing Runs?

When a pitcher takes the mound, he has but one job: to prevent the other team from scoring. For relievers, who often enter the game with men on base, this job can be particularly difficult. Not only do they need to prevent their teammates' bequeathed runners from crossing the plate, but they also have to stop their own batters from circling the bases—while leaving as few runners on base as possible for the next pitcher. How can we evaluate how well a reliever accomplishes all of these tasks? With the help of a new statistic called "Runs Prevented," we can precisely account for the runners a hurler inherits, allows to score, and leaves behind for the next pitcher.

The basis for Runs Prevented is run expectation, which is, simply put, the number of runs that is expected to score in the remainder of an inning given the existing combination of runners on base and remaining outs. According to the classic book *The Hidden Game of Baseball*, the run expectation for the bases loaded and nobody out is 2.25; in other words, given that situation, a team should score, on average, 2.25 runs for the remainder of the inning. If a hitter strikes out with the bases loaded and no outs, the run expectation would decrease to 1.55 runs.

The Runs Prevented concept uses run expectation to determine whether a relief pitcher prevented a greater or lesser number of runs from scoring than would have been expected by an average hurler. A pitcher's Runs Prevented total is tracked through each inning of work by taking the run potential when the pitcher enters the game, subtracting any runs that score during the pitcher's watch, and then subtracting the run expectation when the pitcher leaves the mound. Here are the Runs Prevented values for each of the 24 base/out combinations.

Runs Prevented Values

	Number of Outs		
Runners	0	1	2
None	.45	.25	1.0
1st	.78	.48	.21
2nd	1.07	.70	.35
3rd	1.28	.90	.38
1st & 2nd	1.38	.89	.46
1st & 3rd	1.64	1.09	.49
2nd & 3rd	1.95	1.37	.66
Full	2.25	1.55	.80

(from John Thorn and Pete Palmer's *The Hidden Game of Baseball* [Doubleday, 1984])

These figures can obviously change slightly from year to year, league to league, and ballpark to ballpark, but for simplicity's sake we'll stick with Pete Palmer's original run expectation numbers. There's a lot of merit in measuring all pitchers against the same scale, anyway.

The following details the step-by-step approach that is used to calculate Runs Prevented:

1. Find Runs Prevented Value ("RP Value") when reliever enters game or starts a new inning (the "Initial RP Value").

2a. Subtract one run for every run that scores while the pitcher is on the mound.

2b. If an error is made while the reliever is on the mound, find the RP value for the situation after the error, and subtract from that the RP value for the event that would have occurred but for the error (never assume double plays). The result is the "Error RP Value," which must be added to the RP total.

3. Subtract the RP value when the reliever either: (a) finishes the inning by getting the third out (RP Value = 0); or (b) leaves the mound with less than three outs (including at game's end) (the "End RP Value"). The net result is his total of runs prevented. Repeat steps 1-3 for each inning pitched by the reliever; when the reliever leaves the game, add his RP points for each inning for his RP game total.

Formula: RP = (Initial RP Value) – (runs scored) + (Error RP Value) – (End RP Value)

How about an example? Without further ado. . .

Robb Nen enters the game in the ninth with a runner on first and nobody out (RP value = 0.78). The first batter hits the ball to Craig Grebeck, who boots it, allowing the runner to reach second and the batter to reach first (RP value = 1.38). The scorer determines that the runner from first would have been out (i.e., RP value should have been 0.48). Add 0.90 runs to Nen's RP total (1.38 – 0.48 = 0.90). Nen then surrenders a three-run home run (-3.0 Runs Prevented), ending the game (with nobody retired in the inning, and nobody left on, the RP Value = 0.45).

Robb Nen's runs prevented total for the game is: 0.78 – 3.0 + 0.90 – 0.45 = – 1.77

The beauty of the RP concept is that it isolates the performance of each reliever. Unlike ERAs or win-loss marks, a pitcher's runs prevented are not influenced by what happens to the runners that he leaves on base. In contrast to saves and holds, a pitcher can earn runs prevented regardless of whether his team is leading or trailing. And, unlike the "inherited runners scored/stranded" stat, each inherited runner has a different value: after all, a runner on third with none out is much more likely to score than a runner on first with two outs.

With runs prevented, everything the pitcher does while on the mound is recorded on his ledger and then automatically compared to the league average (which should be zero, though this may differ from year to year based on league offensive performance). Therefore, a typical reliever should have a total of zero runs prevented at the end of the season, while a good pitcher will have a positive score (more runs prevented than average) and a poor pitcher will have a negative figure.

Enough theory. Which 1996 pitchers did the best job of preventing runs from scoring?

Highest Runs Prevented Totals—1996

Pitcher, Team	Runs Prevented
Mariano Rivera, Yanks	27.7
Trevor Hoffman, SD	23.0
Roberto Hernandez, WSox	19.1
Robb Nen, Fla	18.6
Troy Percival, Cal	18.4
Eric Plunk, Cle	17.7
Tim Worrell, SD	16.2
Jeff Shaw, Cin	14.5
Antonio Osuna, LA	14.3
Turk Wendell, Cubs	13.9

Yankee phenom Mariano Rivera led the field in run prevention, proving that, for once at least, the New York media has not been exaggerating about his ability. Rivera's impressive showing was the result of a fine all-around performance: he gave manager Joe Torre a lot of innings (107.2), prevented his teammates' bequeathed runners from scoring (just 6 of 22 scored), and kept his own men from crossing the plate (2.09 ERA, 1.0 baserunners/inning). In contrast, teammate John Wetteland finished 37th overall with 6.4 runs prevented—less than a quarter of Rivera's total.

While more innings help pitchers amass more runs prevented, this is not a "set-up" man stat. Rivera is followed on the leader board by four closers, each of whom had stellar years—though you might not know *how* stellar if you looked only at their save totals. While Trevor Hoffman finished fourth in the majors with 42 saves, Roberto Hernandez, Troy Percival and Robb Nen finished just seventh, eighth, and 10th, respectively. On the other hand, the top three save leaders, Jeff Brantley, Todd Worrell and Wetteland, finished 19th, tied for 155th and 37th, respectively, in runs prevented. Todd Worrell's poor showing (-0.04 runs prevented) was perhaps foreshadowed by his nine blown saves (most in the N.L.). Blown saves do not necessarily translate into a low total of runs prevented, however: Hernandez blew eight saves last season, the third highest figure in the majors.

The news was not all bad for the Worrells. Todd's younger brother Tim teamed with San Diego teammate Trevor Hoffman to form the best one-two run-preventing punch in baseball last season. The two relievers combined for 39.2 runs prevented, which means that they prevented about 39 more runs from scoring than a pair of average hurlers. Maybe Ken Caminiti should lend his MVP trophy to Hoffman and Worrell for a few days. . .

—Steve Schulman

Washington D.C. attorney and avid baseball statistician Steve Schulman is the inventor of the Runs Prevented system and the author of this essay.

A more complete listing for this category can be found on page 293.

Who Throws the Most Strikes?

At some point in every pitcher's career, he's been confronted on the mound by an angry manager with one simple demand: "Throw strikes!" Alas, to the continuing frustration of managers everywhere, throwing strikes requires more than just the will. To deliver a baseball through a 17-inch-by-two-foot box 60 feet away takes considerable *skill*; some have it, and some don't. Let's take a look at the pitchers who threw the most strikes last year, as a percentage of their total pitches:

Strike Percentage Leaders—1996

Player, Team	Strike%
Greg Maddux, Atl	71.5
Dennis Eckersley, StL	70.8
Rod Beck, SF	69.4
Danny Darwin, Pit/Hou	68.7
Mariano Rivera, Yanks	68.7
Gil Heredia, Tex	68.7
Bob Tewksbury, SD	68.0
Mark Wohlers, Atl	67.8
Jeff Shaw, Cin	67.7
Doug Jones, Cubs/Mil	67.7
MLB Average	61.8

(Minimum 200 batters faced)

Anyone who witnessed Greg Maddux' "command performance" in Game 2 of the World Series will understand exactly why he tops this list by a comfortable margin. He shut out the Yankees on six hits over eight innings, and used just 82 pitches to do so—62 of them strikes. And it's no surprise to see Dennis Eckersley show up here, either. He's retained his pinpoint control into his 40s, and issued only four unintentional walks all last season.

Let's all give a tip of the cap to Mark Wohlers, who's come a long way since he broke in as a hard-throwing wild man. He's honed his control to the point where last season, he went over two months—a span of 29 appearances—without issuing an unintentional walk. Of course, if you don't have the stuff of a Mark Wohlers, working within the strike zone doesn't always produce positive results. Texas reliever Gil Heredia's pitches caught plenty of the plate; the trouble was that far too often, they didn't reach the catcher's mitt. He gave up 91 hits and 12 home runs in only 73.1 innings, leading to a fat 5.89 ERA.

Still, for all pitchers, throwing strikes is the first step on the road to success. There were very few successful pitchers among the trailers in strike percentage last year. Who came in last? That would be Milwaukee hurler Steve Sparks, who completely lost control of his knuckleball and threw strikes with only 55.2 percent of his pitches. The results were pretty ugly: 52 walks and a 6.60 ERA in 88.2 innings.

—Mat Olkin

A more complete listing for this category can be found on page 294.

Which Starting Pitchers Are "Bullpen Savers"?

Knowing how tough it is to win with an overused bullpen, managers put a premium on starting pitchers who work deep into games. Here are the starters who've been most successful over the past five years in lasting through the seventh inning:

Highest Percentage of 7+ Inning Starts—1992-96

Pitcher	GS	7-Inning Starts	Pct
Greg Maddux	159	125	78.6
David Cone	132	102	77.3
Kevin Brown	152	108	71.1
Jack McDowell	153	106	69.3
Ismael Valdes	61	41	67.2
Randy Johnson	126	83	65.9
Mike Mussina	149	98	65.8
Curt Schilling	116	76	65.5
Charles Nagy	126	82	65.1
Bret Saberhagen	83	54	65.1

(Minimum 50 games started)

Not surprisingly, Greg Maddux finishes atop the list—thanks in large part to his pinpoint control. Maddux has led the majors in fewest walks per nine innings each of the last two seasons; since '92, he has walked just 1.54 hitters per nine innings. Fewer walks mean fewer pitches per batter—witness Maddux' major league-best 3.10 pitches per hitter last year—and fewer pitches usually means longer outings. Since 1992, the average Greg Maddux start has lasted seven and a half innings but has required just 98 pitches. Maddux is not likely to run out of gas very often.

Perhaps the most impressive thing about Maddux' number-one ranking is the fact that *any* National Leaguer could top our chart. The next three hurlers on the list, David Cone, Kevin Brown and Jack McDowell, all rank highly, in part because they've spent just about all of the last five years in the American League. Other than the 1996 season for Brown and the first half of Cone's 1992 campaign, these hurlers never had to leave games for pinch hitters. Consider these numbers: since '92, Brown is 7-23 when he *doesn't* last at least seven innings, 63-29 when he does go seven. For Cone, those numbers are 7-16 in shorter starts, 62-23 when finishing the seventh. These guys rarely win when they don't pitch seven innings, suggesting that their managers let them work deep into any games where they had shots at earning victories.

But take nothing away from Cone, Brown and McDowell, who certainly have earned the right to stay in games. Cone and McDowell have won Cy Young Awards in the last five years, and Brown probably deserved to win one last year. These 30-something righthanders know how to get opposing hitters out—and to keep themselves in games.

At 23, Ismael Valdes is by far the youngest pitcher to make the top 10—and perhaps the unlikeliest. The nine others on the chart are all veterans, with at least five years of experience through 1996. We'd expect established starters to go seven innings more often than youngsters, as the hook generally comes much quicker for a rookie or second-year pitcher. Valdes also is a National Leaguer on a team with an excellent bullpen—but he defies the odds. In his 61-start, three-season career (including one season in the bullpen), Valdes has demonstrated impressive efficiency with his pitches. He has averaged 6.8 innings per start in his career, on just 101 pitches. If Valdes can rank fifth in seven-inning start percentage at age 23, we can see him ranking even higher in years to come. And how does Valdes do in the starts where he lasts at least seven? How does 24-5 with a 2.16 ERA sound?

One other pitcher who shows up on our list is particularly interesting—Curt Schilling. You wouldn't think of a guy who lost most of the 1994 and 1995 seasons to injury as a durable hurler, but Schilling has pitched at least seven innings in better than 65 percent of his starts. He's worked tirelessly for a pitching-starved Phillie team, partly because he wants to pitch lots of innings—and partly because the team has *needed* him to. In both 1992 and last year, Philadelphia used 15 different starting hurlers, as their starters ranked next-to-last in the N.L. in ERA both seasons. Those just happened to be Schilling's two best years. With a 40-20 mark and 2.17 ERA in games where he went at least seven frames, Schilling couldn't help but stick around until games reached the late innings.

—Ethan D. Cooperson

A more complete listing for this category can be found on page 296.

Which Pitchers Have Misleading Earned Run Averages?

Every statistic has its limitations, but earned run average may be the one with the least imperfections. People rarely take Luis Polonia's batting average or Joe Carter's RBI total as the gospel truth, but a pitcher's ERA is rarely greeted with the same skepticism. Still, no stat is perfect. A pitcher's ERA must be deceptive every now and then, but *when*? If we asked you to name a pitcher whose 1996 ERA was a gross aberration, could you?

We're here to suggest a way of determining when the ERA of a pitcher is misleading. To do so, we'll employ another Bill James creation, the "Runs Created" formula. The formula is usually applied to a batter's stat line, but it can be applied to a pitcher's opposition batting line just as easily. To this point, however, the Runs Created formula has rarely been applied to *pitchers*.

There's a good reason for that: most of the time, it doesn't tell you anything new. Using a pitcher's opposition batting line, you can go through the trouble of calculating a runs created figure and dividing it by the number of innings he threw. In the great majority of cases, the number you come up with (his "Predicted ERA," if you will) nearly matches the pitcher's actual ERA. The reason for that is simple, too: this approach tells you how many runs per game the pitcher's opponents *should have* scored, and the ERA tells you how many they *did* score. The formula works, so the two numbers are usually very close.

But what about when they aren't? There are rare occasions where a pitcher's actual ERA and Predicted ERA differ by a considerable margin. In that case, you've got an interesting situation: you have two very similar measures in substantial disagreement about the quality of the pitcher's work. Which one more accurately predicts what the pitcher's ERA will be in the following season?

To answer that question, we took all the pitchers from 1992 to 1995 who threw 100 innings as a starter or 50 innings as a reliever in two successive seasons (we dropped the minimums to 70 innings for a starter and 35 for a reliever for the strike year of 1994). Then we found the qualifying pitchers whose actual ERA differed the most from their Predicted ERA, and we looked to see which measure better predicted their ERA in the following season.

Here are the pitchers whose Predicted ERAs were the furthest *below* their actual ERAs during each of the four years:

Predicted ERA Furthest Below Actual ERA—1992-95

Year	Player	ERA DIF	ACT ERA	Pred ERA	Next ERA
1992	Tim Leary	–0.97	**5.36**	4.39	5.05
1993	Storm Davis	–0.99	5.05	**4.06**	3.56
1994	Roberto Hernandez	–1.47	4.91	**3.44**	3.92
1995	Juan Guzman	–1.50	6.32	**4.82**	2.93

As you can see, the Predicted ERA was a better predictor in three of the four cases. Now let's do the same for the pitchers whose ERA was the furthest *above* their Predicted ERA:

Predicted ERA Furthest Above Actual ERA—1992-95

Year	Player	ERA DIF	ACT ERA	Pred ERA	Next ERA
1992	Scott Radinsky	+1.05	2.73	**3.78**	4.28
1993	Roger McDowell	+1.81	2.25	**4.06**	5.23
1994	Steve Reed	+1.99	**3.94**	5.93	2.14
1995	Jose Mesa	+1.15	1.13	**2.27**	3.73

Three-for-four again. Taking the two groups together, the Predicted ERA beat the actual ERA in six of eight instances. That's impressive, but you certainly can't base any broad conclusions on only eight examples. To find out if this was just an aberration, we expanded the study to include 10 pitchers from each season, five from each end of the spectrum. The results were equally amazing: out of a group of 40 pitchers, the Predicted ERA was a better indicator of their next year's ERA in 28 cases. That's a success rate of *70 percent!* After seeing that, we began to consider that Predicted ERA may be a better predictor of ERA than ERA itself.

Why is it able to outperform ERA? Perhaps it's because the Predicted ERA eliminates some of the outside influences that can contaminate a pitcher's ERA. One thing that it removes is the illusion created by a starting pitcher's bullpen support. If a starter leaves the game with runners on base, and the bullpen subsequently allows those runners to score, that impacts the starter's ERA—even though it has little to do with his ability to get batters out. For example, in 1995 Darryl Kile was victimized by incredibly poor bullpen support. He "bequeathed" a total of 23 runners when he left games in mid-inning. His bullpen allowed 18 of those 23 runners to score, which was the highest percentage in the majors by a wide margin. This was reflected in Kile's ERA, which was a bloated 4.96. However, his Predicted ERA of 3.59 indicated that he'd actually pitched rather well. Not surprisingly, his ERA dropped by over three-quarters of a run last year.

Another factor is the disrupting influence of random chance. Relief pitchers are particularly susceptible to this influence, since a modern reliever will often throw as few as 60 innings in a season. When a pitcher throws that few innings, each run's impact on his ERA is enormous. Suppose that while a reliever is on the mound, some freak thing happens—something that has absolutely nothing to do with his ability to get hitters out. Let's say that an outfielder goes into the corner in pursuit of a catchable fly ball, but he falls down (with no error charged), the ball kicks around, and eventually three runs score as a result. Now consider this: those three runs will inflate that reliever's seasonal ERA by *almost half a run.*

The Predicted ERA doesn't fall victim to either of these outside influences. The bullpen's success or failure can't affect the Predicted ERA of a starter. For relievers, the Predicted ERA relies not upon the 20 or 30 runs that pitcher allows on the season, but rather upon *every single plate appearance* against the pitcher. It depends entirely upon the pitcher's ability to prevent hitters from reaching base and hitting for power. Those are the two abilities that largely determine the pitcher's actual ERA; illusions may prevent the ERA from accurately reflecting those abilities over the course of a single season, but the pitcher's ERA will eventually fall into line with his level of ability. The Predicted ERA just gives you a head start, that's all.

The only drawback with the Runs Created-based method is that it's annoyingly cumbersome. Pitchers' opposition batting lines are not widely disseminated, and plugging all those stats into the Runs Created formula can be daunting even for the most determined number-cruncher. So we simplified it. Bill James once gave us a shortcut to the Runs Created formula, explaining that you can get a reasonable approximation of a Runs Created total by multiplying (On-Base) times (Slugging) times (at-bats). Based on that, we came up with the formula:

(Opponent On-Base) x (Opponent Slugging) x (31) = Predicted ERA

Why 31? Good question. The number 31 represents the average number of at-bats a team gets in a nine-inning game, with one small adjustment. Remember, we're trying to simulate *earned* run average, and to do that, we're using the Runs Created formula, which deals with *all* runs, earned or not. About nine percent of all runs are unearned, so we have to adjust our formula downward by nine percent, just so the results correspond with actual ERAs. The average number of at-bats in a nine-inning game last year was 34.8; when you subtract nine percent, you get a figure a little bit above 31. The formula makes sense on more than just a theoretical level, though. When we tested it, we found that it worked just fine, and we used it to produce the Predicted ERAs in the charts above.

The best part is that it's so simple that you can easily use it yourself. Pitchers' opponent On-Base and Slugging are available throughout the season in *Baseball Weekly*, as well as on STATS On-Line and STATS' area on America Online (we also offer Predicted ERA). For now, let us do the math. Here are the five pitchers whose ERA should drop the most next year:

Predicted ERA Furthest Below Actual ERA—1996

Player, Team	ERA DIF	ACT ERA	Pred ERA
Bobby Ayala, Sea	−1.60	5.88	4.29
Jason Grimsley, Cal	−1.58	6.84	5.26
Jim Bullinger, Cubs	−1.57	6.54	4.97
Brad Clontz, Atl	−1.48	5.69	4.21
Jim Abbott, Cal	−1.38	7.48	6.10

Bobby Ayala, though beset by all sorts of problems, actually didn't pitch all that poorly—his Predicted ERA was over a half-run *below* the American League average. We expect him to rebound, along with Bruce Ruffin, William VanLandingham, Paul Wilson and Jason Isringhausen.

Here are the top five pitchers whose ERAs were deceptively *low*:

Predicted ERA Furthest Above Actual ERA—1996

Player, Team	ERA DIF	ACT ERA	Pred ERA
Jim Poole, Cle/SF	+1.33	2.86	4.19
John Franco, Mets	+1.29	1.83	3.12
Scott Radinsky, LA	+1.25	2.41	3.65
Mike Mohler, Oak	+1.07	3.67	4.73
Dave Mlicki, Mets	+1.01	3.30	4.31

Mike Mohler posted an impressive ERA over the first half of the season, but Art Howe wasn't fooled, and instead gave the closer's duties to Billy Taylor, who had a worse ERA (4.33) but pitched much more effectively overall (3.34 Predicted ERA). Some whose ERA should worsen include: Jeff Shaw, Randy Myers, Steve Trachsel, Mike Stanton, Dennis Eckersley and Mike Hampton.

We can't promise a 100 percent success rate, but we're confident that if you check back at these lists at the close of the season, you'll find that Predicted ERA outperformed ERA in the majority of cases. After all, it's been the better of the two for four years running.

—Mat Olkin

A more complete listing for this category can be found on page 298.

Is Anyone on Track to Win 300?

Hi; this is Bill James. Many years ago, I developed the system called The Favorite Toy, the function of which is to estimate a hitter's chances of reaching some very difficult career goal, such as 500 homers, 3,000 hits, or 478 grounded into double plays. I have always wanted some way to estimate a pitcher's chances of winning 300 games, but the method that works for hitters doesn't work at all for pitchers, nor can it be made to work by any simple adjustments. The task is a lot more complicated, for pitchers, and until now I had just never found the time to do the background work to develop such a method.

I got to it last December, after I finished the manager's book, so Don asked me to write an article, explaining the system for the *Scoreboard.* It's a five-step process:

1) Identify the candidates.

2) Find each pitcher's Established Win Level.

3) Figure how many years away from 300 the pitcher is.

4) Figure the pitcher's per-season chance of continuing to move toward the goal.

5) Calculate the result.

All the work is in Steps 2 and 4. If I was writing this up for one of my own books I would report all of my research, explain and justify the full details of the system, show dozens of real-life examples, and burn up about 15,000 words. This being the *Scoreboard*, we cut to the chase with less ceremony, so I won't be able to give you a full understanding of how this is done, but I'll try to do enough to give you at least a feel for it.

Step One: Identify the Candidates

If a pitcher's total of Innings Pitched in 1996 plus his Career Wins is 300 or greater, we'll consider him a candidate. If a pitcher's total of '96 IP + Wins is less than 300, he is either

a) finished, or

b) so far away from 300 that he's not yet a viable candidate.

There are, at the moment, 32 candidates worthy of consideration, all of whom will be given in the chart at the end of the article. About one-fourth of the candidates at any moment will turn out to have less than a 1% chance of getting 300 wins anyway, some of them much, much less.

Step Two: Find Each Pitcher's Established Win Level

The elements used to calculate the pitcher's established win level are

1-4. His wins in each of the last four seasons.

5. His strikeouts last year.

6. His "virtual wins" last year, based on his innings pitched, his ERA, and the league ERA.

I combined these elements in hundreds of different weighting patterns, trying to see which method would most accurately predict the next season's wins. The resulting formula (for a pitcher from 1996) was

1993 Wins,

Plus 1994 Wins,

Plus (Five Times 1995 Wins),

Plus (10 Times 1996 Wins),

Plus (10 Times 1996 Virtual Wins),

Plus (.60 Times 1996 strikeouts),

The sum multiplied by .0264.

Plus at the moment, of course, you have to adjust for the strike in 1994-1995.

The highest established win level among the 32 current 300-win candidates was by John Smoltz, 17.96. The lowest was 7.52, by Dennis Martinez.

Step Three: Figuring Years Away from 300 Wins

This one's dead simple. John Smoltz needs 186 more wins to get 300, and he is moving at a rate of 17.96 wins per season, so he needs to continue on at that pace for 10.36 more seasons in order to get 300 wins. Dennis Martinez needs 60 more wins and is moving at a pace of 7.52 wins per season, so he needs to keep going for 7.98 more seasons to get to 300. Despite his low established win level, Martinez is closer to 300 wins, at his current pace, than any other major league pitcher. On the other end of that scale is Scott Erickson, who, at his current pace, would have to keep on keeping on for 20.31 more seasons.

Step Four: Figuring the Pitcher's Per-Season Chance of Continuing to Move Toward the Goal

I call this the P Factor, P standing for "Persistence", or "Probability of continuing to make progress", or "Per Season washout rate"—whatever you want. Calculating the P Factor is the most complex step of the process, and I can't really tell you how to do it in the space I have. What I can tell you is that we look at a variety of "indicators" of a pitcher's forward momentum. If the pitcher is young, the P Factor is relatively high; if he is older, the P Factor is lower. If he's a power pitcher, the P Factor is high, since power pitchers tend to last much longer than finesse pitchers. If he doesn't get many strikeouts, the P Factor is lower.

If the pitcher has pitched 200 innings in each of the last four seasons, that will help his P Factor significantly. If not, then the more times he has pitched 200 innings, the better off he will be.

We ask this question: at the rate this man is progressing, how old would he be when he gets to 300 wins? If the answer is "36", obviously that improves his P Factor; if the answer is "50", obviously that wouldn't be an indication in his favor.

The pitcher's ERA is a factor here—a minor factor, because ERAs go up and down, but if a pitcher's ERA is very high, his career may end suddenly, and we need to account for that.

An average P Factor is a little below .80. The highest P Factor at the moment is by Alex Fernandez, .868; the lowest, among the 32 pitchers under consideration, is .626, by Danny Darwin.

Step Five: Calculating the Results

This, again, is essentially simple: If a pitcher's P Factor is .80 and he is two seasons away from 300 wins, his chance of winning 300 games is 64%. We take the P Factor to the power represented by the number of seasons that the pitcher must continue to win.

Well, not quite that simple. We figure that the first .25 seasons are free, because it's not that likely that somebody will retire with 297 career wins. Actually, the pitcher above would be at .64 if he was 2.25 seasons away from 300 wins.

The best 300-win candidate, at the moment, is pretty obvious: Greg Maddux. Maddux has 165 career wins and is moving forward at a rate estimated at 15.52 wins per season. Thus, he is 8.70 years away from 300 wins, or 8.45 if you give him a quarter of a season free. His P Factor is high, .861—thus, his chance of winning 300 games can be estimated at 28%, which is .861 to the power 8.45.

There are three other pitchers, two of them his teammates, whose chances of winning 300 games are similar to Maddux'. The complete chart:

Greg Maddux	28%
Roger Clemens	26%
John Smoltz	23%
Tom Glavine	20%
Mike Mussina	13%
Alex Fernandez	13%
Chuck Finley	11%
Kevin Appier	10%
Pat Hentgen	10%
Dennis Martinez	9%
Kevin Brown	6%
Andy Benes	6%

Others above 1%: Orel Hershiser and Ken Hill, 4%; Jaime Navarro, Jack McDowell and Todd Stottlemyre, 3%, John Smiley, 2%, Dwight Gooden and Tom Gordon, 1%.

Others qualifying for the study, but below 1%: Fernando Valenzuela, John Burkett, Jimmy Key, Tim Belcher, Bobby Witt, Erik Hanson, Kevin Tapani, Scott Erickson, Doug Drabek, David Wells, Bob Tewksbury, Danny Darwin.

— Bill James

V. QUESTIONS ON DEFENSE

Who's Best In The Infield Zone?

A fielder's responsibility, quite simply, is to field the balls that are hit to him and turn them into outs. For most of baseball's history, there has been no accurate and reliable way to measure a player's performance in that regard. The number of balls a player fielded has always been recorded (total chances), but until recently, there hasn't been any attempt to record the number of balls a player had an *opportunity* to field. Therefore, evaluating fielders on total chances alone is an inherently limited approach—it's like counting hits without counting at-bats. That problem was never addressed until the zone rating was invented.

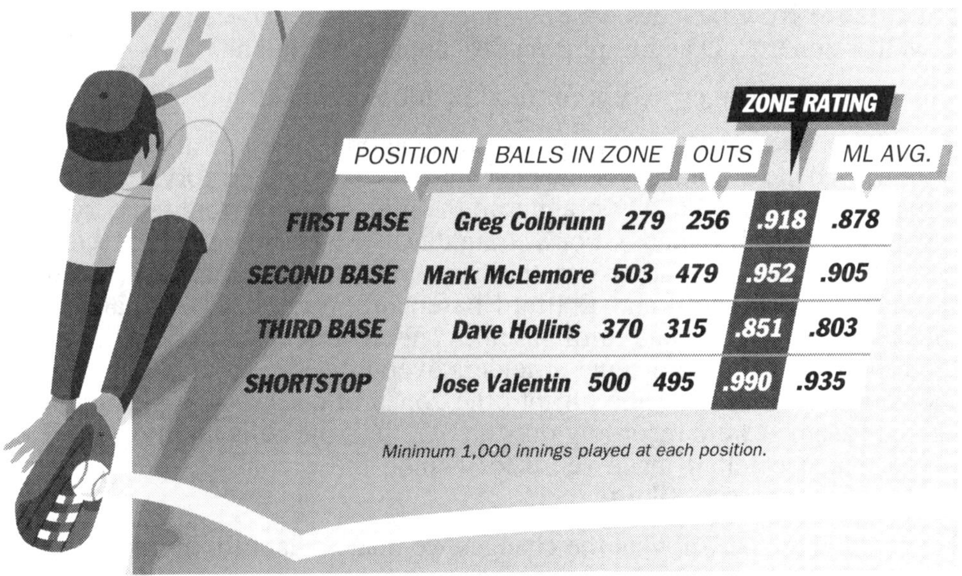

POSITION		BALLS IN ZONE	OUTS	ZONE RATING	ML AVG.
FIRST BASE	Greg Colbrunn	279	256	.918	.878
SECOND BASE	Mark McLemore	503	479	.952	.905
THIRD BASE	Dave Hollins	370	315	.851	.803
SHORTSTOP	Jose Valentin	500	495	.990	.935

Minimum 1,000 innings played at each position.

STATS reporters record the distance and direction of every batted ball, and using that data, we calculate the number of balls that were hit into each fielder's "zone"—the area he's expected to cover. The zone rating simply represents the percentage of those balls that the fielder turned into outs (including double plays started). Like any fielding statistic, zone ratings are subject to outside influences, and when we evaluate a fielder, we don't rely on zone ratings to the exclusion of all other information. Still, they've proven to be one of the best ways to measure a player's ability to cover ground.

Before we begin, we wanted to point out that we've modified our method for keeping infield zone ratings a little since the last edition of the book.

(The outfield zone rating formula remained unchanged.) What we've done is to expand the zones at first base, second base and third a little bit, making them a little more accurate in terms of where balls are actually hit and outs actually made. We also eliminated a bug which was causing the occasional flyball hit to be erroneously charged against a fielder's zone. This is how the zones were altered:

First base: Now includes all balls in 1B zone which traveled greater than 40 feet (previously was 60 feet), plus modification on flyball hits.

Second base: Now includes zone T (more of the hole between 2B and 1B) as well as zones O, P, Q, R and S, plus modification on flyball hits.

Third base: Now includes zone F (more of the hole between SS and 3B) as well as zones C, D and E, plus modification on flyball hits.

Shortstop: Unchanged except for modification on flyball hits.

If you're a bit confused by this, it's pretty simple. We use a letter-grade system to denote wedges of the field from A (foul territory by third-base/left-field stands) to M (straight up the middle) to Z (foul territory by first-base/right-field stands). For a straightaway hitter, the infielders would usually be stationed at approximately zones W (first baseman), R (second baseman), I (shortstop) and D (third baseman). Why did we expand the zones for first, second and third basemen? Well, a detailed review of each zone showed that major league infielders overall were recording outs on at least 50 percent of the balls hit into the zones in question—for example, second basemen were recording outs on over half the balls hit into zone T. Given that, we felt it made sense to include those zones as part of the fielders' area of responsibility.

To give you an idea of what the changes we made meant for individuals at each position, the average zone rating for a first baseman in 1995, using our old formula, was .829; in 1996 it was .878. At second base the average went from .889 (1995) to .905 (1996); at third base from .837 (1995) to .803 (1996) and at shortstop from .883 (1995) to .935 (1996). The numbers for the leaders at each position don't look a whole lot different than they did before, but we're confident that we're tracking infielders with more precision than ever before. Note that when we present three- or five-year ratings, those numbers are now based on the redefined zones.

Now let's take a look at last year's leaders at each infield position (minimum 1,000 innings played):

First Basemen—1996 Zone Ratings

Player, Team	Rtg
Greg Colbrunn, Fla	.918
Rafael Palmeiro, Bal	.898
Wally Joyner, SD	.895
John Mabry, StL	.893
Hal Morris, Cin	.889
Worst	
Paul Sorrento, Sea	.816

Greg Colbrunn seems to have a flair for knocking down hard smashes down the line. That isn't too surprising—after all, he came up as a catcher. Bringing up the rear was Paul Sorrento, who seemed to have a tough time making the adjustment from the Jacobs Field grass to the Kingdome's artificial turf.

Second Basemen—1996 Zone Ratings

Player, Team	Rtg
Mark McLemore, Tex	.952
Jody Reed, SD	.950
Fernando Vina, Mil	.941
Mickey Morandini, Phi	.940
Roberto Alomar, Bal	.933
Worst	
Craig Biggio, Hou	.849

Craig Biggio won his third straight Gold Glove last season—how in the world does he come out *last?* Well, in all fairness, we will readily admit that Biggio *looks* like a good second baseman. He makes all the plays, and appears to have good range. But it can be surprisingly difficult to rate a second baseman with the naked eye. A second sacker's ability to flag down grounders depends not only on his range, but on his *positioning*. Note that the list is headed by two savvy veterans, Mark McLemore and Jody Reed. We submit that Biggio was diving for balls last year that McLemore or Reed might have been in position to field cleanly. Perhaps that's one reason why the Houston pitching staff gave up more hits than any other N.L. staff except for Pittsburgh and Colorado.

Third Basemen—1996 Zone Ratings

Player, Team	Rtg
Dave Hollins, Min/Sea	.851
Robin Ventura, WSox	.842
Vinny Castilla, Col	.841
Ed Sprague, Tor	.835
Jeff Cirillo, Mil	.823
Worst	
Dean Palmer, Tex	.761

Dave Hollins? Now *that's* a surprise. Philadelphia fans will groan in recollection of his fielding woes in 1993 and '94. But in all fairness, Hollins was playing through wrist and shoulder injuries that seriously impaired his throwing. He had been a pretty decent third baseman before the injuries, and he improved by leaps and bounds last year after wrist surgery late in '95 finally corrected the problem. He had the best defensive year of his career, finishing just ahead of A.L. Gold Glover Robin Ventura in the zone ratings.

Shortstops—1996 Zone Ratings

Player, Team	Rtg
Jose Valentin, Mil	.990
David Howard, KC	.981
Greg Gagne, LA	.975
Alex Gonzalez, Tor	.964
Omar Vizquel, Cle	.962
Worst	
Mark Grudzielanek, Mon	.875

Jose Valentin—despite his sometimes-erratic arm—has as much range as any shortstop in the game, and we expect to see his name here for years to come. For the first time in three years, Cal Ripken missed the list, although his zone rating of .961 placed him just behind Gold Glover Omar Vizquel. Mark Grudzielanek got good reviews for his glovework, but it must have been easy to look good compared to the man he replaced, Wil Cordero.

Which of the above players are likely to remain in the top five next year? The following chart should give you a better idea of who's a fluke and who's for real. Here are the top three at each infield position over the last three years (minimum 1,000 innings played):

1994-96 Infield Zone Ratings Leaders

Player	Rtg	Player	Rtg
First Base		**Third Base**	
John Jaha	.923	Jeff Branson	.871
Scott Stahoviak	.916	Jeff Cirillo	.851
John Olerud	.914	Scott Brosius	.849
Second Base		**Shortstop**	
Keith Lockhart	.947	David Howard	.993
Delino DeSheilds	.934	Cal Ripken	.991
Jody Reed	.932	Gary DiSarcina	.981

Now it's time to present the winners of the 1996 STATS infield Gold Gloves. First-hand observation plays a big part in the selection process, but unlike those *other* Gold Gloves, it's not the only criterion.

We give ample weight to the zone ratings and other defensive stats, just to make sure that consistency counts as much as the eye-catching plays. Here are the winners:

First Base. Rafael Palmeiro, A.L., and Mark Grace, N.L. Grace is a long-time glove wizard who just missed the 1996 leaders list with a zone rating of .881. In the A.L., Palmeiro was among the league leaders in assists, fielding percentage and zone rating.

Second Base. Fernando Vina, A.L., and Bret Boone, N.L. Vina has great range and one of the best double-play pivots in the game, so we don't mind overlooking his errors. In the N.L., Boone has everything but flash, just like Jody Reed, who got our vote last year.

Third Base. Robin Ventuta, A.L., and Ken Caminiti, N.L. Ventura has been one of the best-fielding third basemen of the 1990s, and he improved his one weak point—too many careless errors—last year. Caminiti's glove finally received national recognition the last couple of years, although his heavy hitting and determination to play through injuries had a lot to do with him winning his second consecutive Gold Glove. Intestinal fortitude aside, we think his play afield merited the award.

Shortstop. Omar Vizquel, A.L., and Greg Gagne, N.L. There were a number of worthy candidates at shortstop, but both Vizquel and Gagne are widely admired for their all-around work at the position, and both ranked in the top five in zone rating last year.

—Mat Olkin

A more complete listing for this category can be found on page 300.

Who Are the Prime Pivot Men?

How important is it to have a second baseman who can turn the double play? The 1996 Boston Red Sox provided a good illustration. When they opened the season, their second baseman was Wil Cordero, a converted shortstop who was known for his throwing problems and had very limited experience at the keystone. Through May 20th, Cordero was hitting .287 and was on a pace to drive in 111 runs, but he'd turned only 18 double plays. The Red Sox were seven games under .500 and had a team ERA of 5.17. On that evening, Cordero tried to turn two, but neglected to clear out of the way after making the pivot. The baserunner slid into him and broke his leg, and he didn't play much for the rest of the year.

A couple weeks later, the Red Sox picked up Jeff Frye to play second base. Frye was their regular the rest of the way, and turned 70 double plays in 100 games. He didn't hit any better than Cordero had, but after Frye took over at second base, the Red Sox went 63-43 and their team ERA dropped by over one-third of a run.

If you need some more proof of the DP's importance, take a look at the chart below. We've listed last year's top 10 second basemen in double plays per opportunity, or "Pivot Percentage." (An "opportunity" is any situation where the double play is in order, the ball is hit to another infielder and the second baseman takes the throw.) You'll notice that the second basemen from five of the six division-winning teams make the list:

Best Pivot Men—1996

Player, Team	DP	Opp	Pct
Fernando Vina, Mil	59	83	71.1
Jose Vizcaino, Mets/Cle	56	81	69.1
Quilvio Veras, Fla	33	50	66.0
Roberto Alomar, Bal	56	89	62.9
Jody Reed, SD	42	67	62.7
Luis Alicea, StL	48	77	62.3
Eric Young, Col	60	97	61.9
Mariano Duncan, Yanks	33	55	60.0
Mark McLemore, Tex	59	99	59.6
Joey Cora, Sea	54	91	59.3

(minimum 50 opportunities)

In case you were wondering, Jeff Frye's Pivot Percentage was a respectable 56.3, while Wil Cordero's was only 52.0—the second-worst percentage in the A.L. for any second baseman with at least 25 opportunities.

It's no surprise to find Fernando Vina atop this list—he topped the charts in '95 as well. As anyone who's witnessed Vina's speedy pivot will agree, his skill around the bag is a major reason that the Brewers have turned the most double plays of any major league team over the last two years.

Here are baseball's best pivot men over the last six seasons:

Best Pivot Men—1991-1996

Player, Team	DP	Opp	Pct
Robby Thompson	164	249	65.9
Bret Boone	179	272	65.8
Luis Alicea	183	286	64.0
Carlos Garcia	175	278	62.9
Joey Cora	178	283	62.9
Jody Reed	231	371	62.3
Mark McLemore	153	241	62.2

(minimum 210 opportunities)

Again, we see how winners follow these guys around. Five of these seven second basemen have seen the postseason at least once in the last two seasons; Alicea made it both times, with two different teams.

Vina would top this list too, but he's only played regularly for a year and a half, so he comes up short of qualifying. Still, his career percentage is currently 75.6, so if he keeps up his pace, he figures to lock up the top spot on the career list as soon as he logs enough time to qualify.

—Mat Olkin

A more complete listing for this category can be found on page 302.

Which Catchers Catch Thieves?

One of the most important assets for a catcher to possess is the ability to shut down enemy basestealers. By gunning down an opponent on the basepaths, a backstop not only erases the threat of a potential run, but he also hurts the scoring chances of *every other* player who comes to bat in that same inning. Countless rallies have been squelched by the efforts of strong-armed catchers who were able to punish overzealous thieves.

Which catchers proved to be the most lethal to opposing running games? Let's take a look at last season's best- and worst-throwing catchers:

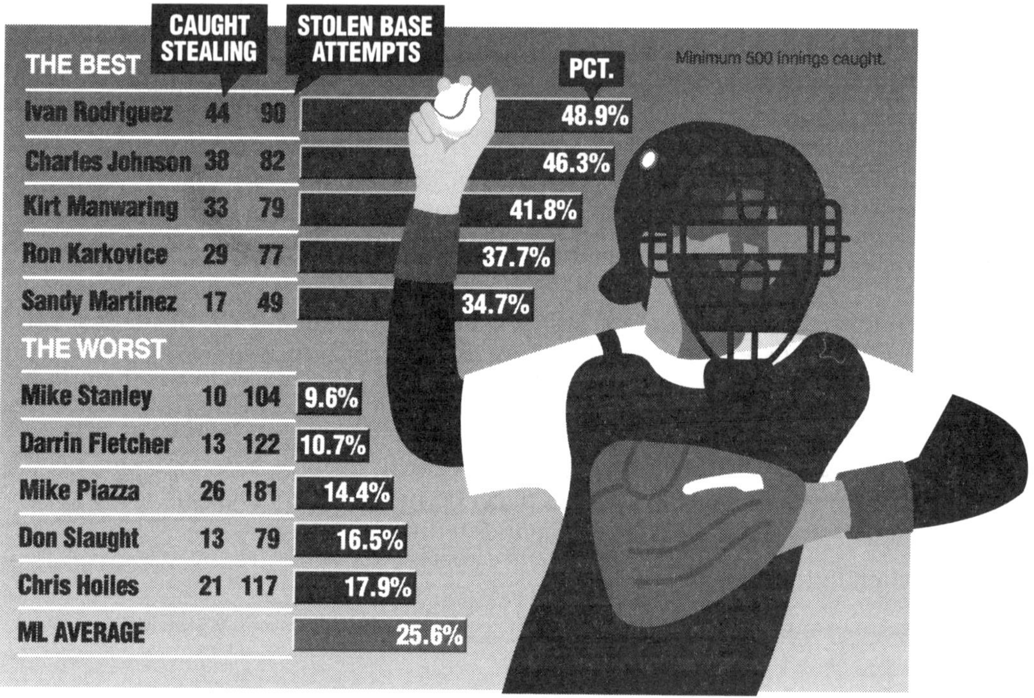

Minimum 500 innings caught.

	CAUGHT STEALING	STOLEN BASE ATTEMPTS	PCT.
THE BEST			
Ivan Rodriguez	44	90	48.9%
Charles Johnson	38	82	46.3%
Kirt Manwaring	33	79	41.8%
Ron Karkovice	29	77	37.7%
Sandy Martinez	17	49	34.7%
THE WORST			
Mike Stanley	10	104	9.6%
Darrin Fletcher	13	122	10.7%
Mike Piazza	26	181	14.4%
Don Slaught	13	79	16.5%
Chris Hoiles	21	117	17.9%
ML AVERAGE			25.6%

In last year's *Scoreboard*, we focused on how the Rangers' Ivan Rodriguez returned to the top of the charts after a two-year absence, as his teammates started to focus more of their attention on holding baserunners. Obviously, that strategy has continued to pay off, as "Pudge" once again nabbed the top spot on our leader board. Interestingly enough, in 1996 we *also* focused on Charlie O'Brien's terrible throwing performance during the '95 season (8-for-71, 10.1 percent). O'Brien has rebounded strongly since he signed with Toronto—but most of the improvement is probably due to the Blue Jays staff; O'Brien's 33.3 percent CS rate (20-for-60) wasn't too far behind that of teammate Sandy Martinez, who placed fifth in 1996.

Which catcher was the league's best "turnstile"? That dubious honor would have to go to Mike Stanley of the Boston Red Sox. Stanley threw out just 10 of 104 runners, or 9.6 percent—the lowest figure in the majors. Stanley has had decent success against the running game over most of his career, but his numbers have plummeted in the last two seasons. As long as he's hitting 24 homers and racking up an OBP of .383 (as he did last season), however, we're sure the Red Sox or some other team will be willing to put up with his defensive shortcomings.

Both Rodriguez and Charles Johnson, owners of the top two throwing arms behind the plate in '96, won Gold Gloves for their efforts. While the award was Johnson's second in a row, the Gold Glove was Pudge's fifth straight. Some observers claimed that Rodriguez shouldn't have received the award, based on his shaky handling of the Texas pitching staff last season. There's definitely some validity to this point: over the last two years, Rangers' hurlers have compiled higher ERAs with Rodriguez catching than with other receivers behind the plate.

Gold Gloves seem to be awarded in the same manner as All-Star roster spots—once a player develops a strong reputation and becomes entrenched at his position, it becomes very tough to unseat him. It's simply more common to win a string of three or four Gold Gloves in a row than it is to pass the torch off to another player after capturing just a single award. But certainly Rodriguez' outstanding throwing arm makes the Texas backstop a dangerous defensive weapon—and worthy of perennial Gold Glove recognition.

—Kevin Fullam

A more complete listing for this category can be found on page 303.

Which Outfielders Intimidate Enemy Runners?

A major argument against the sole use of assist totals to rate outfielders' arms is the fact that not every player gets the same number of throwing opportunities. "If everyone in the league knows Raul Mondesi has a rocket for an arm, who's going to run on him?"—or so the debate goes. To answer this puzzling question, we compiled a list of outfielders who can shut down enemy runners *without* gunning them down on the basepaths, outfielders whose mere presence and reputation make opponents think twice about attempting to take that extra base. Historically, the voting media has always been more than willing to overlook a player's lack of range if he possesses a top-caliber throwing arm and can intimidate opponents on the basepaths. After all, Jay Buhner didn't win a Gold Glove last season for running down gappers in the Kingdome.

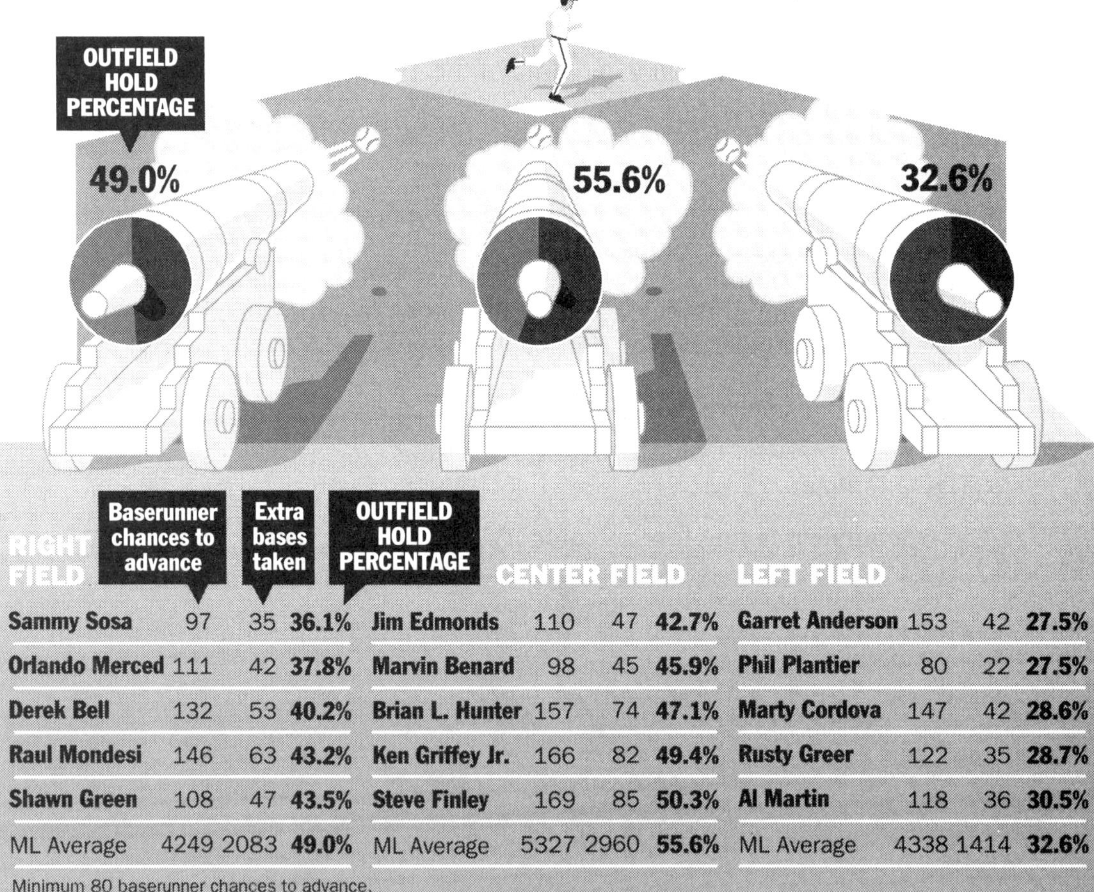

RIGHT FIELD	Baserunner chances to advance	Extra bases taken	OUTFIELD HOLD PERCENTAGE
Sammy Sosa	97	35	**36.1%**
Orlando Merced	111	42	**37.8%**
Derek Bell	132	53	**40.2%**
Raul Mondesi	146	63	**43.2%**
Shawn Green	108	47	**43.5%**
ML Average	4249	2083	**49.0%**

CENTER FIELD	Baserunner chances to advance	Extra bases taken	OUTFIELD HOLD PERCENTAGE
Jim Edmonds	110	47	**42.7%**
Marvin Benard	98	45	**45.9%**
Brian L. Hunter	157	74	**47.1%**
Ken Griffey Jr.	166	82	**49.4%**
Steve Finley	169	85	**50.3%**
ML Average	5327	2960	**55.6%**

LEFT FIELD	Baserunner chances to advance	Extra bases taken	OUTFIELD HOLD PERCENTAGE
Garret Anderson	153	42	**27.5%**
Phil Plantier	80	22	**27.5%**
Marty Cordova	147	42	**28.6%**
Rusty Greer	122	35	**28.7%**
Al Martin	118	36	**30.5%**
ML Average	4338	1414	**32.6%**

Minimum 80 baserunner chances to advance.

In the preceding chart, we highlight the players with the best "outfield hold percentages" at each position. A hold is credited whenever a runner fails to take an extra base on a hit to that particular outfielder. For example, if a batter doubles down the left field line with a runner on first, the left fielder is given a hold if the runner stops at third base. Typically, left fielders have the best hold percentages and center fielders have the worst ones, since there's an inverse relationship between the average distance an outfielder must throw the ball and his ability to hold baserunners. The chart lists the top five at each outfield position last year.

Sammy Sosa's cannon may be the most impressive in the game. Not only did he register 25 percent more holds than the average outfielder at his position, but he also eliminated many of the runners who *did* try to test his arm. Few dared to run on Sosa last season, but he made the most of his opportunities, as you can see by the following table:

Outfield Assist Leaders—1996

Left Field		Center Field		Right Field	
Bernard Gilkey, Mets	18	Rich Becker, Min	18	Manny Ramirez, Cle	19
Tony Phillips, WSox	13	Kenny Lofton, Cle	13	Derek Bell, Hou	16
Albert Belle, Cle	11	Brian L. Hunter, Hou	11	Sammy Sosa, Cubs	15

With all of Cleveland's regular outfielders ranking in the top three in outfield assists at their positions, we're surprised *any* of their opponents dared to take an extra base. The trio combined to erase 43 runners off the basepaths last season, tying the Indians for the top spot in the American League. By contrast, the San Diego Padres, led by pea-shooting Tony Gwynn (two assists in RF) and Rickey Henderson (three assists in LF) racked up the fewest total of "baserunner kills" in the majors, gunning down just 15 men all season. Interestingly enough, *none* of the high-ranking Indians made our outfield hold percentage leader board. Only Derek Bell, Brian L. Hunter, and Sammy Sosa were able to nab spots on both charts.

Since outfield hold percentage is based as much on reputation as on anything else, we decided to track the players who rated the highest in this category over the past three seasons to see if any significant differences occurred. Take a look:

Outfield Hold Percentage—1994-96

Left Field	Pct	Center Field	Pct	Right Field	Pct
Barry Bonds	29.2	Marquis Grissom	46.3	Orlando Merced	38.1
Garret Anderson	29.2	Brian L. Hunter	47.3	Mark Whiten	38.9
Derrick May	30.1	Brett Butler	47.4	Raul Mondesi	43.2
Trailer		**Trailer**		**Trailer**	
Mike Greenwell	41.9	Rich Becker	62.2	Dante Bichette	57.5

(Minimum 200 baserunner chances to advance)

Not only did Dante Bichette trail the three-year RF hold percentage board for the second straight season, but he also served up just four assists in 1996—the lowest total in the majors for right fielders with at least 1,000 innings played. However, it was a shock to see Minnesota center fielder Rich Becker on this list. Becker led all center fielders in assists last season with 18, but he obviously hasn't commanded the respect of enemy baserunners just yet. After his performance last season, *that* should definitely change—or Twins opponents will suffer the consequences.

—Kevin Fullam

A more complete listing for this category can be found on page 304.

Which Players Turn the Outfield into a "No Fly" Zone?

Fielding percentage marks have always been a very unreliable method of rating outfielders' defensive skills. Since players usually don't commit errors on balls they can't reach, baseball fans are left with data proclaiming that Kenny Lofton doesn't hold a candle to Brady Anderson—which only serves to erode people's faith in statistics. You can put Cecil Fielder in center field and he may register a 1.000 fielding percentage, but he'll probably only snare the 10 fly balls a season that are hit directly to him.

As an alternative method of measuring an outfielder's defensive contributions, zone ratings help identify those players who cover the most ground—and reel in those potential extra-base gappers. The ratings measure the number of outs recorded by a fielder in relation to the number of balls that are hit into his defensive area. In addition, they also credit players for reaching balls hit *outside* of their particular areas. Here are last season's zone-rating leaders at each outfield spot (minimum 1,000 innings), starting in left:

Left Field—1996 Zone Ratings

Player, Team	Zone Rating
Rusty Greer, Tex	.868
Tony Phillips, WSox	.856
Garret Anderson, Cal	.840
Bernard Gilkey, Mets	.831
Marty Cordova, Min	.828
MLB Average	.812
Trailer	
Al Martin, Pit	.715

Rusty Greer posted only mediocre numbers in right field in 1995, but as you can see, he quickly acclimated himself to left. Not only did Greer step it up in the field, but he also posted monster numbers at the plate, increasing his batting and slugging averages by 61 and 106 points, respectively. However, for a truly amazing performance, we have to turn to Pittsburgh's Al Martin, who not only compiled the lowest zone rating in '96, but also finished 60 points behind the *second-lowest* player on the list, Greg Vaughn (.775). Could Martin's lack of range have something to do with the rumor that the Pirates will go with four regulars rotating in the outfield next season? Just a hunch. . .

Center Field—1996 Zone Ratings

Player, Team	Zone Rating
Steve Finley, SD	.858
Lance Johnson, Mets	.855
Kenny Lofton, Cle	.846
Brian McRae, Cubs	.842
Brian L. Hunter, Hou	.840
MLB Average	.816
Trailer	
Marquis Grissom, Atl	.766

After finishing third on this list a year ago, Steve Finley climbed to the top of the charts with his outstanding performance in the field. When combined with Rickey Henderson in left and Tony Gwynn in right, both of whom would have made our leader boards had they played enough innings, there's no question that the Padres' outfielders were the best in the majors at tracking down opponents' flies. However, there *is* the matter of their throwing arms—but that's discussed in a separate essay (p. 214).

Right Field—1996 Zone Ratings

Player, Team	Zone Rating
Brian Jordan, StL	.849
Paul O'Neill, Yanks	.849
Sammy Sosa, Cubs	.849
Manny Ramirez, Cle	.831
Tim Salmon, Cal	.821
MLB Average	.813
Trailer	
Dante Bichette, Col	.711

By the smallest of margins, Cardinals outfielder Brian Jordan edged out both Paul O'Neill and Sammy Sosa in last season's right field "zone wars." While he's not listed on the board, Montreal's Moises Alou deserves a special mention for his fielding performance last season. Alou made a complete recovery from the rotator cuff injuries he suffered in '95, but because he split his time between all three outfield positions, he couldn't garner quite enough innings at the right field slot to place on the list. However, Alou's sparkling .866 zone rating would have topped the field had he been eligible.

To continue a longtime STATS tradition, we'll award STATS Gold Gloves to the top two fielders at each outfield position. The awards are based on a combination of zone ratings, throwing arms and general observation. Drum roll, please:

Left Field: Tony Phillips, A.L., and Bernard Gilkey, N.L. After deferring to Garret Anderson last season, Phillips made a defensive comeback at age 37 to snare his second career STATS Gold Glove. He placed second among left fielders in zone rating *and* assists—a deadly combination. Always a capable glove man, Gilkey recorded 18 assists from LF last season—too impressive a figure not to recognize.

Center Field: Kenny Lofton, A.L., and Steve Finley, N.L. Lofton has been perennially recognized as one of the game's best center fielders, whereas Finley finally nabbed his first STATS Gold Glove after eight long seasons in the majors. Not only did Finley explode offensively with the bat last year (slamming a career-high 30 home runs), but he also shined in the field, posting the top center field zone rating in the majors.

Right Field: Paul O'Neill, A.L., and Sammy Sosa, N.L. Picking this year's winners was difficult, since the vast majority of top right fielders all reside in the N.L. O'Neill, however, earned the award on the basis of his work in helping solidify the Yankees' outfield defense for their championship run. Sosa, whose exploits have been documented elsewhere, can not only run down the gappers (he was third in zone rating) but also strike with his powerful throwing arm, as evidenced by his 15 assists and top-ranked hold percentage.

—Kevin Fullam

A more complete listing for this category can be found on page 305.

Which Fielders Have the Best "Defensive Batting Average"?

The *Scoreboard* has popularized several tools for identifying the best fielders, including zone ratings, pivot ratings and outfield arm ratings. "Defensive batting average" is an attempt to use those tools, along with that old reliable, fielding average, to create one easy-to-understand number that will help identify the top fielders at each infield and outfield position. The formulas are complex, but not the end product, a rating system in which—just like batting average—.300 is good and .200 very bad. That's something every baseball fan can understand.

Because the responsibilities of each infield and outfield position are different, we weigh the various categories differently at each position:

Pos	Weighting
1B	Zone Rating 75%, Fielding Pct. 25%
2B	Zone Rating 60%, Fielding Pct. 15%, Pivot Rating 25%
3B	Zone Rating 60%, Fielding Pct. 40%
SS	Zone Rating 80%, Fielding Pct. 20%
LF	Zone Rating 65%, Fielding Pct. 15%, OF Arm 20%
CF	Zone Rating 55%, Fielding Pct. 15%, OF Arm 30%
RF	Zone Rating 50%, Fielding Pct. 15%, OF Arm 35%

Let's look at the best five, and single worst, players at each position in DBA last year. Infielders need to have played 900 innings at a position to qualify, outfielders 800 innings:

First Base	Zone	FPct	DBA
Scott Stahoviak, Min	.314	.293	.309
Greg Colbrunn, Fla	.308	.301	.306
Wally Joyner, SD	.290	.320	.298
Rafael Palmeiro, Bal	.292	.295	.293
Mark Grace, Cubs	.279	.317	.289
Worst			
Paul Sorrento, Sea	.228	.248	.233

In his first full season in the big leagues, Scott Stahoviak of the Twins performed very well with the bat. . . and quite well with the glove, also. A former third baseman, he displayed fine range at his new position, as shown by these numbers, which are weighted heavily by zone ratings. The big news at first base is that Frank Thomas, who's worked hard on his defense, finally escaped last place after three straight years of bringing up the bottom in DBA. Paul Sorrento of the Mariners will attempt to escape the cellar next year.

Second Base	Zone	FPct	Pivot	DBA
Fernando Vina, Mil	.309	.275	.327	.309
Jody Reed, SD	.317	.307	.290	.309
Mark McLemore, Tex	.318	.298	.276	.305
Randy Velarde, Cal	.325	.286	.263	.304
Roberto Alomar, Bal	.302	.299	.291	.299
Worst				
Craig Biggio, Hou	.233	.309	.242	.247

Fernando Vina of the Brewers has developed into a fine defensive second baseman; he has good range, and he's slick on the pivot as well. Vina tied for the top spot with Jody Reed of the Padres, another fine glove man. We were a little surprised to find Gold Glove second sacker Craig Biggio in last place, but the numbers say fielding percentage is the only category he excels in. On the other hand, American League Gold Glove winner Roberto Alomar, who's often ranked well down the list in our ratings, finished in the top five in 1996.

Third Base	Zone	FPct	DBA
Scott Brosius, Oak	.337	.309	.326
Robin Ventura, WSox	.306	.319	.312
Travis Fryman, Det	.283	.331	.302
Wade Boggs, Yanks	.287	.320	.300
Dave Hollins, Min/Sea	.313	.278	.299
Worst			
Dean Palmer, Tex	.249	.273	.259

Robin Ventura and Wade Boggs always rank highly at third base, but the top spot last year—and by a good margin—went to Scott Brosius of the A's. Dean Palmer of the Rangers is a strong hitter, but he's erratic in the field, and our numbers show him as the worst full-time performer at his position last year.

Shortstop	Zone	FPct	DBA
David Howard, KC	.321	.311	.319
Jose Valentin, Mil	.330	.238	.312
Edgar Renteria, Fla	.312	.304	.310
Greg Gagne, LA	.317	.273	.308
Cal Ripken, Bal	.303	.307	.304
Worst			
Mark Grudzielanek, Mon	.225	.259	.232

You think David Howard of the Royals, a .227 lifetime hitter, gets playing time because of his *bat*? Not exactly. . . Howard is a top defensive shortstop, as these figures indicate. Neither Gold Glove winner at shortstop made the top five—Omar Vizquel of the Indians just missed with a .300 mark, but Barry Larkin of the Reds was well down the list with a .256 mark.

Left Field	Zone	FPct	OFArm	DBA
Rusty Greer, Tex	.321	.300	.303	.315
Rickey Henderson, SD	.319	.304	.239	.300
Tony Phillips, WSox	.312	.291	.269	.300
Garret Anderson, Cal	.298	.281	.311	.298
Marty Cordova, Min	.289	.322	.300	.296
Worst				
Al Martin, Pit	.197	.239	.290	.222

Rusty Greer of the Rangers is a solid .300 hitter on offense, and he's a solid ".300 fielder" as well—good in every category. Better-than-average range is essential to be a good left fielder, and all the top guys, including Greer, have it. Al Martin of the Pirates *doesn't* have good range, and that's why he's on the bottom of the list.

Center Field	Zone	FPct	OFArm	DBA
Jim Edmonds, Cal	.285	.311	.347	.307
Steve Finley, SD	.307	.269	.302	.300
Darren Lewis, WSox	.302	.290	.297	.299
Ken Griffey Jr, Sea	.286	.290	.316	.296
Ernie Young, Oak	.293	.313	.273	.290
Worst				
Ricky Otero, Phi	.232	.275	.232	.238

Jim Edmonds of the Angels hasn't won a Gold Glove yet, but he's been the top center fielder in DBA two straight years. . . perhaps his day will come soon. Gold Glovers Steve Finley and Ken Griffey Jr. both cracked the top five—an impressive showing for Griffey, who, like Roberto Alomar, has often fared poorly in our ratings. *Not* doing very well in the ratings was Gold Glover Marquis Grissom, whose DBA was a so-so .269.

Right Field	Zone	FPct	OFArm	DBA
Paul O'Neill, Yanks	.305	.325	.294	.304
Sammy Sosa, Cubs	.305	.253	.322	.303
Moises Alou, Mon	.318	.315	.266	.300
Orlando Merced, Pit	.285	.301	.318	.299
Tony Gwynn, SD	.313	.303	.276	.299
Worst				
Dante Bichette, Col	.203	.251	.272	.234

Paul O'Neill of the Yankees has always been a fine glove man, and he took the top spot in DBA in last year's RF rankings. Sammy Sosa and Orlando Merced, who both made the top five in 1995, repeated in '96. As for Dante Bichette, we think he's overrated as a hitter *and* a fielder.

— Don Zminda

A more complete listing for this category can be found on page 307.

Who Led the League in Fumbles?

In our evaluation of fielders, a player's ability to avoid errors is important, but not *overly* important. A perfect example is the case of Ken Caminiti, last season's National League MVP and a Gold Glove winner in each of the last two years. In 1995, Caminiti led major league third basemen in errors with 27; in '96, only Sean Berry and Jeff Kent had more miscues at the hot corner than Caminiti's 20. Yet Caminiti took home the Gold Glove in both seasons simply because the voters felt his other assets more than made up for the errors.

We'll keep that in mind as we do our annual survey of the players with "Stone Hands" (many errors) and "Soft Hands" (few errors). The chart shows the positional leaders in each category, in terms of most and fewest games per error. Let's run down the positions:

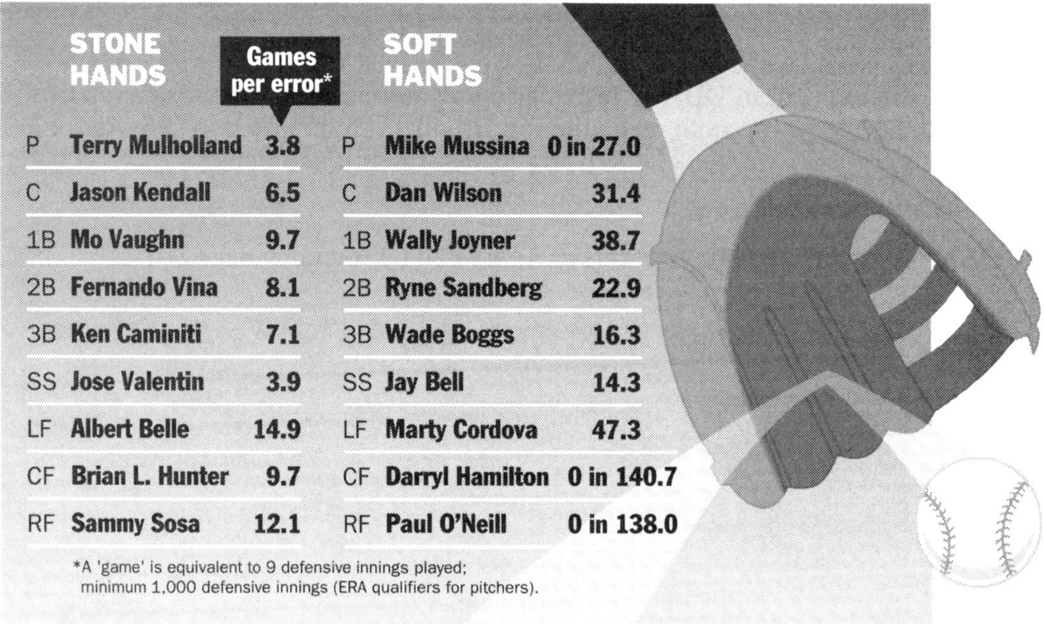

	STONE HANDS	Games per error*		SOFT HANDS	
P	Terry Mulholland	3.8	P	Mike Mussina	0 in 27.0
C	Jason Kendall	6.5	C	Dan Wilson	31.4
1B	Mo Vaughn	9.7	1B	Wally Joyner	38.7
2B	Fernando Vina	8.1	2B	Ryne Sandberg	22.9
3B	Ken Caminiti	7.1	3B	Wade Boggs	16.3
SS	Jose Valentin	3.9	SS	Jay Bell	14.3
LF	Albert Belle	14.9	LF	Marty Cordova	47.3
CF	Brian L. Hunter	9.7	CF	Darryl Hamilton	0 in 140.7
RF	Sammy Sosa	12.1	RF	Paul O'Neill	0 in 138.0

*A 'game' is equivalent to 9 defensive innings played; minimum 1,000 defensive innings (ERA qualifiers for pitchers).

Pitcher. Mike Mussina of the Orioles has more going for him than just his outstanding pitching ability. A deft, mobile fielder, he wound up winning his first Gold Glove last year. The National League Gold Glove winner, Greg Maddux, committed only one error in 245 innings last year, but that's not the only reason why he won the award. In 1994, Maddux committed four errors and had a subpar .934 fielding average, yet he *still* took home a Gold Glove.

Catcher. If you're wondering why Jason Kendall of the Pirates didn't win the National League Rookie of the Year award despite hitting .300, the answer is poor defense. Kendall threw out only 19 percent of opposing baserunners last year, and he also committed 18 errors. No other catcher in the big leagues committed more than 11. On the other hand, the "Soft Hands" guy, Dan Wilson, is solid all-around and a potential Gold Glove winner someday.

First Base. Wally Joyner of the Padres has long been one of the best defensive players at first base, even though he's never won a Gold Glove. Just as good, if not better, is the runner-up for the Soft Hands position, Mark Grace of the Cubs. The Stone Hands guy at first base, Mo Vaughn, gives it his best shot, but his stiff hands often betray him. Fortunately he can hit a little.

Second Base. Coming back after more than a year away from the game, Ryne Sandberg showed last year that he hadn't lost much—either on offense or defense. His counterpart on the Stone Hands team, Fernando Vina, is an outstanding fielder overall with excellent range and superior ability on the double play (see the pivot rating essay on p. 210). All he needs to do is cut down on his errors a little.

Third Base. We've discussed Caminiti already; despite the errors, he's one of the best in the business. On the Soft Hands side, the top three men were Wade Boggs (slipping a little, but still solid), Travis Fryman (outstanding in all areas) and Robin Ventura (a four-time Gold Glove winner).

Shortstop. Jay Bell, now with the Royals, led all shortstops with an average of 14.3 games per error last year. The number-three man, David Howard (11.2) is also a Royal, and probably a better glove man than Bell. . . but, of course, he can't hit like Jay can. In between Bell and Howard was Ozzie Guillen of the White Sox (12.1 games per error), who remains surehanded even though he's lost some range. The Stone Hands representative is Jose Valentin of the Brewers, part of a Stone Hands DP combo with Fernando Vina. Like Vina, Valentin has great range, but 37 errors is simply too many, and we can't rate him as highly as we do Vina.

Left Field. Marty Cordova of the Twins is a solid ballplayer both offensively and defensively. His top ranking at this position is one more sign of what an effective player he is. Albert Belle is not *that* bad in left field, but he was the only left fielder in baseball to reach double figures in errors last year. No one else had more than seven, so we'd have to say that Albert is close to being a defensive liability.

Center Field. Darryl Hamilton set a record by playing errorless ball last year, but he's *not* that good a center fielder; we prefer Marquis Grissom (one error in 1,380 innings). The Stone Hands man, Brian L. Hunter, committed 12 errors last year, and we'd say that's a problem. The Astros thought so, too, and Hunter's miscues were one reason the 'Stros were willing to deal him to the Tigers after the season.

Right Field. One of the memorable moments of the 1996 season was Paul O'Neill, on a bad hamstring, chasing down Luis Polonia's liner in the gap to preserve the Yankees' 1-0 victory in Game 5 of the World Series. He's an excellent all-around right fielder. So is the Stone Hands representative, Sammy Sosa; yes, he makes some dumb mistakes, but we think his range and awesome arm more than compensate for that.

— Don Zminda

A more complete listing for this category can be found on page 309.

Which Players Cleaned Up at the Awards Banquet?

Flip to the back of any baseball reference book, and you're likely to find a list of past MVPs and Cy Young Award winners. For the last eight years, we've been giving out our *own* awards, and this is the part of the book where you'll find the yearly recipients. Our unique STATS awards include the esteemed FlatBat (best bunter), the coveted Slidin' Billy Trophy (best leadoff man), and the control artist's prize, the Red Barrett Trophy (for the fewest pitches in a nine-inning game). We also award STATS Gold Gloves; the concept is hardly original, but the approach—namely, rewarding consistent excellence over flashiness—certainly is. Here are yesteryear's winners:

STATS FlatBat

The STATS FlatBat goes to the game's best bunter. To get the nod, a player must be able to bunt for a base hit as well as a sacrifice, and he must do both often and effectively. Here are the annual winners:

1989	Brett Butler	1993	Omar Vizquel
1990	Brett Butler	1994	Kenny Lofton
1991	Steve Finley	1995	Otis Nixon
1992	Brett Butler	1996	Kenny Lofton

Can you imagine playing third base when Kenny Lofton is up to bat? He's always a threat to lay one down, but when he takes a full cut, he hits the ball *hard*—after all, he reached the seats 14 times last year. Before you creep in on the grass against him, make sure your health insurance is all paid up.

Slidin' Billy Trophy

Nineteenth-century star Slidin' Billy Hamilton was perhaps the consummate leadoff hitter: he hit for a terrific average, he drew walks, he stole bases, and above all else, he scored tons of runs. In his honor, the Slidin' Billy Trophy goes to the top leadoff hitter each season. Perhaps no one will ever fulfill the responsibilities of a leadoff man as perfectly as Hamilton did; the one who comes the closest each season gets the prize. Here are the annual winners:

1989	Rickey Henderson	1993	Lenny Dykstra
1990	Rickey Henderson	1994	Kenny Lofton
1991	Paul Molitor	1995	Chuck Knoblauch
1992	Brady Anderson	1996	Chuck Knoblauch

Brady Anderson's 50 home runs are tough to beat, but Knoblauch had quite a year himself, actually *improving* on his award-winning 1995 campaign. With Anderson, Knoblauch and Kenny Lofton in the league, there figures to be stiff competition for this award for years to come.

Hottest Heaters

It doesn't take a genius to know that the best way to get to strike three is with sheer heat. The winner of each year's "Hottest Heaters" award is the pitcher with the highest strikeout rate:

Year	Pitcher	K/9	Year	Pitcher	K/9
1989	Rob Dibble	12.8	1993	Duane Ward	12.2
1990	Rob Dibble	12.5	1994	Bobby Ayala	12.1
1991	Rob Dibble	13.6	1995	Roberto Hernandez	12.7
1992	Rob Dibble	14.1	1996	Randy Johnson	12.5

How's *that* for heat? Last year, Randy Johnson was the first starting pitcher to win in the award's eight-year history (though he did pitch out of the bullpen a bit in 1996). We can't wait to see what he can do if he stays healthy this year.

Red Barrett Trophy

In 1944, Red Barrett threw a complete game using only 58 pitches. We can't even imagine that happening today! The pitcher who uses the fewest pitches in a nine-inning game each season receives the Red Barrett Trophy as a testament to his efficiency:

Year	Pitcher	#Pitches	Year	Pitcher	#Pitches
1989	Frank Viola	85	1993	Tom Glavine	79
1990	Bob Tewksbury	76	1994	Bobby Munoz	80
1991	Chris Bosio	82	1995	Greg Maddux	88
1992	John Smiley	80	1996	Bob Wolcott	79

Last year's surprise winner was Bob Wolcott, who five-hit the A's with only 79 pitches on July 15. Alas, it was one of the few highlights in an otherwise dismal season. His ERA for the year was 5.73, and he didn't throw another complete game all season.

STATS Gold Gloves

Traditionally, defense has been the most poorly-understood aspect of baseball. We've been doing our best to correct that, though, by awarding STATS Gold Gloves. We don't automatically award them to the most exciting performers or the guys with the best reputations—we're more concerned with finding the players who cover their positions with the greatest efficiency. The winners:

First Base

Year	American	National	Year	American	National
1989	Don Mattingly	Will Clark	1993	Don Mattingly	Mark Grace
1990	Mark McGwire	Sid Bream	1994	Don Mattingly	Jeff Bagwell
1991	Don Mattingly	Mark Grace	1995	Wally Joyner	Jeff Bagwell
1992	Wally Joyner	Mark Grace	1996	Rafael Palmeiro	Mark Grace

Wally Joyner moved to the National League last year, where he was edged out by Mark Grace. Joyner's absence and Mattingly's retirement left a void in the American League, and Rafael Palmeiro seized the moment.

Second Base

Year	American	National	Year	American	National
1989	Harold Reynolds	Ryne Sandberg	1993	Harold Reynolds	Robby Thompson
1990	Billy Ripken	Ryne Sandberg	1994	Jody Reed	Mickey Morandini
1991	Mike Gallego	Ryne Sandberg	1995	Carlos Baerga	Jody Reed
1992	Carlos Baerga	Ryne Sandberg	1996	Fernando Vina	Bret Boone

In coming years, Vina and Boone should get their due. In our eyes, their performance already places them at the top of the heap.

Third Base

Year	American	National	Year	American	National
1989	Gary Gaetti	Tim Wallach	1993	Robin Ventura	Matt Williams
1990	Gary Gaetti	Charlie Hayes	1994	Wade Boggs	Matt Williams
1991	Wade Boggs	Steve Buechele	1995	Travis Fryman	Charlie Hayes
1992	Robin Ventura	Terry Pendleton	1996	Robin Ventura	Ken Caminiti

Unlike many other well-regarded fielders, Ken Caminiti's defense actually stands up to close scutiny. He makes all the plays, torn rotator cuff or not. Travis Fryman has developed into an exceptional third baseman, but this year we gave the nod to Robin Ventura.

Shortstop

Year	American	National	Year	American	National
1989	Ozzie Guillen	Ozzie Smith	1993	Ozzie Guillen	Ozzie Smith
1990	Ozzie Guillen	Ozzie Smith	1994	Gary DiSarcina	Barry Larkin
1991	Cal Ripken	Ozzie Smith	1995	Gary DiSarcina	Kevin Stocker
1992	Cal Ripken	Ozzie Smith	1996	Omar Vizquel	Greg Gagne

Ozzie Smith's retirement leaves an obvious void in the National League. Who will fill it? Some say Rey Ordonez, but for now, our pick is Greg Gagne. Over in the American League, Omar Vizquel re-created his 1995 postseason wizardry on a nightly basis.

Left Field

Year	American	National	Year	American	National
1989	Rickey Henderson	Barry Bonds	1993	Greg Vaughn	Barry Bonds
1990	Rickey Henderson	Barry Bonds	1994	Tony Phillips	Moises Alou
1991	Dan Gladden	Bernard Gilkey	1995	Garret Anderson	Luis Gonzalez
1992	Greg Vaughn	Barry Bonds	1996	Tony Phillips	Bernard Gilkey

Ageless wonder Tony Phillips settled down in one position—left field—last year and turned in an award-winning performance. But with Albert Belle arriving in Chicago this year, the versatile Phillips will probably be shifted to another spot. Bernard Gilkey's hitting overshadowed his fielding, but his glove was an asset as well.

Center Field

Year	American	National	Year	American	National
1989	Devon White	Eric Davis	1993	Kenny Lofton	Darren Lewis
1990	Gary Pettis	Lenny Dykstra	1994	Devon White	Marquis Grissom
1991	Devon White	Brett Butler	1995	Jim Edmonds	Marquis Grissom
1992	Devon White	Darrin Jackson	1996	Kenny Lofton	Steve Finley

In the pastures of center field, there's no greater asset than raw speed, and Kenny Lofton could cover the state of Rhode Island by himself. Steve Finley can go get 'em too, and he's just as good as Lofton at climbing the wall to take away home runs.

Right Field

Year	American	National	Year	American	National
1989	Jesse Barfield	Andre Dawson	1993	Paul O'Neill	Tony Gwynn
1990	Jesse Barfield	Tony Gwynn	1994	Paul O'Neill	Reggie Sanders
1991	Joe Carter	Larry Walker	1995	Tim Salmon	Reggie Sanders
1992	Mark Whiten	Larry Walker	1996	Paul O'Neill	Sammy Sosa

At long last, Sammy Sosa has grown up and started to play defense like he means it. Paul O'Neill is a pleasure to watch, but sadly, a balky hamstring prevented him from proving it to the world in the postseason. He's got a cannon arm and perfect fundamentals, and his last error was 213 games ago.

Who'll be the next STATS winners? Tune in next year.

— Mat Olkin

What Do the Readers Have to Say?

The *Scoreboard* is the favorite book of many of us at STATS, and it's the favorite book of many of our readers as well. We get lots of letters from our readership, and we thought we'd use this essay to highlight some of the more interesting questions and comments we've received over the last couple of years.

The first letter is from Greg Crouse of Cuyahoga, OH:

Your article on successful bunting lists attempts and sacrifices, but it does not list how many times a hitter tried (or squared) to bunt and either took a strike (or ball) or missed the bunt attempt. These unsuccessful attempts put the hitter in a hole. We know hitters starting at 0-1 counts are much worse than even counts, so the act of a missed bunt on 0-0 reduces the hitter's effectiveness for the whole at-bat.

This is interesting, and we confess we hadn't thought of it before Greg's letter. He's right that any fouled or missed bunt attempt puts the hitter at a disadvantage, and you could quantify that and build that into the stat (actually two stats, bunting for a sacrifice per opportunity and bunting for a hit per opportunity). But we like the simplicity of the stat as it is, so we decided not to go quite that far just yet. It's definitely worthy of study in the future, however. In the meantime Greg's letter caused us to make a change in the stat which is simply common sense: when a bunter in a sacrifice situation gets to two strikes because of fouled or missed bunts, we consider that a failed attempt unless he actually succeeds in laying down a sacrifice.

From Craig S. Tyle of Washington, D.C.:

With respect to the Scoreboard, the one area you don't seem to cover is baserunning. I'd be very interested in seeing percentages showing how often individual runners take third on a single, score on a double, advance on a fly, etc.

Good suggestion. We've run this in previous editions, and we hope to get to this again next year. STATS keeps a leaders list called "Extra Bases Taken as a Runner," which is basically what Craig is describing; the top five in 1996 in extra bases taken per opportunity were Raul Mondesi (75.0%), Bernard Gilkey (74.5), Ray Durham (72.5), Roberto Alomar (72.3) and Todd Hollandsworth (72.1). One potential weakness with this stat is that it doesn't break down the opportunities by the field the ball was hit to; as Craig points out, runners who have a right-handed pull hitter hitting behind them would be at a disadvantage compared to guys who bat in front of a *left*-handed pull hitter. But it's still an interesting list, and we hope to get into this subject, perhaps in modified form, next year.

David Smyth of Lincolnshire, IL annually sends us a four-or-five page letter commenting on and criticizing various articles. Here are a couple of his comments from last year's letter:

I think CERA (catchers' ERA) is like pitchers' won-lost records, only more so: a valuable evaluator over a long period but very unreliable over a single season.

Excellent comment, and we're probably not as careful about this as we could be. One example: we sung the praises of Seattle's Dan Wilson last year because the Mariner pitchers had a much lower ERA with Wilson catching than they did with their other catchers. But in 1996 the Mariner pitchers were better—though not by much—with John Marzano and Chris Widger catching than they were with Wilson. We doubt that Wilson forgot how to handle pitchers from '95 to '96; the truth is probably that he wasn't as good as he looked in '95, and that he was better than he looked in '96. A look over a two- or three-year period would be more useful, and that's a great idea for a future *Scoreboard* essay.

David also commented on our article, "Is (Frank) Thomas Too Selective in RBI Situations?"

It's not the walks that are relevant here. Nobody with any sense would recommend that he swing at bad pitches. What some people are trying to say is that Thomas is letting too many good pitches go by in RBI situations. The way to investigate this is not to look at his walks, but at the pattern of his called strikes.

We're not sure we can agree with this. A lot of people say exactly the same thing about Thomas that they did about Ted Williams: if there's a chance to drive in a run, swing at that pitch an inch (or two or three) outside! More to the point, it's simply *not* true that Thomas takes an abnormal amount of called strikes. According to the numbers shown in STATS On-Line, 16.3 percent of all pitches in the American League last year were taken for called strikes. Thomas took a called strike on 14.6 percent of his pitches, which is well under the average. He was also under the average in '95: league 16.0 percent, Thomas 15.3 percent. Admittedly Thomas takes more strikes than more aggressive swingers like Juan Gonzalez (12.0 percent in '96) or Joe Carter (9.0 percent), but their low walk rate is convincing proof that these guys also swing at more pitches out of the strike zone. . . which is what Thomas' critics want him to do. We think that would be a mistake.

Issac W. Stephenson (who unfortunately didn't put his address on his letter) was the first person to suggest the effect of mid-game pitching changes on switch-hitters which appears on page 118. Issac also had this suggestion:

One (idea) concerns when everyday players are rested. . . . It seems as though Sunday is the most common day for rest due to the usual Monday off-day. It would be interesting to know if there is a pattern. This would also be something further to include in the manager profiles (of the Major League Handbook).

Neat idea, and we're kind of sorry we didn't get to it this year. There are all kinds of interesting issues that could be discussed. For instance, which managers *don't* rest their regulars? Is the typical pattern for rest when there's a day game after a night game, or do some managers do it differently? And what's the effect on the team—how much more likely are they to lose? And does a day's rest help a player perform better afterward? We promise to get into this subject in the near future.

Finally, Tom Hanrahan of Lexington Park, MD commented on our article from the 1995 *Scoreboard*, "Can You Bet on a Streak to Continue?"

I believe you created a good set of data to answer your question. However, I find you analysis faulty. . . . Your method of totaling all games by all teams showed that winning clubs have more opportunities to be coming off a 3-plus game winning streak, and thus will contribute more to that part of the data set.

Tom suggested that a better method would be to consider each team against itself when losing or winning, developing 28 matched pairs. He did that and came up with a difference in winning percentage after a winning streak of .029 instead of the .044 from our study. That's a fairly negligible difference, probably attributable, as Tom put it, "not to a team being hot, but a team playing two bad teams in a three- or four-game series. . . making it more likely to go on a streak." After looking at Tom's data, we think his analysis is absolutely right.

Thanks to our readers for your sharp questions and comments. We plan to feature your letters in this space in future editions of the *Scoreboard.*

— Don Zminda

APPENDIX

Since I helped assemble the Appendix this year, I was given the honor of writing this introduction. This is my first attempt at writing any prose for a STATS, Inc. publication, so hopefully I will do this book justice. The following explanation should be familiar to longtime readers of the *Scoreboard.*

Each Appendix has two pieces of information to help reference it to its corresponding essay. The "Title" matches the title in the Table of Contents, and the "Page" refers to the page number of the corresponding essay. Most appendices will be accompanied by a brief explanation describing the order of the list as well as any minimum requirements used. Also note that in some appendices, we could not include every team for players who played with more than one club in 1996. In those cases, the player is listed with the last team he played for.

—Jeff Schinski

The team abbreviation following a player's name refers to the team with which he accumulated the most playing time. Here are the abbreviations:

American League Teams		**National League Teams**	
Bal	Baltimore Orioles	Atl	Atlanta Braves
Bos	Boston Red Sox	ChN	Chicago Cubs
Cal	California Angels	Cin	Cincinnati Reds
ChA	Chicago White Sox	Col	Colorado Rockies
Cle	Cleveland Indians	Fla	Florida Marlins
Det	Detroit Tigers	Hou	Houston Astros
KC	Kansas City Royals	LA	Los Angeles Dodgers
Mil	Milwaukee Brewers	Mon	Montreal Expos
Min	Minnesota Twins	NYN	New York Mets
NYA	New York Yankees	Phi	Philadelphia Phillies
Oak	Oakland Athletics	Pit	Pittsburgh Pirates
Sea	Seattle Mariners	StL	St. Louis Cardinals
Tex	Texas Rangers	SD	San Diego Padres
Tor	Toronto Blue Jays	SF	San Francisco Giants

Anaheim Angels: Should it Be "An' a Home Run!" Stadium? (p. 4)

Park Index - Home Runs (1994-1996)
(* index since 1995)
(# index for 1996 only)

A.L. Park	Index
Anaheim Stadium	118
Tiger Stadium	114
Hubert H. Humphrey Metrodome	109
Oriole Park at Camden Yards	109
SkyDome	108
The Kingdome*	107
Yankee Stadium	101
Fenway Park	98
The Ballpark in Arlington	95
Jacobs Field	94
County Stadium	90
Oakland-Alameda County Coliseum#	88
Ewing M. Kauffman Stadium*	85
Comiskey Park	83

N.L. Park	Index
Coors Field*	176
Atlanta-Fulton County Stadium	117
Wrigley Field	105
San Diego/Jack Murphy Stadium#	104
Three Rivers Stadium	102
3 Com Park	99
Veterans Stadium	97
Cinergy Field	94
Busch Stadium#	93
Shea Stadium	93
Pro Player Stadium	90
Olympic Stadium	89
The Astrodome	80
Dodger Stadium	78

Baltimore Orioles: Did Brady Have the Biggest Home Run Jump Ever? (p. 6)

Largest 1 year increase in home runs (minimum 20 HR Increase and 100 Games played in previous year)

Hitter	Year	HR	Prev Year	Jump
Dave Johnson	1973	43	5	38
Brady Anderson	1996	50	16	34
Harmon Killebrew	1969	49	17	32
Lou Gehrig	1927	47	16	31
Johnny Mize	1947	51	22	29
Andre Dawson	1987	49	20	29
Jimmie Foxx	1932	58	30	28
Ralph Kiner	1947	51	23	28
Kevin Mitchell	1989	47	19	28
Carl Yastrzemski	1967	44	16	28
Rico Petrocelli	1969	40	12	28
Bob Cerv	1958	38	11	27
Phil Plantier	1993	34	7	27
Kirby Puckett	1986	31	4	27
Cito Gaston	1970	29	2	27
Dick Stuart	1963	42	16	26
Ellis Burks	1996	40	14	26
Dusty Baker	1977	30	4	26
Phil Bradley	1985	26	0	26
Babe Ruth	1920	54	29	25
Jim Gentile	1961	46	21	25
Ernie Banks	1955	44	19	25
Ripper Collins	1934	35	10	25
Mike Schmidt	1979	45	21	24
Mel Ott	1929	42	18	24
Greg Vaughn	1996	41	17	24
Darrell Evans	1985	40	16	24
Ted Kluszewski	1953	40	16	24
Dave Winfield	1982	37	13	24
Will Clark	1987	35	11	24
Lefty O'Doul	1929	32	8	24
Bobby Grich	1979	30	6	24
George Foster	1977	52	29	23
Jeff Burroughs	1977	41	18	23
Norm Cash	1961	41	18	23
Roger Maris	1960	39	16	23
Dale Murphy	1982	36	13	23
Willard Marshall	1947	36	13	23
Ken Harrelson	1968	35	12	23
Rusty Staub	1969	29	6	23
Al Kaline	1955	27	4	23
Roger Maris	1961	61	39	22
Eddie Mathews	1953	47	25	22
Orlando Cepeda	1961	46	24	22
Darrell Evans	1973	41	19	22
Hank Sauer	1954	41	19	22
Wally Post	1955	40	18	22
Dave Kingman	1984	35	13	22
Sal Bando	1969	31	9	22
Tommy Harper	1970	31	9	22
Woodie Held	1959	29	7	22
Billy Williams	1970	42	21	21
Duke Snider	1953	42	21	21
Rogers Hornsby	1922	42	21	21
Willie McCovey	1965	39	18	21
Bob Meusel	1925	33	12	21
Tommie Agee	1969	26	5	21
Dave Kingman	1979	48	28	20
Mark McGwire	1992	42	22	20
Dick Allen	1966	40	20	20
Stan Musial	1948	39	19	20
Terry Steinbach	1996	35	15	20
Ben Oglivie	1982	34	14	20
Steve Garvey	1977	33	13	20
Jimmie Foxx	1929	33	13	20
Cecil Cooper	1982	32	12	20
Ken Keltner	1948	31	11	20
Earl Averill	1934	31	11	20
Steve Finley	1996	30	10	20
Hal McRae	1982	27	7	20
Von Hayes	1989	26	6	20
Toby Harrah	1982	25	5	20
Al Cowens	1977	23	3	20
Bert Campaneris	1970	22	2	20
Dan Meyer	1977	22	2	20

Kansas City Royals: Relatively Speaking, Can They Slug? (p. 20)

Top 25 Relative Slugging Percentage

Team	Year	Rel SLG	SLG	BA	HR	W	L
New York Yankees	1927	1.223	.488	.307	158	110	44
Cincinnati Reds	1976	1.175	.424	.280	141	102	60
Pittsburgh Pirates	1902	1.174	.374	.286	19	103	36
Cincinnati Reds	1965	1.173	.439	.273	183	89	73
New York Giants	1947	1.163	.454	.271	221	81	73
New York Yankees	1930	1.159	.488	.309	152	86	68
Colorado Rockies	1996	1.158	.472	.287	221	83	79
Colorado Rockies	1995	1.155	.471	.282	200	77	67
New York Yankees	1931	1.155	.457	.297	155	94	59
Boston Red Sox	1950	1.152	.464	.302	161	94	60
Brooklyn Dodgers	1953	1.152	.474	.285	208	105	49
New York Yankees	1936	1.149	.484	.300	182	102	51
Boston Red Sox	1977	1.147	.465	.281	213	97	64
Detroit Tigers	1908	1.144	.347	.264	19	90	63
Cincinnati Reds	1969	1.144	.422	.277	171	89	73
Cincinnati Reds	1968	1.140	.389	.273	106	83	79
St. Louis Browns	1922	1.140	.453	.310	98	93	61
Boston Red Sox	1903	1.138	.392	.272	48	91	47
New York Yankees	1921	1.138	.465	.301	134	98	55
San Francisco Giants	1963	1.137	.414	.258	197	88	74
Cincinnati Reds	1902	1.137	.362	.282	18	70	70
Pittsburgh Pirates	1971	1.136	.416	.274	154	97	65
Detroit Tigers	1968	1.136	.385	.235	185	103	59
Philadelphia Athletics	1910	1.135	.356	.266	19	102	48
Atlanta Braves	1973	1.135	.427	.266	206	76	85

Worst 25 Relative Slugging Percentage

Team	Year	Rel SLG	SLG	BA	HR	W	L
Houston Astros	1963	.826	.301	.220	62	66	96
Chicago White Sox	1910	.834	.261	.211	7	68	85
Boston Braves	1924	.835	.327	.256	25	53	100
Baltimore Orioles	1955	.839	.320	.240	54	57	97
Houston Astros	1964	.841	.315	.229	70	66	96
Boston Braves	1922	.843	.341	.263	32	53	100
Texas Rangers	1972	.846	.290	.217	56	54	100
Oakland Athletics	1979	.848	.346	.239	108	54	108
St. Louis Cardinals	1986	.859	.327	.236	58	79	82
Pittsburgh Pirates	1954	.861	.350	.248	76	53	101
California Angels	1969	.863	.319	.230	88	71	91
Boston Red Sox	1930	.865	.364	.263	47	52	102
Pittsburgh Pirates	1953	.865	.356	.247	99	50	104
Detroit Tigers	1902	.866	.320	.251	22	52	83
Chicago White Sox	1931	.866	.343	.260	27	56	97
New York Mets	1963	.866	.315	.219	96	51	111
California Angels	1975	.867	.328	.246	55	72	89
Boston Red Sox	1932	.867	.351	.251	53	43	111
Washington Senators	1948	.867	.331	.244	31	56	97
Chicago White Sox	1948	.867	.331	.251	55	51	101
Oakland Athletics	1977	.868	.352	.240	117	63	98
Florida Marlins	1993	.869	.346	.248	94	64	98
St. Louis Browns	1911	.870	.312	.239	17	45	107
Philadelphia Athletics	1920	.870	.337	.252	44	48	106
Philadelphia Athletics	1943	.871	.297	.232	26	49	105

Milwaukee Brewers: Were Vaughn and Fielder the Biggest "Hired Guns" of All Time? (p. 23)

Most Home Runs in a Year—Midseason Acquisitions

Player, Teams	Year	HR
Greg Vaughn, Mil-SD	1996	41
Cecil Fielder, Det-NYA	1996	39
Goose Goslin, Was-STL	1930	37
Fred McGriff, SD-Atl	1993	37
Ralph Kiner, Pit-ChN	1953	35
Gus Zernial, ChA-Phi	1951	33
Hank Sauer, Cin-ChN	1949	31
Bobby Bonds, ChA-Tex	1978	31
Rico Carty, Tor-Oak	1978	31
Andy Pafko, ChN-Bro	1951	30
Ken Harrelson, Bos-Cle	1969	30
Walt Dropo, Bos-Det	1952	29
Roger Maris, Cle-KCA	1958	28
Bobby Bonilla, NYN-Bal	1995	28
Frank Thomas, ChN-Mil	1961	27
Gary Alexander, Oak-Cle	1978	27
Ray Boone, Cle-Det	1953	26
Joe Pepitone, Hou-ChN	1970	26
Dave Kingman, NYN-SD-Cal-NYA	1977	26
Jose Canseco, Oak-Tex	1992	26
Chuck Klein, ChN-Phi	1936	25
Fred Lynn, Bal-Det	1988	25
Todd Zeile, Phi-Bal	1996	25
Johnny Rizzo, Pit-Cin-Phi	1940	24
Lee Thomas, NYA-LAA	1961	24
Ken Phelps, Sea-NYA	1988	24
Dale Murphy, Atl-Phi	1990	24
Babe Dahlgren, Bos-ChN	1941	23
Vic Wertz, Det-STL	1952	23
Steve Balboni, KC-Sea	1988	23
Tom Brunansky, Min-StL	1988	23
Jesse Barfield, Tor-NYA	1989	23
Buster Adams, Phi-StL	1945	22
Wally Westlake, Pit-StL	1951	22
Hector Lopez, KCA-NYA	1959	22
Frank Robinson, Cal-Cle	1974	22
Cliff Johnson, Hou-NYA	1977	22
Gorman Thomas, Mil-Cle	1983	22
John Shelby, Bal-LA	1987	22
Kevin Mitchell, SD-SF	1987	22
Steve Buechele, Tex-Pit	1991	22
Eddie Murray, Cle-Bal	1996	22
Mark Whiten, Phi-Atl-Sea	1996	22
Rudy York, Bos-ChA	1947	21
Eddie Robinson, Was-ChA	1950	21
Smoky Burgess, Phi-Cin	1955	21
Dale Long, Pit-ChN	1957	21
Don Demeter, LA-Phi	1961	21
John Briggs, Phi-Mil	1971	21

Player, Teams	Year	HR
Champ Summers, Cin-Det	1979	21
Jason Thompson, Det-Cal	1980	21
Ken Griffey Sr, NYA-Atl	1986	21
Ron Kittle, ChA-NYA	1986	21
Dave Winfield, NYA-Cal	1990	21
Rickey Henderson, Oak-Tor	1993	21
Rob Deer, Det-Bos	1993	21
Walker Cooper, NYG-Cin	1949	20
Woodie Held, NYA-KCA	1957	20
Charley Smith, ChA-NYN	1964	20
Orlando Cepeda, SF-StL	1966	20
Bob Oliver, Cal-KC	1972	20
Deron Johnson, Phi-Oak	1973	20
George Hendrick, SD-StL	1978	20
Cliff Johnson, NYA-Cle	1979	20
Roy Smalley, Min-NYA	1982	20
Eric Davis, LA-Det	1993	20
Gary Sheffield, SD-Fla	1993	20
George Harper, NYG-StL	1928	19
Vince DiMaggio, Cin-Pit	1940	19
Jake Jones, ChA-Bos	1947	19
Pat Seerey, Cle-ChA	1948	19
Johnny Mize, NYG-NYA	1949	19
Wally Post, Phi-Cin	1960	19
Aurelio Rodriguez, Cal-Was	1970	19
Mike Epstein, Was-Oak	1971	19
Deron Johnson, ChA-Bos	1975	19
Oscar Gamble, Tex-NYA	1979	19
Ruben Sierra, Oak-NYA	1995	19
Smead Jolley, ChA-Bos	1932	18
Moose Solters, Bos-STL	1935	18
Roy Cullenbine, Cle-Det	1945	18
Reggie Smith, StL-LA	1976	18
Doug Rader, SD-Tor	1977	18
Ron Kittle, ChA-Bal	1990	18
Mark Parent, Pit-ChN	1995	18
Pete Incaviglia, Phi-Bal	1996	18
Ed Coleman, Phi-STL	1935	17
Wally Berger, Bos-NYG	1937	17
Joe Medwick, StL-Bro	1940	17
Bill Wilson, ChA-Phi	1954	17
Jim Baxes, LA-Cle	1959	17
Carl Warwick, StL-Hou	1962	17
Gene Oliver, StL-Mil	1963	17
Bill Skowron, Was-ChA	1964	17
Jim Gentile, KCA-Hou	1965	17
Earl Williams, Atl-Mon	1976	17
Bill Madlock, LA-Det	1987	17
Ruben Sierra, Tex-Oak	1992	17

Minnesota Twins: Can Molitor Keep Holding Off Father Time? (p. 25)

Top 50 in hits, age 35-39.

Player	Hits	Hits (Age 40+)
Sam Rice	1023	551
Pete Rose	1010	699
Paul Molitor	928	0
Tris Speaker	887	51
Bill Terry	865	0
Ty Cobb	847	289
Doc Cramer	846	102
Eddie Collins	846	87
Jake Daubert	825	114
Lave Cross	824	162
Cap Anson	816	822
Honus Wagner	809	479
George Brett	786	149
Babe Ruth	784	13
Nap Lajoie	771	242
Zack Wheat	763	0
Jose Cruz	760	16
Carl Yastrzemski	742	410
Dave Parker	742	120
Mickey Vernon	730	125
Eddie Murray	719	147
Hank Aaron	717	262
Patsy Donovan	712	5
Lou Brock	706	123
Luis Aparicio	702	0
Ozzie Smith	697	95
Stan Musial	697	336
Cy Williams	695	88
Minnie Minoso	694	80
Jim O'Rourke	694	458
Tony Perez	686	256
Rico Carty	685	0
Willie Mays	684	218
Ted Williams	683	167
Brett Butler	672	0
Maury Wills	672	0
Dummy Hoy	671	81
Andre Dawson	663	74
Joe Kuhel	662	68
Dwight Evans	661	0
Rod Carew	659	0
Hal McRae	657	80
Deacon White	657	328
Brian Downing	652	202
Kiki Cuyler	651	0
Kid Gleason	649	19
Jimmy Dykes	646	53
Ernie Banks	632	16
Dave Winfield	614	413
Jimmy Ryan	613	109

New York Yankees: Do Old Pennant-Winners Just Fade, Fade Away? (p. 27)

Oldest Teams to Play in a World Series (>28 Years Old)
(* Indicates World Series Winner)

Team, Year	Combined Age	Team, Year	Combined Age
Detroit Tigers, 1945*	32.0	Detroit Tigers, 1935*	28.9
Philadelphia Phillies, 1983	31.9	Philadelphia Athletics, 1929*	28.8
Brooklyn Dodgers, 1956	30.8	Chicago Cubs, 1932	28.8
New York Yankees, 1981	30.7	New York Yankees, 1951*	28.8
Philadelphia Phillies, 1980*	30.6	Baltimore Orioles, 1970*	28.8
Los Angeles Dodgers, 1978	30.4	Cincinnati Reds, 1939	28.8
Washington Senators, 1933	30.2	Washington Senators, 1924*	28.8
Boston Red Sox, 1986	30.2	San Francisco Giants, 1989	28.8
New York Yankees, 1947*	30.2	Chicago Cubs, 1908*	28.7
Brooklyn Dodgers, 1920	30.1	Milwaukee Braves, 1958	28.7
Cleveland Indians, 1954	30.0	New York Yankees, 1949*	28.7
New York Yankees, 1996*	30.0	Detroit Tigers, 1984*	28.7
Kansas City Royals, 1985*	30.0	New York Yankees, 1937*	28.7
St. Louis Cardinals, 1931*	30.0	Pittsburgh Pirates, 1960*	28.7
Chicago Cubs, 1945	30.0	New York Giants, 1933*	28.6
St. Louis Browns, 1944	30.0	Cleveland Indians, 1948*	28.6
Washington Senators, 1925	29.9	New York Yankees, 1953*	28.6
Baltimore Orioles, 1971	29.9	Chicago White Sox, 1919	28.6
Chicago White Sox, 1959	29.8	Brooklyn Dodgers, 1941	28.6
Chicago Cubs, 1929	29.8	St. Louis Cardinals, 1968	28.5
St. Louis Cardinals, 1930	29.7	Brooklyn Dodgers, 1916	28.5
Milwaukee Brewers, 1982	29.6	Baltimore Orioles, 1979	28.5
New York Yankees, 1978*	29.6	Pittsburgh Pirates, 1909*	28.5
Boston Braves, 1948	29.6	New York Yankees, 1942	28.5
Oakland Athletics, 1990	29.5	Cincinnati Reds, 1975*	28.5
New York Giants, 1905*	29.5	New York Yankees, 1938*	28.4
Brooklyn Dodgers, 1955*	29.5	New York Giants, 1954*	28.4
Toronto Blue Jays, 1992*	29.4	New York Yankees, 1932*	28.4
New York Yankees, 1950*	29.4	New York Yankees, 1976	28.4
Baltimore Orioles, 1983*	29.4	New York Yankees, 1943*	28.4
Chicago Cubs, 1938	29.4	Oakland Athletics, 1974*	28.4
Oakland Athletics, 1989*	29.4	New York Giants, 1936	28.3
Pittsburgh Pirates, 1979*	29.3	Atlanta Braves, 1992	28.3
Philadelphia Athletics, 1905	29.3	St. Louis Cardinals, 1934*	28.3
Cleveland Indians, 1920*	29.3	New York Giants, 1917	28.2
Toronto Blue Jays, 1993*	29.3	New York Yankees, 1957	28.2
Detroit Tigers, 1940	29.2	Los Angeles Dodgers, 1966	28.2
Los Angeles Dodgers, 1977	29.2	Minnesota Twins, 1987*	28.2
Boston Red Sox, 1903*	29.2	San Diego Padres, 1984	28.2
Philadelphia Phillies, 1993	29.2	New York Yankees, 1936*	28.2
Cleveland Indians, 1995	29.2	St. Louis Cardinals, 1987	28.2
Chicago White Sox, 1906*	29.2	Boston Red Sox, 1918*	28.1
Brooklyn Dodgers, 1952	29.1	Baltimore Orioles, 1969	28.1
St. Louis Cardinals, 1928	29.1	New York Yankees, 1923*	28.1
Los Angeles Dodgers, 1988*	29.1	New York Yankees, 1962*	28.1
Boston Red Sox, 1946	29.1	New York Yankees, 1964	28.1
Chicago Cubs, 1910	29.0	Milwaukee Braves, 1957*	28.1
Cincinnati Reds, 1976*	29.0	New York Yankees, 1928*	28.1
Philadelphia Athletics, 1931	29.0	New York Yankees, 1961*	28.1
New York Yankees, 1977*	29.0	Pittsburgh Pirates, 1925*	28.1
Los Angeles Dodgers, 1981*	29.0	Detroit Tigers, 1934	28.1
Cincinnati Reds, 1919*	29.0	Oakland Athletics, 1988	28.1
Brooklyn Dodgers, 1953	29.0	Philadelphia Phillies, 1915	28.1
Cincinnati Reds, 1940*	28.9	St. Louis Cardinals, 1964*	28.1
Minnesota Twins, 1991*	28.9	Oakland Athletics, 1973*	28.1
Philadelphia Athletics, 1930*	28.9	Los Angeles Dodgers, 1959*	28.1

Seattle Mariners: Where Will Griffey Rank in History? (p. 32)

Most HR at Age 26

Player	HR	Season
Jimmie Foxx	266	1934
Eddie Mathews	253	1958
Mickey Mantle	249	1958
Mel Ott	242	1935
Frank Robinson	241	1962
Ken Griffey Jr	238	1996
Orlando Cepeda	222	1964
Hank Aaron	219	1960
Juan Gonzalez	214	1996
Johnny Bench	212	1974

Most HR at Age 27

Player	HR	Season
Jimmie Foxx	302	1935
Eddie Mathews	299	1959
Mickey Mantle	280	1959
Mel Ott	275	1936
Frank Robinson	262	1963
Hank Aaron	253	1961
Johnny Bench	240	1975
Jose Canseco	235	1992
Orlando Cepeda	223	1965
Harmon Killebrew	223	1963

Most HR at Age 28

Player	HR	Season
Jimmie Foxx	343	1936
Eddie Mathews	338	1960
Mickey Mantle	320	1960
Mel Ott	306	1937
Hank Aaron	298	1962
Frank Robinson	291	1964
Harmon Killebrew	272	1964
Ralph Kiner	257	1951
Johnny Bench	256	1976
Darryl Strawberry	252	1990

Most HR at Age 29

Player	HR	Season
Jimmie Foxx	379	1937
Mickey Mantle	374	1961
Eddie Mathews	370	1961
Hank Aaron	342	1963
Mel Ott	342	1938
Frank Robinson	324	1965
Harmon Killebrew	297	1965
Ralph Kiner	294	1952
Johnny Bench	287	1977
Babe Ruth	284	1924

Most HR at Age 30

Player	HR	Season
Jimmie Foxx	429	1938
Mickey Mantle	404	1962
Eddie Mathews	399	1962
Frank Robinson	373	1966
Mel Ott	369	1939
Hank Aaron	366	1964
Harmon Killebrew	336	1966
Ralph Kiner	329	1953
Willie Mays	319	1961
Duke Snider	316	1957

Most HR at Age 31

Player	HR	Season
Jimmie Foxx	464	1939
Eddie Mathews	422	1963
Mickey Mantle	419	1963
Frank Robinson	403	1967
Hank Aaron	398	1965
Mel Ott	388	1940
Harmon Killebrew	380	1967
Willie Mays	368	1962
Babe Ruth	356	1926
Ralph Kiner	351	1954

Toronto Blue Jays: How Long Can "The Rocket" Keep Launching? (p. 36)

Top 25 K/9 at age 33 (minimum 160 IP)

Player	Year	K/9 IP
Roger Clemens	1996	9.53
Jeff Fassero	1996	8.62
Bob Veale	1969	8.48
Jim Bunning	1965	8.29
Chuck Finley	1996	8.13
Tom Seaver	1978	7.82
Mike Scott	1988	7.82
Bob Gibson	1969	7.71
Nolan Ryan	1980	7.69
Dazzy Vance	1924	7.65
Jerry Koosman	1976	7.29
Mark Leiter	1996	7.20
Doug Drabek	1996	7.03
Sam Jones	1959	6.94
Mike Krukow	1985	6.93
Earl Wilson	1968	6.75
Mel Queen	1951	6.59
Jack Morris	1988	6.43
Tom Candiotti	1991	6.32
Woodie Fryman	1973	6.30
Fred Norman	1976	6.30
Bobo Newsom	1941	6.30
Gary Peters	1970	6.29
Bert Blyleven	1984	6.24
Connie Johnson	1956	6.24

Atlanta Braves: The Best Pitching Staff of All Time? (p. 39)

Top 50 Biggest Team/League ERA Differentials—6 Year Period

Years	Team	ERA	LgERA	Diff
1934-39	New York Yankees	3.74	4.67	–0.93
1935-40	New York Yankees	3.76	4.65	–0.89
1936-41	New York Yankees	3.75	4.60	–0.85
1937-42	New York Yankees	3.53	4.37	–0.83
1938-43	New York Yankees	3.41	4.14	–0.73
1933-38	New York Yankees	3.91	4.61	–0.70
1948-53	Cleveland Indians	3.44	4.14	–0.70
1905-10	Chicago Cubs	1.99	2.67	–0.69
1947-52	Cleveland Indians	3.41	4.09	–0.68
1902-07	Chicago Cubs	2.12	2.80	–0.68
1949-54	Cleveland Indians	3.37	4.05	–0.68
1904-09	Chicago Cubs	1.95	2.62	–0.67
1942-47	St. Louis Cardinals	2.93	3.60	–0.67
1926-31	Philadelphia Athletics	3.58	4.24	–0.66
1941-46	St. Louis Cardinals	2.87	3.53	–0.65
1972-77	Los Angeles Dodgers	2.99	3.64	–0.65
1953-58	Milwaukee Braves	3.35	4.00	–0.64
1953-58	New York Yankees	3.26	3.90	–0.64
1932-37	New York Yankees	3.92	4.56	–0.64
1952-57	New York Yankees	3.24	3.88	–0.64
1951-56	Cleveland Indians	3.30	3.94	–0.64
1962-67	Chicago White Sox	2.92	3.56	–0.64
1950-55	Cleveland Indians	3.37	4.01	–0.63
1963-68	Chicago White Sox	2.76	3.39	–0.63
1922-27	Cincinnati Reds	3.37	3.99	–0.63
1921-26	Cincinnati Reds	3.35	3.97	–0.62
1903-08	Chicago Cubs	2.11	2.73	–0.62
1973-78	Los Angeles Dodgers	3.04	3.66	–0.61
1906-11	Chicago Cubs	2.13	2.74	–0.61
1946-51	Cleveland Indians	3.46	4.06	–0.60
1991-96	Atlanta Braves	3.38	3.98	–0.60
1951-56	New York Yankees	3.34	3.94	–0.60
1939-44	New York Yankees	3.32	3.92	–0.60
1925-30	Philadelphia Athletics	3.65	4.24	–0.59
1940-45	St. Louis Cardinals	3.01	3.60	–0.59
1920-25	Cincinnati Reds	3.27	3.85	–0.59
1968-73	Baltimore Orioles	2.88	3.46	–0.58
1950-55	New York Yankees	3.43	4.01	–0.58
1969-74	Baltimore Orioles	2.99	3.56	–0.57
1971-76	Los Angeles Dodgers	2.99	3.56	–0.57
1901-06	Chicago Cubs	2.38	2.94	–0.56
1948-53	New York Yankees	3.58	4.14	–0.56
1951-56	Chicago White Sox	3.38	3.94	–0.55
1919-24	Cincinnati Reds	3.09	3.64	–0.55
1954-59	Milwaukee Braves	3.39	3.94	–0.55
1939-44	St. Louis Cardinals	3.06	3.62	–0.55
1943-48	St. Louis Cardinals	3.15	3.70	–0.55
1954-59	New York Yankees	3.33	3.88	–0.55
1964-69	Los Angeles Dodgers	2.90	3.44	–0.55
1939-44	Cincinnati Reds	3.07	3.62	–0.55

Colorado Rockies: What if McGwire (Thomas, Belle, Sheffield...) Called Coors Home? (p. 48)

1996 Coors Projections for selected players

Player, Team	R	2B	HR	Avg	OBP	SLG
Anderson B, Bal	168	47	65	.319	.414	.733
Bagwell, Hou	163	53	48	.365	.488	.704
Belle, Cle	164	40	68	.343	.430	.740
Berroa, Oak	138	36	50	.326	.377	.629
Bonds, SF	166	31	49	.325	.470	.668
Bonilla, Bal	154	34	38	.320	.389	.574
Buhner, Sea	150	32	59	.314	.399	.664
Caminiti, SD	158	45	52	.354	.431	.706
Canseco, Bos	87	22	35	.318	.425	.663
Carter, Tor	113	37	43	.290	.339	.570
Castilla, Col	97	34	40	.304	.343	.548
Clark T, Det	77	17	34	.279	.323	.578
Conine, Fla	122	41	36	.333	.392	.570
Davis E, Cin	110	22	37	.326	.417	.627
Edmonds, Cal	102	34	32	.330	.399	.639
Elster, Tex	100	38	34	.275	.334	.542
Fielder, NYA	117	24	51	.284	.373	.567
Gaetti, StL	99	30	32	.307	.353	.552
Gant, StL	103	16	41	.277	.380	.604
Gilkey, NYN	162	57	47	.366	.434	.710
Gonzalez J, Tex	113	39	67	.343	.391	.772
Griffey Jr, Sea	175	29	59	.316	.400	.684
Higginson, Det	103	42	32	.345	.422	.642
Hoiles, Bal	92	16	34	.294	.385	.567
Hundley, NYN	127	41	61	.295	.384	.693
Jaha, Mil	144	33	44	.330	.416	.621
Jones C, Atl	150	38	36	.341	.420	.589
Karros, LA	128	39	52	.306	.357	.611
King, Pit	121	39	41	.304	.368	.577
Klesko, Atl	118	25	37	.297	.376	.556
Larkin, Cin	159	35	46	.339	.433	.668
Lopez J, Atl	74	22	30	.318	.355	.540
Martinez E, Sea	169	57	35	.378	.498	.696
Martinez T, NYA	111	33	29	.300	.367	.490
McGriff, Atl	106	44	30	.311	.378	.520
McGwire, Oak	142	24	72	.350	.499	.886
Mondesi, LA	149	54	36	.350	.385	.621
Murray E, Bal	96	24	30	.288	.347	.482
Nieves, Det	98	27	31	.274	.341	.562
Palmeiro R, Bal	158	50	51	.310	.396	.622
Palmer, Tex	124	31	54	.306	.367	.627
Piazza, LA	132	22	55	.397	.473	.716
Ramirez, Cle	125	47	47	.341	.419	.679
Ripken C, Bal	135	50	36	.317	.373	.552
Rodriguez A, Sea	197	59	48	.414	.462	.737
Rodriguez H, Mon	105	46	39	.279	.321	.573
Salmon, Cal	125	33	36	.328	.424	.583
Sheffield, Fla	172	42	58	.357	.490	.745
Sosa, ChN	112	25	48	.313	.360	.646
Sprague, Tor	118	37	51	.283	.357	.599
Steinbach, Oak	108	28	48	.307	.375	.627
Tartabull, ChA	86	30	37	.285	.363	.579
Tettleton, Tex	99	31	31	.266	.375	.510
Thomas, ChA	163	34	55	.389	.488	.742
Thome, Cle	162	29	55	.330	.455	.717
Vaughn G, SD	133	23	53	.286	.382	.623
Vaughn M, Bos	151	29	53	.332	.426	.621
Ventura, ChA	143	41	50	.309	.385	.623
Williams B, NYA	146	31	38	.327	.405	.610
Williams M, SF	94	18	30	.342	.401	.601

Florida Marlins: Was Kevin Brown the Best Pitcher in Baseball Last Year? (p. 51)

Best predicted W-L percentage, MLB (Minimum 20 GS)

Pitcher, Team	ERA	Actual W-L	WPct	Expected W-L	EWP
Brown, Fla	1.89	17-11	.607	21-6	.774
Leiter A, Fla	2.93	16-12	.571	17-9	.658
Maddux G, Atl	2.72	15-11	.577	19-10	.654
Guzman, Tor	2.93	11-8	.579	14-8	.634
Smoltz, Atl	2.94	24-8	.750	19-11	.629
Schilling, Phi	3.19	9-10	.474	13-8	.616
Glavine, Atl	2.98	15-10	.600	17-11	.603
Hentgen, Tor	3.22	20-10	.667	19-13	.593
Ashby, SD	3.23	9-5	.643	10-7	.589
Trachsel, ChN	3.03	13-9	.591	14-10	.587
Nagy, Cle	3.41	17-5	.773	15-11	.586
Astacio, LA	3.44	9-8	.529	14-10	.580
Nomo, LA	3.19	16-11	.593	16-11	.578
Neagle, Atl	3.50	16-9	.640	15-11	.577
Fassero, Mon	3.30	15-11	.577	16-12	.575
Appier, KC	3.62	14-11	.560	14-11	.573
Valdes I, LA	3.32	15-7	.682	15-11	.566
Fernandez A, ChA	3.45	16-10	.615	17-13	.556
Reynolds, Hou	3.65	16-10	.615	15-13	.551
Clemens, Bos	3.63	10-13	.435	16-13	.544
Osborne, StL	3.53	13-9	.591	13-11	.543
Hill, Tex	3.63	16-10	.615	16-14	.542
Stottlemyre, StL	3.87	14-11	.560	14-12	.532
Martinez R, LA	3.42	15-6	.714	10-9	.528
Valenzuela, SD	3.62	13-8	.619	11-10	.524
Darwin D, Hou	3.77	10-11	.476	10-9	.520
Smiley, Cin	3.64	13-14	.481	13-12	.518
Clark M, NYN	3.43	14-11	.560	13-12	.516
Martinez P, Mon	3.70	13-10	.565	13-12	.516
Benes An, StL	3.83	18-10	.643	14-13	.513
McDonald, Mil	3.90	12-10	.545	13-13	.508
Hamilton, SD	4.17	15-9	.625	13-12	.505
Pettitte, NYA	3.87	21-8	.724	13-13	.502
Alvarez W, ChA	4.22	15-10	.600	13-13	.489
Navarro, ChN	3.92	15-12	.556	14-14	.486
Belcher, KC	3.92	15-11	.577	14-14	.486
Burba, Cin	3.83	11-13	.458	11-12	.484
Hampton, Hou	3.59	10-10	.500	9-10	.484
Portugal, Cin	3.98	8-9	.471	9-9	.483
Cormier, Mon	4.17	7-10	.412	9-10	.475
Kile, Hou	4.19	12-11	.522	12-14	.461
Baldwin, ChA	4.42	11-6	.647	9-11	.456
Finley, Cal	4.16	15-16	.484	13-15	.456
Jones B, NYN	4.42	12-8	.600	10-13	.456
Burkett, Tex	4.24	11-12	.478	12-14	.453
Prieto, Oak	4.15	6-7	.462	7-8	.452
Harnisch, NYN	4.21	8-12	.400	10-13	.448
Avery, Atl	4.47	7-10	.412	7-9	.443
Moyer, Sea	3.98	13-3	.813	8-11	.443
Morgan, Cin	4.63	6-11	.353	7-9	.441
Radke, Min	4.46	11-16	.407	12-15	.439
Rogers, NYA	4.68	12-8	.600	9-12	.437
Tapani, ChA	4.59	13-10	.565	11-15	.433

Pitcher, Team	ERA	Actual W-L	WPct	Expected W-L	EWP
Key, NYA	4.68	12-11	.522	9-11	.430
Mulholland, Sea	4.66	13-11	.542	10-14	.427
Fernandez O, SF	4.61	7-13	.350	9-12	.426
Hershiser, Cle	4.24	15-9	.625	10-14	.422
Oliver, Tex	4.66	14-6	.700	9-12	.422
Ogea, Cle	4.79	10-6	.625	7-10	.421
Wall, Hou	4.56	9-8	.529	7-10	.420
Tewksbury, SD	4.31	10-10	.500	10-14	.419
Martinez D, Cle	4.50	9-6	.600	6-8	.418
Olivares, Det	4.89	7-11	.389	8-11	.418
Mussina, Bal	4.81	19-11	.633	12-17	.418
Watson, SF	4.61	8-12	.400	9-13	.416
Reynoso, Col	4.96	8-9	.471	8-12	.408
Drabek, Hou	4.57	7-9	.438	8-12	.402
Rapp, Fla	5.10	8-16	.333	8-11	.399
Gardner, SF	4.42	12-7	.632	8-13	.399
Wells D, Bal	5.14	11-14	.440	10-16	.397
Gooden, NYA	5.01	11-7	.611	8-12	.394
Haney, KC	4.70	10-14	.417	10-16	.390
Pavlik, Tex	5.19	15-8	.652	9-14	.390
Candiotti, LA	4.49	9-11	.450	7-11	.389
Karl, Mil	4.86	13-9	.591	9-15	.389
Isringhausen, NYN	4.77	6-14	.300	8-12	.387
Robertson, Min	5.12	7-17	.292	8-14	.382
Coppinger, Bal	5.18	10-6	.625	6-9	.381
Castillo F, ChN	5.28	7-16	.304	8-13	.376
Leiter M, Mon	4.92	8-12	.400	9-15	.376
Erickson, Bal	5.02	13-12	.520	10-16	.375
McDowell J, Cle	5.11	13-9	.591	8-14	.372
Rodriguez F, Min	5.05	13-14	.481	9-15	.369
Benes Al, StL	4.90	13-10	.565	8-14	.366
Lira, Det	5.22	6-14	.300	8-15	.363
Wengert, Oak	5.58	7-11	.389	7-12	.363
Ritz, Col	5.28	17-11	.607	9-16	.362
Williams M, Phi	5.44	6-14	.300	7-13	.357
Thompson M, Col	5.30	9-11	.450	7-13	.355
Witt, Tex	5.41	16-12	.571	8-15	.353
Gordon, Bos	5.59	12-9	.571	9-17	.341
Boskie, Cal	5.32	12-11	.522	8-15	.339
Hitchcock, Sea	5.35	13-9	.591	8-15	.339
Hanson, Tor	5.41	13-17	.433	9-17	.339
Quantrill, Tor	5.43	5-14	.263	5-10	.336
Wolcott, Sea	5.73	7-10	.412	6-12	.332
VanLandingham, SF	5.40	9-14	.391	7-14	.332
Wilson, NYN	5.38	5-12	.294	6-12	.327
Aldred, Min	6.21	6-9	.400	6-13	.323
Sele, Bos	5.32	7-11	.389	6-13	.318
Johns, Oak	5.98	6-12	.333	6-13	.312
Wakefield, Bos	5.14	14-13	.519	8-17	.309
Wasdin, Oak	5.96	8-7	.533	5-11	.299
Bones, NYA	6.22	7-14	.333	5-13	.296
Jarvis, Cin	5.98	8-9	.471	4-10	.276
Freeman, ChA	6.15	7-9	.438	4-11	.274
Bullinger, ChN	6.54	6-10	.375	4-11	.272
Grimsley, Cal	6.84	5-7	.417	4-12	.242
Abbott J, Cal	7.48	2-18	.100	4-13	.219

Los Angeles Dodgers: Will Piazza Be the Best-Hitting Catcher Ever? (p. 56)

All-Time Great Catchers: Through First 500+ Games (OBS .700 or better)

Player	Avg	OBP	SLG
Mike Piazza	.326	.388	.559
Roy Campanella	.287	.370	.510
Gabby Hartnett	.287	.364	.489
Spud Davis	.330	.381	.472
Bubbles Hargrave	.314	.375	.474
Mickey Cochrane	.309	.393	.456
Yogi Berra	.299	.347	.498
Bill Dickey	.322	.368	.476
Babe Phelps	.315	.367	.476
Chris Hoiles	.263	.368	.473
Joe Torre	.300	.361	.478
Carlton Fisk	.277	.349	.480
Earl Smith	.310	.380	.449
Smoky Burgess	.301	.375	.446
Stan Lopata	.258	.353	.467
John Romano	.265	.358	.461
Ernie Lombardi	.311	.355	.461
Gene Tenace	.244	.381	.431
Ed Bailey	.260	.364	.446
King Kelly	.308	.368	.440
Dick Dietz	.259	.382	.424
Walker Cooper	.296	.334	.470
Chief Meyers	.317	.391	.412
Frankie Hayes	.278	.355	.447
Aaron Robinson	.265	.378	.422
Mike Grady	.294	.374	.425
Johnny Bench	.271	.323	.476
Butch Henline	.300	.368	.428
Mike Stanley	.271	.365	.430
Shanty Hogan	.308	.359	.436
Lance Parrish	.266	.320	.468
Bob O'Farrell	.287	.372	.415
Jocko Milligan	.291	.345	.439
Gary Carter	.267	.340	.444
Buck Ewing	.295	.335	.448
Johnny Bassler	.311	.414	.369
Jim Pagliaroni	.261	.353	.430
Roger Bresnahan	.289	.391	.391
Wally Schang	.278	.388	.392
Wes Westrum	.224	.374	.405
Harry Danning	.295	.338	.440
Art Wilson	.275	.376	.401
Elston Howard	.285	.325	.451
Ted Simmons	.296	.349	.424
Tom Haller	.247	.339	.434
Rick Ferrell	.291	.386	.387
Rick Wilkins	.252	.344	.425
Rich Gedman	.274	.323	.444
Gus Triandos	.253	.331	.434
Earl Battey	.269	.345	.418
Thurman Munson	.283	.355	.407
Sherm Lollar	.262	.360	.403
Joe Ferguson	.239	.356	.406
Tony Pena	.296	.332	.427
Charlie Bennett	.273	.338	.418
Duke Sims	.241	.345	.410

Player	Avg	OBP	SLG
Andy Seminick	.242	.342	.412
Mickey Tettleton	.236	.348	.406
Frankie Pytlak	.298	.372	.382
Matt Nokes	.256	.311	.442
Mike Macfarlane	.255	.321	.431
Ozzie Virgil	.242	.326	.424
Bob Brenly	.254	.338	.410
Manny Sanguillen	.309	.332	.415
Brian Harper	.295	.326	.421
Glenn Myatt	.280	.337	.409
Ed McFarland	.289	.348	.392
Bill Freehan	.262	.337	.401
Brian Downing	.264	.366	.371
Todd Hundley	.238	.311	.425
John Roseboro	.241	.331	.405
Heinie Peitz	.275	.354	.381
Jody Davis	.255	.313	.422
Ivan Rodriguez	.281	.318	.416
Joe Garagiola	.255	.350	.382
Sammy White	.273	.316	.416
Terry Kennedy	.275	.322	.410
Hal Smith	.277	.324	.407
Clint Courtney	.279	.341	.387
Darrell Porter	.238	.338	.390
Duke Farrell	.269	.334	.391
Tim McCarver	.278	.325	.399
Terry Steinbach	.272	.326	.399
Don Slaught	.270	.314	.408
Johnny Edwards	.259	.327	.394
Ken O'Dea	.260	.337	.384
Gus Mancuso	.280	.335	.384
Ron Hassey	.272	.346	.373
Hank Foiles	.245	.325	.393
John Stearns	.253	.342	.375
Mike Scioscia	.267	.357	.358
Ernie Whitt	.243	.316	.400
Red Wilson	.264	.348	.367
Sandy Alomar Jr	.270	.313	.400
Darrin Fletcher	.260	.316	.397
Benito Santiago	.265	.301	.412
Del Crandall	.247	.302	.410
Al Lopez	.284	.340	.372
Jimmie Wilson	.284	.339	.371
Johnny Gooch	.287	.347	.362
Geno Petralli	.269	.343	.364
Rollie Hemsley	.272	.318	.390
Steve Yeager	.243	.318	.389
Tommy Clarke	.263	.351	.355
Jack Clements	.273	.325	.380
Bob Stinson	.252	.341	.363
Russ Nixon	.279	.317	.387
Charlie Berry	.271	.326	.377
Ed Herrmann	.241	.323	.380
Al Todd	.283	.314	.388
Deacon McGuire	.259	.335	.367

Montreal Expos: Were Lansing and Grudzielanek "Identical Twins"? (p. 58)

Top 50 Most Similar Double Play Combos

Sim Score	Year	Team	Second Baseman	Shortstop
974	1917	Pittsburgh Pirates	Jake Pitler	Chuck Ward
974	1942	Brooklyn Dodgers	Billy Herman	Pee Wee Reese
974	1981	Cleveland Indians	Duane Kuiper	Tom Veryzer
973	1903	Chicago Cubs	Johnny Evers	Joe Tinker
973	1942	Pittsburgh Pirates	Frankie Gustine	Pete Coscarart
973	1968	Pittsburgh Pirates	Bill Mazeroski	Gene Alley
973	1984	Cincinnati Reds	Ron Oester	Dave Concepcion
971	1954	Boston Red Sox	Ted Lepcio	Milt Bolling
971	1959	Baltimore Orioles	Billy Gardner	Chico Carrasquel
971	1980	Oakland Athletics	Dave McKay	Mario Guerrero
970	1941	Cincinnati Reds	Lonny Frey	Eddie Joost
969	1905	Brooklyn Dodgers	Charlie Malay	Phil Lewis
967	1953	Washington Senators	Wayne Terwilliger	Pete Runnels
967	1954	Chicago Cubs	Gene Baker	Ernie Banks
967	1966	Philadelphia Phillies	Cookie Rojas	Dick Groat
967	1971	Boston Red Sox	Doug Griffin	Luis Aparicio
966	1913	Boston Braves	Bill Sweeney	Rabbit Maranville
966	1927	Boston Braves	Doc Gautreau	Dave Bancroft
966	1981	New York Mets	Doug Flynn	Frank Taveras
965	1967	Washington Senators	Bernie Allen	Ed Brinkman
964	1904	Detroit Tigers	Bobby Lowe	Charley O'Leary
964	1908	Chicago White Sox	George Davis	Freddy Parent
964	1963	New York Yankees	Bobby Richardson	Tony Kubek
964	1974	California Angels	Denny Doyle	Dave Chalk
963	1914	Pittsburgh Rebels	Jack Lewis	Ed Holly
963	1939	Brooklyn Dodgers	Pete Coscarart	Leo Durocher
963	1945	Chicago White Sox	Roy Schalk	Cass Michaels
963	1950	Boston Red Sox	Bobby Doerr	Vern Stephens
962	1915	Newark Peppers	Frank LaPorte	Jimmy Esmond
962	1956	Cleveland Indians	Bobby Avila	Chico Carrasquel
961	1966	Cleveland Indians	Pedro Gonzalez	Larry Brown
960	1906	Chicago White Sox	Frank Isbell	George Davis
960	1908	St. Louis Browns	Jimmy Williams	Bobby Wallace
960	1922	New York Yankees	Aaron Ward	Everett Scott
960	1927	St. Louis Browns	Ski Melillo	Wally Gerber
960	1963	San Francisco Giants	Chuck Hiller	Jose Pagan
960	1981	Detroit Tigers	Lou Whitaker	Alan Trammell
960	1993	Milwaukee Brewers	Bill Spiers	Pat Listach
960	1994	San Francisco Giants	John Patterson	Royce Clayton
959	1930	Cincinnati Reds	Hod Ford	Leo Durocher
959	1943	Boston Braves	Connie Ryan	Whitey Wietelmann
959	1975	Detroit Tigers	Gary Sutherland	Tom Veryzer
959	1976	Atlanta Braves	Rod Gilbreath	Darrel Chaney
959	1986	Detroit Tigers	Lou Whitaker	Alan Trammell
958	1944	Philadelphia Athletics	Irv Hall	Ed Busch
958	1962	Houston Astros	Joey Amalfitano	Bob Lillis
958	1977	Baltimore Orioles	Billy Smith	Mark Belanger
958	1978	Oakland Athletics	Mike Edwards	Mario Guerrero
958	1989	Boston Red Sox	Marty Barrett	Luis Rivera
958	1990	Philadelphia Phillies	Tom Herr	Dickie Thon

New York Mets: Who Are the Fastest Players in Baseball? (p. 61)

Speed Scores (minimum 450 PA)

Player, Team	Score	Player, Team	Score	Player, Team	Score
Alomar R, Bal	5.99	Gonzalez L, ChN	5.22	O'Leary, Bos	4.95
Alou, Mon	4.92	Goodwin T, KC	8.28	O'Neill, NYA	2.95
Anderson B, Bal	5.93	Grace, ChN	3.07	Offerman, KC	6.40
Anderson G, Cal	4.73	Green, Tor	5.51	Olerud, Tor	2.85
Baerga, NYN	3.17	Greer, Tex	6.73	Ordonez, NYN	5.25
Bagwell, Hou	4.36	Griffey Jr, Sea	7.11	Palmeiro R, Bal	4.95
Baines, ChA	2.47	Grissom, Atl	7.01	Palmer, Tex	3.70
Becker, Min	6.50	Grudzielanek, Mon	7.20	Paquette, KC	4.53
Bell D, Hou	6.16	Guillen, ChA	6.82	Pendleton, Atl	2.87
Bell J, Pit	5.19	Gwynn T, SD	4.69	Phillips T, ChA	6.20
Belle, Cle	5.33	Hamilton, Tex	6.22	Piazza, LA	1.34
Benard, SF	7.24	Hayes, NYA	4.17	Ramirez, Cle	4.17
Berroa, Oak	3.06	Henderson, SD	6.93	Reed J, SD	3.53
Berry, Hou	4.73	Higginson, Det	4.94	Renteria, Fla	6.39
Bichette, Col	5.76	Hoiles, Bal	2.50	Ripken C, Bal	3.13
Biggio, Hou	6.41	Hollandsworth, LA	6.80	Rodriguez A, Sea	6.01
Boggs, NYA	4.29	Hollins, Sea	4.04	Rodriguez H, Mon	3.79
Bonds, SF	6.27	Howard D, KC	6.58	Rodriguez I, Tex	5.06
Bonilla, Bal	4.96	Hundley, NYN	2.97	Salmon, Cal	5.12
Boone, Cin	5.02	Hunter B, Hou	7.89	Sandberg, ChN	5.75
Bordick, Oak	5.45	Jaha, Mil	3.15	Santangelo, Mon	6.00
Bragg, Bos	6.35	Jeter, NYA	6.12	Santiago, Phi	3.76
Brosius, Oak	4.25	Johnson L, NYN	8.50	Segui, Mon	4.00
Buhner, Sea	3.31	Jones C, Atl	5.53	Seitzer, Cle	4.24
Burks, Col	7.36	Jordan B, StL	6.98	Servais, ChN	1.27
Caminiti, SD	4.45	Joyner, SD	3.99	Sheffield, Fla	4.27
Carreon, Cle	4.06	Karros, LA	3.50	Sierra, Det	3.62
Carter, Tor	5.71	Kendall, Pit	5.17	Snow, Cal	2.59
Castilla, Col	4.06	Kent, Cle	4.74	Sorrento, Sea	2.92
Cirillo, Mil	4.93	King, Pit	5.18	Sosa, ChN	5.80
Clark W, Tex	3.33	Klesko, Atl	4.84	Sprague, Tor	3.91
Clayton, StL	6.41	Knoblauch, Min	7.77	Stahoviak, Min	4.43
Colbrunn, Fla	2.67	Lankford, StL	7.65	Stanley, Bos	3.60
Conine, Fla	3.65	Lansing, Mon	5.85	Steinbach, Oak	2.16
Cora, Sea	6.34	Larkin, Cin	6.53	Stocker, Phi	6.32
Cordova, Min	5.17	Lemke, Atl	5.07	Surhoff, Bal	4.86
Curtis, LA	5.67	Lewis M, Det	5.15	Tartabull, ChA	4.22
Damon, KC	7.37	Lockhart, KC	5.78	Tettleton, Tex	2.81
Davis C, Cal	2.51	Lofton, Cle	8.42	Thomas, ChA	1.70
Davis E, Cin	6.02	Lopez J, Atl	2.32	Thome, Cle	4.30
Delgado C, Tor	2.54	Mabry, StL	2.74	Valentin J, Bos	5.22
DeShields, LA	7.47	Martin A, Pit	6.68	Valentin J, Mil	7.44
DiSarcina, Cal	5.00	Martinez D, ChA	7.67	Vaughn G, SD	5.44
Durham, ChA	6.90	Martinez E, Sea	3.31	Vaughn M, Bos	2.88
Edmonds, Cal	5.86	Martinez T, NYA	2.67	Velarde, Cal	5.34
Elster, Tex	5.30	McGriff, Atl	3.01	Ventura, ChA	3.54
Fielder, NYA	2.42	McGwire, Oak	1.33	Vina, Mil	6.98
Finley, SD	6.95	McLemore, Tex	5.89	Vizcaino, Cle	6.61
Franco J, Cle	3.25	McRae, ChN	7.05	Vizquel, Cle	7.21
Frye, Bos	6.79	Meares, Min	6.06	Weiss, Col	5.95
Fryman, Det	4.16	Merced, Pit	5.18	White D, Fla	6.90
Gaetti, StL	4.43	Miller, Hou	4.17	Whiten, Sea	4.96
Gagne, LA	5.09	Molitor, Min	5.33	Wilkins, SF	3.67
Galarraga, Col	5.84	Mondesi, LA	6.84	Williams B, NYA	6.57
Gant, StL	5.20	Morandini, Phi	6.50	Williams M, SF	3.82
Giambi, Oak	3.76	Morris, Cin	4.49	Wilson D, Sea	1.72
Gilkey, NYN	5.19	Murray E, Bal	2.99	Young E, Col	7.51
Girardi, NYA	5.27	Naehring, Bos	3.60	Young E, Oak	5.62
Gomez C, SD	3.73	Nieves, Det	5.18	Zeile, Bal	2.64
Gonzalez A, Tor	5.90	Nilsson, Mil	5.30		
Gonzalez J, Tex	4.25	Nixon O, Tor	7.68		

Philadelphia Phillies: How Bad Was Their Injury Problem? (p. 63)

Days Lost to Players on the DL—1996

Team	Days
Philadelphia Phillies	1,700
Boston Red Sox	1,173
California Angels	1,083
Seattle Mariners	930
New York Yankees	919
San Francisco Giants	807
Florida Marlins	780
Los Angeles Dodgers	752
Milwaukee Brewers	727
Kansas City Royals	721
Colorado Rockies	654
Atlanta Braves	641
Montreal Expos	629
Texas Rangers	553
Cincinnati Reds	548
New York Mets	506
Baltimore Orioles	494
Oakland Athletics	484
Minnesota Twins	479
Pittsburgh Pirates	476
St. Louis Cardinals	465
Houston Astros	446
Detroit Tigers	441
Chicago Cubs	385
Chicago White Sox	381
San Diego Padres	360
Toronto Blue Jays	307
Cleveland Indians	306

St. Louis Cardinals: Is La Russa the Master of the "One-Batter Match-Up"? (p. 69)

Mangers' Results in One Batter Match-Ups—1996

Manger, Team	Times	AB	H	RBI	Avg	SLG
Felipe Alou, Mon	31	25	4	7	.160	.160
Dusty Baker, SF	35	32	3	5	.094	.281
Don Baylor, Col	31	30	2	2	.067	.167
Buddy Bell, Det	34	30	9	8	.300	.533
Terry Bevington, ChA	48	44	7	4	.159	.182
Bruce Bochy, SD	21	17	2	2	.118	.176
John Boles, Fla	10	10	2	1	.200	.300
Bob Boone, KC	29	23	4	2	.174	.217
Terry Collins, Hou	27	24	5	6	.208	.333
Bobby Cox, Atl	24	24	1	0	.042	.042
Jim Fregosi, Phi	26	23	0	3	.000	.000
Phil Garner, Mil	26	19	2	5	.105	.263
Cito Gaston, Tor	17	15	1	3	.067	.067
Dallas Green, NYN	20	18	3	3	.167	.333
Mike Hargrove, Cle	43	39	5	6	.128	.205
Art Howe, Oak	35	29	11	9	.379	.690
Davey Johnson, Bal	28	25	2	2	.080	.200
Tom Kelly, Min	33	30	10	7	.333	.667
Kevin Kennedy, Bos	41	33	5	5	.152	.273
Ray Knight, Cin	24	21	6	5	.286	.333
Tony La Russa, StL	47	44	7	3	.159	.182
Marcel Lachemann, Cal	23	22	7	6	.318	.500
Rene Lachemann, Fla	19	17	3	2	.176	.176
Tom Lasorda, LA	11	9	2	2	.222	.222
Jim Leyland, Pit	27	24	4	3	.167	.417
John McNamara, Cal	15	13	1	2	.077	.077
Johnny Oates, Tex	44	40	5	1	.125	.125
Lou Piniella, Sea	23	23	5	5	.217	.304
Jim Riggleman, ChN	34	30	1	1	.033	.033
Cookie Rojas, Fla	0	0	0	0	-	-
Bill Russell, LA	10	10	4	3	.400	.800
Joe Torre, NYA	36	31	7	4	.226	.226
Bobby Valentine, NYN	3	3	0	0	.000	.000

San Diego Padres: Are Things Heating Up at the Hot Corner? (p. 71)

Highest On-Base + Slugging Pct as 3B—1990-1996 (Minimum 400 AB)

Player, Team	Year	OBS	Player, Team	Year	OBS
Jim Thome, Cle	1996	1.061	Ken Caminiti, Hou	1992	.796
Ken Caminiti, SD	1996	1.032	Chipper Jones, Atl	1995	.795
Jim Thome, Cle	1995	1.002	Steve Buechele, ChN	1993	.792
Gary Sheffield, SD	1992	.965	Todd Zeile, Phi-Bal	1996	.789
Chipper Jones, Atl	1996	.946	Todd Zeile, StL	1993	.784
Matt Williams, SF	1994	.930	Steve Buechele, Tex-Pit	1991	.783
Scott Brosius, Oak	1996	.924	Leo Gomez, Bal	1992	.782
Vinny Castilla, Col	1995	.904	Charlie Hayes, Col	1994	.781
Jeff Cirillo, Mil	1996	.898	Terry Pendleton, Fla	1995	.779
Ken Caminiti, SD	1995	.894	Gary Sheffield, Mil	1990	.771
Matt Williams, SF	1993	.888	Todd Zeile, StL	1991	.764
Vinny Castilla, Col	1996	.887	Travis Fryman, Det	1996	.763
Robin Ventura, ChA	1996	.885	Jeff King, Pit	1993	.763
Robin Ventura, ChA	1995	.884	Wade Boggs, NYA	1996	.757
Charlie Hayes, Col	1993	.882	Travis Fryman, Det	1995	.756
Dean Palmer, Tex	1996	.881	Chris Sabo, Cin	1993	.755
Terry Pendleton, Atl	1991	.881	Kelly Gruber, Tor	1991	.750
Wade Boggs, Bos	1991	.878	Scott Cooper, Bos	1993	.750
Bobby Bonilla, NYN	1994	.876	Charlie Hayes, Phi	1995	.746
Tim Naehring, Bos	1995	.867	Wade Boggs, NYA	1993	.732
Tim Wallach, LA	1994	.861	Gregg Jefferies, KC	1992	.731
Ken Caminiti, Hou	1994	.860	Ed Sprague, Tor	1995	.728
Chris Sabo, Cin	1991	.859	Kevin Seitzer, KC	1990	.723
Gary Gaetti, KC	1995	.856	Dean Palmer, Tex	1992	.721
Edgar Martinez, Sea	1991	.854	Terry Pendleton, Atl	1993	.721
Kelly Gruber, Tor	1990	.852	Todd Zeile, StL	1992	.720
Dave Hollins, Phi	1992	.839	Wade Boggs, Bos	1992	.716
Gary Sheffield, SD-Fla	1993	.837	Ken Caminiti, Hou	1993	.713
Wade Boggs, NYA	1995	.829	Charlie Hayes, NYA	1992	.705
Edgar Martinez, Sea	1990	.828	Steve Buechele, ChN-Pit	1992	.704
B.J. Surhoff, Bal	1996	.827	Kevin Seitzer, Mil	1992	.702
Dean Palmer, Tex	1993	.826	Ken Caminiti, Hou	1991	.697
Mike Blowers, Sea	1995	.823	Ed Sprague, Tor	1993	.696
Todd Zeile, StL	1994	.822	Carney Lansford, Oak	1992	.694
Terry Pendleton, Atl	1992	.821	Jim Presley, Atl	1990	.692
Chris Sabo, Cin	1990	.820	B.J. Surhoff, Mil	1993	.689
Wade Boggs, Bos	1990	.817	Matt Williams, SF	1992	.673
Matt Williams, SF	1991	.816	Charlie Hayes, Pit-NYA	1996	.671
Dave Hollins, Phi	1993	.814	Gary Gaetti, Cal	1991	.669
Ed Sprague, Tor	1996	.814	Craig Worthington, Bal	1990	.658
Robin Ventura, ChA	1993	.813	Gary Gaetti, Min	1990	.653
Tim Naehring, Bos	1996	.812	Terry Pendleton, Fla-Atl	1996	.640
Sean Berry, Hou	1996	.811	Robin Ventura, ChA	1990	.638
Tim Wallach, Mon	1990	.810	Carney Lansford, Oak	1990	.636
Robin Ventura, ChA	1991	.810	Charlie Hayes, Phi	1990	.635
Robin Ventura, ChA	1992	.806	Kelly Gruber, Tor	1992	.628
Matt Williams, SF	1990	.805	Tim Wallach, Mon	1991	.626
Gary Gaetti, StL	1996	.803	Ken Caminiti, Hou	1990	.618
Travis Fryman, Det	1994	.801	Charlie Hayes, Phi	1991	.609
Dave Hollins, Min-Sea	1996	.799	Tim Wallach, LA	1993	.609

Is This Another Golden Age? (p. 80)

Major League Baseball Runs/Game 1901-1996

Year	R/G	Year	R/G	Year	R/G	Year	R/G
1930	11.10	1926	9.27	1985	8.66	1946	8.01
1936	10.38	1953	9.21	1960	8.63	1981	8.00
1929	10.37	1949	9.21	1991	8.62	1976	7.99
1925	10.25	1993	9.20	1983	8.62	1966	7.99
1996	10.07	1948	9.16	1957	8.61	1965	7.98
1901	9.98	1951	9.09	1982	8.60	1963	7.89
1994	9.85	1912	9.08	1980	8.58	1943	7.82
1932	9.82	1961	9.05	1958	8.57	1905	7.78
1934	9.81	1911	9.03	1984	8.51	1971	7.78
1935	9.79	1941	8.98	1990	8.51	1919	7.75
1938	9.79	1955	8.97	1973	8.43	1914	7.73
1937	9.75	1933	8.96	1975	8.43	1910	7.67
1922	9.73	1977	8.94	1945	8.36	1915	7.62
1921	9.71	1962	8.92	1952	8.35	1967	7.54
1950	9.70	1979	8.92	1944	8.33	1904	7.45
1995	9.69	1956	8.90	1988	8.28	1972	7.37
1939	9.65	1902	8.88	1989	8.26	1918	7.28
1931	9.63	1903	8.87	1974	8.25	1906	7.23
1923	9.63	1986	8.82	1992	8.23	1917	7.18
1924	9.52	1959	8.77	1978	8.21	1916	7.13
1927	9.50	1954	8.76	1942	8.17	1909	7.09
1928	9.46	1920	8.72	1969	8.14	1907	7.05
1987	9.45	1947	8.71	1913	8.08	1968	6.84
1940	9.36	1970	8.68	1964	8.07	1908	6.77

Is Coors Field the Best Hitters' Park of All Time? (p. 84)

Highest Home Park Scoring Indexes — 1901-96

Year	Home Team	Index	Year	Home Team	Index
1996	Colorado Rockies	171.9	1936	Philadelphia Phillies	127.7
1995	Colorado Rockies	164.4	1917	Cleveland Indians	127.5
1955	Boston Red Sox	155.5	1926	Pittsburgh Pirates	127.5
1933	Philadelphia Phillies	153.3	1972	Chicago Cubs	127.2
1993	Colorado Rockies	151.8	1976	Atlanta Braves	127.2
1900	Boston Braves	148.3	1972	Detroit Tigers	127.1
1925	Philadelphia Phillies	144.5	1920	Philadelphia Phillies	126.7
1923	Philadelphia Phillies	144.3	1961	Los Angeles Angels	126.7
1970	Chicago Cubs	143.0	1964	St Louis Cardinals	126.7
1922	Philadelphia Phillies	142.7	1981	Toronto Blue Jays	126.5
1985	Chicago Cubs	140.4	1906	Detroit Tigers	126.2
1933	St Louis Browns	138.5	1918	Philadelphia Phillies	126.2
1906	New York Yankees	138.5	1934	Philadelphia Phillies	126.1
1916	Chicago Cubs	138.4	1911	New York Yankees	125.9
1906	Cincinnati Reds	138.3	1920	St Louis Browns	125.6
1935	Philadelphia Phillies	136.8	1966	Boston Red Sox	125.4
1977	Boston Red Sox	136.5	1934	St Louis Cardinals	125.3
1977	Atlanta Braves	135.1	1928	Philadelphia Phillies	125.3
1950	Boston Red Sox	135.0	1951	Pittsburgh Pirates	125.3
1973	Atlanta Braves	134.4	1978	Chicago Cubs	125.2
1910	Boston Braves	133.9	1919	Philadelphia Phillies	125.1
1945	St Louis Browns	133.8	1939	Detroit Tigers	125.0
1966	Cincinnati Reds	133.7	1911	Boston Braves	124.9
1926	Philadelphia Athletics	133.2	1970	Boston Red Sox	124.7
1967	Boston Red Sox	133.2	1927	St Louis Browns	124.3
1970	Cleveland Indians	133.1	1930	Philadelphia Phillies	124.2
1904	Cincinnati Reds	133.1	1979	Atlanta Braves	124.1
1932	Philadelphia Phillies	133.0	1962	Detroit Tigers	124.0
1957	Brooklyn Dodgers	132.9	1965	Boston Red Sox	123.9
1938	St Louis Cardinals	132.8	1984	Chicago White Sox	123.9
1968	Cincinnati Reds	132.6	1925	St Louis Browns	123.9
1946	Boston Red Sox	132.4	1937	Philadelphia Phillies	123.8
1945	Boston Braves	132.3	1957	Boston Red Sox	123.7
1994	Colorado Rockies	131.7	1982	Pittsburgh Pirates	123.6
1968	Chicago Cubs	131.6	1971	Atlanta Braves	123.6
1977	Chicago Cubs	131.6	1976	Chicago Cubs	123.5
1960	Los Angeles Dodgers	131.5	1912	Boston Braves	123.4
1952	Philadelphia Athletics	130.4	1976	Boston Red Sox	123.4
1978	Atlanta Braves	130.4	1919	Philadelphia Athletics	123.3
1914	Indianapolis Hoosiers	130.1	1984	Boston Red Sox	123.3
1961	St Louis Cardinals	130.0	1950	St Louis Browns	123.1
1932	Philadelphia Athletics	129.7	1966	Minnesota Twins	122.9
1991	Atlanta Braves	129.5	1924	St Louis Browns	122.8
1981	Philadelphia Phillies	129.2	1910	Pittsburgh Pirates	122.2
1929	Philadelphia Phillies	129.1	1987	Atlanta Braves	122.0
1924	Philadelphia Phillies	128.7	1903	Washington Senators	122.0
1959	Detroit Tigers	128.3	1942	Detroit Tigers	121.9
1907	New York Yankees	128.0	1902	Cincinnati Reds	121.9
1979	Chicago Cubs	127.9	1940	Detroit Tigers	121.7
1915	Baltimore Terrapins	127.8	1995	Milwaukee Brewers	121.6

Who Went to the Moon in '96? (p. 88)

Both Leagues — 1996 Home Runs Listed by Distance (450+ Feet)

Dis	Batter, Team	Pitcher, Team	Date	Site
500	Sosa, ChN	Watson, SF	4/19	ChN
490	Colbrunn, Fla	Watson, SF	6/26	Fla
480	Walker L, Col	Morgan, StL	5/18	Col
480	Lankford, StL	Thompson M, Col	5/19	Col
480	McGwire, Oak	Rodriguez F, Min	6/9	Min
480	McGwire, Oak	Flener, Tor	7/25	Tor
480	Carter, Tor	Wasdin, Oak	7/27	Tor
470	Lankford, StL	Darwin D, Pit	4/17	StL
470	Rodriguez H, Mon	Stottlemyre, StL	4/8	StL
470	Nieves, Det	Nagy, Cle	5/25	Det
470	McGwire, Oak	Baldwin, ChA	7/24	ChA
460	Hayes, Pit	Reed, Col	5/22	Col
460	Bagwell, Hou	Darwin D, Pit	5/29	Pit
460	Caminiti, SD	Reed, Col	7/11	Col
460	Sosa, ChN	Jarvis, Cin	4/17	ChN
460	Galarraga, Col	Telemaco, ChN	7/27	Col
460	Munoz P, Oak	Bones, Mil	4/22	Oak
460	McGwire, Oak	Hershiser, Cle	5/7	Oak
460	Munoz P, Oak	Wells D, Bal	5/25	Bal
460	Vaughn M, Bos	Myers R, Bal	7/7	Bal
460	Vaughn M, Bos	Aguilera, Min	7/28	Min
460	Valentin J, Mil	Wells B, Sea	7/30	Mil
460	Whiten, Sea	Parra, Min	9/13	Min
450	Jones C, NYN	Shaw, Cin	4/23	NYN
450	Burks, Col	Isringhausen, NYN	4/21	NYN
450	Karros, LA	Brown, Fla	4/21	Fla
450	Lankford, StL	Bullinger, ChN	4/30	ChN
450	Hill, SF	Tewksbury, SD	4/30	SD
450	Reed J, Col	Burkett, Fla	5/3	Col
450	Klesko, Atl	Lilliquist, Cin	5/17	Atl
450	Burks, Col	Benes A, StL	5/17	Col
450	Vander Wal, Col	Eckersley, StL	5/18	Col
450	Karros, LA	Schilling, Phi	5/19	LA
450	Mondesi, LA	Harnisch, NYN	5/21	LA
450	Sheffield, Fla	Rueter, Mon	6/4	Fla
450	Walker L, Col	Glavine, Atl	6/8	Col
450	Castilla, Col	Williams M, Phi	6/14	Col
450	Gant, StL	Isringhausen, NYN	6/14	StL
450	Burks, Col	Isringhausen, NYN	7/24	Col
450	Burks, Col	Martinez P, Mon	6/19	Col
450	Walker L, Col	Harnisch, NYN	4/14	Col
450	Newfield, SD	Holmes, Col	4/16	Col
450	Galarraga, Col	Wendell, ChN	7/27	Col
450	Williams M, SF	Woodall, Atl	7/27	SF
450	Johnson M, Pit	Martinez R, LA	8/7	Pit
450	Galarraga, Col	Jones T, Hou	9/15	Col
450	Fielder, Det	Reyes C, Oak	4/6	Oak
450	Williams B, NYA	Radke, Min	4/26	NYA
450	Fielder, Det	Key, NYA	5/9	NYA
450	Vaughn M, Bos	Wengert, Oak	5/29	Oak
450	Gonzalez J, Tex	Milchin, Min	6/2	Tex
450	Delgado C, Tor	Bones, Mil	6/30	Tor
450	Vaughn M, Bos	Olivares, Det	7/12	Det
450	McGwire, Oak	Fernandez A, ChA	7/23	ChA
450	Giles, Cle	Mussina, Bal	7/26	Bal
450	Williams B, NYA	Valera, KC	7/26	NYA
450	Fielder, NYA	Wells D, Bal	9/19	NYA

Who Had the Best Months of the Year? (p. 90)

The Top Batting and Pitching Months of 1996

Batting (75 or more Plate Appearances)

Player, Team	Month	AVG	SLG	OBP	AB	R	H	2B	3B	HR	RBI	SB	BB
McLemore, Tex	June	.472	.597	.563	72	24	34	4	1	1	11	7	15
Eisenreich, Phi	August	.446	.639	.460	83	13	37	11	1	1	14	1	3
Rodriguez A, Sea	August	.435	.758	.474	124	30	54	11	1	9	28	5	11
Alomar R, Bal	May	.421	.621	.491	95	22	40	4	0	5	25	3	16
Mueller, SF	August	.417	.514	.494	72	15	30	5	1	0	6	0	12
Kendall, Pit	August	.413	.560	.477	75	12	31	8	0	1	9	1	6
Joyner, SD	April	.407	.605	.528	86	17	35	12	1	1	14	1	20
Thome, Cle	August	.407	.813	.538	91	27	37	4	0	11	32	1	26
Gonzalez J, Tex	July	.407	.917	.472	108	22	44	10	0	15	38	0	14
Johnson L, NYN	Sep/Oct	.405	.595	.426	111	20	45	10	4	1	10	2	4
Jefferson, Bos	June	.403	.722	.442	72	11	29	4	2	5	18	0	5
Cordova, Min	April	.403	.642	.506	67	22	27	8	1	2	18	2	13
Gwynn T, SD	April	.403	.486	.457	72	12	29	6	0	0	8	2	7
Bell J, Pit	Sep/Oct	.403	.675	.484	77	17	31	6	0	5	21	1	12
Knoblauch, Min	July	.402	.706	.520	102	40	41	13	3	4	15	9	22
O'Neill, NYA	April	.400	.600	.500	85	17	34	8	0	3	14	0	17
Vaughn M, Bos	May	.396	.811	.488	106	24	42	6	1	12	28	0	17
Burks, Col	Sep/Oct	.395	.630	.479	81	16	32	7	0	4	17	9	12
Higginson, Det	June	.394	.789	.470	71	19	28	7	0	7	20	4	10
Rodriguez A, Sea	May	.393	.719	.411	89	23	35	8	0	7	25	2	4
Duncan, NYA	Sep/Oct	.390	.545	.413	77	12	30	7	1	1	7	0	3
Burks, Col	June	.389	.708	.457	113	30	44	7	1	9	31	7	14
Young E, Col	June	.388	.463	.460	121	28	47	4	1	1	18	12	13
Molitor, Min	August	.388	.496	.442	121	18	47	8	1	1	21	3	13
Nilsson, Mil	July	.387	.602	.472	93	20	36	8	0	4	20	0	14
Becker, Min	July	.387	.634	.427	93	25	36	5	3	4	24	3	8
Segui, Mon	April	.386	.557	.443	88	18	34	3	0	4	22	0	9
Molitor, Min	April	.386	.535	.439	101	24	39	7	1	2	21	5	11
Seitzer, Cle	Sep/Oct	.386	.542	.480	83	11	32	10	0	1	16	0	14
Lansing, Mon	April	.383	.533	.455	107	23	41	13	0	1	8	7	11
Rodriguez A, Sea	July	.383	.717	.448	120	35	46	13	0	9	25	2	12

Pitching (25 or more Innings Pitched)

Pitcher, Team	Month	ERA	W	L	S	IP	H	R	ER	BB	K
Finley, Cal	May	0.79	4	0	0	45.2	31	5	4	16	45
Fassero, Mon	July	1.00	3	2	0	45.0	31	9	5	15	44
Darwin D, Hou	June	1.06	4	1	0	34.0	27	4	4	4	8
Guzman, Tor	July	1.27	3	0	0	35.1	22	5	5	8	30
Schilling, Phi	May	1.33	2	0	0	27.0	20	5	4	7	28
Glavine, Atl	May	1.36	4	0	0	39.2	30	7	6	11	32
Brown, Fla	June	1.36	4	1	0	39.2	35	8	6	2	27
Trachsel, ChN	June	1.59	4	0	0	45.1	33	9	8	11	28
Maddux G, Atl	August	1.60	3	1	0	45.0	37	9	8	7	30
Martinez P, Mon	Sep/Oct	1.67	2	1	0	32.1	28	7	6	12	39
Brown, Fla	August	1.71	5	1	0	47.1	32	10	9	4	42
Smoltz, Atl	May	1.73	6	0	0	41.2	26	14	8	11	46
Shaw, Cin	August	1.75	2	1	1	25.2	20	6	5	9	13
Hamilton, SD	August	1.76	3	1	0	41.0	32	9	8	14	39
Wilson, NYN	Sep/Oct	1.76	1	1	0	30.2	29	11	6	14	21
Brown, Fla	Sep/Oct	1.77	3	1	0	35.2	29	9	7	8	21
Hill, Tex	May	1.77	4	1	0	45.2	35	11	9	10	33
Hershiser, Cle	June	1.83	5	0	0	39.1	36	9	8	11	20
Clemens, Bos	August	1.85	4	1	0	39.0	35	8	8	13	39
Fassero, Mon	June	1.88	5	0	0	48.0	28	12	10	9	42
Guzman, Tor	April	1.88	3	1	0	43.0	29	9	9	8	39
Reynolds, Hou	August	1.88	4	1	0	48.0	33	11	10	3	34

Do Heavily-Used Catchers Wind Up Paying At The Plate? (p. 96)

Three-Year Percentages of Games Caught (minimum 410 Games Caught) (listed alphabetically)

Player	Gms Caught	Years	Pct
Earl Battey	424	1961-1963	87.4
Johnny Bench	440	1968-1970	90.2
Yogi Berra	427	1953-1955	92.8
Bob Boone	428	1984-1986	88.1
Gary Carter	439	1978-1980	90.7
Del Crandall	411	1958-1960	88.4
Jody Davis	434	1983-1985	89.5
Carlton Fisk	438	1976-1978	90.1
Bill Freehan	417	1966-1968	85.3
George Gibson	433	1908-1910	93.5
Tom Haller	411	1966-1968	84.7
Jim Hegan	427	1947-1949	91.4
Randy Hundley	463	1967-1969	94.9
Terry Kennedy	430	1983-1985	88.3
Thurman Munson	411	1972-1974	85.8
Tony Pena	441	1983-1985	90.9
Cy Perkins	428	1920-1922	91.8
Darrell Porter	411	1977-1979	84.6
Ray Schalk	419	1920-1922	90.5
Ted Simmons	448	1973-1975	92.2
Jim Sundberg	449	1978-1980	92.2
Butch Wynegar	419	1977-1979	86.4

(Only highest figure for each Catcher was used)

Who Were the Best Players Never to Play in the World Series? (p. 100)

Top 50 Pos. Players and Pitchers who never played in a World Series Game (Pos. Players Ranked by Games; Pitchers Ranked by Innings Pitched)

Position Player	Games Played	Pitcher	Innings Pitched
Andre Dawson	2627	Pud Galvin	5941.1
Ernie Banks	2528	Phil Niekro	5403.2
Billy Williams	2488	Gaylord Perry	5352.0
Nap Lajoie	2480	Kid Nichols	5057.0
Rod Carew	2469	Tim Keefe	5052.1
Luke Appling	2422	Mickey Welch	4802.0
Mickey Vernon	2409	John Clarkson	4536.1
Buddy Bell	2405	Old Hoss Radbourn	4535.1
Jake Beckley	2386	Tony Mullane	4531.1
Bobby Wallace	2383	Fergie Jenkins	4500.2
Jose Cruz	2353	Jack Powell	4388.0
Brian Downing	2344	Gus Weyhing	4324.1
Cap Anson	2276	Jim McCormick	4275.2
Chris Speier	2260	Frank Tanana	4186.2
Ron Santo	2243	Ted Lyons	4161.2
Tim Wallach	2212	Amos Rusie	3769.2
Joe Torre	2209	Jim Bunning	3759.1
Tommy Corcoran	2200	Will White	3542.2
Tony Taylor	2195	Adonis Terry	3523.0
Dale Murphy	2180	Jim Whitney	3496.1
Toby Harrah	2155	Wilbur Cooper	3482.0
Harry Heilmann	2148	Mel Harder	3425.2
Bid McPhee	2135	Charlie Buffinton	3404.0
Willie Keeler	2123	Hooks Dauss	3390.1
Eddie Yost	2109	Clark Griffith	3387.0
Roy McMillan	2093	Chick Fraser	3355.2
Don Kessinger	2078	Al Orth	3354.0
Jesse Burkett	2067	Larry Jackson	3262.0
George Sisler	2055	Dutch Leonard	3220.0
Ryne Sandberg	2029	Silver King	3190.2
Jimmy Ryan	2012	Milt Pappas	3186.1
Bobby Grich	2008	Bill Hutchison	3078.0
Cy Williams	2002	Pink Hawley	3012.2
Roger Connor	1997	Red Donahue	2975.2
Fred Tenney	1994	Ted Breitenstein	2964.1
George Van Haltren	1984	Rube Waddell	2961.1
Clyde Milan	1981	Guy Hecker	2906.0
Bob Elliott	1978	Jack Chesbro	2896.2
Kid Gleason	1966	Jack Stivetts	2887.2
Al Lopez	1950	Dave Stieb	2845.1
Dave Kingman	1941	Steve Rogers	2839.1
Bob Bailey	1931	Bob Caruthers	2828.2
Hal Chase	1917	Frank Dwyer	2819.0
Jim Fregosi	1902	Mark Baldwin	2811.1
Larry Parrish	1891	Bill Doak	2782.0
Roy Sievers	1887	Tommy Bond	2779.2
Johnny Callison	1886	Earl Moore	2775.2
Rick Ferrell	1884	Mark Langston	2772.0
Herman Long	1874	Red Ehret	2754.1
Bob Johnson	1863	Jesse Tannehill	2750.2

Are Smaller Parks Causing the Home Run Explosion? (p. 110)

All Parks

Year	HR	Games	HR/Gm
1989	3083	2106	1.46
1990	3317	2105	1.58
1991	3383	2104	1.61
1992	3038	2106	1.44
1993	4030	2269	1.78
1994	3306	1600	2.07
1995	4081	2017	2.02
1996	4962	2267	2.19

Unchanged Parks

Year	HR	Games	HR/Gm
1989	1519	970	1.57
1990	1624	972	1.67
1991	1727	979	1.76
1992	1319	971	1.36
1993	1727	973	1.77
1994	1439	701	2.05
1995	1734	865	2.00
1996	2083	970	2.15

New Parks

Year	HR	Games	HR/Gm
1989	84	55	1.53
1990	175	81	2.16
1991	300	162	1.85
1992	399	244	1.64
1993	791	405	1.95
1994	874	397	2.20
1995	1140	503	2.27
1996	1347	567	2.38

Changed Parks

Year	HR	Games	HR/Gm
1989	1564	1136	1.38
1990	1693	1133	1.49
1991	1656	1125	1.47
1992	1719	1135	1.51
1993	2303	1296	1.78
1994	1867	899	2.08
1995	2347	1152	2.04
1996	2897	1297	2.22

Who Gets the "Slidin' Billy Trophy"? (p. 114)

Both Leagues — Listed Alphabetically
(Players with 100+ Plate Appearances Batting Leadoff in 1996)

Player, Team	OBP	AB	R	H	BB	HBP	SB
Allensworth, Pit	.340	227	32	60	23	4	11
Alomar R, Bal	.405	197	52	63	29	0	6
Amaral, Sea	.375	166	35	46	22	4	17
Anderson B, Bal	.402	402	87	117	59	18	17
Batista, Oak	.401	139	24	47	15	1	6
Benard, SF	.330	470	83	115	56	4	24
Boggs, NYA	.384	309	42	91	47	0	1
Bragg, Bos	.374	291	57	79	48	2	13
Brumfield, Tor	.303	183	31	44	15	2	5
Cangelosi, Hou	.401	189	40	54	34	3	15
Castillo L, Fla	.320	164	26	43	14	0	17
Clayton, StL	.314	284	43	78	16	1	20
Cora, Sea	.362	417	78	128	31	7	1
Curtis, LA	.332	307	49	72	47	0	12
DeShields, LA	.273	184	24	42	12	0	17
Dykstra, Phi	.381	129	20	33	24	2	3
Erstad, Cal	.338	193	32	55	17	0	3
Fonville, LA	.237	123	17	23	8	0	4
Frye, Bos	.354	194	38	47	32	2	4
Garcia C, Pit	.344	231	40	70	14	1	10
Goodwin C, Cin	.331	109	19	26	15	0	13
Grissom, Atl	.350	671	106	207	41	3	28
Grudzielanek, Mon	.329	597	95	179	19	8	26
Hamilton, Tex	.348	626	94	184	53	2	15
Henderson, SD	.409	447	103	108	118	9	36
Herrera, Oak	.302	208	28	53	12	2	6
Higginson, Det	.500	126	32	53	23	0	3
Hollandsworth, LA	.360	128	22	41	8	0	3
Howard T, Cin	.292	208	32	55	6	3	6
Hudler, Cal	.342	153	33	48	4	3	6
Hunter B, Hou	.313	427	66	124	15	1	29
Javier, SF	.304	123	14	29	11	1	6
Jeter, NYA	.379	174	37	57	14	3	3
Johnson L, NYN	.362	661	112	220	32	1	50
Knoblauch, Min	.448	577	140	197	97	19	45
Listach, Mil	.304	196	27	47	18	1	9
Lofton, Cle	.371	662	131	210	60	0	75
McRae, ChN	.361	620	111	171	73	12	37
Nixon O, Tor	.377	496	87	142	71	1	54
Offerman, KC	.373	344	58	105	37	1	17
Otero, Phi	.331	407	54	112	33	2	16
Owens E, Cin	.250	119	16	22	10	1	8
Phillips T, ChA	.403	578	118	160	123	4	13
Pride, Det	.376	186	37	58	19	0	8
Raines, NYA	.376	154	35	44	22	1	7
Roberts, KC	.354	179	20	55	14	0	4
Smith O, StL	.379	141	26	41	18	2	5
Velarde, Cal	.354	310	50	84	36	4	4
Veras, Fla	.383	211	33	56	39	2	8
Vina, Mil	.345	284	55	82	21	5	6
White D, Fla	.307	208	23	53	12	4	5
Young E, Col	.392	547	109	178	44	19	49
Young E, Oak	.309	182	29	43	18	2	1
AL Team Avg	**.362**	**686**	**124**	**196**	**80**	**7**	**29**
NL Team Avg	**.338**	**684**	**110**	**186**	**64**	**7**	**36**

Who Rose from the Ashes—and Who Crashed to Earth—in 1996? (p. 120)

Both Leagues — Listed Alphabetically (Minimum 425 PA in 1995 and 1996)

Player, Team	'95	'96	+/–
Alicea, StL	.270	.258	–12
Alomar R, Bal	.300	.328	+28
Anderson B, Bal	.262	.297	+35
Baerga, NYN	.314	.254	–60
Bagwell, Hou	.290	.315	+25
Baines, ChA	.299	.311	+12
Becker, Min	.237	.291	+54
Bell D, Hou	.334	.263	–71
Bell J, Pit	.262	.250	–12
Belle, Cle	.317	.311	–6
Berroa, Oak	.278	.290	+12
Bichette, Col	.340	.313	–27
Biggio, Hou	.302	.288	–14
Boggs, NYA	.324	.311	–13
Bonds, SF	.294	.308	+14
Bonilla, Bal	.329	.287	–42
Boone, Cin	.267	.233	–34
Bordick, Oak	.264	.240	–24
Brosius, Oak	.262	.304	+42
Brumfield, Tor	.271	.255	–16
Buhner, Sea	.262	.271	+9
Caminiti, SD	.302	.326	+24
Canseco, Bos	.306	.289	–17
Carreon, Cle	.301	.281	–20
Carter, Tor	.253	.253	+0
Castilla, Col	.309	.304	–5
Clark W, Tex	.302	.284	–18
Clayton, StL	.244	.277	+33
Colbrunn, Fla	.277	.286	+9
Conine, Fla	.302	.293	–9
Cora, Sea	.297	.291	–6
Cordova, Min	.277	.309	+32
Curtis, LA	.268	.252	–16
Davis C, Cal	.318	.292	–26
DeShields, LA	.256	.224	–32
Durham, ChA	.257	.275	+18
Edmonds, Cal	.290	.304	+14
Fielder, NYA	.243	.252	+9
Finley, SD	.297	.298	+1
Fryman, Det	.275	.268	–7
Gaetti, StL	.261	.274	+13
Gagne, LA	.256	.255	–1
Galarraga, Col	.280	.304	+24
Gant, StL	.276	.246	–30
Gilkey, NYN	.298	.317	+19
Girardi, NYA	.262	.294	+32
Gomez C, SD	.223	.257	+34
Gonzalez L, ChN	.276	.271	–5
Goodwin T, KC	.288	.282	–6
Grace, ChN	.326	.331	+5
Greer, Tex	.271	.332	+61
Grissom, Atl	.258	.308	+50
Guillen, ChA	.248	.263	+15
Gwynn T, SD	.368	.353	–15
Hamilton, Tex	.271	.293	+22
Hayes, NYA	.276	.253	–23
Henderson, SD	.300	.241	–59
Higginson, Det	.224	.320	+96
Hoiles, Bal	.250	.258	+8
Jefferies, Phi	.306	.292	–14
Johnson L, NYN	.306	.333	+27
Jones C, Atl	.265	.309	+44
Jordan B, StL	.296	.310	+14
Joyner, SD	.310	.277	–33
Karros, LA	.298	.260	–38
Kent, Cle	.278	.284	+6
King, Pit	.265	.271	+6
Knoblauch, Min	.333	.341	+8
Lankford, StL	.277	.275	–2
Lansing, Mon	.255	.285	+30
Larkin, Cin	.319	.298	–21
Lemke, Atl	.253	.255	+2
Lofton, Cle	.310	.317	+7
Martin A, Pit	.282	.300	+18
Martinez E, Sea	.356	.327	–29
Martinez T, NYA	.293	.292	–1
McGriff, Atl	.280	.295	+15
McLemore, Tex	.261	.290	+29
McRae, ChN	.288	.276	–12
Merced, Pit	.300	.287	–13
Molitor, Min	.270	.341	+71
Mondesi, LA	.285	.297	+12
Morandini, Phi	.283	.250	–33
Murray E, Bal	.323	.260	–63
Naehring, Bos	.307	.288	–19
Nixon O, Tor	.295	.286	–9
O'Leary, Bos	.308	.260	–48
O'Neill, NYA	.300	.302	+2
Offerman, KC	.287	.303	+16
Olerud, Tor	.291	.274	–17
Palmeiro R, Bal	.310	.289	–21
Pendleton, Atl	.290	.238	–52
Phillips T, ChA	.261	.277	+16
Piazza, LA	.346	.336	–10
Ramirez, Cle	.308	.309	+1
Reed J, SD	.256	.244	–12
Ripken C, Bal	.262	.278	+16
Rodriguez I, Tex	.303	.300	–3
Salmon, Cal	.330	.286	–44
Segui, Mon	.309	.286	–23
Seitzer, Cle	.311	.326	+15
Sierra, Det	.263	.247	–16
Snow, Cal	.289	.257	–32
Sosa, ChN	.268	.273	+5
Sprague, Tor	.244	.247	+3
Stanley, Bos	.268	.270	+2
Steinbach, Oak	.278	.272	–6
Stocker, Phi	.218	.254	+36
Surhoff, Bal	.320	.292	–28
Tettleton, Tex	.238	.246	+8
Thomas, ChA	.308	.349	+41
Thome, Cle	.314	.311	–3
Valentin J, Bos	.298	.296	–2
Vaughn G, SD	.224	.260	+36
Vaughn M, Bos	.300	.326	+26
Velarde, Cal	.278	.285	+7
Ventura, ChA	.295	.287	–8
Vizcaino, Cle	.287	.297	+10
Vizquel, Cle	.266	.297	+31
Weiss, Col	.260	.282	+22
White D, Fla	.283	.274	–9
Williams B, NYA	.307	.305	–2
Wilson D, Sea	.278	.285	+7
Zeile, Bal	.246	.263	+17
AL Avg	**.270**	**.277**	**+7**
NL Avg	**.263**	**.262**	**–1**

Will Belle and Thomas Be the Greatest Single-Season Power Duo Ever? (p. 122)

Top 50 Single-Season HR Duos in ML History

Players		Year	Team	Combined HR
Roger Maris	Mickey Mantle	1961	New York Yankees	115
Babe Ruth	Lou Gehrig	1927	New York Yankees	107
Hack Wilson	Gabby Hartnett	1930	Chicago Cubs	93
Jimmie Foxx	Al Simmons	1932	Philadelphia Athletics	93
Ken Griffey Jr	Jay Buhner	1996	Seattle Mariners	93
Lou Gehrig	Babe Ruth	1931	New York Yankees	92
Hank Greenberg	Rudy York	1938	Detroit Tigers	91
Willie Mays	Willie McCovey	1965	San Francisco Giants	91
Babe Ruth	Lou Gehrig	1930	New York Yankees	90
Brady Anderson	Rafael Palmeiro	1996	Baltimore Orioles	89
Mark McGwire	Geronimo Berroa	1996	Oakland Athletics	88
Johnny Mize	Willard Marshall	1947	New York Giants	87
Ted Kluszewski	Wally Post	1955	Cincinnati Reds	87
Andres Galarraga	Ellis Burks	1996	Colorado Rockies	87
Rocky Colavito	Norm Cash	1961	Detroit Tigers	86
Orlando Cepeda	Willie Mays	1961	San Francisco Giants	86
Albert Belle	Jim Thome	1996	Cleveland Indians	86
Eddie Mathews	Hank Aaron	1959	Milwaukee Braves	85
Johnny Bench	Tony Perez	1970	Cincinnati Reds	85
Juan Gonzalez	Dean Palmer	1996	Texas Rangers	85
Willie Mays	Orlando Cepeda	1962	San Francisco Giants	84
Dave Johnson	Darrell Evans	1973	Atlanta Braves	84
Barry Bonds	Matt Williams	1993	San Francisco Giants	84
Babe Ruth	Bob Meusel	1921	New York Yankees	83
Joe DiMaggio	Lou Gehrig	1937	New York Yankees	83
Duke Snider	Roy Campanella	1953	Brooklyn Dodgers	83
Frank Robinson	Boog Powell	1966	Baltimore Orioles	83
George Foster	Johnny Bench	1977	Cincinnati Reds	83
Juan Gonzalez	Rafael Palmeiro	1993	Texas Rangers	83
Ted Williams	Vern Stephens	1949	Boston Red Sox	82
Gil Hodges	Duke Snider	1954	Brooklyn Dodgers	82
Mickey Mantle	Yogi Berra	1956	New York Yankees	82
Willie McCovey	Willie Mays	1963	San Francisco Giants	82
Babe Ruth	Lou Gehrig	1928	New York Yankees	81
Babe Ruth	Lou Gehrig	1929	New York Yankees	81
Harmon Killebrew	Tony Oliva	1964	Minnesota Twins	81
Albert Belle	Manny Ramirez	1995	Cleveland Indians	81
Harmon Killebrew	Bob Allison	1963	Minnesota Twins	80
Hank Aaron	Joe Torre	1966	Atlanta Braves	80
Carl Yastrzemski	Rico Petrocelli	1969	Boston Red Sox	80
Hank Aaron	Earl Williams	1971	Atlanta Braves	80
Mark McGwire	Jose Canseco	1987	Oakland Athletics	80
Matt Williams	Barry Bonds	1994	San Francisco Giants	80
Mickey Mantle	Roger Maris	1960	New York Yankees	79
Hank Aaron	Eddie Mathews	1960	Milwaukee Braves	79
Ben Oglivie	Gorman Thomas	1980	Milwaukee Brewers	79
Hack Wilson	Rogers Hornsby	1929	Chicago Cubs	78
Jimmie Foxx	Bob Johnson	1934	Philadelphia Athletics	78
Lou Gehrig	Joe DiMaggio	1936	New York Yankees	78
Willie Mays	Jim Ray Hart	1964	San Francisco Giants	78
Reggie Jackson	Sal Bando	1969	Oakland Athletics	78
Frank Howard	Mike Epstein	1969	Washington Senators	78
Fred Lynn	Jim Rice	1979	Boston Red Sox	78

You Gotta' Have "Heart," But Can You Live Without One? (p. 125)

Team total statistics for the Number 3, 4, and 5 hitters:

American League — Sorted by Most RBI

Team	Avg	HR	RBI	Slg	Main 3-4-5 Hitters
Seattle	.299	128	419	.578	Griffey Jr, Martinez E, Buhner
Chicago	.306	111	388	.539	Thomas, Baines, Ventura
Cleveland	.294	103	371	.524	Baerga, Belle, Ramirez
Texas	.290	104	368	.524	Greer, Gonzalez J, Tettleton
Baltimore	.287	90	364	.492	Alomar R, Palmeiro R, Bonilla
Milwaukee	.295	87	363	.495	Seitzer, Vaughn G, Jaha
Boston	.301	101	362	.518	Vaughn M, Canseco, Naehring
Oakland	.287	122	354	.543	Giambi, McGwire, Berroa
New York	.284	82	344	.474	O'Neill, Fielder, Martinez T
Minnesota	.303	46	336	.453	Molitor, Cordova, Myers G
Toronto	.255	97	324	.475	Delgado C, Carter, Sprague
Detroit	.254	88	316	.451	Fryman, Fielder, Clark T
California	.282	80	293	.461	Salmon, Davis C, Snow
Kansas City	.249	58	269	.402	Lockhart, Vitiello, Tucker
AL Average	**.285**	**93**	**348**	**.495**	

National League — Sorted by Most RBI

Team	Avg	HR	RBI	Slg	Main 3-4-5 Hitters
Colorado	.307	126	443	.572	Bichette, Walker L, Galarraga
San Francisco	.282	93	367	.494	Bonds, Williams M, Carreon
Houston	.278	66	354	.466	Bagwell, Bell D, Berry
San Diego	.304	84	354	.505	Finley, Caminiti, Joyner
Atlanta	.292	89	329	.494	Jones C, McGriff, Klesko
Florida	.295	86	322	.496	Sheffield, Conine, White D
Cincinnati	.284	95	316	.502	Larkin, Sanders R, Davis E
Los Angeles	.292	93	312	.489	Piazza, Karros, Mondesi
St. Louis	.273	79	310	.457	Gant, Jordan B, Gaetti
Montreal	.277	78	307	.470	Rodriguez H, Alou, Segui
New York	.276	81	307	.470	Gilkey, Hundley, Kent
Pittsburgh	.263	68	306	.437	King, Merced, Hayes
Chicago	.279	75	300	.463	Grace, Sosa, Gonzalez L
Philadelphia	.288	61	275	.441	Jefferies, Zeile, Eisenreich
NL Average	**.285**	**84**	**329**	**.483**	

Who Puts Their Team Ahead? (p. 128)

In the chart below, **Tot RBI** is a player's Total RBI for the season; **GA RBI** is his total number of RBI in plate appearances in which he drove in the go-ahead run; **GA Opp** is the number of times a player drove in the go-ahead run plus the number of times he stranded the go-ahead run in scoring position; **GA DI** is the number of times the player drove in the go-ahead run; **DI%** is the percentage of times a player drove in the go-ahead run divided by his opportunities (**GA Opp**).

Both Leagues — Listed Alphabetically (Minimum 75 Total RBI in 1996)

Player, Team	Tot RBI	GA RBI	GA Opp	GA DI	DI%
Alomar R, Bal	94	17	89	12	13
Alou, Mon	96	41	120	31	26
Anderson B, Bal	110	25	84	21	25
Bagwell, Hou	120	39	106	28	26
Baines, ChA	95	33	111	26	23
Bell D, Hou	113	42	139	29	21
Belle, Cle	148	55	105	33	31
Berroa, Oak	106	24	102	19	19
Berry, Hou	95	23	85	18	21
Bichette, Col	141	49	128	35	27
Biggio, Hou	75	17	97	13	13
Bonds, SF	129	48	96	30	31
Bonilla, Bal	116	22	103	15	15
Buhner, Sea	138	44	111	26	23
Burks, Col	128	42	116	32	28
Caminiti, SD	130	42	94	24	26
Canseco, Bos	82	21	76	16	21
Carter, Tor	107	37	126	27	21
Castilla, Col	113	35	95	19	20
Cirillo, Mil	83	20	84	18	21
Conine, Fla	95	36	120	27	23
Cordova, Min	111	29	119	24	20
Davis C, Cal	95	25	97	20	21
Davis E, Cin	83	25	79	18	23
Delgado C, Tor	92	26	92	15	16
Elster, Tex	99	15	74	9	12
Fielder, NYA	117	39	112	26	23
Finley, SD	95	41	102	28	27
Franco J, Cle	76	22	74	18	24
Fryman, Det	100	28	142	22	15
Gaetti, StL	80	29	81	22	27
Galarraga, Col	150	40	124	29	23
Gant, StL	82	35	78	23	29
Giambi, Oak	79	12	97	10	10
Gilkey, NYN	117	44	113	34	30
Gonzalez J, Tex	144	47	104	30	29
Gonzalez L, ChN	79	28	79	17	22
Grace, ChN	75	20	85	18	21
Greer, Tex	100	32	89	21	24
Griffey Jr, Sea	140	41	121	26	21
Hayes, NYA	75	13	86	10	12
Higginson, Det	81	17	64	15	23
Hollins, Sea	78	19	92	13	14
Hundley, NYN	112	30	113	21	19
Jaha, Mil	118	33	90	19	21
Jeter, NYA	78	21	99	14	14
Jones C, Atl	110	39	108	30	28
Jordan B, StL	104	26	85	19	22
Karros, LA	111	35	112	26	23
King, Pit	111	44	124	30	24
Klesko, Atl	93	27	82	18	22
Lankford, StL	86	28	100	24	24
Larkin, Cin	89	33	92	25	27
Martinez E, Sea	103	29	96	20	21
Martinez T, NYA	117	37	99	22	22
McGriff, Atl	107	35	109	24	22
McGwire, Oak	113	43	77	24	31
Merced, Pit	80	29	75	19	25
Molitor, Min	113	27	131	24	18
Mondesi, LA	88	32	90	22	24
Morris, Cin	80	17	89	10	11
Murray E, Bal	79	18	77	14	18
Nilsson, Mil	84	29	83	18	22
O'Leary, Bos	81	23	64	14	22
O'Neill, NYA	91	38	95	28	29
Palmeiro R, Bal	142	51	119	34	29
Palmer, Tex	107	21	86	14	16
Pendleton, Atl	75	24	86	17	20
Piazza, LA	105	37	96	27	28
Ramirez, Cle	112	36	96	26	27
Ripken C, Bal	102	22	92	16	17
Rodriguez A, Sea	123	34	105	20	19
Rodriguez H, Mon	103	33	97	19	20
Rodriguez I, Tex	86	29	92	21	23
Salmon, Cal	98	31	117	22	19
Sandberg, ChN	92	33	93	19	20
Santiago, Phi	85	29	91	15	16
Seitzer, Cle	78	24	91	20	22
Sheffield, Fla	120	49	100	31	31
Sorrento, Sea	93	26	68	14	21
Sosa, ChN	100	29	101	18	18
Sprague, Tor	101	33	108	23	21
Steinbach, Oak	100	30	90	17	19
Surhoff, Bal	82	22	90	14	16
Tartabull, ChA	101	28	92	16	17
Tettleton, Tex	83	16	70	11	16
Thomas, ChA	134	37	105	28	27
Thome, Cle	116	34	93	23	25
Valentin J, Mil	95	17	93	15	16
Vaughn G, SD	117	32	105	23	22
Vaughn M, Bos	143	42	108	27	25
Ventura, ChA	105	33	102	21	21
White D, Fla	84	24	86	19	22
Williams B, NYA	102	27	90	19	21
Williams M, SF	85	29	92	20	22
Wilson D, Sea	83	21	79	12	15
Zeile, Bal	99	41	129	34	26

Runs Created: Did Bonds Get Robbed of Another MVP Award? (p. 130)

In the chart below, **RC** stands for Runs Created, and **OW%** stands for Offensive Winning Percentage.

Both Leagues — Listed Alphabetically (minimum 350 plate appearances in 1996)

Player, Team	RC	OW%	Player, Team	RC	OW%	Player, Team	RC	OW%
Alfonzo, NYN	39.2	.372	Caminiti, SD	138.7	.802	Gagne, LA	54.2	.466
Alicea, StL	55.7	.535	Canseco, Bos	89.3	.739	Galarraga, Col	136.1	.746
Alomar R, Bal	132.3	.699	Carreon, Cle	64.1	.535	Gant, StL	79.3	.652
Alomar S, Cle	44.0	.306	Carter, Tor	88.6	.450	Garcia C, Pit	52.6	.517
Alou, Mon	82.1	.566	Castilla, Col	111.6	.658	Giambi, Oak	90.1	.558
Amaral, Sea	49.7	.523	Cedeno A, Hou	23.1	.165	Gilkey, NYN	124.0	.739
Anderson B, Bal	149.9	.748	Cirillo, Mil	109.0	.632	Girardi, NYA	55.3	.418
Anderson G, Cal	68.7	.347	Clark T, Det	55.8	.472	Gomez C, SD	53.5	.397
Andrews, Mon	49.2	.480	Clark W, Tex	75.1	.565	Gomez L, ChN	54.8	.538
Aurilia, SF	30.3	.324	Clayton, StL	56.2	.409	Gonzalez A, Tor	61.8	.340
Ausmus, Det	35.1	.257	Colbrunn, Fla	67.9	.493	Gonzalez J, Tex	126.5	.732
Baerga, NYN	51.6	.296	Conine, Fla	101.8	.630	Gonzalez L, ChN	76.1	.575
Bagwell, Hou	155.6	.822	Cora, Sea	74.9	.467	Goodwin T, KC	64.1	.366
Baines, ChA	97.5	.642	Cordova, Min	99.5	.579	Grace, ChN	97.3	.672
Becker, Min	88.0	.549	Curtis, LA	65.5	.398	Green, Tor	65.8	.524
Bell D, Hou	82.0	.480	Damon, KC	63.8	.389	Greer, Tex	119.6	.712
Bell J, Pit	67.9	.464	Davis C, Cal	102.4	.620	Griffey Jr, Sea	141.6	.762
Belle, Cle	155.8	.757	Davis E, Cin	89.9	.727	Grissom, Atl	112.5	.632
Benard, SF	57.2	.413	Delgado C, Tor	85.9	.566	Grudzielanek, Mon	91.2	.550
Berroa, Oak	103.2	.579	DeShields, LA	53.6	.292	Guillen, ChA	47.4	.259
Berry, Hou	66.5	.570	Devereaux, Bal	35.4	.313	Gwynn T, SD	77.1	.658
Bichette, Col	116.6	.667	DiSarcina, Cal	49.8	.248	Hamilton, Tex	84.8	.445
Biggio, Hou	107.1	.639	Duncan, NYA	66.4	.578	Hayes, NYA	57.0	.375
Blowers, LA	42.1	.492	Durham, ChA	87.7	.513	Henderson, SD	81.0	.608
Boggs, NYA	78.8	.542	Edmonds, Cal	93.7	.696	Hernandez J, ChN	35.9	.374
Bonds, SF	162.7	.858	Eisenreich, Phi	68.2	.750	Higginson, Det	106.0	.736
Bonilla, Bal	108.8	.587	Elster, Tex	78.7	.467	Hill, SF	65.6	.638
Boone, Cin	51.1	.326	Fielder, NYA	100.6	.540	Hoiles, Bal	72.5	.567
Bordick, Oak	52.9	.283	Finley, SD	118.7	.657	Hollandsworth, LA	77.2	.615
Bragg, Bos	66.9	.503	Flaherty, SD	52.7	.446	Hollins, Sea	84.2	.520
Branson, Cin	39.4	.444	Fletcher, Mon	50.1	.471	Howard D, KC	39.1	.228
Brosius, Oak	89.3	.666	Franco J, Cle	81.6	.623	Howard T, Cin	46.4	.480
Brumfield, Tor	51.3	.417	Frye, Bos	66.7	.527	Hundley, NYN	106.3	.687
Buhner, Sea	120.0	.659	Fryman, Det	87.0	.449	Hunter B, Hou	58.8	.413
Burks, Col	158.1	.817	Gaetti, StL	79.5	.568	Huskey, NYN	55.2	.505

Player, Team	RC	OW%
Jaha, Mil	119.2	.690
Jefferies, Phi	57.5	.540
Jefferson, Bos	85.6	.721
Jeter, NYA	94.1	.541
Johnson C, Fla	36.9	.296
Johnson L, NYN	121.1	.676
Johnson M, Pit	58.9	.627
Jones C, Atl	130.2	.748
Jordan B, StL	89.9	.655
Joyner, SD	70.6	.608
Karkovice, ChA	34.7	.261
Karros, LA	86.4	.513
Kelly R, Min	52.4	.541
Kendall, Pit	63.9	.592
Kent, Cle	62.0	.520
King, Pit	103.3	.628
Klesko, Atl	102.9	.692
Knoblauch, Min	147.1	.764
Lankford, StL	102.7	.663
Lansing, Mon	86.7	.505
Larkin, Cin	123.6	.760
Lemke, Atl	54.4	.389
Lewis D, ChA	38.0	.295
Lewis M, Det	71.0	.420
Listach, Mil	36.8	.342
Lockhart, KC	56.9	.423
Lofton, Cle	119.4	.600
Lopez J, Atl	66.2	.502
Mabry, StL	74.5	.519
Macfarlane, KC	64.5	.564
Martin A, Pit	104.7	.624
Martinez D, ChA	84.8	.647
Martinez E, Sea	144.3	.803
Martinez T, NYA	100.0	.558
McGriff, Atl	108.0	.645
McGwire, Oak	149.1	.856
McLemore, Tex	81.5	.512
McRae, ChN	102.1	.601
Meares, Min	55.7	.314
Merced, Pit	74.5	.616
Mieske, Mil	53.9	.463

Player, Team	RC	OW%
Miller, Hou	50.5	.379
Molitor, Min	118.5	.614
Mondesi, LA	103.8	.628
Morandini, Phi	60.9	.397
Morris, Cin	94.1	.658
Murray E, Bal	76.5	.422
Myers G, Min	42.4	.418
Naehring, Bos	68.9	.527
Newfield, Mil	55.2	.509
Nieves, Det	66.5	.490
Nilsson, Mil	100.2	.720
Nixon O, Tor	70.8	.462
O'Brien, Tor	44.8	.425
O'Leary, Bos	68.2	.438
O'Neill, NYA	109.3	.641
Offerman, KC	94.6	.561
Olerud, Tor	74.1	.605
Ordonez, NYN	40.8	.264
Otero, Phi	48.6	.443
Pagnozzi, StL	52.7	.483
Palmeiro R, Bal	137.5	.690
Palmer, Tex	106.2	.594
Paquette, KC	54.6	.393
Pendleton, Atl	53.9	.315
Phillips T, ChA	105.4	.587
Piazza, LA	124.6	.773
Ramirez, Cle	127.0	.705
Randa, KC	50.3	.494
Reed J, Col	52.9	.574
Reed J, SD	48.4	.323
Renteria, Fla	62.8	.566
Ripken C, Bal	94.4	.476
Roberts, KC	38.9	.351
Rodriguez A, Sea	156.7	.779
Rodriguez H, Mon	94.9	.652
Rodriguez I, Tex	101.0	.541
Salmon, Cal	118.2	.657
Sandberg, ChN	77.4	.504
Santangelo, Mon	63.6	.589
Santiago, Phi	80.9	.622
Segui, Mon	70.4	.632

Player, Team	RC	OW%
Seitzer, Cle	117.2	.665
Servais, ChN	53.3	.426
Sheffield, Fla	158.5	.848
Sierra, Det	62.9	.366
Snow, Cal	68.4	.360
Sorrento, Sea	89.0	.614
Sosa, ChN	86.8	.628
Sprague, Tor	99.1	.539
Stahoviak, Min	72.4	.586
Stanley, Bos	81.0	.647
Steinbach, Oak	89.2	.564
Stocker, Phi	52.0	.482
Surhoff, Bal	91.6	.579
Tartabull, ChA	79.1	.536
Taubensee, Cin	50.7	.586
Tettleton, Tex	86.2	.547
Thomas, ChA	149.9	.799
Thome, Cle	146.0	.801
Tucker, KC	54.3	.508
Valentin J, Bos	85.4	.528
Valentin J, Mil	93.1	.544
Vaughn G, SD	107.2	.658
Vaughn M, Bos	159.0	.757
Velarde, Cal	87.5	.547
Ventura, ChA	110.9	.608
Vina, Mil	73.5	.424
Vizcaino, Cle	68.9	.463
Vizquel, Cle	87.8	.522
Wallach, LA	38.4	.349
Weiss, Col	81.8	.579
White D, Fla	83.7	.560
White R, Mon	45.9	.521
Whiten, Sea	74.7	.589
Wilkins, SF	60.2	.513
Williams B, NYA	117.9	.675
Williams G, Mil	35.1	.302
Williams M, SF	75.1	.677
Wilson D, Sea	68.1	.443
Young E, Col	100.2	.655
Young E, Oak	63.3	.417
Zeile, Bal	93.8	.548

Who's the Best Bunter? (p. 133)

The following table shows: **SH** = Sac Hits, **FSH** = Failed Sac Hits; and **BH**= Bunt Hits, **FBH** = Failed Bunt Hits

Both Leagues — Listed Alphabetically
(minimum 12 bunts in play)

Batter, Team	SH	FSH	%	BH	FBH	%
Allensworth, Pit	2	1	67	7	3	70
Alomar R, Bal	8	2	80	9	4	69
Aurilia, SF	6	3	67	3	2	60
Bartee, Det	12	0	100	8	7	53
Benard, SF	6	1	86	6	8	43
Biggio, Hou	7	1	87	5	0	100
Bournigal, Oak	8	1	89	2	2	50
Cedeno D, ChA	8	1	89	1	4	20
Clayton, StL	2	1	67	10	8	56
Cora, Sea	5	1	83	4	4	50
Cuyler, Bos	7	0	100	1	4	20
Damon, KC	9	1	90	8	6	57
DeShields, LA	2	2	50	5	8	38
DiSarcina, Cal	16	4	80	0	3	0
Durham, ChA	7	3	70	6	10	37
Elster, Tex	16	1	94	0	1	0
Fassero, Mon	14	6	70	3	1	75
Fonville, LA	3	1	75	5	13	28
Fox, NYA	9	1	90	1	1	50
Girardi, NYA	10	2	83	6	0	100
Glavine, Atl	15	6	71	3	0	100
Gonzalez A, Tor	7	4	64	1	3	25
Goodwin C, Cin	1	0	100	6	6	50
Goodwin T, KC	21	4	84	15	12	56
Guillen, ChA	12	1	92	7	3	70
Hamilton, Tex	7	0	100	6	7	46
Hamilton, SD	11	1	92	1	0	100
Herrera, Oak	3	3	50	3	7	30
Hollins, Sea	1	0	100	12	2	86
Howard D, KC	15	1	94	6	7	46
Javier, SF	5	2	71	1	5	17
Jeter, NYA	5	0	100	3	5	37
Lewis D, ChA	15	2	88	2	9	18
Listach, Mil	5	2	71	1	6	14
Lofton, Cle	7	1	87	21	8	72
Maddux G, Atl	10	1	91	0	1	0
Martinez P, Mon	16	3	84	0	0	0
McCracken, Col	11	1	92	3	4	43
McRae, ChN	2	0	100	9	17	35
Morandini, Phi	5	4	56	3	1	75
Morris, Cin	5	0	100	8	0	100
Neagle, Atl	16	3	84	0	0	0
Nixon O, Tor	7	1	87	20	15	57
Offerman, KC	6	2	75	3	4	43
Osborne, StL	10	2	83	1	0	100
Otero, Phi	0	2	0	11	6	65
Perez R, Tor	4	1	80	6	2	75
Perez T, Tor	6	3	67	4	6	40
Reynolds, Hou	14	1	93	0	0	0
Ritz, Col	10	3	77	1	0	100
Sanchez, ChN	8	1	89	2	3	40
Santangelo, Mon	8	1	89	4	0	100
Smoltz, Atl	14	0	100	0	1	0
Sojo, NYA	8	1	89	2	3	40
Stottlemyre, StL	9	2	82	3	0	100
Valdes I, LA	13	2	87	1	0	100
Valentin J, Mil	6	2	75	9	1	90
Vina, Mil	5	3	62	9	11	45
Vizcaino, Cle	9	1	90	12	5	71
Vizquel, Cle	12	3	80	13	2	87
Weiss, Col	14	1	93	3	4	43
MLB Totals	**1489**	**359**	**81**	**538**	**487**	**52**

Who's First in the Secondary? (p. 136)

Both Leagues — Listed Alphabetically
(minimum 340 plate appearances in 1996)

Player, Team	SA	Player, Team	SA	Player, Team	SA	Player, Team	SA
Abbott, Fla	.244	Duncan, NYA	.185	Joyner, SD	.291	Phillips T, ChA	.346
Alfonzo, NYN	.158	Durham, ChA	.282	Karkovice, ChA	.214	Piazza, LA	.369
Alicea, StL	.282	Edmonds, Cal	.383	Karros, LA	.319	Ramirez, Cle	.433
Alomar R, Bal	.371	Eisenreich, Phi	.237	Kelly R, Min	.230	Randa, KC	.234
Alomar S, Cle	.182	Elster, Tex	.317	Kendall, Pit	.193	Reed J, Col	.261
Alou, Mon	.276	Fielder, NYA	.382	Kent, Cle	.224	Reed J, SD	.166
Amaral, Sea	.276	Finley, SD	.340	King, Pit	.369	Renteria, Fla	.200
Anderson B, Bal	.494	Flaherty, SD	.192	Klesko, Atl	.383	Ripken C, Bal	.278
Anderson G, Cal	.161	Fletcher, Mon	.216	Knoblauch, Min	.400	Roberts, KC	.156
Andrews, Mon	.301	Franco J, Cle	.289	Lankford, StL	.407	Rodriguez A, Sea	.389
Aurilia, SF	.145	Frye, Bos	.265	Lansing, Mon	.212	Rodriguez H, Mon	.359
Ausmus, Det	.176	Fryman, Det	.263	Larkin, Cin	.505	Rodriguez I, Tex	.239
Baerga, NYN	.168	Gaetti, StL	.266	Lemke, Atl	.177	Salmon, Cal	.379
Bagwell, Hou	.518	Gagne, LA	.231	Lewis D, ChA	.264	Sandberg, ChN	.305
Baines, ChA	.343	Galarraga, Col	.377	Lewis M, Det	.213	Santangelo, Mon	.262
Becker, Min	.299	Gant, StL	.453	Listach, Mil	.249	Santiago, Phi	.345
Bell D, Hou	.260	Garcia C, Pit	.197	Lockhart, KC	.219	Segui, Mon	.300
Bell J, Pit	.247	Giambi, Oak	.284	Lofton, Cle	.308	Seitzer, Cle	.300
Belle, Cle	.495	Gilkey, NYN	.387	Lopez J, Atl	.231	Servais, ChN	.182
Benard, SF	.232	Girardi, NYA	.173	Mabry, StL	.204	Sheffield, Fla	.597
Berroa, Oak	.317	Gomez C, SD	.202	Macfarlane, KC	.306	Sierra, Det	.243
Berry, Hou	.278	Gomez L, ChN	.331	Martin A, Pit	.279	Snow, Cal	.216
Bichette, Col	.319	Gonzalez A, Tor	.260	Martinez D, ChA	.286	Sorrento, Sea	.335
Biggio, Hou	.281	Gonzalez J, Tex	.416	Martinez E, Sea	.515	Sosa, ChN	.386
Blowers, LA	.246	Gonzalez L, ChN	.304	Martinez T, NYA	.289	Sprague, Tor	.350
Boggs, NYA	.210	Goodwin T, KC	.206	Matheny, Mil	.185	Stahoviak, Min	.331
Bonds, SF	.663	Grace, ChN	.236	McGriff, Atl	.316	Stanley, Bos	.416
Bonilla, Bal	.326	Green, Tor	.256	McGwire, Oak	.693	Steinbach, Oak	.350
Boone, Cin	.183	Greer, Tex	.328	McLemore, Tex	.290	Stocker, Phi	.239
Bordick, Oak	.175	Griffey Jr, Sea	.495	McRae, ChN	.311	Surhoff, Bal	.276
Bragg, Bos	.321	Grissom, Atl	.267	Meares, Min	.166	Tartabull, ChA	.367
Branson, Cin	.270	Grudzielanek, Mon	.170	Merced, Pit	.291	Taubensee, Cin	.248
Brosius, Oak	.362	Guillen, ChA	.126	Mieske, Mil	.251	Tettleton, Tex	.399
Brumfield, Tor	.294	Gwynn T, SD	.191	Miller, Hou	.182	Thomas, ChA	.484
Buhner, Sea	.433	Hamilton, Tex	.190	Molitor, Min	.230	Thome, Cle	.545
Burks, Col	.437	Hayes, NYA	.203	Mondesi, LA	.260	Tucker, KC	.319
Caminiti, SD	.449	Henderson, SD	.419	Morandini, Phi	.213	Valentin J, Bos	.258
Canseco, Bos	.481	Hernandez J, ChN	.224	Morris, Cin	.265	Valentin J, Mil	.359
Carreon, Cle	.242	Herrera, Oak	.191	Mouton J, Hou	.253	Vaughn G, SD	.450
Carter, Tor	.294	Higginson, Det	.411	Murray E, Bal	.272	Vaughn M, Bos	.409
Castilla, Col	.308	Hill, SF	.314	Myers G, Min	.198	Velarde, Cal	.274
Cedeno A, Hou	.176	Hoiles, Bal	.354	Naehring, Bos	.272	Ventura, ChA	.363
Cirillo, Mil	.272	Hollandsworth, LA	.264	Newfield, Mil	.238	Vina, Mil	.193
Clark T, Det	.327	Hollins, Sea	.312	Nieves, Det	.339	Vizcaino, Cle	.146
Clark W, Tex	.300	Howard D, KC	.179	Nilsson, Mil	.318	Vizquel, Cle	.271
Clayton, StL	.198	Howard T, Cin	.208	Nixon O, Tor	.266	Wallach, LA	.222
Colbrunn, Fla	.200	Hundley, NYN	.433	O'Brien, Tor	.259	Weiss, Col	.263
Conine, Fla	.290	Hunter B, Hou	.169	O'Leary, Bos	.264	White D, Fla	.279
Cora, Sea	.192	Huskey, NYN	.220	O'Neill, NYA	.357	White R, Mon	.225
Cordova, Min	.272	Jaha, Mil	.403	Offerman, KC	.271	Whiten, Sea	.403
Curtis, LA	.278	Jefferies, Phi	.233	Olerud, Tor	.352	Wilkins, SF	.311
Damon, KC	.195	Jefferson, Bos	.311	Ordonez, NYN	.086	Williams B, NYA	.403
Davis C, Cal	.372	Jeter, NYA	.210	Otero, Phi	.173	Williams G, Mil	.191
Davis E, Cin	.439	Johnson C, Fla	.246	Pagnozzi, StL	.219	Williams M, SF	.302
Delgado C, Tor	.338	Johnson L, NYN	.251	Palmeiro R, Bal	.422	Wilson D, Sea	.222
DeShields, LA	.229	Johnson M, Pit	.318	Palmer, Tex	.352	Young E, Col	.239
Devereaux, Bal	.245	Jones C, Atl	.388	Paquette, KC	.252	Young E, Oak	.299
DiSarcina, Cal	.132	Jordan B, StL	.263	Pendleton, Atl	.178	Zeile, Bal	.306

Who Are the Human Air Conditioners? (p. 138)

The table below shows swings missed (**Sw**) as a % of total pitches swung at (**Pit**).

Both Leagues — Listed Alphabetically (minimum 350 plate appearances in 1996)

Player, Team	Sw	Pit	%	Player, Team	Sw	Pit	%	Player, Team	Sw	Pit	%
Alfonzo, NYN	112	714	16	Canseco, Bos	187	730	26	Gant, StL	226	812	28
Alicea, StL	109	659	17	Carreon, Cle	101	801	13	Garcia C, Pit	122	709	17
Alomar R, Bal	144	1187	12	Carter, Tor	289	1400	21	Giambi, Oak	185	1105	17
Alomar S, Cle	101	783	13	Castilla, Col	291	1177	25	Gilkey, NYN	254	1078	24
Alou, Mon	201	1049	19	Cedeno A, Hou	184	674	27	Girardi, NYA	154	776	20
Amaral, Sea	69	544	13	Cirillo, Mil	140	1016	14	Gomez C, SD	97	794	12
Anderson B, Bal	210	1120	19	Clark T, Det	281	780	36	Gomez L, ChN	147	732	20
Anderson G, Cal	191	1039	18	Clark W, Tex	141	854	17	Gonzalez A, Tor	287	1094	26
Andrews, Mon	241	785	31	Clayton, StL	200	975	21	Gonzalez J, Tex	216	1011	21
Aurilia, SF	105	581	18	Colbrunn, Fla	212	1091	19	Gonzalez, ChN	106	911	12
Ausmus, Det	115	667	17	Conine, Fla	256	1206	21	Goodwin T, KC	137	873	16
Baerga, NYN	75	847	9	Cora, Sea	57	852	7	Grace, ChN	95	932	10
Bagwell, Hou	258	1137	23	Cordova, Min	280	1215	23	Green, Tor	209	854	24
Baines, ChA	132	863	15	Curtis, LA	161	959	17	Greer, Tex	165	1019	16
Becker, Min	205	1011	20	Damon, KC	160	1000	16	Griffey Jr, Sea	216	1100	20
Bell D, Hou	343	1250	27	Davis C, Cal	211	1006	21	Grissom, Atl	195	1228	16
Bell J, Pit	215	1131	19	Davis E, Cin	229	790	29	Grudziel., Mon	195	1198	16
Belle, Cle	195	1129	17	Delgado C, Tor	298	1047	28	Guillen, ChA	75	841	9
Benard, SF	140	905	15	DeShields, LA	163	1028	16	Gwynn T, SD	49	730	7
Berroa, Oak	309	1185	26	Devereaux, Bal	107	556	19	Hamilton, Tex	102	1142	9
Berry, Hou	178	848	21	DiSarcina, Cal	80	838	10	Hayes, NYA	207	1021	20
Bichette, Col	303	1351	22	Duncan, NYA	216	828	26	Henderson, SD	110	819	13
Biggio, Hou	177	1157	15	Durham, ChA	199	1071	19	Hernand., ChN	195	684	29
Blowers, LA	161	627	26	Edmonds, Cal	188	811	23	Higginson, Det	132	890	15
Boggs, NYA	37	791	5	Eisenreich, Phi	78	623	13	Hill, SF	233	812	29
Bonds, SF	135	948	14	Elster, Tex	246	1050	23	Hoiles, Bal	196	819	24
Bonilla, Bal	218	1201	18	Fielder, NYA	351	1268	28	Hollandsw., LA	221	929	24
Boone, Cin	218	969	22	Finley, SD	188	1194	16	Hollins, Sea	212	1066	20
Bordick, Oak	89	882	10	Flaherty, SD	119	760	16	Howard D, KC	132	803	16
Bragg, Bos	136	796	17	Fletcher, Mon	74	701	11	Howard T, Cin	139	690	20
Branson, Cin	162	688	24	Franco J, Cle	122	821	15	Hundley, NYN	282	1058	27
Brosius, Oak	179	825	22	Frye, Bos	65	708	9	Hunter B, Hou	205	968	21
Brumfield, Tor	167	734	23	Fryman, Det	252	1232	20	Huskey, NYN	218	816	27
Buhner, Sea	383	1160	33	Gaetti, StL	284	1055	27	Jaha, Mil	244	1020	24
Burks, Col	248	1233	20	Gagne, LA	202	844	24	Jefferies, Phi	57	677	8
Caminiti, SD	234	1088	22	Galarraga, Col	394	1325	30	Jefferson, Bos	222	781	28

Player, Team	Sw	Pit	%
Jeter, NYA	178	1105	16
Johnson C, Fla	223	810	28
Johnson L, NYN	103	1104	9
Johnson M, Pit	159	742	21
Jones C, Atl	213	1087	20
Jordan B, StL	240	1024	23
Joyner, SD	139	823	17
Karkovice, ChA	191	704	27
Karros, LA	252	1201	21
Kelly R, Min	143	704	20
Kendall, Pit	78	770	10
Kent, Cle	214	883	24
King, Pit	181	1107	16
Klesko, Atl	306	1093	28
Knoblauch, Min	117	1107	11
Lankford, StL	317	1178	27
Lansing, Mon	163	1153	14
Larkin, Cin	131	953	14
Lemke, Atl	95	802	12
Lewis D, ChA	61	591	10
Lewis M, Det	183	1022	18
Listach, Mil	84	562	15
Lockhart, KC	125	798	16
Lofton, Cle	117	1159	10
Lopez J, Atl	184	932	20
Mabry, StL	180	1052	17
Macfarlane, KC	147	701	21
Martin A, Pit	286	1238	23
Martinez D, ChA	79	781	10
Martinez E, Sea	110	872	13
Martinez T, NYA	165	1092	15
McGriff, Atl	276	1184	23
McGwire, Oak	246	861	29
McLemore, Tex	121	790	15
McRae, ChN	173	1228	14
Meares, Min	185	997	19
Merced, Pit	134	795	17
Mieske, Mil	159	707	22
Miller, Hou	269	975	28
Molitor, Min	180	1218	15
Mondesi, LA	348	1239	28
Morandini, Phi	128	997	13
Morris, Cin	137	950	14
Murray E, Bal	281	1198	23
Myers G, Min	141	635	22
Naehring, Bos	91	704	13
Newfield, Mil	184	760	24
Nieves, Det	293	888	33
Nilsson, Mil	116	823	14
Nixon O, Tor	112	929	12
O'Brien, Tor	137	708	19
O'Leary, Bos	185	921	20
O'Neill, NYA	170	1046	16
Offerman, KC	141	1041	14
Olerud, Tor	74	676	11
Ordonez, NYN	132	852	15
Otero, Phi	47	680	7
Pagnozzi, StL	157	766	20
Palmeiro R, Bal	180	1188	15
Palmer, Tex	298	1180	25
Paquette, KC	234	854	27
Pendleton, Atl	270	1237	22
Phillips T, ChA	268	1187	23
Piazza, LA	254	1057	24
Ramirez, Cle	187	1067	18
Randa, KC	76	586	13
Reed J, Col	96	611	16
Reed J, SD	72	807	9
Renteria, Fla	133	806	17
Ripken C, Bal	169	1166	14
Roberts, KC	91	735	12
Rodriguez, Sea	210	1182	18
Rodriguez, Mon	396	1188	33
Rodriguez I, Tex	164	1248	13
Salmon, Cal	249	1150	22
Sandberg, ChN	241	1059	23
Santang., Mon	105	713	15
Santiago, Phi	228	998	23
Segui, Mon	145	840	17
Seitzer, Cle	113	1063	11
Servais, ChN	171	852	20
Sheffield, Fla	215	1070	20
Sierra, Det	221	1026	22
Snow, Cal	173	1177	15
Sorrento, Sea	223	884	25
Sosa, ChN	382	1137	34
Sprague, Tor	299	1220	25
Stahoviak, Min	211	832	25
Stanley, Bos	134	772	17
Steinbach, Oak	281	1037	27
Stocker, Phi	168	855	20
Surhoff, Bal	138	952	14
Tartabull, ChA	302	937	32
Taubensee, Cin	136	626	22
Tettleton, Tex	246	918	27
Thomas, ChA	150	1003	15
Thome, Cle	257	1016	25
Tucker, KC	163	701	23
Valentin J, Bos	119	927	13
Valentin J, Mil	279	1185	24
Vaughn G, SD	315	1070	29
Vaughn M, Bos	327	1288	25
Velarde, Cal	198	1025	19
Ventura, ChA	219	1150	19
Vina, Mil	65	882	7
Vizcaino, Cle	139	1002	14
Vizquel, Cle	71	945	8
Wallach, LA	168	732	23
Weiss, Col	100	831	12
White D, Fla	275	1135	24
White R, Mon	137	612	22
Whiten, Sea	238	774	31
Wilkins, SF	251	889	28
Williams B, NYA	135	955	14
Williams G, Mil	158	745	21
Williams M, SF	238	899	26
Wilson D, Sea	190	959	20
Young E, Col	89	926	10
Young E, Oak	287	934	31
Zeile, Bal	159	1003	16
MLB Average			**20**

Which Hitters Will Finish with "Immortal" Numbers? (p. 141)

Players With At Least a 5% Chance at 3000 Hits

Player	Age	Current Hits	Proj. Hits	% Chance
Cal Ripken	35	2549	3166	87
Tony Gwynn	36	2560	3139	81
Wade Boggs	38	2697	3025	58
Roberto Alomar	28	1522	2803	37
Rafael Palmeiro	31	1636	2672	26
Chuck Knoblauch	27	1019	2509	25
Alex Rodriguez	20	259	2151	19
Frank Thomas	28	1077	2355	16
Marquis Grissom	29	1096	2328	15
Carlos Baerga	27	1100	2325	14
Barry Bonds	31	1595	2500	14
Travis Fryman	27	1013	2289	14
Craig Biggio	30	1279	2376	14
Albert Belle	29	1014	2272	13
Mark Grace	32	1514	2447	13
Ken Griffey Jr	26	1204	2331	13
Ruben Sierra	30	1675	2506	13
Raul Mondesi	25	499	2055	12
Harold Baines	37	2425	2782	12
Mo Vaughn	28	794	2156	12
Kenny Lofton	29	883	2178	11
Brian McRae	28	966	2205	11
Lance Johnson	32	1258	2310	10
Bobby Bonilla	33	1643	2461	10
Bernie Williams	27	760	2089	9
Jeff Bagwell	28	950	2162	9
Robin Ventura	28	1041	2197	9
Fred McGriff	32	1466	2360	8
Juan Gonzalez	26	887	2100	7
Gregg Jefferies	28	1224	2237	7
Manny Ramirez	24	406	1842	5

Players With At Least a 9% Chance at 500 Home Runs

Player	Age	Current HR	Proj. HR	% Chance
Barry Bonds	31	334	566	89
Albert Belle	29	242	575	79
Mark McGwire	32	329	543	75
Ken Griffey Jr	26	238	561	73
Frank Thomas	28	222	530	61
Juan Gonzalez	26	214	518	56
Jose Canseco	31	328	495	47
Sammy Sosa	27	171	469	40
Cecil Fielder	32	289	478	40
Fred McGriff	32	317	478	38
Mo Vaughn	28	155	455	37
Rafael Palmeiro	31	233	451	32
Jay Buhner	31	213	444	30
Gary Sheffield	27	159	411	24
Matt Williams	30	247	426	21
Manny Ramirez	24	83	373	19
Jim Thome	25	93	375	19
Alex Rodriguez	20	41	358	19
Tim Salmon	27	120	369	15
Joe Carter	36	357	450	15
Jeff Bagwell	28	144	374	15
Dean Palmer	27	140	368	13
Greg Vaughn	30	179	376	11
Robin Ventura	28	144	361	11
Eric Karros	28	123	349	10
Ryan Klesko	25	76	328	9
Andres Galarraga	35	247	396	9

Who Are the Real RBI Kings? (p. 144)

**Both Leagues — Sorted by RBI Percentage
(minimum 500 RBI Opportunities)**

Player, Team	Opp	RBI	Pct
Ken Griffey Jr, Sea	876	131	15.0
Mark McGwire, Oak	664	98	14.8
Juan Gonzalez, Tex	910	133	14.6
Barry Bonds, SF	817	118	14.4
Albert Belle, Cle	1004	139	13.8
Ken Caminiti, SD	889	121	13.6
Frank Thomas, ChA	900	122	13.6
Andres Galarraga, Col	927	121	13.1
Gary Sheffield, Fla	828	108	13.0
Jim Thome, Cle	834	108	12.9
Jay Buhner, Sea	983	127	12.9
Rafael Palmeiro, Bal	1008	128	12.7
Dante Bichette, Col	999	126	12.6
Jose Canseco, Bos	635	80	12.6
Mo Vaughn, Bos	1031	127	12.3
Jeff Bagwell, Hou	943	116	12.3
Brady Anderson, Bal	850	104	12.2
Ron Gant, StL	646	79	12.2
Greg Vaughn, Mil-SD	887	108	12.2
Alex Rodriguez, Sea	938	114	12.2
John Jaha, Mil	930	111	11.9
Danny Tartabull, ChA	812	96	11.8
Eric Davis, Cin	636	75	11.8
Todd Hundley, NYN	864	101	11.7
Cecil Fielder, Det-NYA	943	110	11.7
Tony Clark, Det	601	70	11.6
Bob Higginson, Det	671	77	11.5
Brian Jordan, StL	803	92	11.5
Sean Berry, Hou	734	84	11.4
Jeff King, Pit	913	104	11.4
Ellis Burks, Col	963	109	11.3
Terry Steinbach, Oak	828	93	11.2
Vinny Castilla, Col	946	106	11.2
Bernard Gilkey, NYN	899	100	11.1
Manny Ramirez, Cle	936	104	11.1
Matt Williams, SF	662	73	11.0
Edgar Martinez, Sea	828	91	11.0
Mike Piazza, LA	831	91	11.0
Sammy Sosa, ChN	814	89	10.9
Carlos Delgado, Tor	770	83	10.8
Bobby Bonilla, Bal	956	102	10.7
Henry Rodriguez, Mon	825	88	10.7
Tino Martinez, NYA	1036	109	10.5
Barry Larkin, Cin	736	77	10.5
Dean Palmer, Tex	987	103	10.4
Ed Sprague, Tor	911	95	10.4
Ryan Klesko, Atl	827	86	10.4
Paul Sorrento, Sea	799	83	10.4
Geronimo Berroa, Oak	947	98	10.3
Ryne Sandberg, ChN	824	85	10.3
Kevin Elster, Tex	894	92	10.3
Reggie Jefferson, Bos	642	66	10.3
Eric Karros, LA	1005	103	10.2
Glenallen Hill, SF	619	63	10.2
Chris Hoiles, Bal	639	65	10.2
Mark Whiten, Phi-Atl-Sea	669	68	10.2
Dave Nilsson, Mil	741	75	10.1
Moises Alou, Mon	866	87	10.0
Harold Baines, ChA	857	86	10.0
Benito Santiago, Phi	778	78	10.0
Bernie Williams, NYA	943	94	10.0
Chipper Jones, Atl	917	91	9.9
Tim Salmon, Cal	903	89	9.9
Robin Ventura, ChA	999	98	9.8
Mike Stanley, Bos	658	64	9.7
Chili Davis, Cal	866	84	9.7
Luis Gonzalez, ChN	748	72	9.6
Roberto Alomar, Bal	884	85	9.6
Marty Cordova, Min	969	93	9.6
Shane Andrews, Mon	594	57	9.6
Will Clark, Tex	712	68	9.6
Troy O'Leary, Bos	808	77	9.5
Joe Carter, Tor	976	93	9.5
Mickey Tettleton, Tex	800	76	9.5
Leo Gomez, ChN	558	53	9.5
Orlando Merced, Pit	716	68	9.5
Julio Franco, Cle	681	64	9.4
Rusty Greer, Tex	898	84	9.4
Derek Bell, Hou	1098	102	9.3
Jose Valentin, Mil	902	83	9.2
Craig Paquette, KC	686	63	9.2
Dan Wilson, Sea	828	76	9.2
Travis Fryman, Det	996	91	9.1
Fred McGriff, Atl	989	90	9.1
Paul Molitor, Min	1081	98	9.1
Scott Brosius, Oak	665	60	9.0
Michael Tucker, KC	521	47	9.0
Paul O'Neill, NYA	914	82	9.0
Todd Zeile, Phi-Bal	982	88	9.0
Jeff Conine, Fla	996	88	8.8
Jason Giambi, Oak	809	71	8.8
Jeff Cirillo, Mil	871	76	8.7
Ray Lankford, StL	828	72	8.7
Matt Mieske, Mil	621	54	8.7
Gary Gaetti, StL	817	71	8.7
Jacob Brumfield, Pit-Tor	576	50	8.7
Cal Ripken, Bal	1007	87	8.6
Melvin Nieves, Det	660	57	8.6
Dave Hollins, Min-Sea	826	71	8.6
Steve Finley, SD	1024	88	8.6
Javy Lopez, Atl	770	66	8.6
Hal Morris, Cin	817	70	8.6
Devon White, Fla	867	74	8.5
John Flaherty, Det-SD	668	57	8.5
Jim Edmonds, Cal	646	55	8.5
Tim Naehring, Bos	717	61	8.5

Player, Team	Opp	RBI	Pct
Darren Lewis, ChA	558	47	8.4
Mike Matheny, Mil	500	42	8.4
John Olerud, Tor	608	51	8.4
Raul Mondesi, LA	997	83	8.3
B.J. Surhoff, Bal	829	69	8.3
David Segui, Mon	625	52	8.3
Marc Newfield, SD-Mil	626	52	8.3
Tom Pagnozzi, StL	627	52	8.3
Butch Huskey, NYN	630	52	8.3
Darrin Fletcher, Mon	622	51	8.2
F.P. Santangelo, Mon	611	50	8.2
Mike Macfarlane, KC	588	48	8.2
Wally Joyner, SD	701	57	8.1
Ernie Young, Oak	718	58	8.1
Eddie Murray, Cle-Bal	929	75	8.1
Scott Stahoviak, Min	651	52	8.0
Eric Young, Col	865	69	8.0
Kevin Seitzer, Mil-Cle	868	69	7.9
Mark Carreon, SF-Cle	705	56	7.9
Charlie Hayes, Pit-NYA	821	65	7.9
Rick Wilkins, Hou-SF	645	51	7.9
Scott Servais, ChN	696	55	7.9
Chuck Knoblauch, Min	836	66	7.9
Bip Roberts, KC	526	41	7.8
Ivan Rodriguez, Tex	977	76	7.8
Jay Bell, Pit	801	62	7.7
Greg Myers, Min	547	42	7.7
Mark Grace, ChN	809	62	7.7
Bret Boone, Cin	824	63	7.6
Ruben Sierra, NYA-Det	891	68	7.6
Derek Jeter, NYA	933	71	7.6
Mark Johnson, Pit	529	40	7.6
Dave Martinez, ChA	649	49	7.6
Terry Pendleton, Fla-Atl	899	67	7.5
John Mabry, StL	860	64	7.4
Craig Biggio, Hou	890	66	7.4
Joe Randa, KC	517	38	7.4
Rich Becker, Min	831	61	7.3
Greg Gagne, LA	669	49	7.3
Greg Colbrunn, Fla	820	60	7.3
Gregg Jefferies, Phi	616	45	7.3
Roberto Kelly, Min	522	38	7.3
Pat Meares, Min	856	62	7.2
Tim Wallach, Cal-LA	541	39	7.2
Jose Hernandez, ChN	528	38	7.2
Brian McRae, ChN	851	61	7.2
Jeff Kent, NYN-Cle	692	49	7.1
Alex Gonzalez, Tor	810	57	7.0
Rondell White, Mon	540	38	7.0
Orlando Miller, Hou	725	51	7.0
Charlie O'Brien, Tor	512	36	7.0
Keith Lockhart, KC	658	46	7.0
Mariano Duncan, NYA	663	46	6.9
Tony Phillips, ChA	781	54	6.9
Ray Durham, ChA	877	60	6.8
Todd Hollandsworth, LA	704	48	6.8
A. Cedeno, SD-Det-Hou	500	34	6.8
Jim Eisenreich, Phi	530	36	6.8
Carlos Garcia, Pit	561	38	6.8

Player, Team	Opp	RBI	Pct
Lance Johnson, NYN	940	63	6.7
Darren Bragg, Sea-Bos	583	39	6.7
Garret Anderson, Cal	1001	66	6.6
Luis Alicea, StL	596	39	6.5
J.T. Snow, Cal	909	59	6.5
Carlos Baerga, Cle-NYN	832	54	6.5
Tony Gwynn, SD	663	43	6.5
Dave Howard, KC	666	43	6.5
Thomas Howard, Cin	528	34	6.4
Sandy Alomar, Cle	668	43	6.4
Mike Devereaux, Bal	517	33	6.4
Marquis Grissom, Atl	910	58	6.4
John Valentin, Bos	801	51	6.4
Al Martin, Pit	929	59	6.4
Kenny Lofton, Cle	940	59	6.3
Omar Vizquel, Cle	850	53	6.2
Johnny Damon, KC	774	47	6.1
Ron Karkovice, ChA	551	33	6.0
Chris Gomez, Det-SD	689	41	6.0
Randy Velarde, Cal	757	45	5.9
Joe Girardi, NYA	673	40	5.9
Kevin Stocker, Phi	608	36	5.9
Edgardo Alfonzo, NYN	575	34	5.9
Jeff Frye, Bos	622	36	5.8
Jeff Reed, Col	502	29	5.8
Jason Kendall, Pit	641	37	5.8
Brad Ausmus, SD-Det	565	32	5.7
Shawn Green, Tor	676	38	5.6
Mark Lewis, Det	811	45	5.5
Gerald Williams, NYA-Mil	543	30	5.5
Mike Bordick, Oak	836	46	5.5
Chad Curtis, Det-LA	730	40	5.5
Gary DiSarcina, Cal	845	46	5.4
Jody Reed, SD	762	41	5.4
Joey Cora, Sea	783	41	5.2
Walt Weiss, Col	789	41	5.2
Jose Offerman, KC	803	41	5.1
Ozzie Guillen, ChA	748	38	5.1
Charles Johnson, Fla	613	31	5.1
Ricky Otero, Phi	554	27	4.9
Darryl Hamilton, Tex	918	44	4.8
Fernando Vina, Mil	820	39	4.8
Mike Lansing, Mon	897	42	4.7
Mark McLemore, Tex	817	38	4.7
Wade Boggs, NYA	721	32	4.4
Delino DeShields, LA	838	37	4.4
Mark Lemke, Atl	727	32	4.4
Rich Aurilia, SF	500	22	4.4
Royce Clayton, StL	723	30	4.1
Jose Vizcaino, NYN-Cle	782	32	4.1
Edgar Renteria, Fla	624	25	4.0
Tom Goodwin, KC	750	29	3.9
Brian L. Hunter, Hou	750	29	3.9
Rickey Henderson, SD	603	23	3.8
Mark Grudzielanek, Mon	900	34	3.8
Otis Nixon, Tor	692	26	3.8
Marvin Benard, SF	680	25	3.7
Rey Ordonez, NYN	753	26	3.5
MLB Avg			**9.0**

Who Gets the Green Light on 3-and-0? (p. 146)

Swinging on 3-0 Results (Minimum 25 3-0 Swings from 1992-96)

Player	Times Swung	3-and-0 Counts	Pct Swung	AB	H	HR	RBI	Avg
Andres Galarraga	41	73	.562	18	9	2	6	.500
Albert Belle	84	153	.549	29	8	2	7	.276
Fred McGriff	74	150	.493	40	18	6	19	.450
Vinny Castilla	28	62	.452	13	4	1	4	.308
Juan Gonzalez	49	115	.426	26	12	5	14	.462
Kevin Mitchell	25	64	.391	16	7	1	4	.438
Ken Griffey Jr	62	171	.363	24	10	3	9	.417
Frank Thomas	98	273	.359	54	21	7	17	.389
Eddie Murray	44	137	.321	25	8	0	4	.320
Matt Williams	29	91	.319	9	6	3	6	.667
Greg Vaughn	47	149	.315	25	10	5	7	.400
Paul Sorrento	37	122	.303	24	15	2	8	.625
Dave Justice	47	155	.303	20	8	2	7	.400
Gary Gaetti	27	94	.287	10	4	0	1	.400
Ken Caminiti	43	150	.287	21	10	2	9	.476
Eric Karros	38	133	.286	20	10	3	11	.500
Jeff Bagwell	56	206	.272	26	14	3	10	.538
Jeff Conine	27	102	.265	12	6	3	8	.500
Mark Whiten	35	133	.263	16	6	3	7	.375
Jim Thome	37	144	.257	13	7	4	5	.538
Ron Gant	38	150	.253	15	3	2	9	.200
Danny Tartabull	34	140	.243	15	9	5	7	.600
Jose Canseco	29	120	.242	14	3	1	5	.214
Bobby Bonilla	26	116	.224	16	3	0	3	.188
Ruben Sierra	30	137	.219	9	4	2	5	.444
Charlie Hayes	25	115	.217	11	2	0	3	.182
Mo Vaughn	35	163	.215	13	1	0	3	.077
John Kruk	30	141	.213	14	7	2	6	.500
Chili Davis	32	154	.208	16	5	3	6	.313
Mike Stanley	28	136	.206	17	8	1	14	.471
Chris Hoiles	31	161	.193	18	9	5	12	.500
Barry Bonds	38	214	.178	24	6	2	9	.250
Jay Buhner	28	160	.175	17	6	2	9	.353
Harold Baines	25	145	.172	13	4	1	2	.308
Paul Molitor	27	176	.153	10	4	1	5	.400
Todd Zeile	29	192	.151	9	3	1	4	.333
Cecil Fielder	27	185	.146	11	4	0	5	.364
Paul O'Neill	26	184	.141	14	6	1	5	.429
Robin Ventura	31	231	.134	18	5	3	12	.278

Is the Big Cat Really Just a Nice, Average Kitty? (p. 148)

Offensive Differentials by Park—1996

A.L. Park	Team	Home RC/27	Road RC/27	Pct Diff
Oriole Park at Camden Yards	Bal	5.38	6.01	–10.5
Fenway Park	Bos	6.31	5.33	18.5
Anaheim Stadium	Cal	5.26	5.47	–3.7
Comiskey Park	ChA	4.98	5.87	–15.1
Jacobs Field	Cle	5.61	5.50	2.0
Tiger Stadium	Det	5.59	5.84	–4.2
Ewing M. Kauffman Stadium	KC	4.62	5.02	–7.9
County Stadium	Mil	5.67	5.63	0.6
Hubert H. Humphrey Metrodome	Min	5.80	5.32	9.0
Yankee Stadium	NYA	5.28	5.20	1.6
Oakland-Alameda County Coliseum	Oak	5.55	5.79	–4.2
The Kingdome	Sea	5.99	6.14	–2.5
The Ballpark in Arlington	Tex	6.06	5.26	15.2
SkyDome	Tor	5.04	4.82	4.6

N.L. Park	Team	Home RC/27	Road RC/27	Pct Diff
Atlanta-Fulton County Stadium	Atl	4.40	4.25	3.5
Wrigley Field	ChN	4.57	4.61	–0.9
Cinergy Field	Cin	4.94	4.81	2.5
Coors Field	Col	7.83	4.28	83.1
Pro Player Stadium	Fla	3.97	4.66	–14.7
The Astrodome	Hou	4.55	5.23	–12.9
Dodger Stadium	LA	3.44	4.83	–28.7
Olympic Stadium	Mon	4.61	4.17	10.7
Shea Stadium	NYN	4.25	5.25	–19.0
Veterans Stadium	Phi	4.48	4.71	–4.8
Three Rivers Stadium	Pit	5.24	4.83	8.6
Busch Stadium	StL	4.38	4.53	–3.2
San Diego/Jack Murphy Stadium	SD	4.22	4.43	–4.9
3 Com Park	SF	4.77	4.89	–2.4

Which Pitchers are the Real "Stoppers"? (p. 151)

Pitcher's Record after a Team Loss or Tie—1996
(minimum 5 GS)

Pitcher, Team	W-L	Pct
Nagy, Cle	8-0	1.000
Oliver, Tex	6-0	1.000
Krivda, Bal	2-0	1.000
Ogea, Cle	2-0	1.000
Hutton, Fla	2-0	1.000
Avery, Atl	1-0	1.000
Martinez R, LA	9-1	.900
Pettitte, NYA	13-3	.813
Sanders, SD	4-1	.800
Telemaco, ChN	4-1	.800
Aguilera, Min	4-1	.800
Hamilton, SD	11-3	.786
Valdes I, LA	7-2	.778
Key, NYA	6-2	.750
Coppinger, Bal	6-2	.750
Chouinard, Oak	3-1	.750
Eshelman, Bos	3-1	.750
Martinez D, Cle	3-1	.750
Grace, Phi	3-1	.750
Hentgen, Tor	13-5	.722
Neagle, Atl	10-4	.714
Wells B, Sea	5-2	.714
Nomo, LA	7-3	.700
Pavlik, Tex	7-3	.700
Glavine, Atl	9-4	.692
Belcher, KC	10-5	.667
Hitchcock, Sea	8-4	.667
Smoltz, Atl	8-4	.667
Valenzuela, SD	6-3	.667
Rosado, KC	6-3	.667
Ashby, SD	4-2	.667
Adams W, Oak	2-1	.667
Mussina, Bal	11-6	.647
Benes An, StL	9-5	.643
Alvarez W, ChA	7-4	.636
Haney, KC	7-4	.636
Fernandez A, ChA	12-7	.632
Tapani, ChA	5-3	.625
Moyer, Sea	5-3	.625
Trachsel, ChN	8-5	.615
Jones B, NYN	8-5	.615
Clark M, NYN	9-6	.600
Reynolds, Hou	9-6	.600
Guzman, Tor	6-4	.600
Appier, KC	6-4	.600
Wojciechowski, Oak	3-2	.600
D'Amico, Mil	3-2	.600
Clemens, Bos	3-2	.600
Salkeld, Cin	3-2	.600
McDonald, Mil	10-7	.588
Gardner, SF	7-5	.583
Fassero, Mon	7-5	.583
Navarro, ChN	7-5	.583
Mulholland, Sea	7-5	.583
Ritz, Col	8-6	.571
Witt, Tex	8-6	.571
Schmidt J, Pit	4-3	.571
Urbina, Mon	4-3	.571
Astacio, LA	4-3	.571
Martinez P, Mon	4-3	.571
Wasdin, Oak	4-3	.571
Leiter A, Fla	9-7	.563
Maddux G, Atl	5-4	.556
Burkett, Tex	5-4	.556
Benes Al, StL	5-4	.556
Karl, Mil	6-5	.545
Osborne, StL	7-6	.538
Brown, Fla	8-7	.533
Hershiser, Cle	6-6	.500
Schilling, Phi	6-6	.500
Johns, Oak	5-5	.500
Portugal, Cin	5-5	.500
Gooden, NYA	5-5	.500
McDowell J, Cle	4-4	.500
Hampton, Hou	4-4	.500
Stottlemyre, StL	4-4	.500
Foster, ChN	4-4	.500
Gohr, Cal	4-4	.500
Wolcott, Sea	3-3	.500
Wagner P, Pit	3-3	.500
Gross, Tex	3-3	.500
Mercker, Cle	2-2	.500
Eldred, Mil	2-2	.500
Fernandez S, Phi	2-2	.500
Langston, Cal	2-2	.500
Lieber, Pit	2-2	.500
Jarvis, Cin	2-2	.500
Miranda, Mil	1-1	.500
Beech, Phi	1-1	.500
Bosio, Sea	1-1	.500
Flener, Tor	1-1	.500
Finley, Cal	9-10	.474
Rodriguez F, Min	6-7	.462
Thompson M, Col	6-7	.462
Hill, Tex	5-6	.455
Darwin D, Hou	4-5	.444
Morgan, Cin	4-5	.444
Sele, Bos	4-5	.444
Cormier, Mon	4-5	.444
Rogers, NYA	4-5	.444
Tewksbury, SD	4-5	.444
Isringhausen, NYN	4-5	.444
Boskie, Cal	6-8	.429
Wakefield, Bos	6-8	.429
Bullinger, ChN	3-4	.429
Gordon, Bos	3-4	.429
Linton, KC	3-4	.429
Drabek, Hou	3-4	.429
Harnisch, NYN	5-7	.417
Lira, Det	5-7	.417
Smiley, Cin	6-9	.400
Smith Z, Pit	4-6	.400
Erickson, Bal	4-6	.400
Baldwin, ChA	2-3	.400
Worrell T, SD	2-3	.400
Leiter M, Mon	5-8	.385
Hanson, Tor	6-10	.375
Wengert, Oak	3-5	.375
Quantrill, Tor	3-5	.375
Candiotti, LA	3-5	.375
Hunter, Phi	3-5	.375
Watson, SF	4-7	.364
Kile, Hou	4-7	.364
Wells D, Bal	5-9	.357
Radke, Min	6-11	.353
Williams M, Phi	4-8	.333
Olivares, Det	3-6	.333
Springer D, Cal	2-4	.333
Weathers, NYA	1-2	.333
Sodowsky, Det	1-2	.333
Wilson, NYN	4-9	.308
VanLandingham, SF	4-9	.308
Robertson, Min	4-10	.286
Grimsley, Cal	2-5	.286
Rueter, SF	2-5	.286
Castillo F, ChN	3-9	.250
Aldred, Min	2-6	.250
Mimbs, Phi	2-6	.250
Park, LA	1-3	.250
Freeman, ChA	1-3	.250
Dickson, Cal	1-3	.250
Burba, Cin	3-10	.231
Wall, Hou	2-8	.200
Fernandez O, SF	2-8	.200
Estes, SF	1-4	.200
Telgheder, Oak	1-4	.200
Reyes C, Oak	1-4	.200
Hammond, Fla	1-4	.200
Bones, NYA	2-9	.182
Prieto, Oak	1-5	.167
Van Poppel, Det	1-5	.167
Schourek, Cin	1-5	.167
Williams B, Det	1-6	.143
Sparks, Mil	1-6	.143
Reynoso, Col	1-7	.125
Rapp, Fla	1-7	.125
Gubicza, KC	1-7	.125
Abbott J, Cal	1-7	.125
Rekar, Col	0-1	.000
Paniagua, Mon	0-2	.000
Bailey R, Col	0-3	.000
Keagle, Det	0-4	.000
Wagner M, Sea	0-2	.000
Wright, Col	0-3	.000
Miceli, Pit	0-5	.000
Munoz B, Phi	0-3	.000
Thompson J, Det	0-5	.000

Which Pitchers Find Hitting "Elementary"? (p. 154)

1996 Active Pitchers — Listed Alphabetically
(minimum 50 plate appearances lifetime)

Pitcher, Team	AVG	AB	H	HR	RBI
Ashby, SD	.168	202	34	0	10
Astacio, LA	.111	225	25	0	6
Avery, Atl	.179	408	73	4	31
Bautista, SF	.100	50	5	0	1
Benes Al, StL	.134	67	9	0	5
Benes An, StL	.130	447	58	4	30
Bielecki, Atl	.079	280	22	0	13
Blair, SD	.058	86	5	0	5
Boskie, Cal	.184	141	26	1	8
Bottenfield, ChN	.246	61	15	0	3
Brantley, Cin	.118	68	8	0	5
Brocail, Hou	.164	67	11	0	1
Brown, Fla	.118	76	9	0	3
Bullinger, ChN	.180	122	22	3	17
Burba, Cin	.120	117	14	2	8
Burkett, Tex	.088	419	37	0	14
Candiotti, LA	.117	266	31	0	10
Castillo F, ChN	.108	268	29	0	8
Charlton, Sea	.093	86	8	0	1
Clark M, NYN	.071	112	8	0	3
Cooke, Pit	.171	117	20	0	6
Cormier, Mon	.185	184	34	0	12
Darwin D, Hou	.136	242	33	2	19
Drabek, Hou	.167	714	119	2	46
Eckersley, StL	.133	181	24	3	12
Fassero, Mon	.077	207	16	0	5
Fernandez O, SF	.088	57	5	0	1
Fernandez S, Phi	.182	538	98	1	34
Foster, ChN	.216	116	25	1	15
Freeman, ChA	.114	140	16	2	7
Gardner, SF	.126	269	34	0	12
Glavine, Atl	.199	632	126	1	44
Hamilton, SD	.104	173	18	1	8
Hammond, Fla	.205	229	47	4	14
Hampton, Hou	.187	91	17	0	3
Harnisch, NYN	.119	319	38	0	15
Hill, Tex	.148	324	48	1	19
Honeycutt, StL	.132	182	24	0	9
Isringhausen, NYN	.218	78	17	2	9
Jackson D, StL	.127	408	52	0	28
Jarvis, Cin	.164	61	10	0	2
Jones B, NYN	.121	182	22	0	5
Kile, Hou	.111	279	31	1	17
Leiter A, Fla	.100	70	7	0	1
Leiter M, Mon	.109	128	14	0	10
Lieber, Pit	.125	96	12	0	3
Lilliquist, Cin	.213	108	23	2	8
Loaiza, Pit	.174	69	12	0	3
Maddux G, Atl	.179	784	140	2	37
Martinez P, Mon	.096	177	17	0	11
Martinez R, LA	.149	510	76	1	31
Mimbs, Phi	.132	68	9	0	2

Pitcher, Team	AVG	AB	H	HR	RBI
Mlicki, NYN	.061	49	3	0	2
Morgan, Cin	.087	425	37	0	12
Mulholland, Sea	.091	450	41	2	11
Munoz B, Phi	.174	46	8	1	6
Myers R, Bal	.186	59	11	0	7
Navarro, ChN	.155	142	22	0	10
Neagle, Atl	.138	210	29	2	19
Nied, Col	.141	71	10	0	2
Nomo, LA	.113	141	16	0	7
Olivares, Det	.229	201	46	4	21
Osborne, StL	.178	197	35	1	17
Painter, Col	.164	55	9	0	5
Patterson B, ChN	.127	55	7	0	4
Pena, Fla	.110	181	20	1	7
Petkovsek, StL	.113	53	6	0	2
Portugal, Cin	.193	393	76	2	32
Pugh, Cin	.202	109	22	0	4
Rapp, Fla	.128	188	24	0	11
Rekar, Col	.122	41	5	0	0
Reynolds, Hou	.157	178	28	2	6
Reynoso, Col	.140	171	24	2	6
Ritz, Col	.180	133	24	1	7
Rojas, Mon	.121	58	7	0	3
Rueter, SF	.093	108	10	0	8
Ruffin B, Col	.081	295	24	0	7
Sanders, SD	.180	111	20	0	7
Schilling, Phi	.158	273	43	0	14
Schourek, Cin	.173	197	34	1	15
Smiley, Cin	.149	464	69	2	33
Smith L, Cin	.047	64	3	1	2
Smith Z, Pit	.158	551	87	0	32
Smoltz, Atl	.153	535	82	4	35
Stottlemyre, StL	.224	67	15	0	2
Swift, Col	.215	205	44	1	13
Swindell, Cle	.192	240	46	0	13
Tewksbury, SD	.131	374	49	0	18
Thompson M, Col	.173	75	13	0	2
Trachsel, ChN	.177	164	29	1	11
Urbani, Det	.246	65	16	1	4
Valdes I, LA	.119	134	16	0	3
Valenzuela, SD	.200	914	183	10	82
VanLandingham, SF	.123	138	17	1	6
Wagner P, Pit	.168	149	25	0	9
Wall, Hou	.184	49	9	0	1
Watson, SF	.255	165	42	0	19
Weathers, NYA	.111	99	11	1	3
West, Phi	.182	55	10	1	5
Wetteland, NYA	.146	41	6	1	7
Williams M, Phi	.168	101	17	0	7
Wilson, NYN	.080	50	4	1	4
Worrell T, SD	.093	54	5	0	3
Young, Hou	.160	94	15	0	4

Who Gets the "Red Barrett Trophy"? (p. 156)

Most Pitches In a Game By Starting Pitchers in 1996

Date	Opp	Score	Pitcher	W/L	IP	H	R	ER	BB	SO	#Pit	Time
6/10	@ChA	2-8	Wakefield, Bos	L	8.0	16	8	6	3	0	162	2:29
7/21	Bal	6-10	Clemens, Bos	ND	7.2	8	5	4	4	9	162	4:09
6/13	Tex	8-7	Clemens, Bos	ND	8.0	9	4	4	3	9	157	4:26
9/18	@Det	4-0	Clemens, Bos	W	9.0	5	0	0	0	20	151	2:56
9/24	Bal	13-8	Gordon, Bos	W	7.2	9	6	5	5	6	151	3:39
6/2	Hou	2-0	Stottlemyre, StL	W	9.0	7	0	0	5	5	144	2:43
6/24	Cal	4-2	Alvarez W, ChA	W	8.0	9	2	2	1	6	144	2:45
6/24	NYA	3-0	Robertson, Min	W	9.0	8	0	0	3	4	144	2:40
9/27	@Min	4-2	Fernandez A, ChA	W	8.0	10	2	2	2	6	144	3:03
6/8	Mil	2-3	Clemens, Bos	ND	7.0	5	2	2	3	9	143	3:42
6/15	@Bos	13-3	Gross, Tex	W	9.0	9	3	3	1	7	143	3:22
8/4	Cal	7-1	Flener, Tor	W	7.2	8	1	1	3	6	142	2:48
9/18	Cin	5-3	Schmidt J, Pit	W	7.0	4	3	2	8	4	142	2:53
7/4	@Bal	6-8	Wakefield, Bos	L	6.1	7	6	3	5	6	141	3:04
4/26	Phi	0-2	Burba, Cin	L	7.0	3	1	0	7	3	141	2:36
7/17	Cal	7-3	Hill, Tex	W	8.2	11	3	2	2	4	141	3:01
8/2	@LA	1-2	Smoltz, Atl	L	8.0	9	2	2	2	12	141	2:53
8/11	Det	12-0	Rogers, NYA	W	9.0	6	0	0	4	1	141	3:00
5/1	@LA	4-1	Thompson M, Col	W	8.2	6	1	1	2	3	140	2:43
6/26	Cle	6-4	Clemens, Bos	ND	7.1	7	4	4	3	6	140	5:14
7/5	Sea	3-6	Witt, Tex	L	8.0	14	6	6	3	8	140	2:53
9/20	Tex	6-5	Boskie, Cal	ND	8.0	6	4	3	6	7	140	3:28

Fewest Pitches In a 9-Inning Complete Game By Starting Pitchers in 1996

Date	Opp	Score	Pitcher	W/L	IP	H	R	ER	BB	SO	#Pit	Time
7/15	@Oak	5-1	Wolcott, Sea	W	9.0	5	1	1	0	6	79	2:13
9/2	@Tor	2-0	Belcher, KC	W	9.0	4	0	0	0	5	90	1:53
4/7	Col	9-1	Fassero, Mon	W	9.0	3	1	1	0	6	91	2:27
5/12	@NYN	3-0	Bullinger, ChN	W	9.0	2	0	0	0	4	93	2:00
4/17	@Mon	9-3	Mulholland, Sea	W	9.0	10	3	3	1	1	95	2:58
6/19	SD	5-1	Smoltz, Atl	W	9.0	2	1	1	0	8	95	1:59
9/18	Hou	6-2	Maddux G, Atl	W	9.0	6	2	2	0	3	95	2:01
9/9	Mon	3-1	Foster, ChN	W	9.0	6	1	1	0	2	96	2:31
7/1	@Cle	4-2	Haney, KC	W	9.0	7	2	2	0	1	97	2:23
6/16	Mon	7-0	Salkeld, Cin	W	9.0	4	0	0	1	5	98	2:22
8/30	@Pit	10-0	Wall, Hou	W	9.0	7	0	0	0	4	98	2:44
5/3	@Det	11-0	Hill, Tex	W	9.0	1	0	0	0	7	100	2:19

Which Pitchers Have "Bionic Arms"? (p. 160)

Top 100 in Pitches Thrown—1992-1996

Pitcher	Total # Pitches	Pitcher	Total # Pitches
Chuck Finley	17749	Mike Morgan	11651
Jack McDowell	17159	Mark Portugal	11587
Alex Fernandez	16857	Frank Castillo	11511
Andy Benes	16712	Mark Leiter	11438
Roger Clemens	16600	Greg Swindell	11326
Kevin Appier	16395	Chris Bosio	11258
Tom Glavine	16386	Jose Rijo	11222
John Smoltz	16381	Danny Jackson	11188
Kevin Brown	16119	Roger Pavlik	11043
Tim Belcher	16065	Pedro Astacio	10914
Kevin Tapani	16004	Danny Darwin	10746
Mike Mussina	15941	Mark Gardner	10741
David Cone	15792	Al Leiter	10695
Randy Johnson	15623	Pedro Martinez	10670
Greg Maddux	15598	Mark Gubicza	10619
Bobby Witt	15448	Ron Darling	10517
Scott Erickson	15266	Cal Eldred	10517
Doug Drabek	15261	Mark Clark	10411
Ken Hill	15127	Andy Ashby	10208
Jaime Navarro	15117	Donovan Osborne	9987
Erik Hanson	14986	Dwight Gooden	9971
John Burkett	14826	Chris Hammond	9935
Todd Stottlemyre	14811	Melido Perez	9834
Ramon Martinez	14770	Tim Wakefield	9816
Wilson Alvarez	14763	Sid Fernandez	9810
Juan Guzman	14751	Dave Stewart	9744
Pat Hentgen	14710	Dave Fleming	9711
Ben McDonald	14608	Pete Schourek	9528
Tom Candiotti	14540	Omar Olivares	9437
Mark Langston	14187	Rheal Cormier	9416
Tom Gordon	14101	Pat Rapp	9384
Ricky Bones	14018	Scott Kamieniecki	9375
Jim Abbott	13995	Jose Mesa	9230
Kevin Gross	13880	Kevin Ritz	9156
Dennis Martinez	13791	Bobby Jones	9156
Steve Avery	13655	Dave Burba	8970
Kenny Rogers	13559	Jamie Moyer	8956
Orel Hershiser	13503	Shawn Boskie	8945
Charles Nagy	13295	Paul Quantrill	8928
John Smiley	13077	Bill Swift	8823
David Wells	13020	Shane Reynolds	8690
Jimmy Key	12999	Chris Haney	8633
Darryl Kile	12934	Bill Wegman	8506
Curt Schilling	12905	Jack Morris	8488
Pete Harnisch	12854	Steve Trachsel	8430
Terry Mulholland	12847	Kirk McCaskill	8427
Bob Tewksbury	12667	Zane Smith	8415
Jeff Fassero	11916	Paul Wagner	8281
Mike Moore	11836	Bret Saberhagen	8268
Denny Neagle	11654	Armando Reynoso	8242

Which Starters Combine Quality With Quantity? (p. 165)

Both Leagues — Listed Alphabetically (minimum 15 games started in 1996)

Player,Team	GS	QS	%
Abbott J, Cal	23	4	17.4
Aguilera, Min	19	9	47.4
Aldred, Min	25	7	28.0
Alvarez W, ChA	35	20	57.1
Appier, KC	32	18	56.3
Ashby, SD	24	11	45.8
Astacio, LA	32	22	68.8
Avery, Atl	23	11	47.8
Baldwin, ChA	28	13	46.4
Belcher, KC	35	20	57.1
Benes Al, StL	32	14	43.8
Benes An, StL	34	23	67.6
Bones, NYA	24	10	41.7
Boskie, Cal	28	13	46.4
Brown, Fla	32	25	78.1
Bullinger, ChN	20	5	25.0
Burba, Cin	33	17	51.5
Burkett, Tex	34	20	58.8
Candiotti, LA	27	12	44.4
Castillo F, ChN	33	13	39.4
Clark M, NYN	32	20	62.5
Clemens, Bos	34	19	55.9
Coppinger, Bal	22	9	40.9
Cormier, Mon	27	12	44.4
D'Amico, Mil	17	4	23.5
Darwin D, Hou	25	15	60.0
Drabek, Hou	30	15	50.0
Eldred, Mil	15	6	40.0
Erickson, Bal	34	19	55.9
Fassero, Mon	34	20	58.8
Fernandez A, ChA	35	19	54.3
Fernandez O, SF	28	14	50.0
Finley, Cal	35	18	51.4
Foster, ChN	16	4	25.0
Freeman, ChA	24	8	33.3
Gardner, SF	28	11	39.3
Glavine, Atl	36	24	66.7
Gohr, Cal	16	6	37.5
Gooden, NYA	29	12	41.4
Gordon, Bos	34	15	44.1
Grimsley, Cal	20	6	30.0
Gross, Tex	19	10	52.6
Gubicza, KC	19	7	36.8
Guzman, Tor	27	18	66.7
Hamilton, SD	33	18	54.5
Hampton, Hou	27	15	55.6
Haney, KC	35	17	48.6
Hanson, Tor	35	15	42.9
Harnisch, NYN	31	19	61.3
Hentgen, Tor	35	22	62.9
Hershiser, Cle	33	21	63.6
Hill, Tex	35	23	65.7
Hitchcock, Sea	35	14	40.0
Isringhaus., NYN	27	13	48.1
Jarvis, Cin	20	6	30.0
Johns, Oak	23	8	34.8
Jones B, NYN	31	17	54.8
Karl, Mil	32	17	53.1
Key, NYA	30	13	43.3
Kile, Hou	33	18	54.5
Langston, Cal	18	7	38.9
Leiter A, Fla	33	24	72.7
Leiter M, Mon	34	15	44.1
Lieber, Pit	15	8	53.3
Linton, KC	18	9	50.0
Lira, Det	32	15	46.9
Maddux G, Atl	35	24	68.6
Martinez D, Cle	20	8	40.0
Martinez P, Mon	33	18	54.5
Martinez R, LA	27	17	63.0
McDonald, Mil	35	20	57.1
McDowell J, Cle	30	14	46.7
Mimbs, Phi	17	5	29.4
Morgan, Cin	23	10	43.5
Moyer, Sea	21	10	47.6
Mulholland, Sea	33	19	57.6
Mussina, Bal	36	18	50.0
Nagy, Cle	32	20	62.5
Navarro, ChN	35	18	51.4
Neagle, Atl	33	22	66.7
Nomo, LA	33	24	72.7
Ogea, Cle	21	10	47.6
Olivares, Det	25	8	32.0
Oliver, Tex	30	12	40.0
Osborne, StL	30	23	76.7
Pavlik, Tex	34	15	44.1
Pettitte, NYA	34	18	52.9
Portugal, Cin	26	10	38.5
Prieto, Oak	21	12	57.1
Quantrill, Tor	20	5	25.0
Radke, Min	35	20	57.1
Rapp, Fla	29	13	44.8
Reynolds, Hou	35	21	60.0
Reynoso, Col	30	14	46.7
Ritz, Col	35	15	42.9
Robertson, Min	31	12	38.7
Rodriguez F, Min	33	17	51.5
Rogers, NYA	30	13	43.3
Rosado, KC	16	10	62.5
Rueter, SF	19	8	42.1
Salkeld, Cin	19	6	31.6
Sanders, SD	16	11	68.8
Schilling, Phi	26	18	69.2
Schmidt J, Pit	17	6	35.3
Sele, Bos	29	11	37.9
Smiley, Cin	34	20	58.8
Smith Z, Pit	16	6	37.5
Smoltz, Atl	35	25	71.4
Springer D, Cal	15	5	33.3
Stottlemyre, StL	33	21	63.6
Tapani, ChA	34	19	55.9
Telemaco, ChN	17	7	41.2
Tewksbury, SD	33	15	45.5
Thompson M, Col	28	15	53.6
Trachsel, ChN	31	23	74.2
Urbina, Mon	17	7	41.2
Valdes I, LA	33	26	78.8
Valenzuela, SD	31	15	48.4
Van Poppel, Det	15	3	20.0
VanLanding., SF	32	11	34.4
Wagner P, Pit	15	6	40.0
Wakefield, Bos	32	15	46.9
Wall, Hou	23	11	47.8
Wasdin, Oak	21	8	38.1
Watson, SF	29	13	44.8
Wells B, Sea	16	3	18.8
Wells D, Bal	34	18	52.9
Wengert, Oak	25	11	44.0
Williams B, Det	17	4	23.5
Williams M, Phi	29	14	48.3
Wilson, NYN	26	9	34.6
Witt, Tex	32	12	37.5
Wojciechow., Oak	15	5	33.3
Wolcott, Sea	28	8	28.6
Wright, Col	15	9	60.0
MLB Avg			**45.8**

Could Smiley Have Used Some of Pettitte's Support? (p. 168)

In the table below, **Sup** stands for Run Support Per Nine Innings. **RS** is the total Runs In Support for that pitcher while he was in the game.

As Starters, Both Leagues — Listed Alphabetically (minimum 20 games started in 1996)

Pitcher, Team	W-L	ERA	Sup	IP	RS
Alvarez W, ChA	15-10	4.22	6.34	217.1	153
Appier, KC	14-11	3.62	4.90	211.1	115
Astacio, LA	9-8	3.57	4.14	204.1	94
Baldwin, ChA	11-6	4.42	5.11	169.0	96
Belcher, KC	15-11	3.92	5.09	238.2	135
Benes Al, StL	12-9	4.88	5.46	188.0	114
Benes An, StL	18-10	3.77	5.38	229.1	137
Boskie, Cal	9-10	5.43	5.59	169.0	105
Brown, Fla	17-11	1.89	3.48	233.0	90
Burba, Cin	11-13	3.87	4.71	193.0	101
Burkett, Tex	11-12	4.24	4.37	222.2	108
Candiotti, LA	9-11	4.43	5.28	148.1	87
Castillo F, ChN	7-16	5.28	4.20	182.1	85
Clark M, NYN	14-11	3.43	5.38	212.1	127
Clemens, Bos	10-13	3.63	4.27	242.2	115
Cormier, Mon	7-10	4.27	3.68	154.0	63
Drabek, Hou	7-9	4.57	4.98	175.1	97
Erickson, Bal	13-12	5.02	6.11	222.1	151
Fassero, Mon	15-11	3.30	4.70	231.2	121
Fernandez A, ChA	16-10	3.45	5.06	258.0	145
Fernandez O, SF	7-12	4.42	3.62	169.0	68
Finley, Cal	15-16	4.16	4.24	238.0	112
Gardner, SF	12-7	4.48	6.88	176.2	135
Glavine, Atl	15-10	2.98	4.82	235.1	126
Gooden, NYA	11-7	5.01	5.01	170.2	95
Gordon, Bos	12-9	5.59	7.34	215.2	176
Guzman, Tor	11-8	2.93	4.32	187.2	90
Hamilton, SD	15-9	4.19	4.83	210.2	113
Hampton, Hou	10-10	3.59	5.16	160.1	92
Haney, KC	10-14	4.70	5.09	228.0	129
Hanson, Tor	13-17	5.41	5.24	214.2	125
Harnisch, NYN	8-12	4.21	4.99	194.2	108
Hentgen, Tor	20-10	3.22	5.73	265.2	169
Hershiser, Cle	15-9	4.24	5.72	206.0	131
Hill, Tex	16-10	3.63	6.07	250.2	169
Hitchcock, Sea	13-9	5.35	5.81	196.2	127
Isringhausen, NYN	6-14	4.77	3.51	171.2	67
Jones B, NYN	12-8	4.42	4.60	195.2	100
Karl, Mil	13-9	4.86	6.77	207.1	156
Key, NYA	12-11	4.68	5.74	169.1	108
Kile, Hou	12-11	4.25	4.83	216.0	116
Leiter A, Fla	16-12	2.93	5.22	215.1	125
Leiter M, Mon	8-12	4.77	5.70	203.2	129
Lira, Det	6-14	5.22	4.53	194.2	98
Maddux G, Atl	15-11	2.72	4.08	245.0	111
Martinez P, Mon	13-10	3.70	5.28	216.2	127
Martinez R, LA	15-5	3.39	6.12	164.2	112
McDonald, Mil	12-10	3.90	6.06	221.1	149
McDowell J, Cle	13-9	5.11	5.58	192.0	119
Mulholland, Sea	13-11	4.66	4.80	202.2	108
Mussina, Bal	19-11	4.81	6.84	243.1	185
Nagy, Cle	17-5	3.41	5.51	222.0	136
Navarro, ChN	15-12	3.92	4.56	236.2	120
Neagle, Atl	16-9	3.50	4.47	221.1	110
Nomo, LA	16-11	3.19	4.53	228.1	115
Oliver, Tex	14-6	4.66	6.63	173.2	128
Osborne, StL	13-9	3.53	4.17	198.2	92
Pavlik, Tex	15-8	5.19	6.40	201.0	143
Pettitte, NYA	20-8	3.92	6.28	218.0	152
Portugal, Cin	8-9	3.89	4.88	155.0	84
Radke, Min	11-16	4.46	4.85	232.0	125
Rapp, Fla	8-15	5.10	4.59	160.2	82
Reynolds, Hou	16-10	3.65	4.78	239.0	127
Reynoso, Col	8-9	4.96	5.92	168.2	111
Ritz, Col	17-11	5.28	7.23	213.0	171
Robertson, Min	6-16	5.31	3.71	174.2	72
Rodriguez F, Min	12-14	5.24	5.57	192.1	119
Rogers, NYA	12-8	4.68	4.63	179.0	92
Schilling, Phi	9-10	3.19	3.88	183.1	79
Sele, Bos	7-11	5.32	5.78	157.1	101
Smiley, Cin	13-14	3.61	4.27	217.0	103
Smoltz, Atl	24-8	2.94	5.68	253.2	160
Stottlemyre, StL	14-11	3.90	5.04	221.1	124
Tapani, ChA	13-10	4.59	6.03	225.1	151
Tewksbury, SD	10-10	4.20	4.78	201.1	107
Thompson M, Col	9-11	5.46	5.84	163.1	106
Trachsel, ChN	13-9	3.03	4.61	205.0	105
Valdes I, LA	15-7	3.32	5.08	225.0	127
Valenzuela, SD	13-8	3.58	5.42	171.0	103
VanLanding., SF	9-14	5.40	5.00	181.2	101
Wakefield, Bos	14-13	5.14	5.19	211.2	122
Watson, SF	8-12	4.61	4.80	185.2	99
Wells D, Bal	11-14	5.14	5.18	224.1	129
Williams M, Phi	6-14	5.37	3.80	161.0	68
Wilson, NYN	5-12	5.38	4.59	149.0	76
Witt, Tex	15-12	5.41	6.89	194.2	149
Wolcott, Sea	7-10	5.52	6.21	145.0	100
MLB Average		**4.73**	**5.31**		

Which Pitchers Suffer the Most From Their Bad Outings? (p. 170)

ERA Differential for Pitchers Without Five Worst Games—1996

Player, Team	Actual ERA	Adj. ERA	Diff	Player, Team	Actual ERA	Adj. ERA	Diff
Castillo F, ChN	3.84	5.28	−1.44	Burkett, Tex	3.53	4.24	−0.72
Erickson, Bal	3.58	5.02	−1.44	Nagy, Cle	2.70	3.41	−0.71
Lira, Det	3.81	5.22	−1.42	VanLanding., SF	4.70	5.40	−0.70
Fernandez O, SF	3.12	4.42	−1.30	Mulholland, Sea	3.97	4.66	−0.69
Boskie, Cal	4.20	5.43	−1.23	Martinez R, LA	2.72	3.39	−0.67
Drabek, Hou	3.36	4.57	−1.21	Mussina, Bal	4.15	4.81	−0.66
Wells D, Bal	3.98	5.14	−1.16	Martinez P, Mon	3.04	3.70	−0.65
Witt, Tex	4.25	5.41	−1.16	Hill, Tex	3.00	3.63	−0.63
Aldred, Min	5.44	6.57	−1.13	Ritz, Col	4.68	5.28	−0.60
Darwin D, Hou	2.72	3.82	−1.10	Navarro, ChN	3.32	3.92	−0.60
Osborne, StL	2.44	3.53	−1.10	Valdes I, LA	2.75	3.32	−0.57
Isringhausen, NYN	3.69	4.77	−1.08	Belcher, KC	3.36	3.92	−0.56
Hamilton, SD	3.11	4.19	−1.08	Guzman, Tor	2.37	2.93	−0.56
Thompson M, Col	4.39	5.46	−1.06	Baldwin, ChA	3.87	4.42	−0.55
Rapp, Fla	4.08	5.10	−1.02	Burba, Cin	3.34	3.87	−0.53
Williams M, Phi	4.35	5.37	−1.01	Radke, Min	3.94	4.46	−0.52
Gooden, NYA	4.00	5.01	−1.01	Leiter M, Mon	4.26	4.77	−0.51
Rogers, NYA	3.67	4.68	−1.01	Neagle, Atl	2.99	3.50	−0.51
Robertson, Min	4.30	5.31	−1.00	Schilling, Phi	2.69	3.19	−0.50
Jones B, NYN	3.42	4.42	−1.00	McDonald, Mil	3.41	3.90	−0.49
Finley, Cal	3.17	4.16	−0.99	Fernandez A, ChA	2.96	3.45	−0.49
Reynolds, Hou	2.66	3.65	−0.99	Pavlik, Tex	4.70	5.19	−0.49
Oliver, Tex	3.70	4.66	−0.96	Glavine, Atl	2.51	2.98	−0.47
Benes A, StL	2.81	3.77	−0.96	Tapani, ChA	4.14	4.59	−0.45
Rodriguez F, Min	4.30	5.24	−0.94	Clemens, Bos	3.19	3.63	−0.45
Smiley, Cin	2.69	3.61	−0.92	Leiter A, Fla	2.50	2.93	−0.43
Hershiser, Cle	3.32	4.24	−0.91	Harnisch, NYN	3.78	4.21	−0.43
Pettitte, NYA	3.03	3.92	−0.89	Trachsel, ChN	2.61	3.03	−0.42
Hanson, Tor	4.53	5.41	−0.88	Appier, KC	3.21	3.62	−0.41
Kile, Hou	3.38	4.25	−0.88	Maddux G, Atl	2.33	2.72	−0.39
Stottlemyre, StL	3.03	3.90	−0.87	Tewksbury, SD	3.87	4.20	−0.33
Key, NYA	3.80	4.68	−0.87	Brown, Fla	1.57	1.89	−0.32
Astacio, LA	2.70	3.57	−0.86	Nomo, LA	2.87	3.19	−0.32
Wakefield, Bos	4.33	5.14	−0.82	Alvarez W, ChA	3.94	4.22	−0.28
Gordon, Bos	4.79	5.59	−0.80	McDowell J, Cle	4.86	5.11	−0.25
Fassero, Mon	2.50	3.30	−0.80	Watson, SF	4.38	4.61	−0.23
Haney, KC	3.90	4.70	−0.80	Hitchcock, Sea	5.13	5.35	−0.23
Karl, Mil	4.11	4.86	−0.75	Hentgen, Tor	3.04	3.22	−0.18
Benes A, StL	4.13	4.88	−0.75	Gardner, SF	4.34	4.48	−0.15
Valenzuela, SD	2.83	3.58	−0.74	Clark M, NYN	3.34	3.43	−0.09
Smoltz, Atl	2.22	2.94	−0.73	Reynoso, Col	4.89	4.96	−0.07

Whose Heater is Hottest? (p. 172)

Both Leagues — Listed Alphabetically
(minimum 130 innings pitched or 56 relief games)

Pitcher,Team	IP	K	K/9
Abbott J, Cal	142.0	58	3.7
Adams T, ChN	101.0	78	7.0
Aldred, Min	165.1	111	6.0
Alvarez W, ChA	217.1	181	7.5
Appier, KC	211.1	207	8.8
Ashby, SD	150.2	85	5.1
Assenmacher, Cle	46.2	44	8.5
Astacio, LA	211.2	130	5.5
Avery, Atl	131.0	86	5.9
Baldwin, ChA	169.0	127	6.8
Beck, SF	62.0	48	7.0
Belcher, KC	238.2	113	4.3
Benes Al, StL	191.0	131	6.2
Benes An, StL	230.1	160	6.3
Blair, SD	88.0	67	6.9
Bochtler, SD	65.2	68	9.3
Bones, NYA	152.0	63	3.7
Borland, Phi	90.2	76	7.5
Boskie, Cal	189.1	133	6.3
Bottalico, Phi	67.2	74	9.8
Brantley, Cin	71.0	76	9.6
Brown, Fla	233.0	159	6.1
Burba, Cin	195.0	148	6.8
Burkett, Tex	222.2	155	6.3
Candiotti, LA	152.1	79	4.7
Carrasco, Cin	74.1	59	7.1
Castillo F, ChN	182.1	139	6.9
Charlton, Sea	75.2	73	8.7
Clark M, NYN	212.1	142	6.0
Clemens, Bos	242.2	257	9.5
Clontz, Atl	80.2	49	5.5
Cook, Tex	70.1	64	8.2
Cormier, Mon	159.2	100	5.6
Corsi, Oak	73.2	43	5.3
Creek, SF	48.1	38	7.1
Daal, Mon	87.1	82	8.5
Darwin D, Hou	164.2	96	5.2
DeLucia, SF	61.2	55	8.0
Dewey, SF	83.1	57	6.2
DiPoto, NYN	77.1	52	6.1
Drabek, Hou	175.1	137	7.0
Dyer, Mon	75.2	51	6.1
Eckersley, StL	60.0	49	7.4
Erickson, Bal	222.1	100	4.0
Fassero, Mon	231.2	222	8.6
Fernandez A, ChA	258.0	200	7.0
Fernandez O, SF	171.2	106	5.6
Fetters, Mil	61.1	53	7.8
Finley, Cal	238.0	215	8.1
Fossas, StL	47.0	36	6.9
Freeman, ChA	131.2	72	4.9
Gardner, SF	179.1	145	7.3
Glavine, Atl	235.1	181	6.9
Gooden, NYA	170.2	126	6.6
Gordon, Bos	215.2	171	7.1
Grimsley, Cal	130.1	82	5.7
Groom, Oak	77.1	57	6.6
Guardado, Min	73.2	74	9.0
Guthrie, LA	73.0	56	6.9
Guzman, Tor	187.2	165	7.9
Hamilton, SD	211.2	184	7.8
Hampton, Hou	160.1	101	5.7
Haney, KC	228.0	115	4.5
Hanson, Tor	214.2	156	6.5
Harnisch, NYN	194.2	114	5.3
Henry, NYN	75.0	58	7.0
Hentgen, Tor	265.2	177	6.0
Hernandez R, ChA	84.2	85	9.0
Hernandez X, Hou	78.0	81	9.3
Hershiser, Cle	206.0	125	5.5
Hill, Tex	250.2	170	6.1
Hitchcock, Sea	196.2	132	6.0
Hoffman, SD	88.0	111	11.4
Holmes, Col	77.0	73	8.5
Honeycutt, StL	47.1	30	5.7
Isringhausen, NYN	171.2	114	6.0
Jackson M, Sea	72.0	70	8.8
James, Cal	81.0	65	7.2
Johns, Oak	158.0	71	4.0
Jones B, NYN	195.2	116	5.3
Juden, Mon	74.1	61	7.4
Karl, Mil	207.1	121	5.3
Key, NYA	169.1	116	6.2
Kile, Hou	219.0	219	9.0
Leiter A, Fla	215.1	200	8.4
Leiter M, Mon	205.0	164	7.2
Leskanic, Col	73.2	76	9.3
Lewis, Det	90.1	78	7.8
Lieber, Pit	142.0	94	6.0
Lira, Det	194.2	113	5.2
Lloyd, NYA	56.2	30	4.8
Maddux G, Atl	245.0	172	6.3

Pitcher,Team	IP	K	K/9
Martinez P, Mon	216.2	222	9.2
Martinez R, LA	168.2	133	7.1
Mathews TJ, StL	83.2	80	8.6
Mathews Te, Bal	73.2	62	7.6
McDonald, Mil	221.1	146	5.9
McDowell J, Cle	192.0	141	6.6
McMichael, Atl	86.2	78	8.1
Mesa, Cle	72.1	64	8.0
Mohler, Oak	81.0	64	7.1
Morgan, Cin	130.1	74	5.1
Moyer, Sea	160.2	79	4.4
Mulholland, Sea	202.2	86	3.8
Mussina, Bal	243.1	204	7.5
Myers M, Det	64.2	69	9.6
Myers R, Bal	58.2	74	11.4
Nagy, Cle	222.0	167	6.8
Navarro, ChN	236.2	158	6.0
Neagle, Atl	221.1	149	6.1
Nelson, NYA	74.1	91	11.0
Nen, Fla	83.0	92	10.0
Nomo, LA	228.1	234	9.2
Ogea, Cle	146.2	101	6.2
Olivares, Det	160.0	81	4.6
Oliver, Tex	173.2	112	5.8
Orosco, Bal	55.2	52	8.4
Osborne, StL	198.2	134	6.1
Osuna A, LA	84.0	85	9.1
Patterson B, ChN	54.2	53	8.7
Pavlik, Tex	201.0	127	5.7
Percival, Cal	74.0	100	12.2
Perez Y, Fla	47.2	47	8.9
Pettitte, NYA	221.0	162	6.6
Pichardo, KC	68.0	43	5.7
Plesac, Pit	70.1	76	9.7
Plunk, Cle	77.2	85	9.8
Poole, SF	50.1	38	6.8
Portugal, Cin	156.0	93	5.4
Powell, Fla	71.1	52	6.6
Quantrill, Tor	134.1	86	5.8
Radinsky, LA	52.1	48	8.3
Radke, Min	232.0	148	5.7
Rapp, Fla	162.1	86	4.8
Reed, Col	75.0	51	6.1
Reynolds, Hou	239.0	204	7.7
Reynoso, Col	168.2	88	4.7

Pitcher,Team	IP	K	K/9
Ritz, Col	213.0	105	4.4
Rivera, NYA	107.2	130	10.9
Robertson, Min	186.1	114	5.5
Rodriguez F, Min	206.2	110	4.8
Rogers, NYA	179.0	92	4.6
Rojas, Mon	81.0	92	10.2
Ruffin B, Col	69.2	74	9.6
Ryan, Phi	89.0	70	7.1
Sanders, SD	144.0	157	9.8
Schilling, Phi	183.1	182	8.9
Scott, SF	66.0	47	6.4
Sele, Bos	157.1	137	7.8
Shaw, Cin	104.2	69	5.9
Simas, ChA	72.2	65	8.1
Slocumb, Bos	83.1	88	9.5
Smiley, Cin	217.1	171	7.1
Smoltz, Atl	253.2	276	9.8
Stanton, Tex	78.2	60	6.9
Stottlemyre, StL	223.1	194	7.8
Tapani, ChA	225.1	150	6.0
Tewksbury, SD	206.2	126	5.5
Thomas, ChA	30.2	20	5.9
Thompson M, Col	169.2	99	5.3
Timlin, Tor	56.2	52	8.3
Trachsel, ChN	205.0	132	5.8
Valdes I, LA	225.0	173	6.9
Valenzuela, SD	171.2	95	5.0
VanLandingham, SF	181.2	97	4.8
Veres D, Mon	77.2	81	9.4
Wakefield, Bos	211.2	140	6.0
Wall, Hou	150.0	99	5.9
Wasdin, Oak	131.1	75	5.1
Watson, SF	185.2	128	6.2
Wells B, Sea	130.2	94	6.5
Wells D, Bal	224.1	130	5.2
Wendell, ChN	79.1	75	8.5
Wengert, Oak	161.1	75	4.2
Wetteland, NYA	63.2	69	9.8
Wickman, Mil	95.2	75	7.1
Williams M, Phi	167.0	103	5.6
Wilson, NYN	149.0	109	6.6
Witt, Tex	199.2	157	7.1
Wohlers, Atl	77.1	100	11.6
Wolcott, Sea	149.1	78	4.7
Worrell To, LA	65.1	66	9.1

Who Gets the Easy Saves? (p. 174)

Both Leagues — Listed Alphabetically
(1996 Relievers with a minimum of 5 Save Opportunities)

Reliever	Easy	Regular	Tough
Adams T, ChN	0/0	4/7	0/1
Ayala, Sea	0/1	3/4	0/1
Beck, SF	20/21	9/12	6/9
Benitez, Bal	1/1	1/2	2/2
Blair, SD	0/0	1/4	0/1
Bluma, KC	4/4	1/1	0/0
Bochtler, SD	0/0	2/3	1/4
Bottalico, Phi	19/22	11/12	4/4
Brantley, Cin	25/25	19/22	0/2
Carmona, Sea	0/0	1/4	0/1
Castillo T, ChA	0/1	1/1	1/4
Charlton, Sea	6/7	11/15	3/5
Clontz, Atl	1/1	0/2	0/3
Cordova, Pit	6/6	5/9	1/3
Corsi, Oak	1/1	1/3	1/2
Crabtree, Tor	0/0	1/3	0/2
Dewey, SF	0/0	0/0	0/5
DiPoto, NYN	0/0	0/0	0/5
Dyer, Mon	0/0	1/3	1/3
Eckersley, StL	13/13	15/18	2/3
Ericks, Pit	5/5	1/3	2/2
Fetters, Mil	15/17	13/17	4/4
Fossas, StL	1/1	1/1	0/5
Franco, NYN	13/13	14/18	1/5
Garcia, Mil	0/0	2/4	2/3
Guardado, Min	1/1	2/3	1/3
Henneman, Tex	14/16	15/18	2/3
Henry, NYN	0/0	8/10	1/4
Hernandez R, ChA	19/20	18/22	1/4
Hernandez X, Hou	1/1	5/7	0/2
Hoffman, SD	19/19	19/23	4/7
Holmes, Col	0/0	1/5	0/3
Honeycutt, StL	1/1	2/4	1/2
Hudson, Bos	0/0	1/4	0/1
Jackson M, Sea	2/2	2/3	2/3
James, Cal	1/1	0/1	0/4
Jones D, Mil	1/1	0/2	2/8
Jones T, Hou	10/11	4/7	3/5
Karchner, ChA	0/0	1/7	0/2
Leskanic, Col	3/3	3/6	0/1
Lewis, Det	0/1	1/1	1/4
Lima, Det	2/3	1/2	0/2
Lloyd, NYA	0/0	0/1	0/4
Mathews TJ, StL	0/0	4/6	2/5
Mathews Te, Bal	0/0	4/6	0/0
McDowell R, Bal	1/1	3/5	0/0
McMichael, Atl	0/2	1/3	1/3
Mesa, Cle	25/26	14/18	0/0
Mills, Bal	0/0	2/3	1/5
Mohler, Oak	2/3	4/5	1/5
Montgomery J, KC	14/16	8/15	2/3
Myers M, Det	2/2	2/3	2/3
Myers R, Bal	17/18	13/19	1/1
Naulty, Min	0/0	3/4	1/5
Nen, Fla	19/20	15/18	1/4
Olson, Hou	3/3	5/6	0/1
Osuna A, LA	3/4	1/2	0/3
Patterson B, ChN	3/3	4/5	1/2
Percival, Cal	12/12	17/18	7/9
Pichardo, KC	1/1	2/2	0/2
Plesac, Pit	4/4	6/10	1/3
Powell, Fla	0/0	2/5	0/0
Reed, Col	0/1	0/2	0/3
Rivera, NYA	2/3	2/4	1/1
Rojas, Mon	9/9	21/23	6/8
Ruffin B, Col	16/17	6/7	2/5
Russell, Tex	0/0	2/4	1/2
Ryan, Phi	1/1	7/9	0/3
Scott, SF	0/1	1/2	0/2
Shaw, Cin	0/0	4/8	0/3
Shuey, Cle	3/4	1/3	0/0
Simas, ChA	0/0	2/6	0/2
Slocumb, Bos	20/20	10/16	1/3
Smith L, Cin	1/4	1/3	0/1
Stanton, Tex	1/1	0/3	0/2
Stevens, Min	9/10	2/5	0/1
Taylor, Oak	4/5	8/8	5/6
Timlin, Tor	22/23	7/13	2/2
Trombley, Min	2/2	2/3	2/4
Veres D, Mon	1/1	3/4	0/1
Vosberg, Tex	4/4	4/4	0/1
Wagner B, Hou	2/4	7/8	0/1
Wendell, ChN	8/8	6/9	4/4
Wetteland, NYA	27/29	12/13	4/5
Wilkins, Pit	0/0	1/2	0/3
Wohlers, Atl	18/18	12/14	9/12
Worrell T, LA	23/24	19/26	2/3
AL Totals	**241/266**	**229/353**	**66/190**
NL Totals	**258/280**	**261/396**	**61/191**
MLB Totals	**499/546**	**490/749**	**127/381**

If You Can Hold the Fort, Will You Soon Be Closing the Gate? (p. 177)

A Hold (**H**) is a Save Opportunity passed on to the next pitcher. If a pitcher comes into the game in a Save Situation and leaves the game having gotten at least one out and without having blown the lead, this is a "passed on" Save Opportunity and the pitcher is credited with a Hold.

Both Leagues — Listed By Most Holds
(minimum 3 Holds in 1996)

Pitcher, Team	H	Pitcher, Team	H	Pitcher, Team	H	Pitcher, Team	H
Rivera, NYA	27	DeLucia, SF	11	Heredia G, Tex	7	Jordan, Phi	4
Reed, Col	22	Plesac, Pit	11	Hernandez X, Hou	7	Mahomes, Bos	4
Shaw, Cin	22	Vosberg, Tex	11	Holmes, Col	7	Miceli, Pit	4
Stanton, Tex	22	Bailey C, StL	10	Howe, NYA	7	Naulty, Min	4
Bochtler, SD	20	Borland, Phi	10	McElroy, Cal	7	Painter, Col	4
Russell, Tex	20	Corsi, Oak	10	Morman, Hou	7	Park, LA	4
Honeycutt, StL	19	Groom, Oak	10	Radinsky, LA	7	Polley, NYA	4
Orosco, Bal	19	Nelson, NYA	10	Shuey, Cle	7	Risley, Tor	4
Guardado, Min	18	Perez Y, Fla	10	Thomas, ChA	7	Ruebel, Pit	4
James, Cal	18	Petkovsek, StL	10	Boze, Mil	6	Taylor, Oak	4
McMichael, Atl	18	Poole, SF	10	Garcia, Mil	6	Trombley, Min	4
Clontz, Atl	17	Powell, Fla	10	Hartgraves, Atl	6	Wade, Atl	4
Crabtree, Tor	17	Scott, SF	10	Jacome, KC	6	Wilkins, Pit	4
Lloyd, NYA	17	Wickman, Mil	10	Lewis, Det	6	Bielecki, Atl	3
Myers M, Det	17	Worrell T, SD	10	Lima, Det	6	Blair, SD	3
Osuna A, LA	16	Castillo T, ChA	9	Miranda, Mil	6	Bones, NYA	3
Carrasco, Cin	15	Daal, Mon	9	Ruffin B, Col	6	Byrd, NYN	3
Fossas, StL	15	Leskanic, Col	9	Springer R, Phi	6	Corbin, Bal	3
Jackson M, Sea	15	Lieber, Pit	9	Urbina, Mon	6	Cordova, Pit	3
Mathews T, Bal	15	Mathews T, StL	9	Wendell, ChN	6	Dessens, Pit	3
Patterson B, ChN	15	McDowell R, Bal	9	Casian, ChN	5	DiPoto, NYN	3
Pichardo, KC	15	Mills, Bal	9	Davis, Sea	5	Gunderson, Bos	3
Plunk, Cle	15	Villone, Mil	9	Guetterman, Sea	5	Hansell, Min	3
Ryan, Phi	15	Carmona, Sea	8	Hammond, Fla	5	Hudson, Bos	3
Simas, ChA	15	Charlton, Sea	8	Holtz, Cal	5	Juden, Mon	3
Veres D, Mon	15	Dyer, Mon	8	Magnante, KC	5	Leiper, Mon	3
Assenmacher, Cle	13	Eshelman, Bos	8	Magrane, ChA	5	MacDonald, NYN	3
Karchner, ChA	13	Florie, Mil	8	Scanlan, KC	5	Milchin, Bal	3
Mohler, Oak	13	Henry, NYN	8	Spoljaric, Tor	5	Pugh, Cin	3
Munoz M, Col	13	Mlicki, NYN	8	Boehringer, NYA	4	Sanders, SD	3
Tavarez, Cle	13	Smith L, Cin	8	Borbon, Atl	4	Service, Cin	3
Brandenburg, Bos	12	Ayala, Sea	7	Bottenfield, ChN	4	Veres R, Det	3
Guthrie, LA	12	Belinda, Bos	7	Eckersley, StL	4	Wagner B, Hou	3
Adams T, ChN	11	Creek, SF	7	Frey, Phi	4	Walker M, Det	3
Cook, Tex	11	Dewey, SF	7	Garces, Bos	4	Weathers, NYA	3

Which Relievers Can Be Counted On to Convert? (p. 180)

The table below lists a reliever's Holds (**H**), Saves (**Sv**), Blown Saves (**BS**), and Hold + Save Percentage (**%**), which is Holds plus Saves divided by Holds plus Saves plus Blown Saves.

Both Leagues — Listed Alphabetically
(minimum 5 Holds+Saves+Blown Saves in 1996)

Pitcher	H	Sv	BS	%
Acre, Oak	2	2	1	80
Adams T, ChN	11	4	4	79
Assenmacher, Cle	13	1	2	88
Ayala, Sea	7	3	3	77
Bailey C, StL	10	0	1	91
Beck, SF	0	35	7	83
Belinda, Bos	7	2	2	82
Benitez, Bal	1	4	1	83
Bielecki, Atl	3	2	0	100
Blair, SD	3	1	4	50
Bluma, KC	2	5	0	100
Bochtler, SD	20	3	4	85
Boehringer, NYA	4	0	1	80
Borbon, Atl	4	1	0	100
Borland, Phi	10	0	2	83
Bottalico, Phi	0	34	4	89
Bottenfield, ChN	4	1	2	71
Boze, Mil	6	1	1	88
Brandenburg, Bos	12	0	2	86
Brantley, Cin	0	44	5	90
Byrd, NYN	3	0	2	60
Carmona, Sea	8	1	4	69
Carrasco, Cin	15	0	2	88
Casian, ChN	5	0	1	83
Castillo T, ChA	9	2	4	73
Charlton, Sea	8	20	7	80
Clontz, Atl	17	1	5	78
Cook, Tex	11	0	2	85
Cordova, Pit	3	12	6	71
Corsi, Oak	10	3	3	81
Crabtree, Tor	17	1	4	82
Creek, SF	7	0	1	88
Daal, Mon	9	0	4	69
Davis, Sea	5	0	0	100
DeLucia, SF	11	0	2	85
Dewey, SF	7	0	5	58
DiPoto, NYN	3	0	5	38
Dyer, Mon	8	2	4	71
Eckersley, StL	4	30	4	89
Ericks, Pit	1	8	2	82
Eshelman, Bos	8	0	0	100
Fetters, Mil	1	32	6	85
Florie, Mil	8	0	3	73
Fossas, StL	15	2	5	77
Franco, NYN	0	28	8	78
Garces, Bos	4	0	2	67
Garcia, Mil	6	4	3	77
Groom, Oak	10	2	2	86
Guardado, Min	18	4	3	88
Guetterman, Sea	5	0	0	100
Guthrie, LA	12	1	2	87
Hammond, Fla	5	0	0	100
Hansell, Min	3	3	1	86
Hartgraves, Atl	6	0	0	100
Henneman, Tex	2	31	6	85
Henry, NYN	8	9	5	77
Heredia G, Tex	7	1	3	73
Hernandez R, ChA	0	38	8	83
Hernandez X, Hou	7	6	4	76
Hoffman, SD	0	42	7	86
Holmes, Col	7	1	7	53
Holtz, Cal	5	0	0	100
Honeycutt, StL	19	4	3	88
Howe, NYA	7	1	1	89
Hudson, Bos	3	1	4	50
Jackson M, Sea	15	6	2	91
Jacome, KC	6	1	3	70
James, Cal	18	1	5	79
Jones D, Mil	2	3	8	38
Jones T, Hou	1	17	6	75
Karchner, ChA	13	1	8	64
Leskanic, Col	9	6	4	79
Lewis, Det	6	2	4	67
Lieber, Pit	9	1	3	77
Lima, Det	6	3	4	69
Lloyd, NYA	17	0	5	77
Magnante, KC	5	0	1	83
Magrane, ChA	5	0	0	100
Mahomes, Bos	4	2	0	100
Mathews TJ, StL	9	6	5	75
Mathews Te, Bal	15	4	2	90
McDowell R, Bal	9	4	2	87
McElroy, Cal	7	0	2	78
McMichael, Atl	18	2	6	77
Mesa, Cle	0	39	5	89
Miceli, Pit	4	1	0	100
Mills, Bal	9	3	5	71
Miranda, Mil	6	1	1	88
Mlicki, NYN	8	1	2	82
Mohler, Oak	13	7	6	77
Montgomery J, KC	0	24	10	71
Morman, Hou	7	0	2	78
Munoz M, Col	13	0	3	81
Myers M, Det	17	6	2	92
Myers R, Bal	2	31	7	83
Naulty, Min	4	4	5	62
Nelson, NYA	10	2	2	86
Nen, Fla	0	35	7	83
Olson, Hou	1	8	2	82
Orosco, Bal	19	0	3	86
Osuna A, LA	16	4	5	80
Painter, Col	4	0	1	80
Patterson B, ChN	15	8	2	92
Percival, Cal	2	36	3	93
Perez Y, Fla	10	0	2	83
Petkovsek, StL	10	0	3	77
Pichardo, KC	15	3	2	90
Plesac, Pit	11	11	6	79
Plunk, Cle	15	2	1	94
Poole, SF	10	0	4	71
Powell, Fla	10	2	3	80
Radinsky, LA	7	1	3	73
Reed, Col	22	0	6	79
Risley, Tor	4	0	2	67
Rivera, NYA	27	5	3	91
Rojas, Mon	1	36	4	90
Ruebel, Pit	4	1	0	100
Ruffin B, Col	6	24	5	86
Russell, Tex	20	3	3	88
Ryan, Phi	15	8	5	82
Scanlan, KC	5	0	1	83
Scott, SF	10	1	4	73
Shaw, Cin	22	4	7	79
Shuey, Cle	7	4	3	79
Simas, ChA	15	2	6	74
Slocumb, Bos	2	31	8	80
Smith L, Cin	8	2	6	63
Spoljaric, Tor	5	1	0	100
Springer R, Phi	6	0	3	67
Stanton, Tex	22	1	5	82
Stevens, Min	0	11	5	69
Tavarez, Cle	13	0	0	100
Taylor, Oak	4	17	2	91
Thomas, ChA	7	0	2	78
Timlin, Tor	2	31	7	83
Trombley, Min	4	6	3	77
Urbina, Mon	6	0	1	86
Veres D, Mon	15	4	2	90
Veres R, Det	3	0	2	60
Villone, Mil	9	2	1	92
Vosberg, Tex	11	8	1	95
Wade, Atl	4	1	1	83
Wagner B, Hou	3	9	4	75
Walker M, Det	3	1	1	80
Wendell, ChN	6	18	3	89
Wetteland, NYA	0	43	4	91
Wickman, Mil	10	0	4	71
Wilkins, Pit	4	1	4	56
Wohlers, Atl	0	39	5	89
Worrell Ti, SD	10	1	1	92
Worrell To, LA	0	44	9	83

Which Pitchers Get a Helping Hand From Their Teammates? (p. 182)

The following table lists the Percentage (%) of baserunners that a pitcher "bequeathed" to his bullpen (**Left**), and those that subsequently scored (**Sc**).

Both Leagues — Listed Alphabetically
(minimum 20 runners bequeathed)

Pitcher, Team	Left	Sc	%
Abbott J, Cal	30	16	53.3
Adams T, ChN	33	7	21.2
Aldred, Min	26	12	46.2
Alvarez W, ChA	25	8	32.0
Assenmacher, Cle	33	7	21.2
Astacio, LA	28	11	39.3
Avery, Atl	23	10	43.5
Bailey C, StL	28	11	39.3
Belcher, KC	22	5	22.7
Belinda, Bos	21	10	47.6
Blair, SD	30	10	33.3
Bochtler, SD	20	5	25.0
Bones, NYA	42	20	47.6
Borland, Phi	25	17	68.0
Boskie, Cal	32	13	40.6
Brandenburg, Bos	22	1	4.5
Bullinger, ChN	31	17	54.8
Burba, Cin	26	11	42.3
Burkett, Tex	20	4	20.0
Carmona, Sea	38	11	28.9
Carrasco, Cin	23	8	34.8
Castillo F, ChN	26	11	42.3
Clontz, Atl	32	17	53.1
Cook, Tex	42	11	26.2
Cormier, Mon	21	7	33.3
Corsi, Oak	32	11	34.4
Creek, SF	34	14	41.2
Daal, Mon	31	6	19.4
Davis, Sea	36	6	16.7
DeLucia, SF	27	15	55.6
Dewey, SF	35	11	31.4
Drabek, Hou	21	7	33.3
Dyer, Mon	39	11	28.2
Eischen, Det	23	3	13.0
Erickson, Bal	21	11	52.4
Eshelman, Bos	29	19	65.5
Fernandez O, SF	22	8	36.4
Finley, Cal	32	15	46.9
Florie, Mil	26	13	50.0
Fossas, StL	36	5	13.9
Freeman, ChA	20	6	30.0
Garces, Bos	22	6	27.3
Gardner, SF	21	6	28.6
Glavine, Atl	26	9	34.6
Gohr, Cal	22	10	45.5
Gordon, Bos	26	12	46.2
Grimsley, Cal	41	18	43.9
Groom, Oak	38	9	23.7
Gross, Tex	22	4	18.2
Guardado, Min	53	19	35.8
Guetterman, Sea	21	6	28.6
Gunderson, Bos	20	7	35.0
Haney, KC	22	6	27.3
Hartgraves, Atl	20	7	35.0
Heredia G, Tex	21	9	42.9
Hernandez X, Hou	20	9	45.0
Hershiser, Cle	25	7	28.0
Hill, Tex	28	10	35.7
Hitchcock, Sea	26	8	30.8
Honeycutt, StL	25	5	20.0
Howe, NYA	23	6	26.1
Jackson M, Sea	22	4	18.2
Jacome, KC	28	3	10.7
James, Cal	34	7	20.6
Johns, Oak	36	18	50.0
Juden, Mon	22	8	36.4
Karchner, ChA	24	10	41.7
Karl, Mil	30	15	50.0
Keagle, Det	24	8	33.3
Kile, Hou	27	6	22.2
Leiter A, Fla	27	9	33.3
Leiter M, Mon	24	10	41.7

Pitcher, Team	Left	Sc	%
Lewis, Det	45	13	28.9
Lieber, Pit	22	6	27.3
Lima, Det	20	7	35.0
Lira, Det	33	17	51.5
Lloyd, NYA	47	13	27.7
Magnante, KC	21	6	28.6
Manuel, Mon	23	5	21.7
Martinez P, Mon	20	10	50.0
Mathews T, Bal	26	6	23.1
McDonald, Mil	20	5	25.0
McDowell J, Cle	31	18	58.1
McDowell R, Bal	22	11	50.0
McElroy, Cal	25	3	12.0
McMichael, Atl	20	4	20.0
Milchin, Bal	28	12	42.9
Mimbs, Phi	20	7	35.0
Miranda, Mil	38	8	21.1
Mohler, Oak	25	1	4.0
Morman, Hou	36	7	19.4
Moyer, Sea	22	8	36.4
Mulholland, Sea	27	8	29.6
Munoz M, Col	26	12	46.2
Myers M, Det	56	19	33.9
Naulty, Min	23	9	39.1
Neagle, Atl	22	6	27.3
Nelson, NYA	37	15	40.5
Olivares, Det	22	12	54.5
Oliver, Tex	23	10	43.5
Orosco, Bal	47	9	19.1
Park, LA	22	7	31.8
Patterson B, ChN	46	4	8.7
Pavlik, Tex	30	8	26.7
Pennington, Cal	20	9	45.0
Perez Y, Fla	41	10	24.4
Pichardo, KC	27	13	48.1
Plesac, Pit	27	10	37.0
Plunk, Cle	21	5	23.8
Polley, NYA	24	12	50.0
Poole, SF	37	6	16.2
Potts, Mil	25	13	52.0
Powell, Fla	28	10	35.7

Pitcher, Team	Left	Sc	%
Quantrill, Tor	25	4	16.0
Radke, Min	22	11	50.0
Rapp, Fla	21	7	33.3
Reyes C, Oak	23	1	4.3
Ritz, Col	25	13	52.0
Robertson, Min	35	14	40.0
Rodriguez F, Min	24	10	41.7
Rogers, NYA	34	12	35.3
Russell, Tex	24	6	25.0
Ryan, Phi	27	7	25.9
Sanders, SD	25	13	52.0
Scott, SF	26	7	26.9
Simas, ChA	22	10	45.5
Springer D, Cal	24	14	58.3
Springer R, Phi	21	4	19.0
Stanton, Tex	25	3	12.0
Tapani, ChA	20	7	35.0
Tewksbury, SD	26	11	42.3
Thomas, ChA	50	8	16.0
Thompson M, Col	24	10	41.7
Valenzuela, SD	29	5	17.2
Valera, KC	25	7	28.0
VanLanding., SF	37	17	45.9
Veres D, Mon	36	9	25.0
Villone, Mil	29	5	17.2
Vosberg, Tex	28	9	32.1
Wade, Atl	22	7	31.8
Wakefield, Bos	25	14	56.0
Weathers, NYA	29	8	27.6
Wells B, Sea	23	10	43.5
Wells D, Bal	23	10	43.5
Wendell, ChN	20	7	35.0
Wengert, Oak	31	11	35.5
Wickman, Mil	31	6	19.4
Wilkins, Pit	22	5	22.7
Wilson, NYN	23	7	30.4
Witt, Tex	36	16	44.4
Wolcott, Sea	32	13	40.6
Worrell T, SD	20	5	25.0
MLB Avg			**35.2**

Who Knows How to Handle Their Inheritance? (p. 184)

The table below shows the percentage (**%**) of Inherited Runners (**IR**) each relief pitcher allowed to score (**SC**)

Both Leagues — Listed Alphabetically (minimum 23 inherited runners in 1996)

Pitcher, Team	IR	SC	%
Adams T, ChN	29	8	27.6
Assenmacher, Cle	50	13	26.0
Ayala, Sea	28	8	28.6
Bailey C, StL	27	9	33.3
Bautista, SF	27	13	48.1
Beck, SF	33	10	30.3
Belinda, Bos	24	9	37.5
Bennett, Min	23	4	17.4
Blair, SD	38	13	34.2
Bochtler, SD	40	13	32.5
Borland, Phi	42	18	42.9
Boze, Mil	23	11	47.8
Brandenburg, Bos	39	17	43.6
Byrd, NYN	23	10	43.5
Carmona, Sea	48	15	31.3
Carrasco, Cin	25	12	48.0
Casian, ChN	38	7	18.4
Castillo T, ChA	47	14	29.8
Charlton, Sea	39	8	20.5
Clontz, Atl	54	18	33.3
Cook, Tex	81	16	19.8
Cordova, Pit	23	6	26.1
Corsi, Oak	41	14	34.1
Crabtree, Tor	23	9	39.1
Creek, SF	46	14	30.4
Cummings, Det	33	16	48.5
Daal, Mon	54	15	27.8
Davis, Sea	38	13	34.2
DeLucia, SF	31	11	35.5
Dewey, SF	74	33	44.6
DiPoto, NYN	38	18	47.4
Dyer, Mon	54	19	35.2
Eichhorn, Cal	28	17	60.7
Eischen, Det	39	14	35.9
Embree, Cle	24	5	20.8
Eshelman, Bos	26	8	30.8
Florie, Mil	34	13	38.2
Fossas, StL	40	11	27.5
Frey, Phi	23	12	52.2
Garces, Bos	34	12	35.3
Garcia, Mil	40	11	27.5
Groom, Oak	66	21	31.8
Guardado, Min	58	18	31.0
Gunderson, Bos	24	8	33.3
Guthrie, LA	32	16	50.0
Hansell, Min	37	21	56.8
Heredia G, Tex	40	14	35.0
Hernandez R, ChA	30	9	30.0
Hernandez X, Hou	26	12	46.2
Hoffman, SD	35	6	17.1
Holmes, Col	34	14	41.2
Holtz, Cal	29	6	20.7
Holzemer, Cal	28	9	32.1
Honeycutt, StL	49	17	34.7
Howe, NYA	28	6	21.4
Hudson, Bos	29	9	31.0
Jackson M, Sea	72	24	33.3
Jacome, KC	37	10	27.0
James, Cal	47	17	36.2
Jones D, Mil	43	17	39.5
Jones T, Hou	37	14	37.8
Juden, Mon	26	9	34.6
Karchner, ChA	38	14	36.8
Leiper, Mon	24	6	25.0
Leskanic, Col	23	8	34.8
Lewis, Det	88	32	36.4
Lima, Det	27	9	33.3
Lloyd, NYA	63	21	33.3
MacDonald, NYN	26	7	26.9
Magnante, KC	31	9	29.0
Manuel, Mon	49	17	34.7
Mathews TJ, StL	36	6	16.7
Mathews Te, Bal	46	19	41.3
McDowell R, Bal	44	20	45.5
McElroy, Cal	50	14	28.0
Mecir, NYA	29	15	51.7
Milchin, Bal	28	8	28.6
Mills, Bal	41	15	36.6
Minor, Sea	23	10	43.5
Miranda, Mil	25	11	44.0
Mlicki, NYN	27	5	18.5
Mohler, Oak	46	19	41.3
Morman, Hou	51	18	35.3
Munoz M, Col	23	8	34.8
Myers M, Det	69	17	24.6
Myers R, ChN	28	13	46.4
Naulty, Min	33	13	39.4
Nelson, NYA	33	13	39.4
Nen, Fla	30	8	26.7
Olson, Hou	36	20	55.6
Orosco, Bal	46	10	21.7
Osuna A, LA	45	13	28.9
Parrett, Phi	29	18	62.1
Patterson B, ChN	73	17	23.3
Pavlas, NYA	23	10	43.5
Percival, Cal	28	4	14.3
Perez Y, Fla	58	18	31.0
Petkovsek, StL	28	9	32.1
Pichardo, KC	44	17	38.6
Plesac, Pit	38	11	28.9
Plunk, Cle	49	11	22.4
Polley, NYA	25	4	16.0
Poole, SF	60	15	25.0
Powell, Fla	46	14	30.4
Pugh, Cin	23	9	39.1
Radinsky, LA	30	16	53.3
Reed, Col	48	15	31.3
Reyes C, Oak	34	17	50.0
Rojas, Mon	29	7	24.1
Ruffin B, Col	25	9	36.0
Russell, Tex	48	16	33.3
Scott, SF	44	18	40.9
Service, Cin	23	10	43.5
Shaw, Cin	53	18	34.0
Simas, ChA	49	17	34.7
Slocumb, Bos	30	9	30.0
Springer R, Phi	29	8	27.6
Stanton, Tex	64	21	32.8
Tavarez, Cle	30	12	40.0
Taylor, Oak	34	5	14.7
Thomas, ChA	52	11	21.2
Trombley, Min	51	22	43.1
Valera, KC	30	8	26.7
Van Poppel, Det	25	9	36.0
Veres D, Mon	33	11	33.3
Veres R, Det	23	11	47.8
Villone, Mil	44	22	50.0
Vosberg, Tex	47	17	36.2
Wendell, ChN	31	8	25.8
Wickander, Mil	29	16	55.2
Wickman, Mil	68	34	50.0
Wohlers, Atl	36	6	16.7
Worrell Ti, SD	25	7	28.0
Worrell To, LA	24	10	41.7
MLB Avg			**35.2**

Which Pitchers Really "Lost Out" in 1996? (p. 186)

No Wins after Leaving with Chance to Win 1996 (Minimum 10 times pulled)

Pitcher, Team	No Win	Pulled With Lead	Pct
Astacio, LA	8	17	.471
Radke, Min	8	17	.471
Alvarez W, ChA	8	23	.348
Karl, Mil	7	17	.412
Clemens, Bos	6	11	.545
Leiter M, Mon	6	12	.500
Reynoso, Col	6	14	.429
Burkett, Tex	6	15	.400
Tapani, ChA	6	18	.333
Glavine, Atl	6	21	.286
Benes An, StL	6	21	.286
Drabek, Hou	5	11	.455
Wengert, Oak	5	11	.455
Harnisch, NYN	5	12	.417
Haney, KC	5	12	.417
Gordon, Bos	5	13	.385
Kile, Hou	5	13	.385
Tewksbury, SD	5	15	.333
Osborne, StL	5	16	.313
McDonald, Mil	5	17	.294
Clark M, NYN	5	17	.294
Nagy, Cle	5	18	.278
Avery, Atl	4	10	.400
Wolcott, Sea	4	10	.400
Portugal, Cin	4	11	.364
Darwin D, Hou	4	12	.333
Hill, Tex	4	13	.308
Erickson, Bal	4	13	.308
Rogers, NYA	4	15	.267
Navarro, ChN	4	15	.267
Finley, Cal	4	16	.250
Belcher, KC	4	16	.250
Stottlemyre, StL	4	16	.250
Martinez R, LA	4	17	.235
Neagle, Atl	4	18	.222
Mussina, Bal	4	19	.211
Freeman, ChA	3	10	.300
Bones, NYA	3	10	.300
Sele, Bos	3	10	.300
Watson, SF	3	10	.300
Gardner, SF	3	11	.273
Ashby, SD	3	11	.273
Jones B, NYN	3	12	.250

Pitcher, Team	No Win	Pulled With Lead	Pct
Gooden, NYA	3	13	.231
Fassero, Mon	3	13	.231
Smiley, Cin	3	14	.214
Burba, Cin	3	14	.214
Baldwin, ChA	3	14	.214
Hitchcock, Sea	3	16	.188
Nomo, LA	3	16	.188
Ritz, Col	3	18	.167
Gross, Tex	2	10	.200
Candiotti, LA	2	10	.200
Guzman, Tor	2	10	.200
Sanders, SD	2	10	.200
Wells D, Bal	2	11	.182
Boskie, Cal	2	11	.182
VanLandingham, SF	2	11	.182
Benes Al, StL	2	11	.182
Coppinger, Bal	2	11	.182
Martinez P, Mon	2	12	.167
Wakefield, Bos	2	12	.167
Moyer, Sea	2	13	.154
Appier, KC	2	13	.154
Fernandez A, ChA	2	13	.154
Key, NYA	2	14	.143
Maddux G, Atl	2	14	.143
Hentgen, Tor	2	15	.133
Leiter A, Fla	2	16	.125
Hamilton, SD	2	16	.125
Pettitte, NYA	2	20	.100
Rodriguez F, Min	1	10	.100
Mulholland, Sea	1	11	.091
McDowell J, Cle	1	11	.091
Pavlik, Tex	1	11	.091
Brown, Fla	1	13	.077
Hanson, Tor	1	13	.077
Reynolds, Hou	1	13	.077
Valdes I, LA	1	16	.063
Trachsel, ChN	0	10	.000
Valenzuela, SD	0	13	.000
Witt, Tex	0	13	.000
Oliver, Tex	0	13	.000
Hershiser, Cle	0	15	.000
Smoltz, Atl	0	19	.000

Which Reliever is *Really* the Best at Preventing Runs? (p. 188)

Runs Prevented Point Totals—1996 (Minimum 70 IP)

Reliever, Team	Pts	Reliever, Team	Pts	Reliever, Team	Pts
Rivera, NYA	27.7	Kile, Hou	1.4	Freeman, ChA	–2.5
Hoffman, SD	23.0	Pettitte, NYA	1.4	Abbott J, Cal	–2.5
Hernandez R, ChA	19.1	Tavarez, Cle	1.3	Leiter M, Mon	–2.6
Nen, Fla	18.6	Carrasco, Cin	1.2	Lima, Det	–2.6
Percival, Cal	18.4	Wagner P, Pit	1.2	Bones, NYA	–2.8
Plunk, Cle	17.7	Coppinger, Bal	0.9	Lieber, Pit	–3.0
Worrell T, SD	16.2	Burba, Cin	0.9	Holmes, Col	–3.0
Shaw, Cin	14.5	Stottlemyre, StL	0.9	Schmidt J, Pit	–3.1
Osuna A, LA	14.3	Sager, Det	0.9	Williams M, Phi	–3.5
Wendell, ChN	13.9	Cordova, Pit	0.9	Boskie, Cal	–3.5
Wohlers, Atl	12.9	Flener, Tor	0.8	Wolcott, Sea	–3.5
Ryan, Phi	11.6	Telgheder, Oak	0.7	Johns, Oak	–3.6
Cook, Tex	11.2	Hamilton, SD	0.5	Sparks, Mil	–3.6
Mathews T, StL	11.2	Rueter, SF	0.4	Guardado, Min	–3.7
Guthrie, LA	10.7	DiPoto, NYN	0.3	Wasdin, Oak	–3.8
Manuel, Mon	10.6	Person, NYN	0.1	Bailey R, Col	–3.9
Brantley, Cin	9.9	Martinez R, LA	0.0	Blair, SD	–4.1
Adams T, ChN	9.6	Robertson, Min	–0.2	Wengert, Oak	–4.2
Rojas, Mon	8.5	Rapp, Fla	–0.2	Avery, Atl	–4.2
James, Cal	8.2	Wright, Col	–0.2	Simas, ChA	–4.5
Bielecki, Atl	8.0	Linton, KC	–0.4	Mohler, Oak	–4.6
Slocumb, Bos	7.6	Dyer, Mon	–0.5	Powell, Fla	–4.6
Sanders, SD	7.3	Benes Al, StL	–0.5	Aldred, Min	–5.2
Gross, Tex	7.2	Gardner, SF	–0.5	Henry, NYN	–5.9
Urbina, Mon	5.5	Wojciechowski, Oak	–0.5	Nelson, NYA	–6.0
Salkeld, Cin	5.4	Witt, Tex	–0.7	Hernandez X, Hou	–6.1
Reed, Col	5.2	Springer D, Cal	–1.1	Wilkins, Pit	–6.3
Mlicki, NYN	5.0	Tewksbury, SD	–1.2	Reyes C, Oak	–6.3
Quantrill, Tor	4.7	Moyer, Sea	–1.2	Telemaco, ChN	–6.3
Wells B, Sea	4.7	Smiley, Cin	–1.2	Mimbs, Phi	–6.4
Petkovsek, StL	4.5	Borland, Phi	–1.4	Van Poppel, Det	–6.5
Rodriguez F, Min	4.3	Carmona, Sea	–1.5	Haynes, Bal	–6.9
Park, LA	4.2	Benes An, StL	–1.5	Brandenburg, Bos	–7.1
Daal, Mon	4.1	Portugal, Cin	–1.5	Clontz, Atl	–7.6
Castillo T, ChA	3.9	Darwin D, Hou	–1.6	Miranda, Mil	–8.8
Lewis, Det	3.6	Veres D, Mon	–1.6	Parra, Min	–8.9
Charlton, Sea	3.2	Dewey, SF	–1.6	Ogea, Cle	–9.0
Mesa, Cle	3.2	Hammond, Fla	–1.6	Miceli, Pit	–9.3
Bergman, SD	3.2	Stanton, Tex	–1.6	Mathews T, Bal	–12.1
Juden, Mon	2.7	Wall, Hou	–1.7	Grimsley, Cal	–12.6
Bullinger, ChN	2.7	Weathers, NYA	–1.8	Garcia, Mil	–13.3
McMichael, Atl	2.5	Fernandez O, SF	–2.0	Williams B, Det	–13.4
Astacio, LA	2.4	Groom, Oak	–2.1	Eshelman, Bos	–13.7
Janzen, Tor	2.4	Valenzuela, SD	–2.1	Gohr, Cal	–13.9
Corsi, Oak	2.4	Foster, ChN	–2.1	Heredia G, Tex	–14.0
Cormier, Mon	1.9	Hutton, Fla	–2.1	Hansell, Min	–15.7
Thompson M, Col	1.5	Candiotti, LA	–2.2	Keagle, Det	–17.8
Jarvis, Cin	1.5	Springer R, Phi	–2.2	Leskanic, Col	–19.2
Jackson M, Sea	1.5	Plesac, Pit	–2.3	Wickman, Mil	–21.9
Krivda, Bal	1.4	Wagner M, Sea	–2.4		

Who Throws the Most Strikes? (p. 192)

Strike Percentage (Minimum 200 BFP)

Player, Team	Strike%
Abbott J, Cal	60.2
Adams T, ChN	59.6
Adams W, Oak	62.4
Aguilera, Min	62.6
Aldred, Min	59.7
Alvarez W, ChA	61.8
Anderson, Cle	61.4
Appier, KC	63.5
Ashby, SD	64.8
Assenmacher, Cle	65.7
Astacio, LA	62.7
Avery, Atl	63.6
Ayala, Sea	64.2
Bailey C, StL	58.7
Bailey R, Col	55.6
Baldwin, ChA	60.9
Bautista, SF	66.2
Beck, SF	69.4
Belcher, KC	64.0
Benes Al, StL	59.9
Benes An, StL	61.4
Bergman, SD	64.5
Bielecki, Atl	62.2
Blair, SD	62.5
Bochtler, SD	58.9
Boehringer, NYA	61.1
Bones, NYA	57.5
Borland, Phi	59.7
Bosio, Sea	60.0
Boskie, Cal	64.0
Bottalico, Phi	63.8
Bottenfield, ChN	63.5
Brandenburg, Bos	64.9
Brantley, Cin	64.0
Brocail, Hou	61.4
Brown, Fla	66.0
Bullinger, ChN	58.8
Burba, Cin	60.1
Burkett, Tex	62.5
Byrd, NYN	63.3
Candiotti, LA	61.7
Carmona, Sea	59.8
Carrasco, Cin	59.4
Castillo F, ChN	61.7
Castillo T, ChA	62.8
Charlton, Sea	59.0
Chouinard, Oak	60.6
Christiansen, Pit	62.0
Clark M, NYN	64.5
Clemens, Bos	60.5
Clontz, Atl	63.5
Cone, NYA	59.0
Cook, Tex	60.4
Coppinger, Bal	60.0
Cordova, Pit	66.9
Cormier, Mon	61.4
Corsi, Oak	57.2
Crabtree, Tor	65.4
Creek, SF	57.4
D'Amico, Mil	62.8
Daal, Mon	61.6
Darwin D, Hou	68.7
DeLucia, SF	62.8
Dewey, SF	62.1
DiPoto, NYN	59.5
Drabek, Hou	61.3
Dyer, Mon	61.7
Eckersley, StL	70.8
Eischen, Det	62.2
Eldred, Mil	59.2
Ericks, Pit	63.6
Erickson, Bal	62.1
Eshelman, Bos	59.7
Estes, SF	57.7
Fassero, Mon	67.2
Fernandez A, ChA	63.8
Fernandez O, SF	61.0
Fernandez S, Phi	64.3
Fetters, Mil	62.3
Finley, Cal	60.7
Flener, Tor	59.8
Florie, Mil	59.5
Fossas, StL	62.9
Foster, ChN	63.0
Franco, NYN	61.7
Freeman, ChA	62.3
Garces, Bos	58.1
Garcia, Mil	61.8
Gardner, SF	63.6
Glavine, Atl	61.4
Gohr, Cal	61.6
Gooden, NYA	58.3
Gordon, Bos	60.7
Grace, Phi	64.6
Grimsley, Cal	57.5
Groom, Oak	62.2
Gross, Tex	60.7
Guardado, Min	63.6
Gubicza, KC	60.2
Guthrie, LA	63.0
Guzman, Tor	62.5
Hamilton, SD	62.6
Hammond, Fla	64.7
Hampton, Hou	63.5
Haney, KC	64.2
Hansell, Min	62.2
Hanson, Tor	58.0
Harnisch, NYN	63.5
Haynes, Bal	59.2
Henry, NYN	60.7
Hentgen, Tor	61.8
Heredia G, Tex	68.7
Hernandez R, ChA	65.2
Hernandez X, Hou	62.7
Hershiser, Cle	62.4
Hill, Tex	62.5
Hitchcock, Sea	59.6
Hoffman, SD	65.8
Holmes, Col	63.7
Hudson, Bos	55.4
Hunter, Phi	59.2
Hurtado, Sea	58.2
Hutton, Fla	63.6
Isringhausen, NYN	60.2
Jackson M, Sea	61.0
Jacome, KC	63.7
James, Cal	61.4
Janzen, Tor	60.6
Jarvis, Cin	61.7
Johns, Oak	60.4
Johnson R, Sea	60.9
Jones B, NYN	64.7
Jones D, Mil	67.7
Jones T, Hou	60.3
Juden, Mon	62.4
Karchner, ChA	58.7
Karl, Mil	61.5
Keagle, Det	57.4
Key, NYA	60.8
Keyser, ChA	59.4
Kile, Hou	60.9
Krivda, Bal	61.7
Langston, Cal	61.8
Leiter A, Fla	57.2
Leiter M, Mon	63.7
Leskanic, Col	60.4
Lewis, Det	57.8
Lieber, Pit	66.5
Lima, Det	65.8
Linton, KC	64.8
Lira, Det	59.8
Lloyd, NYA	61.3
Loaiza, Pit	63.4
Lopez, Cle	62.2
Maddux G, Atl	71.5
Maddux M, Bos	60.7

Player, Team	Strike%
Magnante, KC	61.7
Magrane, ChA	59.5
Mahomes, Bos	57.5
Manuel, Mon	62.8
Martinez D, Cle	61.3
Martinez P, Mon	64.2
Martinez R, LA	58.3
Mathews TJ, StL	64.8
Mathews Te, Bal	62.9
McCaskill, ChA	59.2
McDonald, Mil	60.6
McDowell J, Cle	63.6
McDowell R, Bal	62.9
McElroy, Cal	62.4
McMichael, Atl	65.4
Mendoza, NYA	65.0
Mercker, Cle	56.9
Mesa, Cle	64.1
Miceli, Pit	62.7
Miller K, Fla	58.7
Mills, Bal	58.0
Mimbs, Phi	60.5
Minor, Sea	61.6
Miranda, Mil	57.0
Mlicki, NYN	61.9
Mohler, Oak	59.5
Montgomery J, KC	64.8
Morgan, Cin	61.2
Moyer, Sea	61.5
Mulholland, Sea	65.5
Munoz M, Col	62.0
Mussina, Bal	65.6
Myers M, Det	61.2
Myers Ra, Bal	61.4
Myers Ro, ChN	58.9
Nagy, Cle	62.3
Naulty, Min	58.4
Navarro, ChN	62.3
Neagle, Atl	64.8
Nelson, NYA	60.8
Nen, Fla	67.3
Nitkowski, Det	55.7
Nomo, LA	62.1
Ogea, Cle	64.5
Olivares, Det	58.0
Oliver, Tex	61.1
Olson, Hou	57.6
Orosco, Bal	61.6
Osborne, StL	63.3
Osuna A, LA	64.0
Painter, Col	59.7
Paniagua, Mon	60.0
Park, LA	58.3
Parra, Min	62.6
Parrett, Phi	62.0
Patterson B, ChN	65.8

Player, Team	Strike%
Pavlik, Tex	62.0
Percival, Cal	65.4
Perez Y, Fla	60.7
Person, NYN	60.4
Peters, Pit	61.1
Petkovsek, StL	59.7
Pettitte, NYA	62.8
Pichardo, KC	63.0
Plesac, Pit	66.9
Plunk, Cle	62.3
Poole, SF	60.5
Portugal, Cin	64.6
Potts, Mil	56.1
Powell, Fla	60.7
Prieto, Oak	58.3
Pugh, Cin	61.5
Quantrill, Tor	61.0
Radinsky, LA	66.0
Radke, Min	64.9
Rapp, Fla	58.4
Reed, Col	64.7
Rekar, Col	62.2
Reyes C, Oak	58.7
Reynolds, Hou	67.5
Reynoso, Col	60.6
Rhodes, Bal	63.1
Ritz, Col	59.0
Rivera, NYA	68.7
Robertson, Min	56.5
Rodriguez F, Min	60.8
Rogers, NYA	58.5
Rojas, Mon	65.7
Rosado, KC	64.4
Ruebel, Pit	57.7
Rueter, SF	61.9
Ruffin B, Col	64.4
Ruffin J, Cin	61.1
Russell, Tex	60.7
Ryan, Phi	60.8
Sager, Det	59.7
Salkeld, Cin	59.1
Sanders, SD	63.8
Schilling, Phi	66.9
Schmidt J, Pit	61.1
Schourek, Cin	63.6
Scott, SF	63.4
Sele, Bos	59.3
Service, Cin	63.9
Shaw, Cin	67.7
Shuey, Cle	58.6
Simas, ChA	62.3
Slocumb, Bos	60.1
Smiley, Cin	67.1
Smith L, Cin	61.4
Smith Z, Pit	62.4
Smoltz, Atl	66.6

Player, Team	Strike%
Sparks, Mil	55.2
Springer D, Cal	59.9
Springer R, Phi	65.7
Stanton, Tex	64.8
Stevens, Min	62.7
Stottlemyre, StL	61.4
Swindell, Cle	63.6
Tapani, ChA	62.4
Tavarez, Cle	61.6
Taylor, Oak	63.2
Telemaco, ChN	62.6
Telgheder, Oak	62.2
Tewksbury, SD	68.0
Thompson J, Det	61.7
Thompson M, Col	60.0
Timlin, Tor	67.6
Torres, Sea	58.9
Trachsel, ChN	62.7
Trombley, Min	64.3
Urbina, Mon	64.4
Valdes I, LA	65.4
Valdes M, Fla	58.1
Valenzuela, SD	59.0
Valera, KC	62.7
Van Poppel, Det	58.2
VanEgmond, Mil	59.4
VanLanding., SF	62.0
Veres D, Mon	61.0
Wade, Atl	59.2
Wagner B, Hou	63.9
Wagner M, Sea	61.4
Wagner P, Pit	58.4
Wakefield, Bos	62.9
Wall, Hou	65.4
Wasdin, Oak	64.6
Watson, SF	62.8
Weathers, NYA	59.4
Wells B, Sea	61.7
Wells D, Bal	66.4
Wendell, ChN	61.2
Wengert, Oak	61.1
Wetteland, NYA	64.7
Wickman, Mil	59.1
Wilkins, Pit	60.9
Williams B, Det	56.3
Williams M, Phi	62.2
Williams W, Tor	62.7
Wilson, NYN	60.9
Witt, Tex	61.4
Wohlers, Atl	67.8
Wojciechow., Oak	62.3
Wolcott, Sea	62.3
Worrell Ti, SD	62.1
Worrell To, LA	65.7
Wright, Col	59.6

Which Starting Pitchers Are "Bullpen Savers"? (p. 194)

1992-96 Percentage of Starts of 7+ Innings (Minimum 50 GS)

Pitcher	GS	7-Inning Starts	Pct
Greg Maddux	159	125	.786
David Cone	132	102	.773
Kevin Brown	152	108	.711
Jack McDowell	153	106	.693
Ismael Valdes	61	41	.672
Randy Johnson	126	83	.659
Mike Mussina	149	98	.658
Curt Schilling	116	76	.655
Charles Nagy	126	82	.651
Bret Saberhagen	83	54	.651
Roger Clemens	142	91	.641
Alex Fernandez	152	97	.638
Mark Langston	134	84	.627
Hideo Nomo	61	38	.623
John Smoltz	155	94	.606
Kevin Appier	150	90	.600
Dennis Martinez	138	82	.594
Doug Drabek	152	90	.592
Melido Perez	92	54	.587
Cal Eldred	94	55	.585
Andy Pettitte	60	35	.583
Jose Rijo	109	63	.578
Pat Hentgen	123	71	.577
Tom Glavine	159	91	.572
Chuck Finley	158	90	.570
Brad Radke	63	35	.556
Tim Wakefield	92	51	.554
Bobby Jones	94	52	.553
Juan Guzman	137	75	.547
Andy Benes	158	86	.544
Tim Belcher	155	84	.542
Dwight Gooden	96	52	.542
Orel Hershiser	146	78	.534
Ken Hill	148	79	.534
Jim Abbott	138	73	.529
Jaime Navarro	142	75	.528
Bill Wegman	76	40	.526
John Smiley	137	72	.526
Tom Candiotti	141	74	.525
Wilson Alvarez	128	66	.516
Todd Stottlemyre	138	71	.514
David Wells	123	63	.512
Bob Tewksbury	142	72	.507
Kevin Tapani	158	80	.506
Ramon Martinez	138	69	.500
Jeff Fassero	100	50	.500
Chris Bosio	116	57	.491
Jimmy Key	127	62	.488
Kenny Rogers	118	57	.483
Steve Trachsel	85	41	.482
Joey Hamilton	79	38	.481
Kevin Gross	134	64	.478
Jack Morris	84	40	.476
Charlie Leibrandt	57	27	.474
Pedro Martinez	89	42	.472
Jamie Moyer	87	41	.471
Terry Mulholland	136	64	.471
Shane Reynolds	85	40	.471
Steve Avery	146	68	.466
Mark Portugal	127	59	.465
Bill Swift	95	44	.463
Pedro Astacio	108	50	.463
Danny Darwin	102	47	.461
Frank Tanana	63	29	.460
John Burkett	155	71	.458
Ricky Bones	138	62	.449
Erik Hanson	145	65	.448
Jose Guzman	67	30	.448
Tom Gordon	114	51	.447
Scott Kamieniecki	85	38	.447
Frank Viola	79	35	.443
Scott Erickson	154	68	.442
Charlie Hough	82	36	.439
Steve Cooke	55	24	.436
Bobby Witt	149	65	.436
Bill Gullickson	81	35	.432
Mike Morgan	125	54	.432
Dave Fleming	94	40	.426
Greg W. Harris	80	34	.425
Donovan Osborne	104	44	.423
Greg Swindell	116	49	.422
Danny Jackson	114	48	.421
Dave Stewart	95	40	.421
Scott Karl	50	21	.420

Pitcher	GS	7-Inning Starts	Pct
Ben McDonald	141	59	.418
Denny Neagle	101	42	.416
Rick Sutcliffe	78	32	.410
Sid Fernandez	98	40	.408
Mark Gubicza	98	40	.408
Ron Darling	108	44	.407
Mike Hampton	54	22	.407
Pete Harnisch	133	54	.406
Omar Olivares	82	33	.402
Darryl Kile	126	50	.397
Mike Moore	122	48	.393
Roger Pavlik	114	44	.386
Greg Hibbard	73	28	.384
Jose Mesa	60	23	.383
Randy Tomlin	55	21	.382
Chris Haney	90	34	.378
Pete Schourek	90	34	.378
John Doherty	61	23	.377
Zane Smith	97	36	.371
Sterling Hitchcock	76	28	.368
Tommy Greene	55	20	.364
Andy Ashby	108	39	.361
Mark Clark	108	39	.361
Rheal Cormier	97	35	.361
Frank Castillo	124	44	.355
Mark Leiter	97	33	.340
Bill Krueger	50	17	.340
Tim Leary	53	18	.340
Al Leiter	93	31	.333
Scott Sanders	60	20	.333
Frank Rodriguez	51	17	.333
Bob Walk	51	17	.333
W. VanLandingham	64	21	.328
Trevor Wilson	61	20	.328
Joe Magrane	52	17	.327
Scott Sanderson	87	28	.322
Kirk McCaskill	53	17	.321

Pitcher	GS	7-Inning Starts	Pct
Allen Watson	85	27	.318
Brian Williams	57	18	.316
Bud Black	64	20	.313
Aaron Sele	75	23	.307
Tim Pugh	56	17	.304
Butch Henry	80	24	.300
Chris Hammond	104	31	.298
Jack Armstrong	58	17	.293
Chris Nabholz	65	19	.292
Jason Bere	80	23	.288
Jim Bullinger	63	18	.286
Mark Gardner	99	28	.283
Paul Wagner	75	21	.280
Shawn Boskie	83	23	.277
John Dopson	58	16	.276
Kevin Foster	58	16	.276
Pat Rapp	98	26	.265
Todd Van Poppel	68	18	.265
Armando Reynoso	88	23	.261
Jim Deshaies	73	19	.260
Mike Williams	54	14	.259
Sean Bergman	51	13	.255
Marvin Freeman	60	15	.250
Kent Mercker	61	15	.246
Arthur Rhodes	53	13	.245
Dave Burba	58	14	.241
Joe Hesketh	50	12	.240
F. Valenzuela	84	20	.238
Willie Banks	80	19	.238
Kevin Ritz	89	21	.236
Paul Quantrill	64	15	.234
Bob Welch	56	13	.232
Kirk Rueter	62	13	.210
Mike Harkey	68	14	.206
Felipe Lira	54	11	.204
Pat Mahomes	51	8	.157
Dave Weathers	57	8	.140

Which Pitchers Have Misleading Earned Run Averages? (p. 196)

Predicted ERA versus Actual ERA—1996

Pitcher, Team	ERA DIF	ACT ERA	Pred ERA
Ayala, Sea	-1.60	5.88	4.29
Grimsley, Cal	-1.58	6.84	5.26
Bullinger, ChN	-1.57	6.54	4.97
Clontz, Atl	-1.48	5.69	4.21
Abbott J, Cal	-1.38	7.48	6.10
Ruffin B, Col	-1.30	4.00	2.71
Pichardo, KC	-1.22	5.43	4.20
DeLucia, SF	-1.22	5.84	4.62
Valera, KC	-1.11	6.46	5.34
Guardado, Min	-1.11	5.25	4.15
Garcia, Mil	-1.10	6.66	5.56
Heredia G, Tex	-1.01	5.89	4.88
Cook, Tex	-1.00	4.09	3.10
Taylor, Oak	-0.98	4.33	3.34
Florie, Mil	-0.90	4.74	3.84
Blair, SD	-0.88	4.60	3.72
Plesac, Pit	-0.85	4.09	3.25
Rojas, Mon	-0.84	3.22	2.38
VanLandingham, SF	-0.84	5.40	4.56
Wilson, NYN	-0.79	5.38	4.59
Langston, Cal	-0.76	4.82	4.06
Leskanic, Col	-0.72	6.23	5.51
Lira, Det	-0.71	5.22	4.51
Jarvis, Cin	-0.67	5.98	5.31
Keagle, Det	-0.67	7.39	6.72
Freeman, ChA	-0.65	6.15	5.50
Myers R, ChN	-0.65	4.68	4.03
Wasdin, Oak	-0.63	5.96	5.33
Rogers, NYA	-0.62	4.68	4.05
Aldred, Min	-0.62	6.21	5.59
Magnante, KC	-0.61	5.67	5.06
Park, LA	-0.55	3.64	3.09
Timlin, Tor	-0.54	3.65	3.11
Aguilera, Min	-0.54	5.42	4.88
Isringhausen, NYN	-0.54	4.77	4.24
Karchner, ChA	-0.52	5.76	5.24
Gordon, Bos	-0.52	5.59	5.08
Wells D, Bal	-0.51	5.14	4.62
Carrasco, Cin	-0.49	3.75	3.26
Gooden, NYA	-0.48	5.01	4.53
Powell, Fla	-0.47	4.54	4.07
Johns, Oak	-0.46	5.98	5.52
Daal, Mon	-0.46	4.02	3.56
Rodriguez F, Min	-0.45	5.05	4.60
Tewksbury, SD	-0.45	4.31	3.86
Martinez P, Mon	-0.45	3.70	3.25
Sanders, SD	-0.45	3.38	2.93
McDowell J, Cle	-0.44	5.11	4.67
Orosco, Bal	-0.43	3.40	2.96
Myers M, Det	-0.43	5.01	4.58
Henry, NYN	-0.41	4.68	4.27
Pavlik, Tex	-0.41	5.19	4.78
Naulty, Min	-0.39	3.79	3.40
Castillo F, ChN	-0.39	5.28	4.89
Mussina, Bal	-0.38	4.81	4.43
Lloyd, NYA	-0.38	4.29	3.91
Hanson, Tor	-0.37	5.41	5.04
Bottalico, Phi	-0.36	3.19	2.83
Borland, Phi	-0.35	4.07	3.72
Sele, Bos	-0.34	5.32	4.98
Hoffman, SD	-0.34	2.25	1.91
Key, NYA	-0.34	4.68	4.34
Ritz, Col	-0.33	5.28	4.95
Reynolds, Hou	-0.32	3.65	3.34
Ogea, Cle	-0.31	4.79	4.47
Hamilton, SD	-0.31	4.17	3.85
Percival, Cal	-0.31	2.31	2.00
Burkett, Tex	-0.31	4.24	3.94
Cordova, Pit	-0.30	4.09	3.79
Slocumb, Bos	-0.28	3.02	2.75
Smoltz, Atl	-0.27	2.94	2.67
Rivera, NYA	-0.27	2.09	1.82
Olson, Hou	-0.27	4.99	4.72
Avery, Atl	-0.24	4.47	4.22
Baldwin, ChA	-0.24	4.42	4.18
Hansell, Min	-0.23	5.69	5.46
Benes Al, StL	-0.23	4.90	4.67
Reed, Col	-0.21	3.96	3.75
Karl, Mil	-0.20	4.86	4.66
Nelson, NYA	-0.18	4.36	4.18
Robertson, Min	-0.16	5.12	4.96
Erickson, Bal	-0.16	5.02	4.86
Mathews T, StL	-0.15	3.01	2.86
Portugal, Cin	-0.15	3.98	3.83
Stottlemyre, StL	-0.15	3.87	3.72
Mesa, Cle	-0.15	3.73	3.59
Bones, NYA	-0.15	6.22	6.07
Cormier, Mon	-0.14	4.17	4.03
Williams M, Phi	-0.13	5.44	5.31
Coppinger, Bal	-0.13	5.18	5.06
Radke, Min	-0.12	4.46	4.34
Gubicza, KC	-0.12	5.13	5.01
Springer R, Phi	-0.12	4.66	4.54
Olivares, Det	-0.12	4.89	4.78
Clemens, Bos	-0.12	3.63	3.52
Charlton, Sea	-0.11	4.04	3.94
Nomo, LA	-0.10	3.19	3.09
Schilling, Phi	-0.10	3.19	3.09
Dyer, Mon	-0.10	4.40	4.30
Lima, Det	-0.10	5.70	5.60
Martinez D, Cle	-0.08	4.50	4.42
Simas, ChA	-0.08	4.58	4.51
Tapani, ChA	-0.07	4.59	4.52
Hernandez X, Hou	-0.07	4.62	4.54
Haney, KC	-0.07	4.70	4.63
Mills, Bal	-0.07	4.28	4.21
Fassero, Mon	-0.06	3.30	3.24
Benes An, StL	-0.05	3.83	3.78
Wolcott, Sea	-0.03	5.73	5.70
Darwin D, Hou	-0.03	3.77	3.74
Appier, KC	-0.02	3.62	3.60
Candiotti, LA	-0.02	4.49	4.48

Pitcher, Team	ERA DIF	ACT ERA	Pred ERA
Mulholland, Sea	-0.01	4.66	4.65
Witt, Tex	-0.01	5.41	5.40
Wakefield, Bos	-0.01	5.14	5.14
Jackson M, Sea	-0.01	3.63	3.62
Rapp, Fla	0.00	5.10	5.10
Scott, SF	0.02	4.64	4.66
Oliver, Tex	0.03	4.66	4.69
Dewey, SF	0.03	4.21	4.24
Bochtler, SD	0.03	3.02	3.05
Wall, Hou	0.04	4.56	4.60
Alvarez W, ChA	0.04	4.22	4.26
Maddux G, Atl	0.04	2.72	2.76
Jones T, Hou	0.04	4.40	4.44
Finley, Cal	0.05	4.16	4.21
Lewis, Det	0.05	4.18	4.23
Burba, Cin	0.06	3.83	3.89
Minor, Sea	0.07	4.24	4.30
Harnisch, NYN	0.08	4.21	4.28
Valdes I, LA	0.08	3.32	3.40
Hitchcock, Sea	0.08	5.35	5.44
Thompson M, Col	0.09	5.30	5.40
Osuna A, LA	0.09	3.00	3.09
Leiter M, Mon	0.11	4.92	5.03
Beck, SF	0.12	3.34	3.46
Fernandez O, SF	0.12	4.61	4.73
Ruffin J, Cin	0.13	5.49	5.61
Gross, Tex	0.13	5.22	5.35
Mathews T, Bal	0.13	4.52	4.65
McDonald, Mil	0.13	3.90	4.04
Jones B, NYN	0.14	4.42	4.55
Holmes, Col	0.15	3.97	4.12
Tavarez, Cle	0.15	5.36	5.51
Wickman, Mil	0.15	4.42	4.57
Hentgen, Tor	0.17	3.22	3.39
Martinez R, LA	0.18	3.42	3.60
Leiter A, Fla	0.19	2.93	3.12
Manuel, Mon	0.20	3.24	3.44
Kile, Hou	0.20	4.19	4.39
Smiley, Cin	0.20	3.64	3.84
Plunk, Cle	0.20	2.43	2.64
Rosado, KC	0.20	3.21	3.41
Keyser, ChA	0.21	4.98	5.18
Prieto, Oak	0.21	4.15	4.36
McMichael, Atl	0.21	3.22	3.43
Osborne, StL	0.21	3.53	3.75
Reynoso, Col	0.22	4.96	5.19
Wendell, ChN	0.22	2.84	3.06
Morgan, Cin	0.23	4.63	4.85
Watson, SF	0.23	4.61	4.83
Smith L, Cin	0.24	3.74	3.99
Wohlers, Atl	0.26	3.03	3.28
Pettitte, NYA	0.26	3.87	4.13
Hill, Tex	0.27	3.63	3.89
Trombley, Min	0.27	3.01	3.28
Nagy, Cle	0.27	3.41	3.68
Wengert, Oak	0.28	5.58	5.86
Petkovsek, StL	0.29	3.55	3.84
Hershiser, Cle	0.29	4.24	4.53
Corsi, Oak	0.31	4.03	4.34
Moyer, Sea	0.32	3.98	4.29
Worrell T, SD	0.32	3.05	3.37
Fernandez A, ChA	0.32	3.45	3.77
Parrett, Phi	0.32	3.39	3.72
Guzman, Tor	0.33	2.93	3.25
Wagner B, Hou	0.33	2.44	2.77
Castillo T, ChA	0.33	3.60	3.93
Boskie, Cal	0.33	5.32	5.65
Reyes C, Oak	0.33	4.78	5.11
Adams T, ChN	0.33	2.94	3.27
Juden, Mon	0.34	3.27	3.60
Clark M, NYN	0.34	3.43	3.77
Navarro, ChN	0.35	3.92	4.27
Jones D, Mil	0.37	4.22	4.59
Bautista, SF	0.39	3.36	3.75
Worrell T, LA	0.40	3.03	3.43
Gardner, SF	0.41	4.42	4.83
Astacio, LA	0.42	3.44	3.86
Wilkins, Pit	0.43	3.84	4.27
Drabek, Hou	0.44	4.57	5.01
Brown, Fla	0.45	1.89	2.34
Glavine, Atl	0.45	2.98	3.43
Hernandez R, ChA	0.46	1.91	2.37
Montgomery J, KC	0.46	4.26	4.72
Ashby, SD	0.46	3.23	3.69
Patterson B, ChN	0.47	3.13	3.59
Bailey C, StL	0.48	3.00	3.48
Fetters, Mil	0.49	3.38	3.86
Neagle, Atl	0.51	3.50	4.01
Brantley, Cin	0.52	2.41	2.92
Stevens, Min	0.53	4.66	5.19
McDowell R, Bal	0.53	4.25	4.78
Crabtree, Tor	0.54	2.54	3.08
Bielecki, Atl	0.55	2.63	3.17
Belcher, KC	0.55	3.92	4.48
Hampton, Hou	0.56	3.59	4.16
Veres D, Mon	0.58	4.17	4.75
Groom, Oak	0.59	3.84	4.43
Carmona, Sea	0.59	4.28	4.88
Russell, Tex	0.59	3.38	3.97
Valenzuela, SD	0.60	3.62	4.21
Wetteland, NYA	0.61	2.83	3.44
Nen, Fla	0.62	1.95	2.57
Guthrie, LA	0.62	2.22	2.84
Ryan, Phi	0.66	2.43	3.08
Eckersley, StL	0.66	3.30	3.96
James, Cal	0.67	2.67	3.34
Shuey, Cle	0.68	2.85	3.53
Stanton, Tex	0.69	3.66	4.35
Brandenburg, Bos	0.75	3.43	4.18
Trachsel, ChN	0.77	3.03	3.80
Eischen, Det	0.77	4.21	4.98
Quantrill, Tor	0.77	5.43	6.20
Myers R, Bal	0.81	3.53	4.34
DiPoto, NYN	0.88	4.19	5.07
Bottenfield, ChN	0.98	2.63	3.61
Shaw, Cin	1.00	2.49	3.49
Mlicki, NYN	1.01	3.30	4.31
Mohler, Oak	1.07	3.67	4.73
Radinsky, LA	1.25	2.41	3.65
Franco, NYN	1.29	1.83	3.12
Poole, SF	1.33	2.86	4.19

Who's Best in the Infield Zone? (p. 205)

Zone Ratings — Infielders (minimum 550 defensive innings in 1996)

FIRST BASE		1996			1994-96		
		In		Zone	In		Zone
Player, Team	Innings	Zone	Outs	Rating	Zone	Outs	Rating
King, Pit	683.1	143	142	.993	208	203	.976
Olerud, Tor	823.0	165	158	.958	605	553	.914
Stahoviak, Min	902.2	188	174	.926	320	293	.916
Johnson M, Pit	739.2	161	149	.925	260	233	.896
Colbrunn, Fla	1127.1	279	256	.918	609	548	.900
Palmeiro R, Bal	1418.2	264	237	.898	734	650	.886
Joyner, SD	1044.0	190	170	.895	604	551	.912
Mabry, StL	1198.2	214	191	.893	327	291	.890
Karros, LA	1391.1	288	256	.889	779	699	.897
Morris, Cin	1173.2	225	200	.889	549	493	.898
Carreon, Cle	863.0	168	149	.887	312	278	.891
Bagwell, Hou	1430.0	294	260	.884	751	681	.907
McGriff, Atl	1401.0	233	206	.884	609	527	.865
Franco J, Cle	832.2	195	172	.882	208	181	.870
Grace, ChN	1218.0	277	244	.881	736	644	.875
Jaha, Mil	718.0	148	130	.878	414	382	.923
Galarraga, Col	1378.2	320	280	.875	842	749	.890
Martinez T, NYA	1305.2	231	202	.874	601	529	.880
Clark W, Tex	994.2	208	181	.870	620	522	.842
McGwire, Oak	896.1	174	151	.868	428	365	.853
Fielder, NYA	687.2	134	116	.866	491	426	.868
Offerman, KC	741.0	187	161	.861	187	161	.861
Clark T, Det	760.0	136	117	.860	197	170	.863
Snow, Cal	1339.0	252	216	.857	504	420	.833
Segui, Mon	988.2	158	135	.854	476	412	.866
Seitzer, Cle	576.0	130	109	.838	243	209	.860
Vaughn M, Bos	1309.0	241	202	.838	661	557	.843
Huskey, NYN	575.0	134	111	.828	134	111	.828
Thomas, ChA	1231.0	224	183	.817	493	399	.809

SECOND BASE		1996			1994-96		
		In		Zone	In		Zone
Player, Team	Innings	Zone	Outs	Rating	Zone	Outs	Rating
Lockhart, KC	589.1	220	214	.973	415	393	.947
Velarde, Cal	967.2	252	242	.960	426	390	.915
McLemore, Tex	1279.1	503	479	.952	1001	932	.931
Reed J, SD	1245.0	443	421	.950	1210	1128	.932
Perez T, Tor	625.1	238	226	.950	252	241	.956
Vina, Mil	1165.2	443	417	.941	707	651	.921
Morandini, Phi	1154.0	385	362	.940	990	908	.917
Alomar R, Bal	1217.2	476	444	.933	1221	1102	.903
Alicea, StL	954.0	291	270	.928	912	832	.912
Sandberg, ChN	1234.0	466	430	.923	673	627	.932
Boone, Cin	1205.2	412	376	.913	1084	995	.918
Durham, ChA	1313.0	462	421	.911	808	722	.894
Lemke, Atl	1166.1	466	424	.910	1127	1024	.909
Knoblauch, Min	1267.2	414	376	.908	1161	1050	.904
DeShields, LA	1315.1	455	412	.905	1110	1037	.934
Young E, Col	1169.0	484	436	.901	731	664	.908
Duncan, NYA	774.0	262	235	.897	454	404	.890
Lansing, Mon	1368.0	444	395	.890	1100	978	.889
Vizcaino, Cle	1152.2	414	363	.877	415	364	.877
Baerga, NYN	887.1	356	312	.876	1226	1106	.902
King, Pit	554.2	200	175	.875	221	195	.882
Lewis M, Det	1240.2	475	415	.874	477	417	.874
Cora, Sea	1071.2	347	303	.873	876	760	.868
Veras, Fla	581.0	205	179	.873	556	507	.912
Frye, Bos	872.0	364	315	.865	790	710	.899
Biggio, Hou	1409.1	490	416	.849	1360	1185	.871

THIRD BASE

Player, Team	Innings	1996 In Zone	1996 Outs	1996 Zone Rating	1994-96 In Zone	1994-96 Outs	1994-96 Zone Rating
Brosius, Oak	946.1	321	284	.885	671	570	.849
Arias G, Cal	657.1	256	219	.855	256	219	.855
Hollins, Sea	1226.1	370	315	.851	461	375	.813
Ventura, ChA	1274.1	354	298	.842	892	733	.822
Castilla, Col	1374.0	533	448	.841	922	744	.807
Sprague, Tor	1285.0	315	263	.835	905	731	.808
Williams M, SF	796.1	244	203	.832	789	667	.845
Cirillo, Mil	1243.1	344	283	.823	630	536	.851
Naehring, Bos	989.0	295	242	.820	666	543	.815
Gaetti, StL	1104.0	300	246	.820	830	690	.831
Caminiti, SD	1274.0	426	348	.817	1127	910	.807
Boggs, NYA	1026.2	285	232	.814	830	685	.825
Thome, Cle	1277.1	371	301	.811	910	745	.819
Surhoff, Bal	926.1	275	223	.811	308	241	.782
Pendleton, Atl	1270.0	417	338	.811	963	796	.827
Andrews, Mon	939.0	342	277	.810	462	371	.803
Fryman, Det	1116.1	378	306	.810	1160	949	.818
Gomez L, ChN	854.1	254	204	.803	553	442	.799
Zeile, Bal	1185.2	332	262	.789	834	663	.795
Hayes, NYA	1182.2	444	349	.786	1109	900	.812
Wallach, LA	747.1	206	161	.782	673	533	.792
Jones C, Atl	1037.0	260	203	.781	614	497	.809
Kent, Cle	788.2	286	220	.769	286	220	.769
Palmer, Tex	1321.1	335	255	.761	694	533	.768
Randa, KC	700.1	206	151	.733	246	182	.740
Berry, Hou	871.1	316	225	.712	790	596	.754
Blowers, LA	773.0	185	129	.697	584	408	.699

SHORTSTOP

Player, Team	Innings	1996 In Zone	1996 Outs	1996 Zone Rating	1994-96 In Zone	1994-96 Outs	1994-96 Zone Rating
Valentin J, Mil	1290.1	500	495	.990	1166	1140	.978
Howard D, KC	1109.0	412	404	.981	551	547	.993
Gagne, LA	1126.2	447	436	.975	1225	1168	.953
Renteria, Fla	922.1	370	359	.970	370	359	.970
Gonzalez A, Tor	1316.0	502	484	.964	788	755	.958
Vizquel, Cle	1312.1	468	450	.962	1139	1083	.951
Ripken C, Bal	1379.2	483	464	.961	1260	1249	.991
DiSarcina, Cal	1290.0	504	483	.958	1184	1161	.981
Elster, Tex	1355.0	500	476	.952	584	562	.962
Stocker, Phi	991.2	374	355	.949	1102	1044	.947
Clayton, StL	997.2	388	368	.948	1199	1155	.963
Bordick, Oak	1338.0	526	498	.947	1229	1195	.972
Bell J, Pit	1289.1	531	502	.945	1413	1339	.948
Valentin J, Bos	1043.1	410	386	.941	1134	1083	.955
Rodriguez A, Sea	1267.2	460	430	.935	646	594	.920
Ordonez, NYN	1262.1	501	468	.934	501	468	.934
Sanchez, ChN	768.0	340	317	.932	437	415	.950
Aurilia, SF	678.2	262	244	.931	278	261	.939
Dunston, SF	634.0	263	244	.928	933	849	.910
Guillen, ChA	1197.0	386	357	.925	1019	967	.949
Blauser, Atl	654.1	249	230	.924	968	899	.929
Gomez C, SD	1146.0	430	397	.923	891	830	.932
Meares, Min	1249.1	387	355	.917	996	907	.911
Weiss, Col	1275.0	517	473	.915	1316	1227	.932
Hernandez J, ChN	670.0	244	223	.914	389	363	.933
Larkin, Cin	1242.1	495	445	.899	1209	1115	.922
Jeter, NYA	1370.2	528	471	.892	572	512	.895
Miller, Hou	913.2	362	321	.887	700	626	.894
Grudzielanek, Mon	1328.2	530	464	.875	648	571	.881
Cedeno A, Hou	803.1	340	286	.841	999	887	.888

Who Are the Prime Pivot Men? (p. 210)

Both Leagues — Listed Alphabetically
1996 Active Players with 15 or more DP Opportunities (1991-1996)

Player, Team	DP Opp	DP	Pct
Alexander, Bal	44	30	.682
Alfonzo, NYN	45	24	.533
Alicea, StL	287	184	.641
Alomar R, Bal	610	360	.590
Amaral, Sea	83	47	.566
Arias A, Fla	24	13	.542
Baerga, Cle-NYN	493	306	.621
Barberie, ChN	160	98	.613
Bates, Col	57	40	.702
Batista, Oak	28	18	.643
Bell D, StL	28	18	.643
Belliard, Atl	50	31	.620
Benjamin, Phi	20	12	.600
Biggio, Hou	387	202	.522
Blauser, Atl	47	25	.532
Boone, Cin	272	179	.658
Bordick, Oak	64	42	.656
Bournigal, Oak	42	29	.690
Branson, Cin	62	40	.645
Candaele, Cle	85	54	.635
Canizaro, SF	15	9	.600
Castillo L, Fla	32	20	.625
Cedeno D, Tor-ChA	56	37	.661
Cirillo, Mil	17	12	.706
Cora, Sea	326	204	.626
Cordero, Bos	28	13	.464
DeShields, LA	450	247	.549
Duncan, NYA	233	128	.549
Durham, ChA	166	92	.554
Easley, Cal-Det	115	72	.626
Espinoza, Cle-NYN	22	14	.636
Fermin, ChN	28	17	.607
Fonville, LA	30	15	.500
Fox, NYA	21	11	.524
Franco J, Cle	239	122	.510
Frye, Bos	198	107	.540
Gallego, StL	218	134	.615
Garcia C, Pit	278	175	.629
Gates, Oak	214	128	.598
Gomez C, Det-SD	38	24	.632
Gonzales, Tex	81	53	.654
Grebeck, Fla	46	30	.652
Hale, Min	22	15	.682
Haney, ChN	31	11	.355
Harris, Cin	120	57	.475
Hernandez J, ChN	19	10	.526
Howard D, KC	35	16	.457
Hudler, Cal	86	58	.674
Huson, Bal	42	28	.667
Jefferies, Phi	121	47	.388
Kelly P, NYA	281	170	.605
Kent, NYN-Cle	188	125	.665
King, Pit	76	40	.526
Knoblauch, Min	498	305	.612
Lansing, Mon	215	128	.595
Lemke, Atl	398	228	.573
Lewis M, Det	127	71	.559
Liriano, Pit	228	116	.509
Listach, Mil	43	26	.605
Lockhart, KC	77	50	.649
Lopez L, SD	18	8	.444
Lovullo, Oak	69	41	.594
Martin N, ChA	31	15	.484
McLemore, Tex	276	174	.630
Morandini, Phi	364	206	.566
Naehring, Bos	57	28	.491
Offerman, KC	25	16	.640
Pena G, Cle	156	109	.699
Perez T, Tor	50	35	.700
Phillips T, ChA	196	115	.587
Reboulet, Min	21	12	.571
Reed J, SD	576	367	.637
Ripken B, Bal	311	204	.656
Roberts, KC	195	100	.513
Samuel, Tor	228	99	.434
Sanchez, ChN	79	45	.570
Sandberg, ChN	471	265	.563
Scarsone, SF	83	55	.663
Shipley, SD	28	14	.500
Shumpert, ChN	128	74	.578
Sojo, Sea-NYA	199	124	.623
Spiers, Hou	60	34	.567
Stankiewicz, Mon	25	16	.640
Stillwell, Tex	74	37	.500
Strange, Sea	121	74	.612
Thompson R, SF	480	302	.629
Velarde, Cal	122	70	.574
Veras, Fla	120	75	.625
Vina, Mil	156	118	.756
Vizcaino, NYN-Cle	101	70	.693
Young E, Col	191	115	.602
MLB Totals	**12749**	**7577**	**.594**

Which Catchers Catch Thieves? (p. 212)

The chart below lists the Stolen Bases (**SB**) while this catcher was behind the plate, the runners he caught stealing (**CCS**), that percentage (**CS%**), the runners he picked off (**CPk**), the SB allowed per 9 innings (**SB/9**), the runners caught stealing (**PCS**) and picked off (**PPk**) by his pitchers.

Both Leagues — Listed Alphabetically
(Minimum 500 Innings Caught)

Catcher, Team	SB	CCS	CS%	CPk	SB/9	PCS	PPk
Alomar S, Cle	76	25	24.8	1	0.69	10	2
Ausmus, Det	81	34	29.6	2	0.73	6	1
Fabregas, Cal	61	20	24.7	0	0.83	2	3
Flaherty, SD	77	26	25.2	0	0.72	6	0
Fletcher, Mon	109	13	10.7	0	1.14	14	2
Girardi, NYA	90	22	19.6	0	0.83	8	11
Haselman, Bos	44	15	25.4	0	0.72	1	1
Hoiles, Bal	96	21	17.9	0	0.83	7	1
Hundley, NYN	98	32	24.6	0	0.70	0	5
Johnson B, SD	49	11	18.3	0	0.85	5	1
Johnson C, Fla	44	38	46.3	0	0.40	2	4
Karkovice, ChA	48	29	37.7	1	0.49	4	3
Kendall, Pit	136	31	18.6	1	1.15	10	5
Levis, Mil	37	12	24.5	0	0.61	2	2
Lopez J, Atl	97	33	25.4	2	0.78	2	2
Macfarlane, KC	38	20	34.5	0	0.42	4	3
Manwaring, Hou	46	33	41.8	0	0.67	4	4
Martinez S, Tor	32	17	34.7	2	0.49	0	4
Matheny, Mil	52	19	26.8	2	0.57	6	7
Myers G, Min	41	17	29.3	0	0.52	5	0
O'Brien, Tor	40	20	33.3	4	0.45	4	1
Oliver, Cin	58	21	26.6	1	0.72	2	1
Pagnozzi, StL	67	32	32.3	0	0.62	3	7
Piazza, LA	155	26	14.4	1	1.11	8	2
Reed J, Col	75	30	28.6	1	0.79	1	12
Rodriguez I, Tex	46	44	48.9	10	0.34	4	3
Santiago, Phi	64	26	28.9	1	0.59	2	4
Servais, ChN	99	40	28.8	0	0.81	0	3
Slaught, ChA	66	13	16.5	0	1.09	6	2
Stanley, Bos	94	10	9.6	0	1.00	10	2
Steinbach, Oak	83	26	23.9	0	0.65	8	0
Taubensee, Cin	87	26	23.0	0	1.13	0	1
Wilkins, SF	88	36	29.0	3	0.82	4	1
Wilson D, Sea	61	29	32.2	2	0.49	10	4

Which Outfielders Intimidate Enemy Runners? (p. 214)

Both Leagues — 1996 — Listed by Hold Percentage (minimum 30 baserunner opportunities to advance)

Left Field

Player, Team	Opp	XB	Pct
Curtis, LA	37	7	18.9
Higginson, Det	68	15	22.1
Pride, Det	38	9	23.7
Goodwin T, KC	42	10	23.8
Williams G, Mil	41	10	24.4
Rodriguez H, Mon	55	14	25.5
Bragg, Bos	38	10	26.3
Orsulak, Fla	34	9	26.5
Sierra, Det	34	9	26.5
Perez R, Tor	34	9	26.5
Newfield, Mil	59	16	27.1
May, Hou	73	20	27.4
Anderson G, Cal	153	42	27.5
Plantier, Oak	80	22	27.5
Jefferson, Bos	49	14	28.6
Cordova, Min	147	42	28.6
Greer, Tex	122	35	28.7
Hammonds, Bal	55	16	29.1
Whiten, Sea	41	12	29.3
Carter, Tor	79	24	30.4
Martin A, Pit	118	36	30.5
Gilkey, NYN	159	49	30.8
Bonds, SF	160	50	31.3
Paquette, KC	44	14	31.8
Mouton J, Hou	62	20	32.3
Nieves, Det	37	12	32.4
Burks, Col	123	40	32.5
Amaral, Sea	49	16	32.7
Giambi, Oak	48	16	33.3
Belle, Cle	134	45	33.6
Phillips T, ChA	140	48	34.3
Floyd, Mon	46	16	34.8
Vaughn G, SD	131	46	35.1
Gant, StL	98	35	35.7
Klesko, Atl	107	39	36.4
Conine, Fla	96	35	36.5
Henderson, SD	98	38	38.8
Incaviglia, Bal	51	20	39.2
Jefferies, Phi	40	16	40.0
Hollandsworth, LA	87	35	40.2
Polonia, Atl	37	16	43.2
Gonzalez L, ChN	93	41	44.1
Greenwell, Bos	76	35	46.1
O'Leary, Bos	30	16	53.3

Center Field

Player, Team	Opp	XB	Pct
Williams G, Mil	45	19	42.2
Edmonds, Cal	110	47	42.7
Martinez D, ChA	75	34	45.3
Cedeno R, LA	35	16	45.7
Benard, SF	98	45	45.9
Hunter B, Hou	157	74	47.1
Erstad, Cal	37	18	48.6
Griffey Jr, Sea	166	82	49.4
Cole, Bos	30	15	50.0
Finley, SD	169	85	50.3
Grissom, Atl	161	81	50.3
White R, Mon	91	46	50.5
Brumfield, Tor	47	24	51.1
Dykstra, Phi	39	20	51.3
Javier, SF	42	22	52.4
Lewis D, ChA	114	60	52.6
Hamilton, Tex	178	95	53.4
Lofton, Cle	153	82	53.6
McRae, ChN	139	77	55.4
Lankford, StL	126	70	55.6
Johnson L, NYN	179	100	55.9
Bartee, Det	100	56	56.0
Anderson B, Bal	180	101	56.1
Hulse, Mil	39	22	56.4
Bragg, Bos	60	34	56.7
Curtis, LA	139	79	56.8
Young E, Oak	151	86	57.0
Goodwin T, KC	79	45	57.0
Williams B, NYA	202	117	57.9
Kingery, Pit	60	35	58.3
Listach, Mil	97	57	58.8
Santangelo, Mon	81	48	59.3
McCracken, Col	81	49	60.5
Nixon O, Tor	152	92	60.5
White D, Fla	142	86	60.6
Allensworth, Pit	61	37	60.7
Becker, Min	126	77	61.1
Tinsley, Bos	93	57	61.3
Otero, Phi	109	68	62.4
Hosey, Bos	35	22	62.9
Davis E, Cin	105	67	63.8
Devereaux, Bal	47	30	63.8
Kelly R, Min	39	25	64.1
Damon, KC	74	48	64.9
Walker L, Col	63	41	65.1
Cuyler, Bos	30	22	73.3

Right Field

Player, Team	Opp	XB	Pct
Whiten, Sea	52	17	32.7
Kelly R, Min	36	12	33.3
Sosa, ChN	97	35	36.1
Merced, Pit	111	42	37.8
Bell D, Hou	132	53	40.2
Mondesi, LA	146	63	43.2
Green, Tor	108	47	43.5
Bonilla, Bal	110	48	43.6
O'Neill, NYA	128	57	44.5
Ochoa, NYN	67	30	44.8
Nilsson, Mil	52	24	46.2
Lawton, Min	52	24	46.2
Ramirez, Cle	124	58	46.8
Buhner, Sea	128	60	46.9
Tartabull, ChA	114	54	47.4
Newson, Tex	38	18	47.4
Eisenreich, Phi	52	25	48.1
Sanders, Cin	64	31	48.4
Gwynn T, SD	78	38	48.7
Dye, Atl	39	19	48.7
Bichette, Col	151	74	49.0
Gonzalez J, Tex	112	55	49.1
Mieske, Mil	77	38	49.4
Hill, SF	88	44	50.0
Sheffield, Fla	127	64	50.4
Jordan B, StL	79	40	50.6
Brumfield, Tor	41	21	51.2
Alou, Mon	87	46	52.9
Higginson, Det	64	34	53.1
Nieves, Det	84	46	54.8
Damon, KC	64	36	56.3
Tucker, KC	56	32	57.1
Salmon, Cal	182	105	57.7
O'Leary, Bos	96	58	60.4
Hocking, Min	38	24	63.2
Herrera, Oak	69	45	65.2
Berroa, Oak	39	26	66.7
Obando, Mon	35	25	71.4
Mitchell K, Cin	30	24	80.0

Which Players Turn the Outfield into a "No Fly" Zone? (p. 217)

Zone Ratings — Outfielders (minimum 550 defensive innings in 1996)

LEFT FIELD	1996				1994-96		
Player, Team	Innings	In Zone	Outs	Zone Rating	In Zone	Outs	Zone Rating
Greer, Tex	1187.1	326	283	.868	439	378	.861
Henderson, SD	932.1	214	185	.864	567	472	.832
Newfield, Mil	623.2	160	138	.863	239	204	.854
Phillips T, ChA	1309.0	383	328	.856	766	655	.855
Rodriguez H, Mon	702.0	121	103	.851	277	232	.838
Anderson G, Cal	1247.1	349	293	.840	606	509	.840
Gilkey, NYN	1290.2	372	309	.831	806	659	.818
Cordova, Min	1278.1	377	312	.828	745	631	.847
Gonzalez L, ChN	1124.0	271	222	.819	841	687	.817
Belle, Cle	1343.0	367	298	.812	970	790	.814
Hollandsworth, LA	930.0	213	172	.808	217	176	.811
Klesko, Atl	1211.1	233	188	.807	454	363	.800
Bonds, SF	1272.2	324	258	.796	882	699	.793
Carter, Tor	935.2	201	160	.796	459	373	.813
Incaviglia, Bal	574.1	117	93	.795	226	182	.805
Conine, Fla	1063.0	226	179	.792	678	531	.783
Gant, StL	991.2	267	211	.790	485	389	.802
Greenwell, Bos	614.0	170	134	.788	639	467	.731
Burks, Col	1031.1	267	208	.779	301	234	.777
Vaughn G, SD	1130.1	334	259	.775	518	416	.803
Martin A, Pit	1126.1	249	178	.715	528	393	.744

CENTER FIELD	1996				1994-96		
Player, Team	Innings	In Zone	Outs	Zone Rating	In Zone	Outs	Zone Rating
Bartee, Det	593.2	236	211	.894	236	211	.894
Finley, SD	1416.2	437	375	.858	1017	869	.854
Johnson L, NYN	1356.1	448	383	.855	1209	1021	.844
Santangelo, Mon	577.2	213	182	.854	215	184	.856
Damon, KC	669.0	226	193	.854	340	293	.862
Lewis D, ChA	933.0	322	274	.851	1018	849	.834
Lofton, Cle	1334.0	429	363	.846	1036	878	.847
McRae, ChN	1358.2	399	336	.842	1082	907	.838
Hunter B, Hou	1046.2	325	273	.840	557	466	.837
Young E, Oak	1061.2	391	328	.839	412	346	.840
White R, Mon	734.1	218	181	.830	522	429	.822
Griffey Jr, Sea	1173.0	449	372	.829	973	776	.798

Edmonds, Cal	921.2	329	272	.827	783	672	.858
White D, Fla	1200.2	350	287	.820	965	804	.833
Lankford, StL	1242.0	425	348	.819	1120	883	.788
Becker, Min	1012.1	400	327	.818	815	667	.818
Curtis, LA	858.0	299	243	.813	1115	913	.819
Davis E, Cin	893.2	299	243	.813	394	327	.830
Nixon O, Tor	1079.1	417	338	.811	1171	937	.800
Hamilton, Tex	1266.1	468	379	.810	866	693	.800
Benard, SF	848.0	306	246	.804	333	265	.796
Williams B, NYA	1232.0	411	329	.800	1218	1025	.842
Anderson B, Bal	1258.1	423	338	.799	606	489	.807
Goodwin T, KC	613.1	212	169	.797	457	372	.814
Grissom, Atl	1380.0	419	321	.766	1135	931	.820
Otero, Phi	834.1	313	236	.754	329	246	.748
McCracken, Col	557.1	182	121	.665	182	121	.665

RIGHT FIELD		1996				1994-96	
		In		Zone	In		Zone
Player, Team	Innings	Zone	Outs	Rating	Zone	Outs	Rating
Sanders, Cin	692.1	168	147	.875	658	580	.881
Alou, Mon	947.2	224	194	.866	403	346	.859
Gwynn T, SD	960.0	206	177	.859	703	601	.855
Jordan B, StL	1046.0	318	270	.849	652	548	.840
O'Neill, NYA	1241.2	337	286	.849	800	661	.826
Sosa, ChN	1086.2	284	241	.849	874	757	.866
Herrera, Oak	567.2	184	154	.837	188	156	.830
Whiten, Sea	597.0	153	128	.837	596	501	.841
Ramirez, Cle	1303.1	319	265	.831	746	614	.823
Mieske, Mil	754.2	236	196	.831	612	512	.837
Tartabull, ChA	993.2	288	239	.830	380	307	.808
Nieves, Det	720.1	188	156	.830	207	173	.836
Merced, Pit	994.2	286	235	.822	623	519	.833
Salmon, Cal	1339.2	369	303	.821	996	820	.823
Green, Tor	991.1	300	243	.810	559	448	.801
Sheffield, Fla	1342.0	283	227	.802	607	476	.784
Buhner, Sea	1230.1	306	245	.801	742	576	.776
Ochoa, NYN	633.2	165	132	.800	187	150	.802
Mondesi, LA	1407.1	408	326	.799	902	732	.812
Tucker, KC	571.1	168	132	.786	173	135	.780
Bell D, Hou	1371.1	359	281	.783	528	412	.780
O'Leary, Bos	744.0	183	141	.770	399	312	.782
Gonzalez J, Tex	855.1	206	156	.757	206	156	.757
Hill, SF	826.0	211	157	.744	487	380	.780
Bonilla, Bal	915.1	244	181	.742	332	246	.741
Bichette, Col	1167.0	311	221	.711	620	462	.745

Which Fielders Have the Best "Defensive Batting Average"? (p. 220)

Each chart summarizes, by position, the STATS Defensive Batting Average: a player's zone rating (**ZR**), his fielding percentage (**FP**), his pivot rating (**PR**) if he was a second baseman, and, if he was an outfielder, his outfield arm rating (**OA**). A weighting system (see article on page 224) was used to determine a player's all-around fielding rating (**Rtng**).

Both Leagues — Sorted by Fielding Rating (Minimum 550 Innings Played in 1996)

First Base	ZR	FP	PR	OA	Rtng
King, Pit	.367	.321	—	—	.356
Olerud, Tor	.340	.322	—	—	.335
Stahoviak, Min	.314	.293	—	—	.309
Johnson M, Pit	.314	.290	—	—	.308
Colbrunn, Fla	.308	.301	—	—	.306
Joyner, SD	.290	.320	—	—	.298
Palmeiro R, Bal	.292	.295	—	—	.293
Grace, ChN	.279	.317	—	—	.289
Mabry, StL	.288	.286	—	—	.288
Morris, Cin	.286	.284	—	—	.285
Martinez T, NYA	.274	.309	—	—	.283
Clark W, Tex	.271	.308	—	—	.280
McGriff, Atl	.282	.273	—	—	.280
Karros, LA	.285	.249	—	—	.276
Jaha, Mil	.277	.270	—	—	.275
Franco J, Cle	.280	.256	—	—	.274
Carreon, Cle	.284	.243	—	—	.274
Bagwell, Hou	.282	.246	—	—	.273
Galarraga, Col	.275	.267	—	—	.273
Offerman, KC	.264	.291	—	—	.271
Clark T, Det	.263	.277	—	—	.267
Snow, Cal	.261	.278	—	—	.265
Fielder, NYA	.267	.257	—	—	.265
McGwire, Oak	.269	.251	—	—	.264
Segui, Mon	.258	.282	—	—	.264
Seitzer, Cle	.246	.312	—	—	.262
Vaughn M, Bos	.246	.238	—	—	.244
Thomas, ChA	.229	.275	—	—	.240
Sorrento, Sea	.228	.248	—	—	.233
Huskey, NYN	.238	.197	—	—	.228

Second Base	ZR	FP	PR	OA	Rtng
Lockhart, KC	.335	.261	.311	—	.318
Perez T, Tor	.316	.240	.340	—	.311
Vina, Mil	.309	.275	.327	—	.309
Reed J, SD	.317	.307	.290	—	.309
McLemore, Tex	.318	.298	.276	—	.305
Velarde, Cal	.325	.286	.263	—	.304
Alomar R, Bal	.302	.299	.291	—	.299
Sandberg, ChN	.294	.322	.273	—	.293
Morandini, Phi	.308	.285	.250	—	.290
Boone, Cin	.285	.324	.275	—	.289
Knoblauch, Min	.282	.311	.272	—	.284
Durham, ChA	.284	.293	.269	—	.282
Young E, Col	.276	.297	.286	—	.282
Alicea, StL	.298	.187	.288	—	.279
Vizcaino, Cle	.256	.297	.319	—	.278
Veras, Fla	.253	.304	.305	—	.273
Lansing, Mon	.266	.300	.274	—	.273
Duncan, NYA	.272	.257	.278	—	.272
DeShields, LA	.280	.260	.244	—	.268
Lemke, Atl	.283	.267	.218	—	.264
Cora, Sea	.253	.275	.275	—	.262
Lewis M, Det	.253	.306	.247	—	.260
Frye, Bos	.246	.290	.262	—	.257
King, Pit	.254	.275	.233	—	.252
Baerga, NYN	.255	.244	.243	—	.251
Biggio, Hou	.233	.309	.242	—	.247
Garcia C, Pit	.202	.299	.308	—	.243

Third Base	ZR	FP	PR	OA	Rtng
Brosius, Oak	.337	.309	—	—	.326
Ventura, ChA	.306	.319	—	—	.312
Arias G, Cal	.316	.289	—	—	.305
Fryman, Det	.283	.331	—	—	.302
Boggs, NYA	.287	.320	—	—	.300
Hollins, Sea	.313	.278	—	—	.299
Castilla, Col	.306	.290	—	—	.299
Gaetti, StL	.291	.310	—	—	.298
Gomez L, ChN	.279	.315	—	—	.293
Naehring, Bos	.291	.296	—	—	.293
Sprague, Tor	.302	.280	—	—	.293
Williams M, SF	.299	.268	—	—	.287
Caminiti, SD	.289	.275	—	—	.283
Cirillo, Mil	.293	.268	—	—	.283
Andrews, Mon	.284	.278	—	—	.282
Pendleton, Atl	.284	.277	—	—	.281
Thome, Cle	.285	.274	—	—	.281
Zeile, Bal	.269	.294	—	—	.279
Surhoff, Bal	.284	.262	—	—	.275
Hayes, NYA	.267	.278	—	—	.271
Wallach, LA	.263	.277	—	—	.269
Jones C, Atl	.263	.260	—	—	.262
Palmer, Tex	.249	.273	—	—	.259
Randa, KC	.229	.269	—	—	.245
Kent, Cle	.255	.217	—	—	.239
Blowers, LA	.203	.270	—	—	.230
Berry, Hou	.214	.206	—	—	.211

Shortstop	ZR	FP	PR	OA	Rtng
Howard D, KC	.321	.311	—	—	.319

Shortstop	ZR	FP	PR	OA	Rtng
Valentin J, Mil	.330	.238	—	—	.312
Renteria, Fla	.312	.304	—	—	.310
Gagne, LA	.317	.273	—	—	.308
Ripken C, Bal	.303	.307	—	—	.304
Gonzalez A, Tor	.306	.290	—	—	.303
Vizquel, Cle	.304	.286	—	—	.300
DiSarcina, Cal	.301	.286	—	—	.298
Elster, Tex	.295	.309	—	—	.298
Bell J, Pit	.289	.320	—	—	.295
Stocker, Phi	.293	.296	—	—	.293
Bordick, Oak	.290	.304	—	—	.293
Clayton, StL	.292	.288	—	—	.291
Valentin J, Bos	.286	.287	—	—	.286
Rodriguez A, Sea	.279	.300	—	—	.284
Sanchez, ChN	.277	.299	—	—	.282
Aurilia, SF	.276	.289	—	—	.279
Guillen, ChA	.270	.309	—	—	.278
Ordonez, NYN	.279	.265	—	—	.276
Gomez C, SD	.269	.279	—	—	.271
Dunston, SF	.273	.254	—	—	.269
Meares, Min	.263	.271	—	—	.265
Weiss, Col	.261	.254	—	—	.260
Larkin, Cin	.247	.295	—	—	.256
Hernandez, ChN	.260	.233	—	—	.255
Blauser, Atl	.269	.184	—	—	.252
Jeter, NYA	.240	.281	—	—	.249
Miller, Hou	.235	.255	—	—	.239
Grudzielan., Mon	.225	.259	—	—	.232
Cedeno A, Hou	.194	.232	—	—	.201

Left Field	ZR	FP	PR	OA	Rtng
Newfield, Mil	.317	.328	—	.315	.318
Greer, Tex	.321	.300	—	.303	.315
Henderson, SD	.319	.304	—	.239	.300
Phillips T, ChA	.312	.291	—	.269	.300
Anderson G, Cal	.298	.281	—	.311	.298
Cordova, Min	.289	.322	—	.300	.296
Gilkey, NYN	.291	.295	—	.290	.291
Rodriguez, Mon	.308	.188	—	.311	.290
Gonzalez L, ChN	.282	.311	—	.227	.275
Belle, Cle	.276	.258	—	.280	.274
Klesko, Atl	.272	.274	—	.262	.270
Bonds, SF	.263	.288	—	.279	.270
Hollands., LA	.272	.268	—	.244	.266
Carter, Tor	.263	.233	—	.294	.265
Gant, StL	.258	.282	—	.266	.263
Conine, Fla	.260	.274	—	.254	.261
Burks, Col	.249	.282	—	.277	.260
Incaviglia, Bal	.262	.264	—	.248	.259
Vaughn G, SD	.246	.283	—	.262	.255
Greenwell, Bos	.257	.269	—	.212	.249
Martin A, Pit	.197	.239	—	.290	.222

Center Field	ZR	FP	PR	OA	Rtng
Bartee, Det	.334	.293	—	.275	.310
Edmonds, Cal	.285	.311	—	.347	.307
Finley, SD	.307	.269	—	.302	.300
Lewis D, ChA	.302	.290	—	.297	.299
Griffey Jr, Sea	.286	.290	—	.316	.296
White R, Mon	.287	.290	—	.303	.292
Young E, Oak	.293	.313	—	.273	.290
Hunter B, Hou	.294	.202	—	.325	.290
Benard, SF	.268	.287	—	.329	.289
McRae, ChN	.296	.279	—	.282	.289
Lofton, Cle	.299	.246	—	.289	.288
Johnson L, NYN	.305	.234	—	.275	.285
Santangelo, Mon	.305	.260	—	.262	.285
Lankford, StL	.279	.313	—	.280	.284
Hamilton, Tex	.272	.321	—	.288	.284
Damon, KC	.304	.279	—	.224	.276
Becker, Min	.278	.304	—	.250	.274
White D, Fla	.280	.282	—	.254	.272
Nixon O, Tor	.273	.304	—	.255	.272
Anderson B, Bal	.264	.296	—	.274	.272
Grissom, Atl	.240	.313	—	.301	.269
Williams B, NYA	.265	.278	—	.268	.268
Goodwin T, KC	.263	.270	—	.276	.268
Curtis, LA	.274	.228	—	.271	.266
Davis E, Cin	.274	.286	—	.241	.266
Otero, Phi	.232	.275	—	.232	.238
McCracken, Col	.167	.208	—	.255	.199

Right Field	ZR	FP	PR	OA	Rtng
O'Neill, NYA	.305	.325	—	.294	.304
Sanders, Cin	.325	.301	—	.274	.304
Sosa, ChN	.305	.253	—	.322	.303
Whiten, Sea	.296	.202	—	.354	.303
Alou, Mon	.318	.315	—	.266	.300
Merced, Pit	.285	.301	—	.318	.299
Gwynn T, SD	.313	.303	—	.276	.299
Jordan B, StL	.306	.311	—	.267	.293
Mieske, Mil	.292	.315	—	.279	.291
Green, Tor	.277	.310	—	.301	.290
Tartabull, ChA	.291	.271	—	.288	.287
Ramirez, Cle	.292	.264	—	.282	.284
Bell D, Hou	.256	.279	—	.318	.281
Buhner, Sea	.270	.302	—	.282	.279
Mondesi, LA	.268	.258	—	.295	.276
Ochoa, NYN	.269	.257	—	.292	.275
Sheffield, Fla	.271	.277	—	.269	.271
Nieves, Det	.291	.222	—	.252	.267
Salmon, Cal	.285	.274	—	.235	.266
Tucker, KC	.259	.310	—	.250	.263
Herrera, Oak	.297	.264	—	.211	.262
Bonilla, Bal	.226	.274	—	.300	.259
Gonzalez J, Tex	.237	.301	—	.271	.259
O'Leary, Bos	.247	.271	—	.231	.245
Hill, SF	.228	.243	—	.268	.244
Bichette, Col	.203	.251	—	.272	.234

Who Led the League in Fumbles? (p. 224)

Both Leagues — Listed by Fewest Games per Error (G/E) — 1996
(minimum 600 defensive innings played)

Catchers

Name, Team	Inn	E	G/E
Kendall, Pit	1060.1	18	6.5
Taubensee, Cin	693.0	11	7.0
Reed J, Col	850.1	11	8.6
Stanley, Bos	846.2	10	9.4
Myers G, Min	714.0	8	9.9
Flaherty, SD	963.2	10	10.7
Santiago, Phi	982.0	10	10.9
Ausmus, Det	993.2	10	11.0
Servais, ChN	1097.1	11	11.1
Matheny, Mil	826.2	8	11.5
Alomar S, Cle	992.0	9	12.2
Fabregas, Cal	665.0	6	12.3
Wilkins, SF	970.1	8	13.5
Pagnozzi, StL	974.2	8	13.5
Rodriguez I, Tex	1222.2	10	13.6
Piazza, LA	1255.2	9	15.5
Fletcher, Mon	857.0	6	15.9
Oliver, Cin	724.0	5	16.1
Hoiles, Bal	1036.0	7	16.4
Hundley, NYN	1265.1	8	17.6
Steinbach, Oak	1140.2	7	18.1
Karkovice, ChA	890.1	5	19.8
Lopez J, Atl	1112.2	6	20.6
Macfarlane, KC	819.1	4	22.8
Manwaring, Hou	618.0	3	22.9
Johnson C, Fla	998.0	4	27.7
O'Brien, Tor	801.0	3	29.7
Wilson D, Sea	1130.0	4	31.4
Girardi, NYA	973.2	3	36.0

First Basemen

Name, Team	Inn	E	G/E
Carreon, Cle	863.0	10	9.6
Vaughn M, Bos	1309.0	15	9.7
Bagwell, Hou	1430.0	16	9.9
McGwire, Oak	896.1	10	10.0
Franco J, Cle	832.2	9	10.3
Karros, LA	1391.1	15	10.3
Fielder, NYA	687.2	7	10.9
Galarraga, Col	1378.2	14	10.9
Sorrento, Sea	1099.1	11	11.1
McGriff, Atl	1401.0	12	13.0
Jaha, Mil	718.0	6	13.3
Clark T, Det	760.0	6	14.1
Snow, Cal	1339.0	10	14.9
Thomas, ChA	1231.0	9	15.2
Segui, Mon	988.2	7	15.7
Morris, Cin	1173.2	8	16.3
Johnson M, Pit	739.2	5	16.4
Offerman, KC	741.0	5	16.5
Mabry, StL	1198.2	8	16.6
Palmeiro R, Bal	1418.2	8	19.7
Stahoviak, Min	902.2	5	20.1
Colbrunn, Fla	1127.1	6	20.9
Clark W, Tex	994.2	4	27.6
Martinez T, NYA	1305.2	5	29.0
Grace, ChN	1218.0	4	33.8
King, Pit	683.1	2	38.0
Joyner, SD	1044.0	3	38.7
Olerud, Tor	823.0	2	45.0

Second Basemen

Name, Team	Inn	E	G/E
Alicea, StL	954.0	24	4.4
Perez T, Tor	625.1	11	6.3
Baerga, NYN	887.1	15	6.6
Duncan, NYA	774.0	11	7.8
Vina, Mil	1165.2	16	8.1
DeShields, LA	1315.1	17	8.6
Lemke, Atl	1166.1	15	8.6
Cora, Sea	1071.2	13	9.2
Morandini, Phi	1154.0	12	10.7
Frye, Bos	872.0	9	10.8
Young E, Col	1169.0	12	10.8
McLemore, Tex	1279.1	12	11.8
Velarde, Cal	967.2	9	11.9
Alomar R, Bal	1217.2	11	12.3
Vizcaino, Cle	1152.2	10	12.8
Durham, ChA	1313.0	11	13.3
Lansing, Mon	1368.0	11	13.8
Lewis M, Det	1240.2	9	15.3
Reed J, SD	1245.0	9	15.4
Biggio, Hou	1409.1	10	15.7
Knoblauch, Min	1267.2	8	17.6
Boone, Cin	1205.2	6	22.3
Sandberg, ChN	1234.0	6	22.0

Third Basemen

Name, Team	Inn	E	G/E
Kent, Cle	788.2	21	4.2
Berry, Hou	871.1	22	4.4
Williams M, SF	796.1	13	6.8
Andrews, Mon	939.0	15	7.0
Caminiti, SD	1274.0	20	7.1
Hayes, NYA	1182.2	18	7.3
Arias G, Cal	657.1	10	7.3
Surhoff, Bal	926.1	14	7.4
Pendleton, Atl	1270.0	19	7.4
Castilla, Col	1374.0	20	7.6
Cirillo, Mil	1243.1	18	7.7
Hollins, Sea	1226.1	17	8.0
Wallach, LA	747.1	10	8.3
Thome, Cle	1277.1	17	8.3
Randa, KC	700.1	9	8.6
Jones C, Atl	1037.0	13	8.9
Palmer, Tex	1321.1	16	9.2
Sprague, Tor	1285.0	15	9.5
Blowers, LA	773.0	9	9.5
Naehring, Bos	989.0	11	10.0
Zeile, Bal	1185.2	13	10.1
Brosius, Oak	946.1	10	10.5
Gomez L, ChN	854.1	7	13.6
Gaetti, StL	1104.0	9	13.6
Ventura, ChA	1274.1	10	14.2
Fryman, Det	1116.1	8	15.5
Boggs, NYA	1026.2	7	16.0

Shortstops

Name, Team	Inn	E	G/E
Blauser, Atl	654.1	23	3.2
Valentin J, Mil	1290.1	37	3.9
Hernandez J, ChN	670.0	19	3.9
Cedeno A, Hou	803.1	22	4.1
Dunston, SF	634.0	15	4.7
Weiss, Col	1275.0	30	4.7
Ordonez, NYN	1262.1	27	5.2
Miller, Hou	913.2	19	5.3
Grudzielanek, Mon	1328.2	27	5.5
Gagne, LA	1126.2	21	6.0
Meares, Min	1249.1	22	6.3
Gomez C, SD	1146.0	19	6.7
Jeter, NYA	1370.2	22	6.9
Gonzalez A, Tor	1316.0	21	7.0
DiSarcina, Cal	1290.0	20	7.2
Valentin J, Bos	1043.1	16	7.2
Vizquel, Cle	1312.1	20	7.3
Clayton, StL	997.2	15	7.4
Aurilia, SF	678.2	10	7.5
Sanchez, ChN	768.0	11	7.8
Larkin, Cin	1242.1	17	8.1
Stocker, Phi	991.2	13	8.5
Bordick, Oak	1338.0	16	9.3
Renteria, Fla	922.1	11	9.3
Rodriguez A, Sea	1267.2	15	9.4
Elster, Tex	1355.0	14	10.8
Ripken C, Bal	1379.2	14	10.9
Howard D, KC	1109.0	11	11.2
Guillen, ChA	1197.0	11	12.1
Bell J, Pit	1289.1	10	14.0

Left Fielders

Name, Team	Inn	E	G/E
Rodriguez H, Mon	702.0	6	13.0
Carter, Tor	935.2	7	14.9
Belle, Cle	1343.0	10	14.9
Greenwell, Bos	614.0	4	17.1
Martin A, Pit	1126.1	7	17.9
Anderson G, Cal	1247.1	7	19.8
Hollandsworth, LA	930.0	5	20.7
Phillips T, ChA	1309.0	7	20.8
Vaughn G, SD	1130.1	6	20.9
Gant, StL	991.2	5	22.0
Burks, Col	1031.1	5	22.9
Bonds, SF	1272.2	6	23.6
Conine, Fla	1063.0	5	23.6
Gilkey, NYN	1290.2	6	23.9
Greer, Tex	1187.1	5	26.4
Klesko, Atl	1211.1	5	26.9
Henderson, SD	932.1	3	34.5
Gonzalez L, ChN	1124.0	3	41.6
Cordova, Min	1278.1	3	47.3
Newfield, Mil	623.2	1	69.0

Center Fielders

Name, Team	Inn	E	G/E
Hunter B, Hou	1046.2	12	9.7
Curtis, LA	858.0	8	11.9
Johnson L, NYN	1356.1	12	12.6
Lofton, Cle	1334.0	10	14.8
Finley, SD	1416.2	7	22.5
Goodwin T, KC	613.1	3	22.7
Otero, Phi	834.1	4	23.2
Damon, KC	669.0	3	24.8
Williams B, NYA	1232.0	5	27.4
McRae, ChN	1358.2	5	30.2
Benard, SF	848.0	3	31.4
Griffey Jr, Sea	1173.0	4	32.6
Davis E, Cin	893.2	3	33.1
White D, Fla	1200.2	4	33.4
Lewis D, ChA	933.0	3	34.6
White R, Mon	734.1	2	40.8
Anderson B, Bal	1258.1	3	46.6
Becker, Min	1012.1	2	56.2
Nixon O, Tor	1079.1	2	60.0
Edmonds, Cal	921.2	1	102.4
Young E, Oak	1061.2	1	118.0
Lankford, StL	1242.0	1	138.0
Grissom, Atl	1380.0	1	153.3
Hamilton, Tex	1266.1	0	—

Right Fielders

Name, Team	Inn	E	G/E
Nieves, Det	720.1	9	8.9
Sosa, ChN	1086.2	10	12.1
Mondesi, LA	1407.1	12	13.0
Hill, SF	826.0	7	13.1
Ochoa, NYN	633.2	5	14.1
Bichette, Col	1167.0	9	14.4
Tartabull, ChA	993.2	7	15.8
Ramirez, Cle	1303.1	9	16.1
Salmon, Cal	1339.2	8	18.6
Bonilla, Bal	915.1	5	20.3
O'Leary, Bos	744.0	4	20.7
Bell D, Hou	1371.1	7	21.8
Sheffield, Fla	1342.0	6	24.9
Merced, Pit	994.2	3	36.8
Sanders, Cin	692.1	2	38.5
Buhner, Sea	1230.1	3	45.6
Gonzalez J, Tex	855.1	2	47.5
Gwynn T, SD	960.0	2	53.3
Green, Tor	991.1	2	55.1
Jordan B, StL	1046.0	2	58.1
Mieske, Mil	754.2	1	83.9
Alou, Mon	947.2	1	105.3
O'Neill, NYA	1241.2	0	—

Glossary

Batting Average

Hits divided by At Bats.

Bequeathed Runners

Any runner(s) on base when a pitcher leaves a game are considered "bequeathed" to the departing hurler; the opposite of "inherited runners" (see below).

Brock2/Brock6

A complex set of several hundred interlocking formulas devised by Bill James, designed to project a player's final career totals on the basis of his age and past performance. The method was first introduced as Brock2; the most recent version is called Brock6.

Defensive Batting Average

A composite statistic incorporating various defensive statistics to arrive at a number akin to batting average. Zone rating and fielding percentage are the primary determinants.

Earned Run Average

(Earned Runs times nine) divided by Innings Pitched.

Expected Winning Percentage

The offensive winning percentage (see below) compiled by the batters facing a particular pitcher. This estimates what the pitcher's actual winning percentage should be, given average run support.

Favorite Toy

The Favorite Toy is a method that is used to estimate a player's chance of achieving a specific goal—in the following example, we'll say 3,000 hits.

Four things are considered:

1) Need Hits—the number of hits needed to reach the goal. (This, of course, could also be "Need Home Runs" or "Need Doubles"—Whatever.)

2) Years Remaining. The number of years remaining to meet the goal is estimated by the formula 24 - .6(age). This formula assigns a 20-year-old player 12.0 remaining seasons, a 25-year-old player 9.0 remaining seasons, a 30-year-old player 6.0 remaining seasons, a 35-year-old player 3.0 remaining seasons. Any player who is still playing regularly is assumed to have at least 1.5 seasons remaining, regardless of his age.

3) Established Hit Level. For 1997, the established hit level would be found by adding 1994 hits, two times 1995 hits, and three times 1996 hits, and dividing by six. However, a player cannot have an established performance level that is less than three-fourths of his most recent performance—that is, a player who had 200 hits in 1996 cannot have an established hit level below 150.

4) Projected Remaining Hits. This is found by multiplying the second number (ears remaining) by the third (established hit level).

Once you get the projected remaining hits, the chance of getting to the goal is figured by (projected remaining hits) divided by (need hits), minus .5. By this method, if your "need hits" and your "projected remaining hits" are the same, your chance of reaching the goal is 50 percent. If your projected remaining hits are 20 percent more than your need hits, the chance of reaching the goal is 70 percent.

Two special rules, and a note:
1) A player's chance of continuing to progress toward a goal cannot exceed .97 per year. (This rule prevents a player from figuring to have a 148 percent chance of reaching a goal.)
2) If a player's offensive winning percentage is below .500, his chance of continuing to progress toward the goal cannot exceed .75 per season. (That is, if a below-average hitter is two years away from reaching a goal, his chance of reaching that goal cannot be shown as better than nine-sixteenths, or three-fourths times three-fourths, regardless of his age.)
3) For 1994 and 1995, we used projected stats based on a full season of play.

Fielding Percentage

(Putouts plus Assists) divided by (Putouts plus Assists plus Errors).

Game Score

A tool designed by Bill James to quantify how well a starting pitcher performed in a single game. A score of 50 is about average; anything above 90 is outstanding.

Go-Ahead RBI

Any time a player drives in a run which gives his team the lead, he is credited with a go-ahead RBI.

Ground/Fly Ratio (Grd/Fly)

Simply a hitter's ground balls divided by his fly balls. All batted balls except line drives and bunts are included.

Hall Of Fame Career Monitor

A system developed by Bill James to estimate a player's chances of being elected to the Hall of Fame. The system awards a certain number of points for each of the player's seasonal accomplishments throughout his career. Achievements that have carried the most weight in past Hall of Fame balloting (like getting 200 hits in a season) are worth the most points. Any score over 100 means that the player has a better-than-even chance to be elected.

Hold

A Hold is credited any time a relief pitcher enters a game in a Save Situation (see definition below), records at least one out, and leaves the game never having relinquished the lead. Note: a pitcher cannot finish the game and receive credit for a hold, nor can he earn a hold and a save in the same game.

Inherited Runner

Any runner(s) on base when a relief pitcher enters a game are considered "inherited" by that pitcher.

Isolated Power

Slugging Percentage minus Batting Average.

K/BB Ratio

Strikeouts divided by Walks.

No Decision (ND)

The result when a starter is credited with neither a win nor a loss.

OBS

On-base percentage plus slugging percentage.

Offensive Winning Percentage (OWP)

Jeff Bagwell's offensive winning percentage equals the percentage of games a team would win with nine Jeff Bagwells in the lineup (given average pitching and defense). The formula: (Runs Created per 27 outs) divided by the League average of runs scored per game. Square the result and divide it by (1+itself).

On-Base Percentage

(Hits plus Walks plus Hit by Pitcher) divided by (At Bats plus Walks plus Hit by Pitcher plus Sacrifice Flies).

Outfielder Hold Percentage

A statistic used to evaluate outfielders' throwing arms. "Hold Percentage" is computed by dividing extra bases taken by baserunners by the number of opportunities. For example, if a single is lined to center field with men on first and second, and one man scores while the other stops at second, that is one extra base taken on two opportunities, a 50.0 hold percentage.

Park Index

A method of measuring the extent to which a given ballpark favor the pitcher or the hitter in a given category, such as home runs. A park index for home runs is derived by dividing the team's (home runs per game plus home runs allowed per game, at home) by the team's (home runs plus home runs allowed per game, on the road) and multiplying by 100. An index of 100 means the park is completely neutral; anything over 100 indicates that the park favors the pitcher. A park index of 118 (for home runs) means that games played in the home park feature 18% more home runs than the average park.

Pivot Percentage

The number of double plays turned by a second baseman as the pivot man, divided by the number of opportunities. An "opportunity" is any situation where the double play is in order, the ball is hit to an infielder, and the second baseman takes the throw.

Plate Appearances

At Bats plus Total Walks plus Hit By Pitcher plus Sacrifice Hits plus Sacrifice Flies plus Times Reached on Defensive Interference.

Pickoffs (Pk)

The number of times a runner was picked off base by a pitcher.

Predicted ERA

(Opponent on-base percentage) multiplied by (opponent slugging average) multiplied by (31).

Quality Start

Any start in which a pitcher works six or more innings while allowing three or fewer earned runs.

Quick Hooks and Slow Hooks

A Quick Hook is the removal of a pitcher who has pitched less than 6 innings and given up 3 runs or less. A Slow Hook goes to a pitcher who pitches more than 9 innings, or allows 7 or more runs, or whose combined innings pitched and runs allowed totals 13 or more.

RBI Opportunities

The number of RBI a hitter would have accumulated if he had hit a home run every time up, given the total number of men that were on base when he batted. No RBI opportunities are charged if the batter reaches base via a base on balls, a hit batsmen or catcher's interference.

Relative Slugging Percentage

Slugging percentage divided by league slugging percentage.

Relief Conversion Percentage

(Saves plus Holds) divided by (Saves plus Blown Saves plus Holds).

Relief Points (Pts)

Wins plus saves minus losses

Replacement Level

A hypothetical baseline representing the lowest level of offensive production that a player can maintain without being replaced.

Run Support Per 9 IP

The number of runs scored by a pitcher's team while he was still in the game times nine divided by his Innings Pitched.

Runs Created

A way to combine a batter's total offensive contributions into one number. The formula: (H + BB + HBP - CS - GIDP) times (Total Bases + .26(TBB - IBB + HBP) + .52(SH + SF + SB)) divided by (AB + TBB + HBP + SH + SF).

Runs Prevented

A linear weights system that attempts to measure how many runs a reliever prevents, given the opposition's scoring potential both when the reliever enters and exits the game. The scoring potential depends on the number of outs, the number of men on base and the bases they occupy, if any.

Save Percentage

Saves (SV) divided by Save Opportunities (OP).

Save Situation

A Relief Pitcher is in a Save Situation when:

upon entering the game with his club leading, he has the opportunity to be the finishing pitcher (and is not the winning pitcher of record at the time), and meets any one of the three following conditions:

(1) he has a lead of no more than three runs and has the opportunity to pitch for at least one inning, or

(2) he enters the game, regardless of the count, with the potential tying run either on base, at bat, or on deck; or

(3) he pitches three or more innings regardless of the lead and the official scorer credits him with a save.

SBA

Stolen-base attempts against a catcher

Secondary Average

A way to look at a player's extra bases gained, independent of Batting Average. The formula: (Total Bases - Hits + TBB + SB - CS) divided by At Bats.

Similarity Score

A method of measuring the degree of similarity of two statistical lines (the stats may be team stats or player stats). Two identical stat lines would generate a score of 1,000.

Slugging Percentage

Total Bases divided by At Bats.

Zone Rating

The percentage of balls fielded by a player in his typical defensive "zone," as measured by STATS reporters, along with outs recorded on balls hit outside the zone. Players receive additional credit (outs) for starting a double play.

About STATS, Inc.

STATS, Inc. is the nation's leading independent sports information and statistical analysis company, providing detailed sports services for a wide array of clients.

As one of the fastest-growing sports companies—in 1994, we ranked 144th on the "Inc. 500" list of fastest-growing privately held firms—STATS provides the most up-to-the-minute sports information to professional teams, print and broadcast media, software developers and interactive service providers around the country. Some of our major clients are ESPN, the Associated Press, *The Sporting News*, Electronic Arts, Motorola, SONY and Topps. Much of the information we provide is available to the public via STATS On-Line. With a computer and a modem, you can follow action in the four major professional sports, as well as NCAA football and basketball. . . as it happens!

STATS Publishing, a division of STATS, Inc., produces 11 annual books, including the *Major League Handbook*, *The Scouting Notebook*, the *Pro Football Handbook*, the *Pro Basketball Handbook* and the *Hockey Handbook.* These publications deliver STATS' expertise to fans, scouts, general managers and media around the country.

In addition, STATS offers the most innovative—and fun—fantasy sports games around, from *Bill James Fantasy Baseball* and *Bill James Classic Baseball* to *STATS Fantasy Football* and *STATS Fantasy Hoops.*

Information technology has grown by leaps and bounds in the last decade, and STATS will continue to be at the forefront as both a vendor and supplier of the most up-to-date, in-depth sports information available. For those of you on the information superhighway, you can always catch STATS at our site on America Online (Keyword: STATS).

For more information on our products, or on joining our reporter network, write us at:

STATS, Inc.
8131 Monticello Ave.
Skokie, IL 60076-3300

. . . or call us at 1-800-63-STATS (1-800-637-8287). Outside the U.S., dial 1-847-676-3383.

Index

A

B

C

D

K

L

M

N

O

P

Q

R

S

T

W

Z

STATS Fantasy Hoops

Soar into the 1996-97 season with STATS Fantasy Hoops! SFH puts YOU in charge. Don't just sit back and watch Grant Hill, Shawn Kemp, and Michael Jordan—get in the game and coach your team to the top!

How to Play SFH:

1. Sign up to coach a team.
2. You'll receive a full set of rules and a draft form with SFH point values for all eligible players - anyone who played in the NBA in 1995-96, plus all 1996 NBA draft picks.
3. Complete the draft form and return it to STATS.
4. You will take part in the draft with nine other owners, and we will send you league rosters.
5. You make unlimited weekly transactions including trades, free agent signings, activations, and benchings.
6. Six of the 10 teams in your league advance to postseason play, with two teams ultimately advancing to the Finals.

SFH point values are tested against actual NBA results, mirroring the real thing. Weekly reports will tell you everything you need to know to lead your team to the SFH Championship!

STATS Fantasy Football

STATS Fantasy Football puts YOU in charge! You draft, trade, cut, bench, activate players and even sign free agents each week. SFF pits you head-to-head against 11 other owners.

STATS' scoring system applies realistic values, tested against actual NFL results. Each week, you'll receive a superb in-depth report telling you all about both team and league performances.

How to Play SFF:

1. Sign up today!
2. STATS sends you a draft form listing all eligible NFL players.
3. Fill out the draft form and return it to STATS, and you will take part in the draft along with 11 other team owners.
4. Go head-to-head against the other owners in your league. You'll make week-by-week roster moves and transactions through STATS' Fantasy Football experts, via phone, fax, or on-line!

Order from  **Today!**

Use Order Form in This Book, or Call 1-800-63-STATS or 847-676-3383 or e-mail: info@stats.com

Bill James Fantasy Baseball

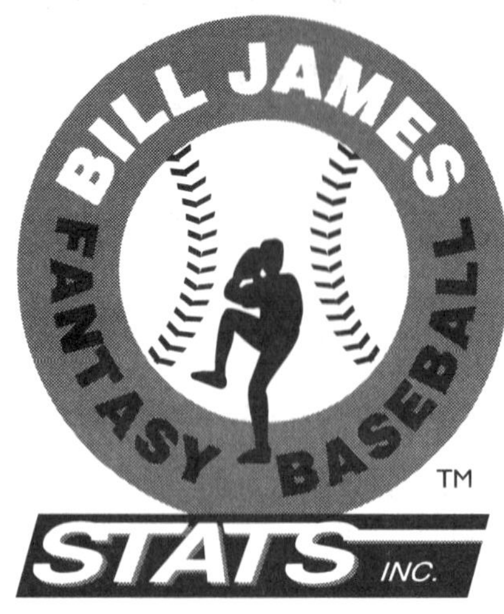

Bill James Fantasy Baseball enters its ninth season of offering baseball fans the most unique, realistic and exciting game fantasy sports has to offer.

You draft a 26-player roster and can expand to as many as 28. Players aren't ranked like in rotisserie leagues—you'll get credit for everything a player does, like hitting homers, driving in runs, turning double plays, pitching quality outings and more!

The team which scores the most points among all leagues, plus wins the World Series, will receive the John McGraw Award, which includes a one-week trip to the Grapefruit League in spring training, a day at the ballpark with Bill James, and a new fantasy league named in his/her honor!

Unique Features Include:

- **Live fantasy experts** — available seven days a week
- **The best weekly reports in the business** — detailing who is in the lead, win-loss records, MVPs, and team strengths and weaknesses
- **On-Line computer system** — a world of information, including daily updates of fantasy standings and stats
- **Over twice as many statistics as rotisserie**
- **Transactions that are effective the very next day!**

PLAYABLE THRU STATS ON-LINE

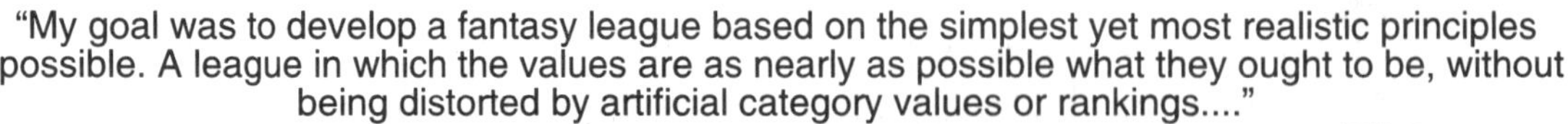

"My goal was to develop a fantasy league based on the simplest yet most realistic principles possible. A league in which the values are as nearly as possible what they ought to be, without being distorted by artificial category values or rankings...."

- Bill James

All this, all summer long...for less than $5 per week!

Order from  **Today!**

Use Order Form in This Book, or Call 1-800-63-STATS or 847-676-3383 or e-mail: info@stats.com

STATS INC.™

Meet the Winning Lineup...

Bill James Presents:

STATS Major League Handbook 1997

- Bill James' exclusive 1997 player projections
- Career data for every 1996 Major League Baseball player
- Leader boards, fielding stats and stadium data
- **Item #HB97, $19.95, Available NOW!**

Bill James Presents:

STATS Minor League Handbook 1997

- Year-by-year career statistical data for AA and AAA players
- Bill James' exclusive Major League Equivalencies
- Complete 1996 Single-A and rookie statistics
- **Item #MH97, $19.95, Available NOW!**

STATS Player Profiles 1997

- Exclusive 1996 breakdowns for pitchers and hitters, over 30 in all: lefty/righty, home/road, clutch situations, ahead/behind in the count, month-by-month, etc.
- Complete breakdowns by player for the last five seasons
- **Item #PP97, $19.95, Available NOW!**

STATS Scouting Notebook: 1997

- Extensive scouting reports on over 700 major league players
- Evaluations of nearly 200 minor league prospects
- **Item #SN97, $18.95, Available NOW!**

STATS Minor League Scouting Notebook 1997

- Evaluation of each organization's top prospects
- Essays, stat lines and grades for more than 400 prospects
- **Item #MN97, $18.95, Available NOW!**

Bill James Presents:

STATS 1997 Batter Versus Pitcher Match-Ups!

- Complete stats for pitchers vs. batters (5+ career AB against them)
- Leader boards and stats for all 1996 major league players
- **Item #BP97, $14.95, Available NOW!**

STATS Baseball Scoreboard 1997

- Lively analysis of all the hottest topics facing baseball today!
- Easy-to-understand charts answer the questions fans always ask
- Specific coverage for each major league team
- **Item #SB97, $18.95, Available NOW!**

STATS Pro Basketball Handbook 1997-98

- Career stats for every player who logged minutes during 1996-97
- Team game logs with points, rebounds, assists and much more
- Leader boards from points per game to triple doubles
- **Item #BH98, $19.95, Available September 1997!**

STATS Pro Football Handbook 1997

- A complete season-by-season register for every active 1995 player
- Numerous statistical breakdowns for hundreds of NFL players
- Leader boards in a number of innovative and traditional categories
- **Item #FH97, $19.95, Available NOW!**

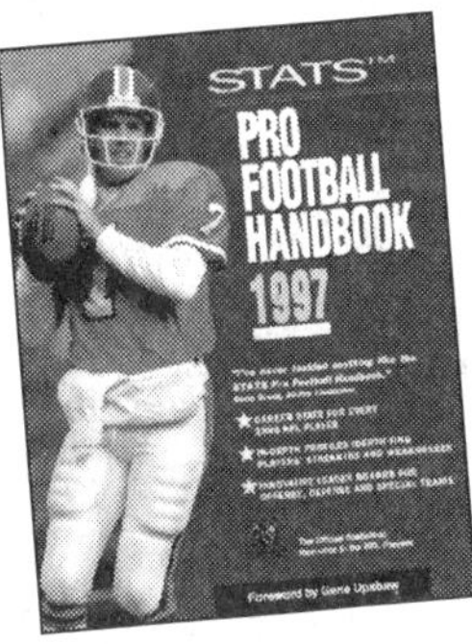

Pro Football Revealed: The 100-Yard War (1997 Edition)

- Profiles each team, complete with essays, charts and play diagrams
- Detailed statistical breakdowns on players, teams and coaches
- Essays about NFL trends and happenings by leading experts
- **Price: $18.95, Item #PF97 , Available July 1997!**

STATS Hockey Handbook 1996-97

- A complete season-by-season register for every active 1996 player
- Numerous statistical breakdowns for hundreds of NHL players
- Leader boards in numerous innovative and traditional categories
- **Item #HH97, $17.95, Available NOW!**
- ***STATS Hockey Handbook 1997-98***

  Price: $19.95, Item #HH98, Available August 1997

STATS On-Line

Now you can have a direct line to a world of sports information just like the pros use with STATS On-Line. If you love to keep up with your favorite teams and players, STATS On-Line is for you. From Charles Barkley's fast-breaking dunks to Mark McGwire's tape-measure blasts — if you want baseball, basketball, football and hockey stats, we put them at your fingertips!

STATS On-Line

- **Player Profiles and Team Profiles** — The #1 resource for scouting your favorite professional teams and players with information you simply can't find anywhere else! The most detailed info you've ever seen, including real-time stats.
- **NO monthly or annual fees**
- **Local access numbers** — avoid costly long-distance charges!
- **Unlimited access** — 24 hours a day, seven days a week
- **Downloadable files** — get year-to-date stats in an ASCII format for baseball, football, basketball, and hockey
- **In-progress box scores** — You'll have access to the most up-to-the-second scoring stats for every team and player. When you log into STATS On-Line, you'll get detailed updates, including player stats while the games are in progress!
- **Other exclusive features** — transactions and injury information, team and player profiles and updates, standings, leader and trailer boards, game-by-game logs, fantasy game features, and much more!

Sign-up fee of $30 (applied towards future use), 24-hour access with usage charges of $.75/min. Mon.-Fri., 8am-6pm CST; $.25/min. all other hours and weekends.

Order from 

Today!

Use Order Form in This Book, or Call 1-800-63-STATS or 847-676-3383 or e-mail: info@stats.com

STATS, Inc. Order Form

me____

ldress____

ty______________________ State__________ Zip__________

ione__________ Fax__________ Internet Address__________

ethod of Payment (U.S. Funds Only):

❑ Check ❑ Money Order ❑ Visa ❑ MasterCard

redit Card Information:

ardholder Name____

redit Card Number______________________ Exp. Date__________

ignature____

OOKS (STATS publications now include free first class shipping)

Qty.	Product Name	Item Number	Price	Total
	STATS Major League Handbook 1997	**HB97**	**$19.95**	
	STATS Major League Handbook 1997 (Comb-bound)	**HC97**	**$21.95**	
	STATS Projections Update 1997	**PJUP**	**$9.95**	
	The Scouting Notebook: 1997	**SN97**	**$18.95**	
	The Scouting Notebook: 1997 (Comb-bound)	**SC97**	**$20.95**	
	STATS Minor League Scouting Notebook 1997	**MN97**	**$18.95**	
	STATS Minor League Handbook 1997	**MH97**	**$19.95**	
	STATS Minor League Handbook 1997 (Comb-bound)	**MC97**	**$21.95**	
	STATS Player Profiles 1997	**PP97**	**$19.95**	
	STATS Player Profiles 1997 (Comb-bound)	**PC97**	**$21.95**	
	STATS 1997 BVSP Match-Ups!	**BP97**	**$14.95**	
	STATS Baseball Scoreboard 1997	**SB97**	**$18.95**	
	Pro Football Revealed: The 100 Yard War (1997 Edition)	**PF97**	**$18.95**	
	STATS Pro Football Handbook 1997	**FH97**	**$19.95**	
	STATS Basketball Handbook 1997-98	**BH98**	**$17.95**	
	STATS Hockey Handbook 1996-97	**HH97**	**$17.95**	
	STATS Hockey Handbook 1997-98	**HH98**	**$19.95**	
	Prior Editions **(Please circle appropriate year)**			
	STATS Major League Handbook	'90 '91 '92 '93 '94 '95 '96	$9.95	
	The Scouting Report/Notebook	'94 '95 '96	$9.95	
	STATS Player Profiles	'93 '94 '95 '96	$9.95	
	STATS Minor League Handbook	'92 '93 '94 '95 '96	$9.95	
	STATS BVSP Match-Ups!	'94 '95 '96	$3.95	
	STATS Baseball Scoreboard	'92 '93 '94 '95 '96	$9.95	
	STATS Basketball Scoreboard/Handbook	'93-'94 '94-'95 '95-'96	$9.95	
	Pro Football Revealed: The 100 Yard War	'94 '95 '96	$9.95	
	STATS Pro Football Handbook	'95 '96	$9.95	
	STATS Minor League Scouting Notebook	'95 '96	$9.95	

MULTIMEDIA PRODUCTS (Prices include shipping & handling charges)

Qty.	Product Name	Item Number	Price	Total
	Bill James Encyclopedia CD-Rom	BJCD	$49.95	
	STATS On-Line	STON	$30.00	

SEASON FINAL & YEAR-END REPORTS (Prices include shipping & handling charges)

Qty.	Product Name	Circle Format	Price	Total
	Season Final Report	Paper 3 1/2" disk 5" disk Mac	$12.95	
	Lefty/Righty Report	Paper 3 1/2" disk 5" disk Mac	$19.95	
	Stolen Base Report	Paper 3 1/2" disk 5" disk Mac	$34.95	
	Defensive Games by Position	Paper 3 1/2" disk 5" disk Mac	$9.95	
	Catcher Report	Paper 3 1/2" disk 5" disk Mac	$49.95	
	Relief Pitching Report	Paper 3 1/2" disk 5" disk Mac	$49.95	
	Zone Ratings/Outfield Arms Report	Paper 3 1/2" disk 5" disk Mac	$99.95	
	End of Season STATpak	Paper 3 1/2" disk 5" disk	$9.95	
	Team(s):			
	STATpak Subscription	Paper 3 1/2" disk 5" disk	$29.95	
	Team(s):			

FANTASY GAMES & STATSfax (STATSfax prices reflect the monthly charge for service)

Qty.	Product Name	Item Number	Price	Total
	Bill James Classic Baseball	BJCB	$129.00	
	How to Win the Classic Game	CGBK	$16.95	
	Classic Game STATSfax	CFX5	$20.00	
	STATS Fantasy Hoops	SFH	$85.00	
	STATS Fantasy Hoops STATSfax—5-Day	SFH5	$20.00	
	STATS Fantasy Hoops STATSfax—7-Day	SFH7	$25.00	
	STATS Fantasy Football	SFF	$69.00	
	STATS Fantasy Football STATSfax—3-Day	SFF3	$15.00	
	Bill James Fantasy Baseball	BJFB	$89.00	
	Fantasy Baseball STATSfax—5-Day	SFX5	$20.00	
	Fantasy Baseball STATSfax—7-Day	SFX7	$25.00	

1st Fantasy Team Name (ex. Colt 45's):________________

What Fantasy Game is this team for?________________

2nd Fantasy Team Name (ex. Colt 45's):________________

What Fantasy Game is this team for?________________

NOTE: $1.00/player is charged for all roster moves and transactions.

For Bill James Fantasy Baseball:

Would you like to play in a league drafted by Bill James? ❑ Yes ❑ No

For faster service, call: 1-800-63-STATS or 847-676-3383, or fax this form to STATS: 847-676-0821

TOTALS	Price	Total
Product Total (excl. Fantasy Games)		
Canada—all orders—add:	$2.50/book	
Order 2 or more books—subtract:	$1.00/book	
(NOT to be combined with other specials)		
IL residents add 8.5% sales tax		
Subtotal		
Fantasy Games Total		
GRAND TOTAL		

All books now include free 1st class shipping!

Thanks for ordering from STATS, Inc.